Data Hiding Techniques in Window

Data Hiding Techniques
in Windows OS
A Practical Approach to Investigation and Defense

Nihad Ahmad Hassan
University of Greenwich
IT Security and Digital Forensics Consultant;
Founder of www.DarknessGate.com

Rami Hijazi
University of Liverpool
Information Security Consultant;
General Manager, MERICLER Inc.,
Candela Drive, Mississauga, Ontario, Canada

Helvi Salminen
Technical Editor

ELSEVIER

AMSTERDAM • BOSTON • HEIDELBERG • LONDON • NEW YORK • OXFORD • PARIS
SAN DIEGO • SAN FRANCISCO • SINGAPORE • SYDNEY • TOKYO

Syngress is an imprint of Elsevier

Syngress is an imprint of Elsevier
50 Hampshire Street, 5th Floor, Cambridge, MA 02139, United States

Library of Congress Cataloging-in-Publication Data
A catalog record for this book is available from the Library of Congress

British Library Cataloguing-in-Publication Data
A catalogue record for this book is available from the British Library

ISBN: 978-0-12-804449-0

For information on all Syngress publications
visit our website at https://www.elsevier.com/

Working together
to grow libraries in
developing countries

www.elsevier.com • www.bookaid.org

Publisher: Todd Green
Acquisition Editor: Chris Katsaropoulos
Editorial Project Manager: Anna Valutkevich
Production Project Manager: Priya Kumaraguruparan
Designer: Mark Rogers

Typeset by TNQ Books and Journals

To my mom, Samiha, thank you for everything.
Without you, I'm nothing.

Nihad A. Hassan

Contents

Biography   xi
Preface   xiii
Acknowledgments   xv

1. Introduction and Historical Background

Introduction   1
Classical Cipher Types   2
  Substitution Cipher   2
  Transposition Cipher   8
  Other Ciphers and Codes   9
  Difference Between Substitution and
  Transposition Cipher   10
  Practicing Old Ciphers Using Modern
  Computing   12
Modern Cryptography Systems   12
  Secret Key Cryptography   13
  Public Key Cryptography   13
  Digital Signature   14
  Cryptographic Hash Function   14
Steganography   15
  What Is Steganography?   15
  Comparing Steganography and
  Cryptography   15
  Steganography Types   15
Watermarking   20
  Watermarking Types   20
  Compare Steganography and
  Watermarking   21
Anonymity   21
Summary   21
References   21
Bibliography   22

2. Data Hiding Using Simple Methods

Introduction   23
Bit-Shifting Data Hiding   23
Hiding Data Inside Rich Text Format
Documents   26

Renaming Files   27
  Matching File Signatures and File
  Extensions   27
Hiding Data in Compressed Files   28
Hiding Data Through File Splitting   31
Hiding Data in Microsoft® Office
Documents   33
  Hidden Text   34
  Hidden Data Within Document
  Attributes (Metadata)   34
  White Font   35
  Hiding Data by Exploiting OLE
  Structured Storage   35
  Self-Encrypt MS Office® Document   37
  Hiding Inside MS Excel® Spreadsheet   38
Data Hiding Inside Image Attributes
(Image Metadata)   40
Summary   43
References   43
Bibliography   43

3. Data Hiding Using Steganographic Techniques

Introduction   45
Text Steganography   46
  Format-Based Steganography   46
  Random and Statistical Generation   47
  Linguistic-Based Methods   48
  Hiding Inside MS Office® Documents
  Based on OOXML File Format   49
  Webpage Text Steganography   64
  Hiding Secret Messages Inside Twitter
  Updates   67
Image Steganography   68
  Digital Image Basic Concepts   69
  Image Steganographic Techniques   73
  Digital Media Steganography Tools   81
Data Hiding Inside Audio Files   81
  Audio Files Basic Concepts   82
  Audio Steganography Types   84
Data Hiding Using Other Digital
Media Types   90
  Data Hiding Inside PDF Documents   91
  Data Hiding Inside Program Binaries   94

Summary   95
References   95
Bibliography   95

4. Data Hiding Under Windows® OS File Structure

Introduction   97
Data Hiding Using Alternate Data Stream   98
  What Is the New Technology File System?   98
  What Is an Alternate Data Stream?   98
  How Can We Use Alternate Data
  Streams to Hide Files?   98
  Hiding Executable Code in Alternate
  Data Stream Files   100
  Important Notes About Using Alternate
  Data Stream in Hiding Files   102
  How to Delete Alternate Data
  Stream Files   104
  Detecting Alternate Data Stream Files   104
Data Hiding Using Stealth Alternate
Data Stream   104
Hiding Data Inside Windows®
Restoration Points   106
Hiding Data Inside Windows® Registry   109
Hiding in a File's Slack Space   112
  Understanding Hard Disk Drives   112
  File Allocation Table   114
Hidden Partitions   117
  Hidden Partitions Under Windows® OS   118
  Creating a Hidden Partition Within a
  USB Zip Drive   118
Data Hiding Within Master File Table   123
Data Hiding in Disk Bad Blocks   127
Data Hiding Under Computer
Hardware Level   128
  Data Hiding Inside Host Protected Area   129
  Hiding Data in Device Configuration
  Overlay   130
Summary   131
References   131
Bibliography   132

5. Data Hiding Using Encryption Techniques

Introduction   134
Security Awareness Corners   134
  Human Security   134
  Device Security   134
  Message Security   135
  Network Security   135
Anonymous Operating System   135
  Tails   135
  Ubuntu Privacy Remix   137

Other Security Distributions   138
Advice When Using Security
Operating Systems   138
Portable Stick Computer   140
Disk Encryption   140
  Encrypting Partitions Using BitLocker   141
  Creating Encrypted Vaults   145
  Single File Encryption   159
  Cloud Storage Encryption   161
  Discussion of Security Level in Disk
  Encryption   162
Anonymize Your Location Online   169
  Using the TOR Browser   169
  Virtual Private Networks   176
  SSH Tunneling   179
  Using Proxy Server   179
  Anonymous Search Engine   180
  Web Browser Privacy Add-Ons   181
  Secure Anonymous File Sharing   183
Encrypting Email Communications   185
  Email Encryption Using Gpg4Win   186
  Open PGP Encryption for Webmail
  Using the Mailvelope Browser Extension   190
  Secure Web Mail Providers   192
Encrypt Instant Messaging, Video Calls,
and VOIP Sessions   195
  What Are the Risks?   195
  Off-the-Record-Messaging and Pidgin   195
  A Secure Video Calling Service
  Using Gruveo   198
  A Secure Anonymous Calling Service
  Using GHOST CALL   199
  Retroshare Secure Social Platform   199
  TOR Messenger   199
  Complete Anonymous IM Using
  Ricochet   201
Create and Maintain Secure Passwords   201
  Password Best Practice   201
  Password Generation Tools   202
  Password-Saving Techniques   202
  Password Manager Tools   202
Miscellaneous Security Hints and Best
Practices   203
Summary   204
References   204
Bibliography   205

6. Data Hiding Forensics

Introduction   207
Understanding Computer Forensics   208
  Computer Forensic Process   208
  Differences Between Computer
  Forensics and Other Computing Domains   209
  The Need for Digital Evidence   209

Steganalysis 210
   Steganalysis Methods 210
   Destroying Hidden Data 211
Steganalysis of Digital Media Files 211
   Text Document Steganalysis 211
   Image Forensics 214
   Audio Forensics 219
   Video Forensics 219
   Digital Files Metadata Forensic 222
Windows Forensics 227
   Capture Volatile Memory 228
   Capture Disk Drive 231
   Deleted Files Recovery 233
   Windows Registry Analysis 239
   Forensic Analysis of Windows
   Prefetch Files 249
   Windows Minidump Files Forensics 250
   Windows Thumbnail Forensics 250
   File Signature Analysis 252
   File Attributes Analysis 252
   Discover Hidden Partitions 252
   Detect Alternative Data Streams 255
   Investigating Windows Volume
   Shadow Copy 255
   Virtual Memory Analysis 257
   Windows Password Cracking 259
   Host Protected Area and Device
   Configuration Relay Forensic 262
   Examining Encrypted Files 262
Summary 264
References 265
Bibliography 265

7. Antiforensic Techniques

Introduction 267
Antiforensics Goals 268
Data Hiding General Advice 268
Data Destruction 268
   Hard Disk Wiping 269
   Manipulating Digital File Metadata 272
Windows Antiforensics Techniques 275
   Configure Windows for Better Privacy 275
   Disable Recycle Bin 276

Registry Antiforensics 276
   Disable Windows Hibernation 278
   Disable Windows Virtual Memory
   (Paging File) 278
   Disable System Restore Points and
   File History 280
   Disable Windows Thumbnail Cache 281
   Disable Windows Prefetch Feature 281
   Disable Windows Logging 285
   Disable Windows® Password
   Hash Extraction 285
Clearing Digital Footprints 287
   Live CDs and Bootable USB Tokens 287
   Virtual Machines 288
   Using Portable Applications 289
Direct Attack Against Forensic Software 289
Summary 289
References 289
Bibliography 290

8. Future Trends

Introduction 291
The Future of Encryption 292
Data Stored in Cloud Computing 293
Virtualization Technology 293
Data Hiding in Enterprise Networks 294
   Data Concealment 294
   Data Leakage Prevention 295
Streaming Protocols 295
Wireless Networks and Future
Networking Protocols 296
Data Hiding in Mobile Devices 297
Anonymous Networks 297
Summary 298
References 298
Bibliography 298

Index 299

Biography

Nihad A. Hassan is an independent computer security and forensic consultant. He has been actively conducting research on computer forensic techniques for more than 8 years, focusing on techniques in Windows® OS, especially digital steganography techniques.

Nihad has completed numerous technical security consulting engagements involving security architectures, penetration testing, Windows® OS diagnostic reviews, disaster recovery planning, and computer crime investigation.

He has written thousands of pages of technical documentation for different global companies in the IT and cybersecurity fields in both Arabic and English. His writing style highlights information that is simplified and presented in an easy manner, which gives him an extensive reputation in this field.

Nihad believes that security concerns are best addressed by well-prepared and security-savvy individuals. Nihad also enjoys being involved in security training, education, and motivation. His current works are focused on network security, penetration testing, computer forensic and antiforensic techniques, and web security assessment. Nihad has a BSc honors degree in computer science from the University of Greenwich, United Kingdom.

You can reach Nihad through:

InfoSecurity blog	http://www.DarknessGate.com
Personal website	http://www.ThunderWeaver.com
Email	nihadhas@gmail.com

Rami Hijazi is the general manager of MERICLER Inc., an education and corporate training firm in Toronto, Canada. Rami is an experienced IT professional who lectures on a wide array of topics, including object-oriented programming, Java, eCommerce, Agile development, database design, and data handling analysis. Rami also works as consultant to Cyber Boundaries Inc., where he is involved in the design of encryption systems and wireless networks, intrusion detection, and data breach tracking, as well as providing planning and development advice for IT departments concerning contingency planning.

Helvi Salminen has worked full-time in information security since June of 1990. Prior to her security career, she had 12 years of experience in systems development. Helvi values lifelong learning and knowledge sharing, which she has practiced by studying and teaching in lifelong learning security education programs at Aalto University and by speaking at security conferences. She was awarded CISO of the year 2014 in Finland by the Finnish Information Security Association.

Preface

ABOUT THIS BOOK

In brief, this book presents a wide array of techniques that could be used to hide digital data under the Windows® OS, in addition to different steganographic techniques to conceal data in multimedia files. The book also presents different ways to investigate and explore hidden data inside digital files and the Windows® OS file structure.

The main focus of this book is teaching Windows® users how they can exploit data hiding techniques within Windows® OS and multimedia files to secure their data and communications. Today, the demand for privacy is a major concern for computer users. This book will help those users learn vast arrays of techniques to better secure their privacy by teaching them how to conceal their personal data. Users also learn how to use different cryptographic anonymity techniques to conceal their identity online.

Many books on data hiding techniques are available in the market. However, none of these books have a practical approach such as this one. The data hiding topic is usually approached in most books in an academic way with long math equations about how each hiding technique algorithm works behind the scene. These books are usually targeted for people who work in the academic arenas. We need a book that teaches professionals and end users alike how they can hide their data and discover the hidden ones using a variety of ways, under the most used operating system on earth, Windows®.

This book will entertain the reader by following a simple writing style. It focuses on approaching the data hiding topic practically and offers plenty of screen captures for each technique used. The book is written as a series of tutorials (you can consider it a cookbook full of delicious recipes, with each task (hence recipe) presenting a different hiding technique). Book contents are completely practical; a user can read a task and then implement it directly on his or her PC. Relevant theoretical information will be presented to enrich the user about terms used in each hiding technique, making this book quite informative for different user populations. Techniques discussed in this book cover all Windows® versions, from Windows® XP to Windows®10.

TARGET AUDIENCE

The topic of digital data hiding is quite stimulating. This book will be valuable for the following user groups:

1. Computer forensic investigators
2. Law enforcement officers and border protection agencies
3. Intelligence services staff
4. Human rights activists
5. Journalists
6. IT professionals
7. Computing and information technology students
8. Business managers in all industries
9. End users

Any computer user will benefit from this book! All people like to obscure their personal data using simple methods and they are eager to become more computer literate and able to override mass surveillance programs deployed by many governments to monitor online traffic. This book will explain these ideas in an easy-to-follow manner, making complex technical ideas easy to assimilate by nontechnical folks.

SUMMARY OF CONTENTS

In the following you will find a brief description about each chapter's contents.

Chapter 1, Introduction and Historical Background: This chapter talks about the history of data hiding since old civilizations, and presents historical events related to this subject. This chapter begins by listing old cryptographic techniques used in ancient times to secure message transmission, and then discusses modern steganography and encryption techniques used in today's world.

Chapter 2, Data Hiding Using Simple Methods: In this chapter, we present many simple techniques that average computer users can use to hide their personal data. The techniques presented in this chapter can be used without using any third-party tool.

Chapter 3, Data Hiding Using Steganographic Techniques: In this chapter, we present different steganographic techniques to conceal our data in multimedia files. We demonstrate how we can use different tools and techniques to conceal data inside e-documents, web files, images, and audio and video files. A brief discussion of how each technique works behind the scene is also included to make this chapter both informative and practical.

Chapter 4, **Data Hiding Under Windows® OS File Structure:** This is an advanced chapter that shows how we can exploit the Windows® OS NTFS file structure to conceal our data. Many data hiding techniques in this chapter can be performed without using third-party tools, mostly by exploiting Windows® OS's own files. This chapter gives insight on how hackers can use data hiding techniques to launch sophisticated attacks against computer systems and private networks.

Chapter 5, Data Hiding Using Encryption Techniques: This chapter presents different techniques to protect your private data using encryption. It covers encrypting a Windows® partition, data disk, and files in addition to emails, IMs, and VOIP calls. Attacks against full disk encryption and countermeasures also are described in this chapter. This chapter also covers using cryptographic anonymity techniques to anonymize your online communications, making them untraceable.

This chapter can be read alone; in fact, you can consider it as a minibook dedicated to teaching you practical tricks and guidelines for online risks and steps to protect yourself against cyberattacks through encryption and cryptographic anonymity tools.

Chapter 6, Data Hiding Forensics: This chapter is the reverse of Chapters 3 and 4 as it looks into how data hiding forensics investigate different methods to detect concealed data in digital files and Windows® file structure. In addition to this the chapter illustrates how we can investigate Windows®-based machines to determine whether any steganography tools have been installed or used.

Chapter 7, Antiforensic Techniques: This chapter discusses techniques and gives advice on eliminating your tracks when using steganography tools to conceal secret data. It also presents ways to prevent general computer forensic tools from investigating and exploring your hidden data. This chapter is the reverse of , Chapter 6.

Chapter 8, Future Trends: We discuss future trends and advancements in digital data hiding and how new IT technology affects this subject.

COMMENTS AND QUESTIONS

To comment or ask technical questions about this book, send email to nihadhas@gmail.com.

We are going to publish a webpage for this book that lists additional references, tools, examples, and other information. You can access this page through the author's InfoSec portal: http://www.DarknessGate.com.

For more information about Syngress books go to http://store.elsevier.com/Syngress/IMP_76/.

Acknowledgments

When I first thought about creating my first book, Rami Hijazi was the first person who came to my mind when seeking advice. I consider him the best man in the field. His precious feedback has always enlightened my road. Even after years of working together, I am constantly surprised by his amazing intelligence, innate humility, and genuine friendship. Looking forward to working with you again on another book, Rami!

It is with a deep sense of appreciation that I want to thank my technical reviewer Helvi Salminen. Helvi plays two roles in this book; first as a proposal reviewer she provided me with excellent feedback. The second role is of course reviewing this text technically. Without her excellent feedback and dedicated work, producing this text would have been difficult. Thank you very much, Helvi; I'm looking forward to working with you again on another book.

Book acquisition editor Chris Katsaropoulos, thank you for believing in my book's idea and for your moral encouragement before and during the writing process. Hope to work with you again.

Book Editorial Project Manager Anna Valutkevich, thank you for your diligent support during the writing process. You make authoring this book a joyful journey! Hope to work with you again, Anna!

Mary Ide, thank you very much for your feedback at the initial stage of book development. Your encouragement gave me a boost to proceed with this project.

Kandy Zabka, I highly appreciate your encouragement and practical advice on my book's proposal. Your initial feedback has guided my way all the way through the end.

I want to thank Jodi L. Colburn for her precious help at the start of my career as a computer security professional. I will always remember your encouragement and faithful advice.

I want to thank all the Syngress staff who worked behind the scenes to make this book possible and ready for launch. I hope you will continue your excellent job in creating highly valued computer security books. You are simply the best in this field.

Naturally, I'm saving the best for last. During this book I use many photos of a baby boy to describe digital steganographic techniques in images. These photos are of my brother's son Omran. I want to thank this little baby boy for adding a pleasant touch to the technical script. I hope he will become an author like his uncle when he grows up!

Nihad A. Hassan

Chapter 1

Introduction and Historical Background

Chapter Outline

Introduction	**1**
Classical Cipher Types	**2**
Substitution Cipher	2
Monoalphabetic Ciphers	2
Polyalphabetic Ciphers	2
Polygraphic Ciphers	5
Mechanical Substitution Ciphers	7
Transposition Cipher	8
Rail Fence	8
Columnar Transposition	8
Double Transposition	9
Other Ciphers and Codes	9
The One-Time Pad	9
Morse Code	9
Book Cipher	10
Difference Between Substitution and Transposition Cipher	10
Practicing Old Ciphers Using Modern Computing	12
Modern Cryptography Systems	**12**
Secret Key Cryptography	13
Public Key Cryptography	13
Digital Signature	14
Cryptographic Hash Function	14
Steganography	**15**
What Is Steganography?	15
Comparing Steganography and Cryptography	15
Steganography Types	15
Technical Steganography	16
Linguistic Steganography	17
Digital Steganography	18
Watermarking	**20**
Watermarking Types	20
Visible Watermark	20
Invisible Watermark	21
Compare Steganography and Watermarking	21
Anonymity	**21**
Summary	**21**
References	**21**
Bibliography	**22**

INTRODUCTION

Throughout history, humankind always tried to find the best ways to communicate efficiently and securely. The evolution of communication began with shouting out words, then quickly evolved to the next stage of sophisticated spoken language; however, the carrier (a human) may forget parts of the message or simply forget the message completely when moving from one place to another. A more refined method was needed, such as writing messages on basic materials such as stones. Writing was more efficient and represented a big milestone in human history.

In the Imperial period, the Persian empire was one of the first civilizations to enhance communications routes; roads were built across the entire empire to make sending messages more quick and efficient. The wealth and power of the Persian empire allowed it to invade more land outside its borders, which meant sending troops far away from their central capital, hence new requirements for secure communication emerged. A method for delivering secure messages through cryptographic and message-hiding techniques was devised.

Many sources give credit to Greece for creating the first known hiding technique by humans, as we will see later. Arabs, Chinese, and Romans also created their own methods to communicate securely, especially during war time.

Cryptography is a type of data hiding by obscuring messages. We begin discussing it in the first pages of this book because it is important to understand how old cryptographic techniques work since new methods are mainly based on these principles.

Steganography is the science of hiding data; there are many types and each type has its own techniques in hiding. Combining steganography with encryption to transmit secret messages is the ideal solution to counter today's online risks.

In this chapter we introduce *Data Hiding*. Interestingly, data hiding combines mystery, fun, history, and new advancements in computing, making it not only a very important topic in computer science, but also a type of art.

Data Hiding Techniques in Windows OS. http://dx.doi.org/10.1016/B978-0-12-804449-0.00001-4

Starting with the Roman emperor, Julius Caesar, and his simple cipher method, to the surveillance programs deployed by National Security Agency (NSA), to monitor communication and online traffic, this chapter introduces the history of secret message concealment from past history to the present.

CLASSICAL CIPHER TYPES

In principle, a *cipher* constitutes text after we have implemented a specific encryption algorithm to plaintext or a message. Each letter of the message is shifted to the left or to the right, making the text unfit for reading. Classical ciphers are encryption algorithms that have been used in the past to secure communications. There are many types of classical cipher methods; however, all of them have become insecure in today's standards in data security. The development of computer technology and the huge increase in computer processing power makes such algorithms breakable in a fraction of a minute.

In the following sections, we are going to give a historical review of the main classical ciphers types used in the past, which are substitution ciphers and transposition ciphers, along with detailed examples on how to use each one to encrypt secret messages.

Substitution Cipher

In this cipher, letters or groups of letters are replaced for other letters or group of letters, thus making the message scrambled and unreadable. We have three main types of this cipher: monoalphabetic, polyalphabetic, and polygraphic.

Monoalphabetic Ciphers

This is a simple substitution cipher where each letter of the plaintext (the secret message) is replaced by another letter from the ciphertext. There are many types of this cipher; the best known are Caesar shift, Atbash, and Keyword.

Caesar Shift

This technique is named after the Roman Emperor Julius Caesar, first invented more than 2000 years ago. It works by substituting one letter of the alphabet by the third letter in succession; for example, according to Table 1.1. If we shift the alphabet by three positions we can have the values shown (the Caesar cipher row) substituted for each letter of alphabet.

A becomes *D*, **B** becomes *E*, and so forth.

For example, encrypting the following message using Caesar shift:

Hello my name is Mary
becomes:
KHOOR PB QDPH LV PDUB

We can shift by any number, of course. In this example we used Caesar shift by three. Remember, Caesar shift does not use a key.

Atbash Cipher

Atbash is a simple substitution cipher for the Hebrew alphabet. It is considered one of the oldest known substitution ciphers used. Hebrew is written from right to left just like Arabic. Naturally, we can use this cipher with different languages in addition to Hebrew.

In Atbash cipher, the letters of the alphabet are simply reversed. For example **A** becomes *Z*, **B** becomes *Y*, and so forth, as it appears in Table 1.2.

For example, encrypting the following message using Atbash cipher:

Hello my name is Kandy
becomes:
SVOOL NB MZNV RH PZMWB

Keyword Cipher

This cipher uses a keyword to rearrange the alphabet. It is similar to the Caesar alphabet with the exception that it uses a predefined keyword for the beginning of the substitution alphabet. Letters used in the keyword are not used in the rest of the cipher alphabet (duplicate letters in the keyword should be omitted). The keyword is needed to decipher the secret message.

Let us use the example in Table 1.3 to more fully explain. We will use the word **Rima** as the keyword.

Encrypting the following message using the Keyword cipher:

Hello my name is Kathy
becomes:
EBJJN KY LRKB FS HRTEY

Polyalphabetic Ciphers

Polyalphabetic cipher is a substitution cipher, where the substituted alphabet is changed multiple times throughout the message. For example, the letter *N* may become *D* after encoding the first part of the message, but encoded as the letter *W* in the next part of the message. The best-known example of a polyalphabetic cipher is the Vigenère cipher. There are many variations of the Vigenère cipher, such as the AutoKey, Beaufort, and Running Key ciphers. Only the Vigenère cipher will be discussed in detail since the other methods are merely variations of it.

Vigenère Cipher

This cipher was invented by a French diplomat, Blaise de Vigenère, in the 16th century. The Vigenère cipher uses a series of different Caesar ciphers based on a keyword or passphrase. In a Caesar cipher the letters of the alphabet are

TABLE 1.1 The Ciphertext Alphabet for the Caesar Cipher

Plain	A	B	C	D	E	F	G	H	I	J	K	L	M	N	O	P	Q	R	S	T	U	V	W	X	Y	Z
Caesar cipher	D	E	F	G	H	I	J	K	L	M	N	O	P	Q	R	S	T	U	V	W	X	Y	Z	A	B	C

TABLE 1.2 The Ciphertext Alphabet for the Atbash Cipher

Plain	A	B	C	D	E	F	G	H	I	J	K	L	M	N	O	P	Q	R	S	T	U	V	W	X	Y	Z
Atbash cipher	Z	Y	X	W	V	U	T	S	R	Q	P	O	N	M	L	K	J	I	H	G	F	E	D	C	B	A

TABLE 1.3 The Ciphertext Alphabet for the Keyword Cipher

Plain	A	B	C	D	E	F	G	H	I	J	K	L	M	N	O	P	Q	R	S	T	U	V	W	X	Y	Z
Keyword cipher	R	I	M	A	B	C	D	E	F	G	H	J	K	L	N	O	P	Q	S	T	U	V	W	X	Y	Z

shifted using one shift value. For example, a Caesar shift by three makes *A* become *D*, *B* become *E*, and so on. The Vigenère cipher uses several Caesar ciphers, and each cipher has a different shift value (one could be shifted by three, the next shifted by five, and so on).

In order to encrypt our secret text we need to have the Vigenère table. This table consists of the entire English alphabet written out 26 times in different rows. Each row is shifted by one position to the left until we reach to the last letter *Z*. This means we have 26 Caesar shifts, and each row is shifted by one as it appears in Vigenère (Table 1.4).

In order to encrypt our secret message using a Vigenère cipher we need to use it (Table 1.5) in conjunction with a key of our choice.

Let us experiment using this cipher by encrypting the following secret message:

MoveAfterMidnight

(Note: I did not use spaces between words to simplify the example; however, we can use spaces as we did in previous ciphers, because spaces do not count in the ciphertext for letters of correspondence.)

The key, **Rima**, will be used in the example in Table 1.5. First, we write our key as many times as necessary to cover all letters of our secret message.

Now, in order to encrypt our text we need to find the intersection in the table between our plaintext letter and the keyword letter. The first letter of the plaintext is **M**. The corresponding letter in the key row is **R**. We check the **M** letter

TABLE 1.4 Vigenère Table

| | | Plain Text Letter | | | | | | | | | | | | | | | | | | | | | | | | |
		A	B	C	D	E	F	G	H	I	J	K	L	M	N	O	P	Q	R	S	T	U	V	W	X	Y	Z
	A	A	B	C	D	E	F	G	H	I	J	K	L	M	N	O	P	Q	R	S	T	U	V	W	X	Y	Z
	B	B	C	D	E	F	G	H	I	J	K	L	M	N	O	P	Q	R	S	T	U	V	W	X	Y	Z	A
	C	C	D	E	F	G	H	I	J	K	L	M	N	O	P	Q	R	S	T	U	V	W	X	Y	Z	A	B
	D	D	E	F	G	H	I	J	K	L	M	N	O	P	Q	R	S	T	U	V	W	X	Y	Z	A	B	C
	E	E	F	G	H	I	J	K	L	M	N	O	P	Q	R	S	T	U	V	W	X	Y	Z	A	B	C	D
	F	F	G	H	I	J	K	L	M	N	O	P	Q	R	S	T	U	V	W	X	Y	Z	A	B	C	D	E
	G	G	H	I	J	K	L	M	N	O	P	Q	R	S	T	U	V	W	X	Y	Z	A	B	C	D	E	F
	H	H	I	J	K	L	M	N	O	P	Q	R	S	T	U	V	W	X	Y	Z	A	B	C	D	E	F	G
	I	I	J	K	L	M	N	O	P	Q	R	S	T	U	V	W	X	Y	Z	A	B	C	D	E	F	G	H
	J	J	K	L	M	N	O	P	Q	R	S	T	U	V	W	X	Y	Z	A	B	C	D	E	F	G	H	I
	K	K	L	M	N	O	P	Q	R	S	T	U	V	W	X	Y	Z	A	B	C	D	E	F	G	H	I	J
	L	L	M	N	O	P	Q	R	S	T	U	V	W	X	Y	Z	A	B	C	D	E	F	G	H	I	J	K
	M	M	N	O	P	Q	R	S	T	U	V	W	X	Y	Z	A	B	C	D	E	F	G	H	I	J	K	L
	N	N	O	P	Q	R	S	T	U	V	W	X	Y	Z	A	B	C	D	E	F	G	H	I	J	K	L	M
	O	O	P	Q	R	S	T	U	V	W	X	Y	Z	A	B	C	D	E	F	G	H	I	J	K	L	M	N
	P	P	Q	R	S	T	U	V	W	X	Y	Z	A	B	C	D	E	F	G	H	I	J	K	L	M	N	O
	Q	Q	R	S	T	U	V	W	X	Y	Z	A	B	C	D	E	F	G	H	I	J	K	L	M	N	O	P
	R	R	S	T	U	V	W	X	Y	Z	A	B	C	D	E	F	G	H	I	J	K	L	M	N	O	P	Q
	S	S	T	U	V	W	X	Y	Z	A	B	C	D	E	F	G	H	I	J	K	L	M	N	O	P	Q	R
	T	T	U	V	W	X	Y	Z	A	B	C	D	E	F	G	H	I	J	K	L	M	N	O	P	Q	R	S
	U	U	V	W	X	Y	Z	A	B	C	D	E	F	G	H	I	J	K	L	M	N	O	P	Q	R	S	T
	V	V	W	X	Y	Z	A	B	C	D	E	F	G	H	I	J	K	L	M	N	O	P	Q	R	S	T	U
	W	W	X	Y	Z	A	B	C	D	E	F	G	H	I	J	K	L	M	N	O	P	Q	R	S	T	U	V
	X	X	Y	Z	A	B	C	D	E	F	G	H	I	J	K	L	M	N	O	P	Q	R	S	T	U	V	W
	Y	Y	Z	A	B	C	D	E	F	G	H	I	J	K	L	M	N	O	P	Q	R	S	T	U	V	W	X
	Z	Z	A	B	C	D	E	F	G	H	I	J	K	L	M	N	O	P	Q	R	S	T	U	V	W	X	Y

Keyword - Password

TABLE 1.5 The Ciphertext Alphabet for the Vigenère Cipher Using the Word *Rima* as a Key

Key	R	I	M	A	R	I	M	A	R	I	M	A	R	I	M	A	R
Plaintext	M	O	V	E	A	F	T	E	R	M	I	D	N	I	G	H	T
Encrypted text	D	W	H	E	R	N	F	E	I	U	U	D	E	Q	S	H	K

FIGURE 1.1   Excerpt from the Vigenère table showing only rows corresponding to our chosen keyword.

in the top horizontal row and move down until we reach the **R** row (keyword row). The intersection takes place at the letter **D** as it appears in Table 1.5. Repeat the same process with the remaining letters.

Decryption is performed by using the keyword and the ciphertext as follows: we search for the position of the ciphertext in the row that corresponds to row of the matched key. For example, to decrypt the first letter we look for the letter **D** in the **R** row of the table; the matched letter is **M** in the top plaintext row (horizontal top row). To decrypt the second letter we search for **W** in the **I** row of the table; the matching letter is **O**. We repeat the same process until we match each letter in the ciphertext with its correspondent in the keyword (Fig. 1.1).

Keyword: **RIMARIMARIMARIMAR**
Ciphertext: **DWHERNFEIUUDEQSHK**

AutoKey Cipher

This cipher uses the same encryption and decryption process of the Vigenère cipher with one exception. Undoubtedly, in the Vigenère cipher we have to repeat the keyword many times, until the number of letters becomes equal with the plaintext that we are going to encrypt. In AutoKey cipher, we incorporate the plaintext into the keyword. For example:

Plaintext: **MoveAfterMidNight**
Keyword: *Rima*
AutoKey Keyword would become:
RimaMoveAfterMidNight
We continue the encryption and decryption as we did in the Vigenère cipher.

Polygraphic Ciphers

In polygraphic ciphers each letter of the plaintext is substituted with two or more groups of letters, numbers, graphic symbols, or other group of characters. By using this cipher each word in the plaintext would be replaced by another word, character, or number, thus making these ciphers very hard to break using frequency analysis techniques.

Polygraphic ciphers were originally developed to hide frequencies of ciphertext characters. Popular phrases are replaced many times randomly during the message; for example, the word *Attack* could be replaced by *SY YF BL* for the first time during the message and then replaced by *FY YF BL* in the next occurrence. This makes analyzing the secret message using frequency analysis techniques very hard to implement.

There are many types of polygraphic ciphers such as Playfair, Bifid, Trifid, and Four-square. The best known one is Playfair cipher, which we describe in detail next.

Playfair Cipher

This cipher was invented by a British scholar, Sir Charles Wheatstone, in 1854; however, the cipher was named after the Scottish scientist and liberal politician, Lord Lyon Playfair. Lord Playfair promoted this cipher technique widely.

It was used for tactical purposes by the British forces in the Second Boer War and in World War I. It was also used again by both British and Australian forces during World War II.

Playfair was preferred by the British forces because it is fast to learn and needs no equipment to implement; however, it was not used for top secret communications. Its use was limited to protecting communications during combat as enemy forces were able to decrypt Playfair cipher, but only after a fair amount of time. It was successful because the information decrypted would be useless to the enemy by then [1].

How to Encrypt Using Playfair Cipher? To encrypt using Playfair, we first need to have a secret key. This key is made up of 25 letters; no repeated letters in sequence are allowed. For example, if two *R*'s happen to occur in sequence only the first one is used; the second one is skipped.

Next, we need to create our Playfair table, which will be a five-by-five table that begins with our chosen key. The rest of the alphabet is inserted into the table without repeating the letters used in the keyword. Make sure that the table consists of only 25 letters. Usually *I* and *J* are combined into one (insert either *I* or *J*) letter, or we have the option to remove *Q* or *X* from the table.

Let us now experiment creating our Playfair table. We first need to have a secret keyword: **London.**

This is not a perfect keyword because it repeats two letters, *O* and *N*, but we will use it to demonstrate how repeated letters in the keyword will be skipped in the table.

Let us now construct our Playfair five-by-five table (Table 1.6). We begin by writing the keyword without modifying its letter order, skipping repeated letters. (We will begin writing from left to right and top to bottom.)

We insert the secret key, **London**, *without repeating letters* (**LOND**). Remember to count the *I* and *J* as only *I*. We insert the remaining alphabet row by row from left to right and top to bottom without repeating the letters that existed previously in the secret key, which were inserted before.

Next, we need to split up the secret message (plaintext) into a group of two letters; if the plaintext consists of an odd number of letters we should add *X* or *Q* at the end to make it even. For example the sentence, **Move after Midnight Rima,** would look like *MO VE AF TE RM ID NI GH TR IM AX*. We then add *X* to the word Rima to make the final plaintext number of letters even. We should also consider not having one pair in the plaintext that contains double letters in succession after splitting it; if we have such a case we should insert the letter *X*. For example, SUMMIT would become *SU MX MI TX*. We separate the *MM* pair with *X* and added *X* to the end of the word in order to complete the last

bigram and make it even. It is not necessary to add the letter *X*; if the pair consists of two *X* letters we can break it using another letter like *Z*, for example.

Now we take each group of letters and find them in the table, first considering the following **three Playfair encryption** rules:

1. If both letters are in the same column, take the letter below each one; if one of the two letters is at the end of the column, go back to the top of the column and take the first letter.

   For example, to encrypt the pair letters *EX*, both are in the same column, the first letter *E* becomes *K* (we took the letter below it directly), and the second letter *X* is at the end of the column, so we return back to the top of the column and select *N*. Now *EX* becomes *KN* after implementing Playfair encryption using the table (see Fig. 1.2).

2. If letters are both in the same row, take the letter to the right of each one. Again if one of the letters is at the end of the row, return to the beginning of that same row from the left and take the first letter in the row.

   For example, to encrypt the pair *FG*, the letter on the right side of *F* is *G*. The second letter *G* is at the end of the row so we return back to the beginning of the same

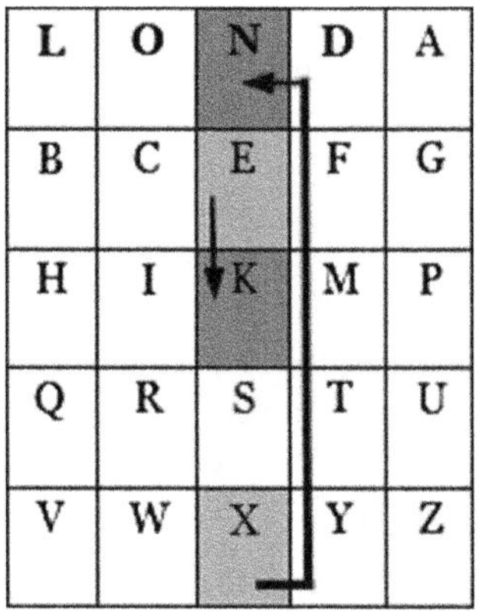

FIGURE 1.2   Letters in the same column case.

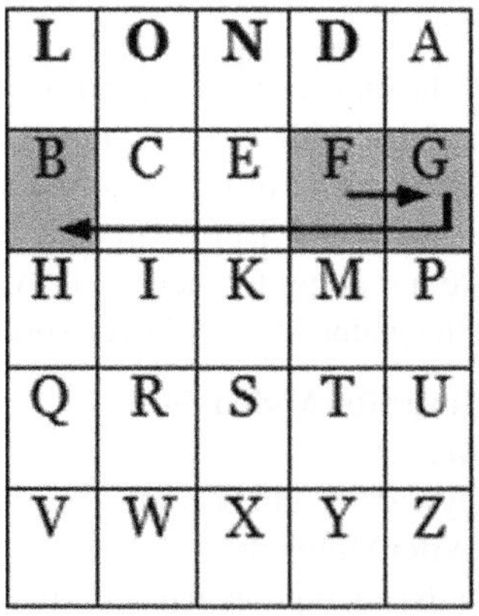

FIGURE 1.3   Letters are in the same row case.

TABLE 1.6 Playfair Table With the Keyword LONDON

L	O	N	D	A
B	C	E	F	G
H	I	K	M	P
Q	R	S	T	U
V	W	X	Y	Z

row from the left and take the letter *B*. Now *FG* becomes *GB* (see Fig. 1.3).

3. If the letters are on different rows and columns of your table, form a rectangle with two letters on the horizontal opposite corners of the rectangle.

According to the previous example (see Fig. 1.4), to encrypt the pair *PV*, we should form a rectangle, where *P* becomes *H* and *V* becomes *Z*. The result of encrypting of *PV* becomes *HZ*. We should pay close attention to the last rule. The order of letters is very important; the letter that comes first in the plaintext is encrypted first, so in the previous example *PV* becomes *HZ*, not *ZH*.

Let us now return to our example: we want to encrypt the text, **Move after Midnight Rima**.

Secret Keyword: **London**

First, divide the text you want to encrypt into pairs. Put *X* at the end of the plaintext if it consists of an odd number of letters. If a pair has repeated letters in succession after splitting it up, you will need to insert *X* inside it. Using Table 1.6, the following applies (Table 1.7):

MO VE AF TE RM ID NI GH TR IM AX

How to Decrypt Using Playfair Cipher? Decrypting the Playfair cipher is easy. We do the same encryption steps but in reverse. Indeed, we need to have the secret key to complete the decryption successfully. The next step would be creating

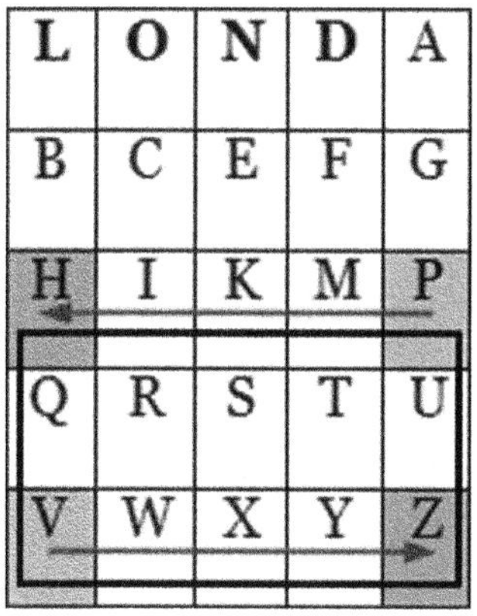

FIGURE 1.4 Letters are on different rows and columns case.

our Playfair five-by-five tables and do the decryption using the reverse steps of encryption.

Mechanical Substitution Ciphers

Mechanical substitution ciphers were invented and used in the period between World War I and the widespread availability of computers (some governments started to take advantage of computers in ciphering in 1950, others waited until 1960). The most famous and secure machine was the Enigma machine, especially versions developed by the German army exclusively for this purpose.

The Enigma Machine

With the increase of wireless communication starting in 1900, the need for a ciphering technique that replaces the old and time-consuming handwritten ciphers to secure communications was essential. From this point in history, different countries seriously started investing in the development of mechanical cipher machines.

As with many modern products, it is difficult to figure out who has invented it before the others, but the concept of using rotating disks to encrypt messages was invented in many countries almost simultaneously. The leading inventors were *Edward Hebern* in the United States, *Arvid Damm* in Sweden, *Hugo Koch* in The Netherlands, and *Arthur Scherbius* in Germany. Many sources reference *Hebern* as the pioneer in this field because he tried to manufacture and market his machines commercially on a wide basis before the others [2].

In 1917, *Hebern* developed his cipher machine with rotating disks; each disk would perform a substitution cipher. He built his machine through combining the mechanical parts of a standard typewriter with the electrical parts of an electric typewriter, connecting the two through a scrambler.

It should be noted that Enigma is the brand name of a series of rotor cipher machines, developed before and during World War II by various countries (United States, Japan, United Kingdom, to name a few). Some of the variations developed were compatible with each other, although many others were not [3].

The famous German Enigma machine was invented by the German engineer *Arthur Scherbius* at the end of World War I in 1918. Its early adoption was for commercial use, but the weight and size of the early models (A and B models) made them unattractive for military use. Enigma

TABLE 1.7 Playfair Ciphertext According to Table 1.6

Plaintext	MO	VE	AF	TE	RM	ID	NI	GH	TR	IM	AX
Rule Number[a]	3	3	3	3	3	3	2	3	2	2	3
Playfair cipher	ID	XB	DG	SF	TI	MO	OK	BP	US	KP	NZ

[a]*We have three rules as we mentioned before: (1) Pairs are on the same column, (2) pairs are on the same row, and (3) pairs are on different rows and on different columns.*

TABLE 1.8 Rail Fence Imaginary Table

M	.	.	A	.	.	.	R	.	.	.	N	.	.	.	T	.	.	.	A
.	O	.	E	.	F	.	E	.	M	.	D	.	I	.	H	.	R	.	M	.
.	.	V	.	.	.	T	.	.	.	I	.	.	.	G	.	.	.	I	.	.

evolved through several stages such as adding a reflector to its engine, making it lighter and smaller in size (Enigma C and D). In 1926, however, the commercial Enigma was purchased by the German navy and adapted for military use. The German army developed many versions of Enigma before and during World War II; the most famous one was Enigma M4, which was used exclusively in the U-Boot division of the German navy. The Enigma M4 played a vital role in the *Battle of the Atlantic*, where many historical sources reference capturing its codebooks as a major turning point in World War II events.

Basically, the Enigma engine was composed mainly of three physical rotors, each one taking a letter and outputting it as a different one to the next rotor in line. The letter passes through all the three rotors and finally bounces off a reflector, which also gives it another letter at the end. The same process is repeated in reverse order, and the last letter passes back through all three rotors in the other direction until reaching the lightboard.

The board then lights up, showing the corresponding encrypted output at the same time, and the first of the three rotors clicks round one position. This results in changing the second letter output even though it was the same letter as the previous one.

You can check the *Cipher Machines* website for an illustration of how Enigma machines work [4].

You can also download an open source exact simulation of the Enigma cipher machine used during World War II from the following link for practice on your own desktop: http://users.telenet.be/d.rijmenants/en/enigmasim.htm.

Transposition Cipher

This is an encryption method where plaintext letters (or group of characters) are reordered according to a predefined system to hide messages sent. Transposition cipher is considered as an alternative type of cipher used in ancient civilizations. It has many different implementations; the following are only a few.

Rail Fence

Considered one of the oldest implementations of transposition ciphers, used by ancient Greeks in a mechanical system called Scytale, Rail Fence derives its name from the way in which it is encoded.

The plaintext is written downward and diagonally on successive *rails* of an imaginary fence, then moving up when we reach the bottom rail. When we reach the top rail, the message is written downward again until the whole plaintext is completed [5].

The key for the rail fence cipher is just the number of rails. The number of practical keys that we can use is small. Let us practice using this cipher by encrypting the following text using a key of three rails, shown in Table 1.8:

Move after midnight Rima

The ciphertext is read off along the rows:

MARNTAOEFEMDIHRMVTIGI

(Note: Spaces between words in plaintext are ignored in ciphertext.)

Decrypting the message is easy if the row boundaries are known. Just write down the rows in order:

MARNTA
OEFEMDIHRM
VTIGI

Then reconstruct the rail again (three rails) and read it as we did in Table 1.8.

Columnar Transposition

This is a fairly easy cipher to implement. In this cipher the message is written out in rows of fixed length. What determines the number of rows and how the column is shifted is the actual *keyword*. Let us practice encryption using this cipher.

Let's select **FRANCE** as a keyword, and encrypt the following text:

Move after midnight Jodi

The row length is the same as the length of the keyword, and the number of columns is also determined according to the number of keyword letters (in this case, 6) (Table 1.9).

We've added three *X*'s to make our secret message fit in the rectangle. This is called regular columnar transposition. An irregular columnar transposition leaves these characters blank.

Now we need to reorder the columns according to the alphabetical order of the keyword (Table 1.10).

The ciphertext is read off along the columns (do not count the keyword letters):

VRGIAITXFDJXMTNOEMHXOEID

To decipher the message, the recipient has to work out the column lengths by dividing the message length by the key

TABLE 1.9 Columnar Transposition Cipher With the Keyword FRANCE

F	R	A	N	C	E
M	O	V	E	A	F
T	E	R	M	I	D
N	I	G	H	T	J
O	D	I	X	X	X

TABLE 1.10 Columnar Transposition Cipher Ordered According to the English Alphabet Order

A	C	E	F	N	R
V	A	F	M	E	O
R	I	D	T	M	E
G	T	J	N	H	I
I	X	X	O	X	D

TABLE 1.11 One-Time Pad Cipher for Encrypting HELLO KANDY

Plaintext	H	E	L	L	O	K	A	N	D	Y
One-time pad	C	Y	H	U	I	P	H	G	T	R
Ciphertext	J	C	S	F	W	Z	H	T	W	P

length. In this case, message length is 24 and the keyword length is 6, so this column length would subsequently be 4.

Now we create our grid with six columns (keyword) while each column contains four characters from the ciphertext. Finally we rearrange the column according to our keyword [6].

Double Transposition

This is just the same as the columnar cipher with an additional layer of security. We run the produced cipher through the encryption again using a different keyword, thus making the message extremely difficult to decipher.

Other implementations of the transposition cipher are Route, Myszkowski transposition, Disrupted transposition, and Grilles.

Other Ciphers and Codes

The One-Time Pad

This ciphering technique is considered one the few ciphering techniques that have been proven to be unbreakable if used correctly. What we mean by *unbreakable if used correctly* is that during the last year of World War II (1943) and shortly after, a counterintelligence project called *Venona* was initiated by the US army's Signal Intelligence Services (this agency is now known by the name NSA) to decrypt the Soviet one-time pad message. Many sources mention that more than 3000 messages were decrypted during the life span of this project (1943–1980). The main reason for cracking this cipher was using a nonrandom key material for encrypting messages sent by the Soviet Union [7]. You can read more about this project in an article published by the *New York Times* [8].

It works by pairing the plaintext with a secret key; now each character from the plaintext is combined with its correspondent from the secret key to produce the ciphertext. Let us practice using it (Table 1.11).

Plaintext: **Hello Kandy**
One-time pad: **CYHUIPHGTR**

The first letter from the plaintext is **H**, its position in the English alphabet is 8, and the one-time pad letter that corresponds to it is **C**, which has the position 3. We calculate both number positions and subtract 1 from the result: $(8+3)-1=10$. The number 10 is equal to the position of letter **J** in the English alphabet and this becomes our first encrypted letter. Each letter is enciphered in this method, with the alphabet wrapping around to the beginning if the addition results in a number beyond 26 (**Z**).

The ciphertext is **JCSFWZHTWP**

To decrypt the message, we subtract the first letter of the ciphertext from the one-time pad and add one to the result. The resulting number will point to the letter in the alphabet that is corresponding to our plaintext letter.

To decrypt the first letter, **J**, we subtract **J** from **C** and add 1 to the result (what we mean by subtraction is the value position of each letter in the alphabet: **J** = 10 AND **C** = 3):

$(10-3)+1=8$, which equals the letter **H** in the alphabet.

One-time pad is considered an impractical ciphering technique as it requires that the key material be as long as the plaintext, and the secret key should be random and used only once. Furthermore, the key should be kept secret, not told to anyone except the sender and receiver, since the key and the ciphertext will reveal the entire secret message.

Morse Code

Morse code, originally named after its inventor, Samuel Finley Breese Morse (1791–1872), an American inventor and painter. is a system in which letters are represented by dots and dashes. Morse code was used over telegraph lines to send messages in the United States since 1835.

Morse's original code was not quite the same as the one in use today as it included pauses as well as dahs and dits. However, a conference in Berlin in 1851 established an international version, shown in Fig. 1.5.

The most well-known use of Morse code is for sending the distress signal: SOS. The SOS signal is sent as:

$$\bullet \; \bullet \; \bullet \quad \blacksquare \; \blacksquare \; \blacksquare \quad \bullet \; \bullet \; \bullet$$

Although the telegraph has fallen out of widespread use since the start of the 21st century, replaced by the telephone, fax machine, and Internet, it set the groundwork for the communications revolution that led to those later innovations.

Book Cipher

Book cipher uses a large text or a complete book to encrypt a secret message. This means the cipher key could be a complete book, and without it the message cannot be decrypted.

Each word in the plaintext message is replaced with a number that represents the location of word from the book being used. For example, the word **Move** could appear in the book as word number 1075; we replace it with this number to form our ciphertext, and then repeat the same process with the remaining words. Finally we will have a cipher similar to this:

Plaintext: **Move after Midnight**
Ciphertext: 1075 **145** 1256

To decrypt the message we count the number of words in the book and write down each one to form our plaintext message again.

Difference Between Substitution and Transposition Cipher

In substitution cipher we replace each letter of the plaintext with another letter, symbol, or number; for the decryption, the reverse substitution has to be performed. However, in

International Morse Code

1. A dash is equal to three dots.
2. The space between parts of the same letter is equal to one dot.
3. The space between two letters is equal to three dots.
4. The space between two words is equal to seven dots.

FIGURE 1.5 Chart of the Morse code letters and numerals [9].

transposition cipher we just rearrange the plaintext letters in a different order; for example, when encrypting the word *Attack* using a Caesar shift (shift of three), it results in *DWWDFN*. In simple transposition cipher we can simply reorder the plaintext, and then *Attack* would become *KCATTA*. We simply reverse the text.

The simplest form of substitution cipher is when each character is replaced by exactly one other character (monoalphabetic ciphers). This encryption can be broken with statistical methods (frequency analysis) because in every language characters appear with a particular probability (Fig. 1.6). Examples of similar weak ciphers are Caesar Shift, Atbash, and Keyword.

The basic use of frequency analysis is to first count the frequency of ciphertext letters and then associate guessed plaintext letters with them (Table 1.12). The first one who

studied frequencies of letters was the Muslim Arab mathematician Al-Kindi (c.801–873 CE), who formally developed this method.

Polyalphabetic cipher was adopted to reduce the effectiveness of frequency analysis attacks on the ciphertext, because each letter in the ciphertext is shifted by a different amount, determined according to the key used. Nonetheless, any resulting frequencies in the ciphertext would not represent the frequencies of the actual message. This makes conducting frequency analysis attacks harder in this cipher but not impossible to crack!

Polygraphic cipher (like the Playfair cipher) is also harder to break using a frequency analysis technique. Playfair encrypts pairs of letters (digraphs) instead of one letter in a monoalphabetic cipher, which means we have more than 600 possible digraphs rather than the 26 possible monographs.

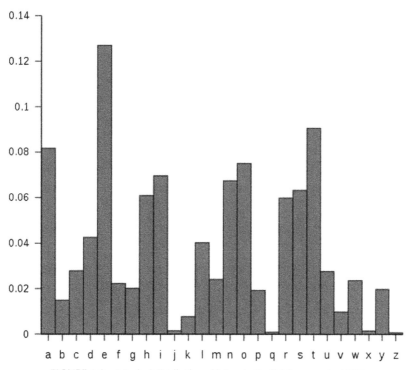

FIGURE 1.6 A typical distribution of letters in English language text [10].

TABLE 1.12 Frequency of Common Letter Combinations in the English Language

Most common trigraphs in order of frequency	THE, AND, THA, ENT, ION, TIO, FOR, NDE, HAS, NCE, TIS, OFT, MEN
The most common two-letter words in order of frequency	of, to, in, it, is, be, as, at, so, we, he, by, or, on, do, if, me, my, up, an, go, no, us, am
The most common four-letter words in order of frequency	That, with, have, this, will, your, from, they, know, want, been, good, much, some, time, very, when, come, here, just, like, long, make, many, more, only, over, such, take, than, them, well, were

Transposition cipher is also susceptible to many different attacks. A single columnar transposition could be attacked by guessing possible column lengths, writing the message out in its columns, and then looking for possible anagrams. Nowadays with the advance of computer systems many classical algorithms mentioned before could be broken in a fraction of a second. The best methods now to secure encryption is to combine both substitution and transposition ciphers to create a powerful encryption schema (AES and DES algorithms combine both ciphers to create very powerful algorithms).

The techniques mentioned earlier are considered obsolete in today's world, but knowing these techniques remain useful for understanding cryptography and the workings of more complex modern ciphers.

Practicing Old Ciphers Using Modern Computing

There are numerous websites that offers functionality for practicing encryption/decryption of different ciphering algorithms. However, I do not recommend using these websites because they may not be accurate enough (although some of them can be professional and are maintained by specialists in the field). CrypTool is a tool developed and maintained by a set of famous German and European universities (Fig. 1.7). The CrypTool website describes this tool as follows:

CrypTool 1 (CT1) is an open-source Windows program for cryptography and cryptanalysis. It's the most wide-spread e-learning software of its kind.

There is another version of this tool with more advanced features and covers more encryption algorithms, defined by its creators as follows:

CrypTool 2 is the modern successor of CrypTool 1, it provides a graphical user interface for visual programming. So workflows can be visualized and controlled to enable intuitive manipulation and interaction of cryptographic functions.

Both tools can be downloaded from https://www.cryptool.org/en/. It should be noted that practicing algorithms using this tool is fun and simple.

MODERN CRYPTOGRAPHY SYSTEMS

Cryptography is the practice of hiding information by obscuring it, thus making it unreadable for any unintended recipients. Modern cryptography intersects the disciplines of mathematics, computer science, and electrical engineering. Applications of cryptography include ATM cards, authentication and digital signatures, secure network communications, disk encryption, electronic commerce, cable television networks, and so on.

Basically there are three types of cryptography systems:

- Secret key cryptography (symmetrical encryption)
- Public key cryptography (asymmetrical encryption)
- Cryptographic hash function

In cryptography, a key is a piece of information used by an algorithm to alter information. This is aimed at making this information scrambled and is visible only to people who have the corresponding key to recover the desired information.

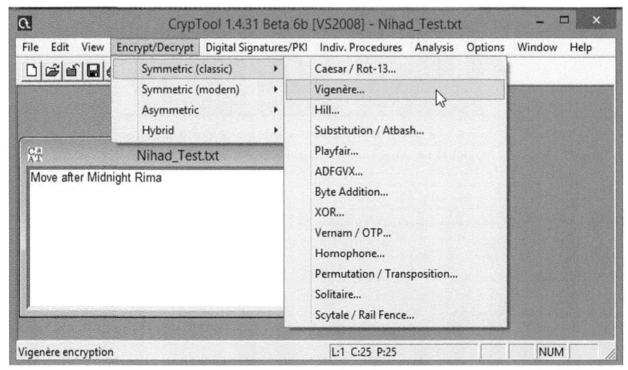

FIGURE 1.7 Screen capture of the CrypTool program.

Secret Key Cryptography

In secret key cryptography, both the sender and receiver must use the same key to encrypt and decrypt a message as shown in Fig. 1.8 (for obvious reasons it was named symmetrical encryption). This imposes a security risk as we need to deliver the key to the recipient of the message in a secure way to decrypt the message. If intruders get hold of the key, they will be able to decrypt the secret message, thus compromising the entire system.

Public Key Cryptography

In public key cryptography, we use two keys: one for encryption and the second for decryption. We can distribute the public key everywhere without compromising the private key. A user will use his friend's public key to encrypt the message. The receiver will use his/her private key (which should be kept secret) to decrypt this message.

Although the two keys are different, two parts of this key pair are mathematically linked. The public key is used to encrypt plaintext or to verify a digital signature, whereas the private key is used to decrypt ciphertext or to create a digital signature. Messages encrypted with a public key can only be decrypted using the same private key pair.

This method is far more secure than the symmetric cryptography, as the sender and receiver can exchange their public keys using any communication method while keeping their private keys secret to decrypt the messages received.

Let us demonstrate how public key cryptography works using this simple example (Fig. 1.9):

1. *Sophy* wants to communicate secretly with *Nihad*, so Sophy encrypts a message using *Nihad's* public key (which he made available to everyone through his website or on his email signature) and sends the encrypted message to him.
2. When *Nihad* receives the encrypted message, he uses his private key to decrypt the message so he can read it.
3. If *Nihad* wants to send an encrypted reply to *Sophy*, he will use her public key to encrypt the message and send it back to her.
4. When *Sophy* receives *Nihad's* reply, she will use her private key to decrypt the message so she is able to read it.

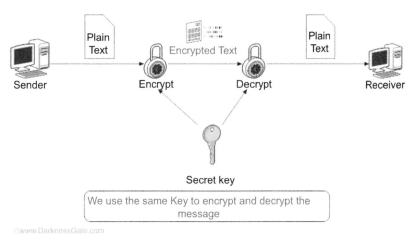

FIGURE 1.8 Demonstration of a secret key cryptography system.

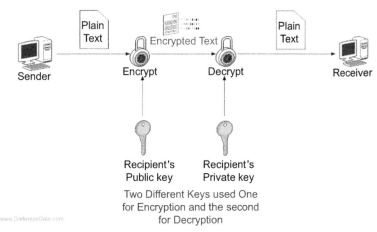

FIGURE 1.9 Demonstration of asymmetric cryptography: public and private key pair.

Digital Signature

After we learned how public/private keypair works, we need a method to make sure that the person who sends us the encrypted message is who he pretends to be. For example in our last demonstration, we said that if *Sophy* wants to send a secure message to *Nihad* she should encrypt it using *Nihad's* public key, and *Nihad* will use his private key to decrypt the received message.

However, how can *Nihad* make sure that this message was sent from *Sophy*? What if another person (*Mary*, for example) sent him the message pretending to be *Sophy*! Here comes the digital signature's role in authenticating the sender of the message.

Sophy can encrypt the message using her private key and send it to *Nihad*. *Nihad* now has to use *Sophy's* public key to decrypt the message. Because *Sophy's* private key is secret (and should always be so), *Nihad* knows that this message originated from *Sophy* and not from anyone else because only *Sophy* knows her private key. This is similar to a paper letter, where a signature on the letter serves as a proof that this message was written by the person who signed it with his own signature. Encrypting with a private key can thus be regarded as an equivalent alternative to placing one's signature on the message. This is why it is being called creating a digital signature for the message (Fig. 1.10).

In order to send the message secretly after signing it, *Sophy* has to encrypt the message again using *Nihad's* public key and then send it to him. On the other end, *Nihad* has to decrypt the message using his private key and then decrypt the result again using *Sophy's* public key so he can read the message and also make sure it originated from *Sophy*.

Cryptographic Hash Function

The hash function is another secure way of encryption. Hashing is the act of generating a number from a string of text. The hash is substantially smaller than the text itself, and is generated by a formula in such a way that it is extremely unlikely that some other text will produce the same hash value.

Hashing is widely used in information security and forensic systems. If we want to send an encrypted file, we will first calculate the file hash. Then we will encrypt the file along with the generated hash number (we can put it in a text file) and send it to the recipient. The recipient will decrypt the file and calculate his hash number. If both hashes are the same there is very high probability that message has not been tampered with [11].

The ideal cryptographic hash function has four main properties [12]:

- It is easy to compute the hash value for any given message.
- It is almost impossible to generate a message from a given hash.
- It is impossible to modify a message without changing the hash.
- It is impossible to find two different messages with the same hash.

There are many different hashing algorithms: MD2, MD5, SHA, and SHA-1 are examples.

How to Calculate File Hash?

Many tools can be used to calculate a file hash under Windows® machines. *Febooti Hash & CRC* is one tool that is very easy to use (Fig. 1.11).

To install it on your PC follow these steps:
1. Go to http://www.febooti.com/downloads (if the link changed search for *Hash & CRC*).
2. Download the file to your PC (it is 0.9 MB and works on both 32- and 64-bit machines).
3. After installing the program, right-click on any file that you want to calculate its hash and select *Properties*.
4. From the Properties window, select the *Hash/CRC* tab.

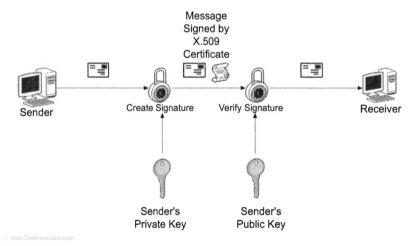

FIGURE 1.10 Digital signature using X.509 certificate.

FIGURE 1.11 Calculate hash using the Hash/CRC tool.

STEGANOGRAPHY

What Is Steganography?

Steganography is the science of hiding information. It is among the few disciplines that have the honor to be described as an *art* in addition to being a *science*. Whereas the goal of cryptography is to make data unreadable by a third party, the goal of steganography is to hide data from a third party. Steganography is usually used in conjunction with encryption for additional security of sensitive data. By hiding encrypted data inside an honest-looking carrier, a secret message has less possibility of being discovered by outside parties during information exchange.

Hiding secret messages inside what seem to be ordinary messages is nothing new. The word steganography itself originated in Greece and it means *covered writing*. It includes a vast array of techniques that could be used to conceal the existence of a hidden message. The first recorded use of this term was in 1499 AD by a German scholar name *Johannes Trithemius* in his *Steganographia*, a three-volume work describing different techniques of concealing secret messages in text. These volumes also suggested different techniques to hide messages using cryptography and a system of rapid learning [13].

Although the term steganography appeared first in the 15th century, throughout history there have been number of techniques used for hiding messages, especially during wars. Different civilizations implemented steganography techniques in different ways. The first recorded one took place in 440 BC in ancient Greece when *Demaratus* sent a warning about a forthcoming attack to Greece by writing it directly on the wooden backing of a wax tablet before applying its beeswax surface [14].

The Roman Empire also used steganography techniques around 300 AD through human skin, where Roman generals used slaves as carriers for their secret messages during wars. The slave's head would be shaved clean, and the secret message is tattooed on his head using small letters. After a month, the slave's hair would grow back, covering the secret message. Then the slave was sent across hostile land with little fear that the secret message may get exposed by the enemy. Upon reaching the final destination, a quick head shave revealed the secret message. The reply could be sent by another slave in the same way.

In ancient China, secret messages were written on fine silk or papers and then rolled it into a ball and covered by a layer of wax. The messenger swallowed the ball and kept it in his stomach until he reached his final destination.

If we compare historical methods of steganography with the new modern ones we are going to see in coming chapters, we find that the major changes between both was in the carrier of secret data only. Historical methods relied on physical steganography (technique) such as invisible ink, animal skin, eggs, human skin, and engraved symbols. Modern methods, however, are heavily dependent on digital media like digital images, audio, video files, transmission protocols, and electronic waves as new carriers of the concealed data.

Comparing Steganography and Cryptography

Both steganography and cryptography share the goal in providing secret communications, but they differ in the methods used to achieve this goal. Some researchers argue that steganography is a form of cryptography because it is used to cover communications. In this book, nonetheless, we will talk about steganography as a separate field to simplify presenting information for readers. Because digital steganography has evolved a lot in the last years, it is only right to put it in its own category in modern computer science.

Table 1.13 describes some main differences between both techniques.

Steganography Types

There are different types of stenography: linguistic, technical, and digital (Fig. 1.12). The focus of this book is on digital stenography used mostly on computers; however, we

If we took the first letter from each word we will have the following message:

Pershing sails from NY June 1.

The Germans returned another message, apparently as a check on the first:

APPARENTLY   NEUTRAL'S   PROTEST   IS THOROUGHLY DISCOUNTED AND IGNORED. ISMAN HARD HIT. BLOCKADE ISSUE AFFECTS PRETEXT FOR EMBARGO ON BYPRODUCTS, EJECTING SUETS AND VEGETABLE OILS.

Taking the second letter in each word the same secret message as the first will emerge:

Pershing sails from NY June 1.

The advantage of this method is that a secret message could be hidden inside another open carrier that contains ordinary text that may not grab the attention of any observer [16].In Chapter 3, we will investigate a modern type of null cipher that allows us to hide our secret message digitally using SPAM messages as a carrier.

Grille Cipher Grille cipher was invented by *Gerolamo Cardano*. Grilles are a kind of transposition cipher that can also include aspects of steganography. They are best thought of as pieces of cardboard with holes cut into them in a specific pattern. The secret message is written in the holes, and then the rest of the message is filled in around it. The only way the message is readable is by the recipient who has the correct grille.

Digital Steganography

The advance of computers and the widespread use of online communication nowadays had allowed us to begin embedding secret messages inside digital files like images and audio files. This could be achieved by adding secret bits or replacing the current bits inside digital files. Such hiding methods are considered difficult to crack and notice for both human observer and automated programs used by governments to monitor online traffic.

Some may argue that using cryptography techniques is more secure for transmitting extremely sensitive information and business documents; however, there are cases when we are not able to use cryptography because it is not allowed by law or simply because we have something to hide and do not want to grab attention. Along comes steganography to solve this problem.

There are basically two popular approaches for implementing steganography in digital files:

1. Adding bits to a file: Hidden messages could be inserted in the *file header* of different digital files. In many image formats *file headers* usually store information like the image's size, resolution, number of colors, and so on. Such places are ideal for storing our hidden messages. In Chapter 2 you will see how you can hide large amounts of data inside an image *header* without tampering the image's appearance or quality. We can also insert secret messages after the *end-of-file* (EOF) marker. Each digital file has an EOF marker that signals the end of file. Everything after this mark will not be read by the program. The disadvantage of this method is that the size of the carrier file will increase if our secret message was large.

2. Using Least Significant Bit (LSB): In this method we do not add new bits to our carrier file, we simply substitute the last significant bit with one bit from our secret message. Each byte is composed of 8 bits, however, the last bit of each byte is not significant to the file itself. Fortunately we can change it without affecting the quality of the original file. This bit is called the LSB and here is where we are going to hide our bit. By using this method the size of the carrier file will not increase.

In this book we will often refer to the secret message (hidden message) by the name *covert file* and the carrier message by the name *overt file*.

Steganography Protocols Types

There are basically three (protocols) in which steganography can be implemented digitally:

1. *Pure steganography:* In this method, steganography is implemented without using a key (stego-key); we just insert the hidden message inside the carrier file. This method is considered the least secure because the security of the system depends entirely on its secrecy.

2. *Private key steganography:* This requires exchanging a secret key between the sender and the receiver before the communication can occur. In this process the secret message is embedded inside the overt file (any supported digital file) using a stego-key and then sent over a public channel like the Internet to the recipient, who also needs to have the same stego-key in order to extract the hidden message and read it. The disadvantage of this protocol is that the stego-key should be transferred in advance between the two parties and in a secure method. If, at any point, an intruder gets hold of the key, bearing in mind that he/she suspects that there is a hidden message transmitted, he/she will be able to decrypt the secret message and thus compromise the whole system.

3. *Public key steganography:* This is similar to the public key cryptography. In this protocol the sender will encrypt the hidden message with the recipient's public key and send it to him/her. The receiver will then use his/her private key in order to reconstruct the hidden message.

This protocol takes advantage of the secret features of the pubic key cryptography (hence no need to exchange private keys between parties, which eliminates the possibility of stealing the key while transmitting it). In order to compromise this protocol an intruder needs first to know about the existence of the hidden message. He/she, then, can find a way to break the encryption algorithm (which is extremely difficult to achieve) in order to extract and read the hidden message.

A major disadvantage of the last two methods is that encrypting secret messages before hiding it inside a carrier file will make it susceptible to an automated monitoring system. Monitoring programs used by governments and big organizations can easily detect encrypted files and steganography embedding algorithm signatures (more on this on Chapter 6), resulting in launching an alarm for further investigation by humans.

Steganography Types According to Host File Type

There are several approaches in categorizing steganographic systems. We can categorize them according to the type of overt file used for secret communication or according to the overt file modifications applied in the embedding process (Fig. 1.13). In this section we will follow the first approach in categorizing steganographic systems. This helps us to keep our approach on data hiding more practical and understood by most computer professionals and end users alike.

We can divide digital steganography according to the host file used (carrier or overt file) as follows.

Text Steganography Text steganography is a type of steganography that uses text to conceal messages inside it. This could be achieved by changing text formatting or the characteristics of the text. This type is considered impractical, though, because it cannot hide large volumes of data without grabbing someone's attention. Some examples are the hidden text feature in MS Office®, which can be applied by inserting small spaces between words to store bits; white space manipulation to store bits in front of each line or section in the document; shifting lines up or down to store bits; making text white on a white background; and storing hidden text inside document metadata.

Image Steganography Image Steganography is a technique that has become more popular in recent years because of the

flood of electronic images available online with the advent of digital cameras, smart phones, and high-speed Internet that simplify distribution of large images. In addition to its popularity among users, digital images have more capability to store large amounts of hidden data inside their structure, as we will see in Chapter 3.

Image steganography works by embedding an encrypted message (or the original message without encryption) into a graphic file. This produces what is called a stego-image.

This stego-image is then transmitted to the receiver, who then extracts the message from the carrier file using a predefined shared secret between the sender and the receiver. During the transmission of the stego-image, unauthenticated persons can only observe the transmission of an image but can't recognize the existence of the hidden message.

Audio/Video Steganography Audio steganography takes advantage of physical characteristics of the human auditory system. For example, the human ear can listen to noise in the audible frequency range between 20 Hz and 20 kHz. Audio steganography works by embedding a secret message inside a digitized audio signal, which results in changing the binary sequence of the corresponding audio file without any noticeable change to the human ear. The human ear is not able to recognize a low tone frequency signal in the presence of a higher frequency; this is called frequency masking. This discovered property is used in different ways to exploit audio files for embedding data inside it secretly.

Audio steganography uses the following techniques for hiding secret messages:

- LSB coding
- Parity coding
- Phase coding
- Spread spectrum
- Echo hiding

Audio steganography is also part of the more common term of digital watermarking (antipiracy techniques), which is widely used in counterpiracy systems. This technique enable us to know whether a specific audio/video is illegally recorded (copy version) and when this happened.

Video uses a combination of both images and audio to deliver its contents. Hidden data is usually embedded inside video images. The continual stream of images and sound will make it very hard for humans to know there is hidden data inside the video file (more on this in Chapter 3).

Network Steganography Network steganography works by exploiting different networking protocol features to hide its secret message. We can also consider concealing data messages inside images, then sending them across the Internet as a kind of networking stego. In this book, however, we will only refer to the methods where we can

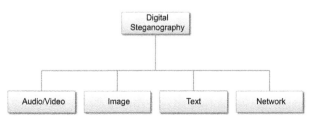

FIGURE 1.13 Classification of digital steganography according to host file type.

exploit hidden areas inside networking protocol channels as networking steganography.

There are basically two ways in which we can hide our secret messages using network steganography:

1. Exploiting some networking protocols in unused header space to conceal data.
2. Masking secret messages as ordinary network traffic.

Some working examples of networking steganography are:

1. Hiding messages inside network protocols, like hiding in IPv4, IPv6, TCP, or UDP headers.
2. Concealing secret messages by masking their contents to appear as a regular traffic, for example, masking a message to appears as HTML code and sending it through port 80 to look like ordinary Internet traffic.
3. Exploiting HTTP GET requests to convey their messages to a web server.
4. Hiding inside DNS queries.

In Chapter 3 we will expand our discussion on hiding data inside digital files to include plenty of working examples on how we can achieve this practically in addition to offering a detailed description of how each technique works behind the scene.

Digital Steganography Techniques

In the previous section we've categorized steganography according to the overt file used. In the digital steganography techniques section we will talk about how this could be achieved with respect to the overt file modifications.

In order to hide our secret message inside digitalized files we need to use one (or more) of the following techniques.

Injunction In this technique we insert our secret message in a trivial location that will not be read by an overt file application. For example, each file has an EOF marker that points where the file ends. Some files allow us to insert secret data beyond the EOF marker, so if we have a JPEG image that contains secret data beyond the EOF, any application (Windows® Photo Viewer, for example) will read the image and stop when it reaches the EOF marker. Everything beyond the EOF marker will be hidden without affecting image quality or appearance. The main drawback of this method is that the size of the overt file will increase dramatically if the volume of secret data is big, thus making it more suspicious for observers. In addition, investigating for hidden data beyond the EOF is very easy and could be done automatically by many tools.

Substitution Substitution works by embedding secret messages inside the overt file without adding any additional bits to it. It looks for insignificant bits in the overt file that will not affect the file itself if replaced with the secret message bits. This technique is more secure than the injunction technique because it does not add anything new to the overt file, making its size the same as the original one. However, the volume of data that can be hidden is limited to the amount of insignificant bits in the overt file. For example, the image file is composed of many bytes, each byte containing 8 bits. If we replace the least bit in each byte of the image with our secret message bit we can have our secret message hidden completely without modifying image appearance or size.

Generation In this method a new overt file will be produced based on the information that existed in the secret message. This will produce a new overt file that contains the secret data. For example, we can hide our secret message by producing another bigger message that looks similar to SPAM messages. A website called *Spammimic* [17] uses such a technique to hide and transmit secret messages.

In Chapter 3 we will expand our discussion on each steganographic technique based on the modifications of the overt file.

WATERMARKING

With the increased number of digital files published online, it is necessary to find a method to identify the legal owner of a specific file. A digital watermark is a kind of marker embedded into audio, video, or image files. A digital watermarks is usually used to verify the content is genuine and from an authorized source and that content has not been altered or reproduced. Furthermore, it is used for protecting against digital piracy by defining ownership and usage rights of digital contents in addition to tracking it online.

Famous artists usually watermark their pictures in case someone tries to steel their work as the watermark will be copied along with the image and reproduce itself with each copy.

Watermarking Types

Watermarks could be categorized in two ways:

● Technique used to embed the watermark in the overt file
● Visibility of the inserted watermark

To simplify the discussion in this section we will categorize it according to its visibility.

Visible Watermark

As its name implies, visible watermarks appear clearly on the digital file that we want to protect. Copyright owners usually use symbols or text to prove the ownership of their files. Fig. 1.14 displays a copyright notice by its owner.

FIGURE 1.14 Demonstration of visible watermark on a picture.

Invisible Watermark

This is a hidden watermark embedded in a digital file's binary data without altering its visual representation. We can store such marks in image EXIF property fields (as we will see in Chapters 2 and 6). Some specialized software can detect and uncover invisible watermarks. Its primary usage is to prove the ownership of the file and to track it online by inserting some metadata. Removing an invisible watermark completely could be done using specialized software (as we will see in Chapters 6 and 7). EXIF metadata can also be removed in Windows® machines by *right-clicking Photo » Properties » Details » Remove Properties and Personal Information* or we can simply (if it is hidden in EXIF property) open the image in any image editor and save it again as a copy to remove the hidden watermark from the photo. The last two methods will not guarantee completely removing all tags.

Compare Steganography and Watermarking

They do not share the same goal, although embedding a hidden watermark inside a digital file is considered a type of steganography, but the ultimate goal is to track copyright infringements and prove the ownership of the file in case of a dispute, and steganography's goal is to hide data secretly. Steganography tries to hide as much data as possible while watermarking tends to hide a small amount of data inside the overt file.

ANONYMITY

The most recent addition to the field of data hiding is anonymity. Anonymity is concerned with hiding any traces between the sender and message receiver. It uses a combination of encryption algorithms to encrypt messages and cryptographic anonymity tools to hide your identity during the transmission.

Shortly after the *Edward Snowden* scandal (he leaked classified information from NSA about running illegal surveillance program to the press in 2013), a mass media campaign was launched inside and outside the United States against this program. Large numbers of privacy groups, social activists, journalists groups, and encryption software vendors began to ask the public to encrypt everything from emails to IM instant messages.

Snowden's scandal raised public awareness toward taking their privacy online seriously. In order to anonymize your online activities you need to follow a set of procedures when surfing the Internet, sending emails, and chatting with friends. In Chapter 5 we will discuss how we can protect ourselves online using a combination of hiding techniques, encryption and cryptographic anonymity tools.

SUMMARY

In this chapter we began our journey from the past to discover the old cryptographic systems, which played vital roles during wars and in sending diplomatic messages in ancient times. This knowledge is crucial to understand the new encryption techniques and how they work in modern time.

After listing the major cryptographic techniques we talked about steganography, its types, and techniques, and how was implemented in ancient civilizations to the present day.

We also talked briefly about digital watermarking and online anonymity. We postpone our deep discussion of these two subjects to Chapters 3 and 5, respectively.

In Chapter 2 we will begin our practical hiding journey by introducing the reader to many simple techniques that could be used to hide our files in Windows®. So let us begin hiding your secret information!

REFERENCES

[1] Wikipedia, Playfair Cipher [Online]. Available from: http://en.wikipedia.org/wiki/Playfair_cipher (accessed 14.03.15).

[2] Wikipedia, Rotor machine [Online]. Available from: https://en.wikipedia.org/wiki/Rotor_machine (accessed 18.03.15).

[3] Wikipedia, Enigma Machine [Online]. Available from: https://en.wikipedia.org/wiki/Enigma_machine (accessed 26.03.15).

[4] Cipher Machines, The History and Technology of the Enigma Cipher Machine [Online]. Available from: http://ciphermachines.com/enigma (accessed 29.03.15).

[5] Wikipedia, Rail Fence [Online]. Available from: http://en.wikipedia.org/wiki/Rail_fence_cipher (accessed 30.03.15).

[6] Wikipedia, Columnar Transposition [Online]. Available from: http://en.wikipedia.org/wiki/Transposition_cipher#Columnar_transposition (accessed 11.05.15).

[7] Wikipedia, Venona project [Online]. Available from: http://en.wikipedia.org/wiki/Venona_project (accessed 14.05.15).

[8] New York Times, Venona Decoding Soviet Espionage in America [Online]. Available from: https://www.nytimes.com/books/first/h/haynes-venona.html (accessed 15.07.15).

[9] Wikimedia Commons: Morse code; copyright James Kanjo GNU Free Documentation License|this is a visually updated/enhanced image based on the original 1922 Chart of the Morse Code Letters and Numerals [Online]. Available from: https://commons.wikimedia.org/wiki/File:International_Morse_Code.PNG (accessed 15.07.15).

[10] Wikipedia, Frequency analysis of English alphabet [Online]. Available from: https://commons.wikimedia.org/wiki/File:English_letter_frequency_(alphabetic).svg#/media/File:English_letter_frequency_(alphabetic).svg (accessed 19.07.15).

[11] Webopedia, Defining computer Hashing [Online]. Available from: http://www.webopedia.com/TERM/H/hashing.html (accessed 17.06.15).

[12] Wikipedia, Cryptographic Hash Function Main Properties [Online]. Available from: http://en.wikipedia.org/wiki/Cryptographic_hash_function (accessed 11.02.15).

[13] Wikipedia, Johannes Trithemius; Steganogrphia book [Online]. Available from: https://en.wikipedia.org/wiki/Johannes_Trithemius (accessed 17.06.15).

[14] Project Gutenberg, The History of Herodotus—Vol. 1 by Herodotus [Online]. Available from: http://www.gutenberg.org/files/2707/2707-h/2707-h.htm (accessed 17.06.15).

[15] Wikipedia, Microdot [Online]. Available from: http://en.wikipedia.org/wiki/Microdot (accessed 17.06.15).

[16] D. Kahn, The Codebreakers, The Macmillan Company, New York, NY, 1967.

[17] Spammimic, Hiding in Spam emails [Online]. Available from: http://www.spammimic.com (accessed 17.06.15).

BIBLIOGRAPHY

[1] Johannes Trithemius Main Page [Online]. Available from: http://www.renaissanceastrology.com/trithemius.html (accessed 17.06.16).

[2] G. Kessler, An Overview of Steganography for the Computer Forensics Examiner [Online]. Available from: http://www.garykessler.net/library/fsc_stego.html (accessed 17.06.15).

[3] Steganography Types and Some Tools. http://www.hackersonlineclub.com/steganography (accessed 17.06.15).

[4] Spy Techniques During USA Revolutionary War [Online]. Available from: http://www.mountvernon.org/george-washington/the-revolutionary-war/george-washington-spymaster/spy-techniques-of-the-revolutionary-war/ (accessed 17.06.15).

[5] Software Anti-Piracy Systems and Methods Utilizing Certificates With Digital Content [Online]. Available from: http://www.google.com/patents/US7639834 (accessed 17.06.15).

Chapter 2

Data Hiding Using Simple Methods

Chapter Outline

Introduction	23	Hidden Data Within Document Attributes (Metadata)	34
Bit-Shifting Data Hiding	23	White Font	35
Hiding Data Inside Rich Text Format Documents	26	Hiding Data by Exploiting OLE Structured Storage	35
Renaming Files	27	Self-Encrypt MS Office® Document	37
Matching File Signatures and File Extensions	27	Hiding Inside MS Excel® Spreadsheet	38
Hiding Data in Compressed Files	28	Data Hiding Inside Image Attributes (Image Metadata)	40
Hiding Data Through File Splitting	31	Summary	43
Hiding Data in Microsoft® Office Documents	33	References	43
Hidden Text	34	Bibliography	43

INTRODUCTION

Most Windows® users use different computer programs on daily basis, especially the MS Office® suite to create documents, Acrobat Reader® to read PDF files, and compression utilities to compress their data. These programs contains many areas a user can exploit to hide data inside them. For example MS office® documents such as MS Word®, MS Excel®, or PowerPoint® can contain considerable amounts of data inside their properties fields such as author name, comments, title, and more; data stored in these areas are called metadata and could be used to hide secret information. Rich text format (RTF) documents created by MS WordPad® can contain hidden information inside its raw source. This data continues to be hidden when viewing the file in the regular viewer.

Computer users have many reasons to hide their personal information. They may use a shared PC with another family member, or they may want to email a file to a friend and hide some information inside it. Whatever their intention is, digital data hiding offers a means to cover communication and make it invisible to a third party. If combined with encryption (which will be explained later in a dedicated chapter), a user can insure a higher level of security when exchanging information across insecure networks such as the Internet.

Businesses too, need to secure their data from outside intruders. Many companies set strict security procedures when exchanging information across the Internet. They use secure socket layer (SSL) technology for online transactions. Other companies use virtual private networks (VPNs) and firewalls on their networks. However, many of them neglect to protect their data internally when used internally. A disgruntled employee can use different techniques to steal company data and smuggle it outside company walls despite all security measures implemented. The development of digital data hiding today imposes more security measures that can be implemented by companies to protect their data from theft. Another task businesses need to worry about is discovering hidden and encrypted data by their own employees and preventing any internal information from leaving company systems and walls without permission.

In this chapter we will describe many simple but efficient techniques to obscure data. All the techniques discussed can be implemented using a common computer system running Windows® with ease.

BIT-SHIFTING DATA HIDING

Bit order refers to the direction in which bits are represented in a byte of memory. The bit order we see most commonly used is the one in which the zeroth, or least significant bit, is the first bit read in a byte. This is referred to as up-bit ordering or normal bit direction. When the seventh, or most significant, bit is the first one stored in a byte, we call this down-bit ordering, or reverse bit direction [1].

Many programmers developed a way to create encryption programs using low level assembly language based on the principle of changing the direction of bits inside binary files. For example, if we have a file that we want to hide, we can run a bit shifting program that changes the direction of the bits inside that. As a result the file contents become scrambled and unreadable. To access the original file content again we need to run another program (or the same one if it supports this feature) to restore the scrambled bits to their original order.

A computer savvy user can achieve the bit shifting by scrambling a file using specially written software using any high level programming language such as PERL, Python, C#, and so on. Any person inspecting the bit-shifted file will think it is damaged. This makes this technique effective for hiding data without drawing any attention to confidential files.

Hex Workshop® [2] is a program that allows us to perform bit shifting to change the bytes values of data. This method changes data from readable text to data that looks like binary executable code. The following small exercise uses this technique:

1. Start your Notepad editor (or any editor that produces pure text files), create a new text file, name it *Original_File.txt*, and type some text of your choice inside it.
2. Open Hex Workshop®, select *Options*, and then select the *Toolbars* option as shown in Fig. 2.1.
3. Check the option *Data Operation*; a new toolbar appears for shifting bits.
4. From Hex Workshop, select *File*, then select *Open* from the drop-down menu, navigate to where you have stored your text file *Original_File.txt*, and open it (Fig. 2.2).
5. Click the *shift left* button (≪) on the data operation toolbar (see Fig. 2.3). A new dialog window appears (see Fig. 2.4). You can now specify how you treat your shifted data—the order schema for byte shift and whether you want to shift data for the entire file or only for a highlighted section within text.
6. Click *OK* to proceed with the default settings and shift the bits in your text file *Original_File.txt* to the left.
7. After completing shifting the bits, the text inside the text file will be scrambled and will become unreadable. Notice how it contains many @ symbols, which means bits were shifted successfully in this document (see Fig. 2.5).

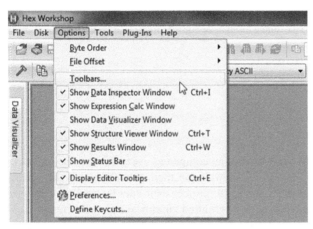

FIGURE 2.1 Activating bit-shifting toolbar in Hex Workshop.

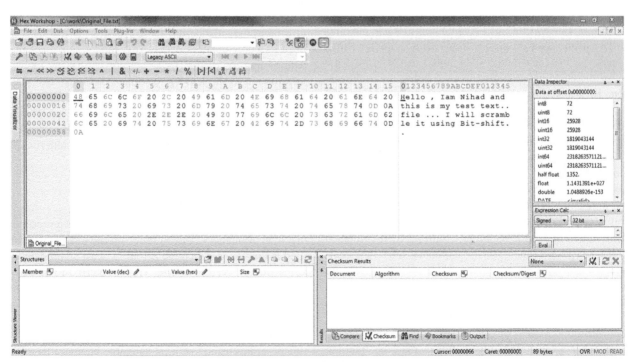

FIGURE 2.2 Open text file using Hex Workshop.

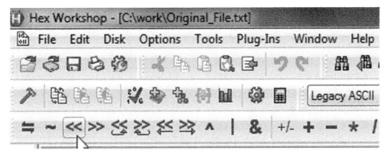

FIGURE 2.3   Click the Shift Left button to shift data.

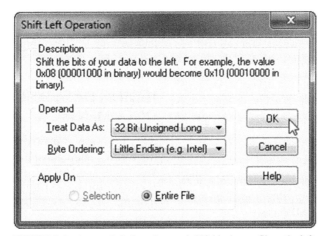

FIGURE 2.4   Accept default settings and shift bits in text file to the left.

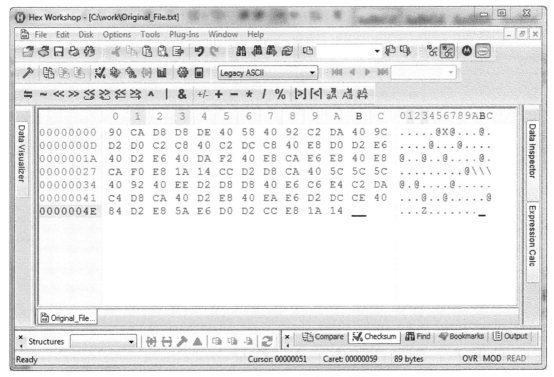

FIGURE 2.5   Text scrambled after bit shifting.

8. Save the new file as *Bit_Shift_Left.txt* in your work folder (by clicking *File* then *Save as* within Hex Workshop®).

9. To restore our file *Bit_Shift_Left.txt* to its original status, we need to shift the data back by clicking the *Shift Right* button (≫) on the data operation toolbar (see previous Fig. 2.3, but here you click the ≫ button).

10. In the same way as we did in step 6, click *OK* to accept the default settings. Our data are shifted back to the original order and the text becomes readable again.

Now, let's check the hash values of these two files and compare whether they changed after shifting the bits. There are many free tools for calculating hash value of a file (see the section, "Cryptographic Hash Function" in Chapter 1 for a free MD5 calculator tool); however, you can still use Hex Workshop® for the same reason as follows:

1. Open the first file, *Original_File.txt*, in Hex Workshop®; select *Tools* then *Generate Checksum* as in Fig. 2.6. A new dialog appears; select *MD5 (128 bit)* and click the *Generate* button.

2. The generated MD5 hash will appears in the lower window of Hex Workshop® as in Fig. 2.7.

3. Repeat the same process with the second file, *Bit_Shift_Left.txt*. First, open it in Hex Workshop® and then repeat the same steps to calculate its MD5 hash.

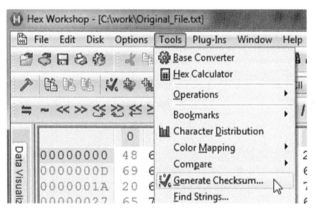

FIGURE 2.6   Generate checksum for opened files.

4. Copy both results to new text file and compare them. You will find the following results:

File Name	MD5(128 bit) Hash value
Original_File.txt	7D47B9D750C4718A3CAD3B-87571C9FAC
Bit_Shift_Left.txt	6B807174E82523C899E34F-4D1A07D6BD

You will notice that although we did not make any modifications to our original text file it ended up with a different value after shifting bits to the left is complete.

Malware writers use the bit shifting technique to obscure their code and make it harder to reverse engineer, thus making it almost impossible to detect by normal antivirus engines.

HIDING DATA INSIDE RICH TEXT FORMAT DOCUMENTS

RTF files are property file documents developed by Microsoft. They can be opened and edited using both WordPad® and MS Word® programs (all versions). There are many versions of RTF specifications, which are continually developed with each release of Microsoft Office® suites.

RTF uses a markup language similar to HTML. This leaves room for hiding data inside some of its tags. It is seldom that a user checks the raw data of an RTF file, which makes it ideal for hiding data. This leaves very small chances of your data being discovered.

To view the raw source data of an RTF file, we can open it using Windows Notepad®. We notice that RTF source files begin with **{\rtf1** and end with **}**. Any data after the closing bracket is ignored. The data will not be displayed when viewing the RTF file using MS Word® or WordPad®. RTF also ignores any text located between **{** and **}** inside the document body, which makes this location also suitable for hiding data (Fig. 2.8).

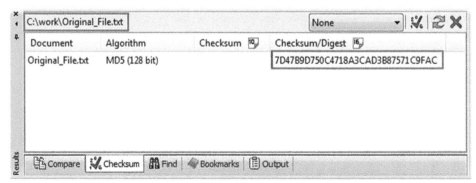

FIGURE 2.7   Showing MD5 hash using Hex Workshop.

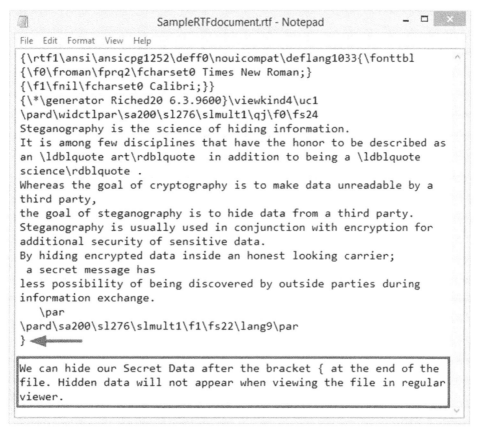

FIGURE 2.8   Hiding data inside the RTF source file.

RENAMING FILES

We can change the file extension and store it inside the *C:\ Windows\System32* directory. For example, if we want to hide an MS Word® file called *invoice.doc*, we can change its name to *MSDOS386.dll* and store it inside the *System32* directory. The *System32* directory is full of DLL files and Windows® by default changes the icon and default associated program used to open the file according to its new extension, thus making it nearly impossible for a casual user to track it down.

The only possible way to recognize renamed files is to check the file signature. Under Windows® OS each file type has a unique signature, usually stored in the first 20 bytes of the file. We can check the original file signature of any file by examining it with Notepad®. For example, EXE, DLL, and SYS extensions have the signature (MZ). RTF documents (**{\rtf1**), Windows Bitmap files with the file extension bmp contain (424D) hexadecimal in the first 20 bytes.

Matching File Signatures and File Extensions

If you are suspicious of a specific file and believe its extension was changed, you can open the file using Notepad®

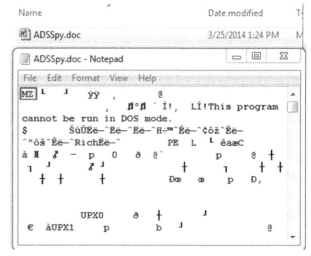

FIGURE 2.9   Check *ADSSpy.doc* signature to check if its extension is false.

and check the first character that appears. You can access a database of about 512 signatures on the website http://www. filesignatures.net. Enter file extensions in the search box and check to see its associated file signatures. Remember

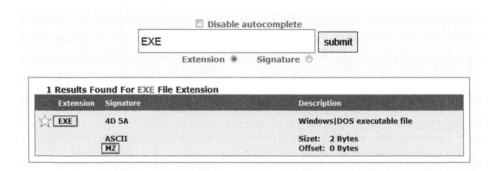

FIGURE 2.10 Searching for EXE shows its file signature is MZ.

to omit the point when you type the extension letters in the search text box.

If you did not find the signature you are searching for on *filesignatures.net*, point your browser to http://www. garykessler.net/library/file_sigs.html (created by Gary Kessler) and try searching for it again.

In the next screen (Fig. 2.9) I will change a file with an EXE extension to one with a doc extension and open it using Notepad. As we note, the first 20 bytes of the file contains the letters (MZ), so I went to www.filesignatures. net and searched for this file signature to see that it belongs to an EXE file type (Fig. 2.10).

There are automated tools to perform a comparison between a file extension and its associated signature. Two of these tools are *ProDiscover Basic®* and *Hex Browser* (http://hexbrowser.com). More details can be found in Chapter 6, where we will describe thoroughly how we can use such tools to automate finding files with false extensions in a specific directory.

HIDING DATA IN COMPRESSED FILES

Another sophisticated way to hide your files without using any third-party tool is by using the command line in

Windows® OS. In this section we will look into how you can hide a file inside an image using only the DOS command.

First we need to create a compressed file (ZIP extension). This compressed file will hold your secret file(s), which can then be hidden inside an image.

We can create compressed files using different tools; we chose Windows® built-in compression utility. It can be accessed by right-clicking on the file or folder you want to compress. You then select *send to*, and then *Compressed (zipped folder)*, as shown in Fig. 2.11. Other well-known tools for creating zipped folders are 7-zip (http://www.7-zip.org) and WinRAR (http://www.win-rar.com); the latter is commercial.

We will first create the file that we need to hide. We can make any dummy file; for this experiment we will create an RTF file and name it *secret.rtf* (Fig. 2.12).

Next we will create a new folder with the name *Secret-Folder*. We will put our newly created RTF document inside it and then zip its contents as shown in Fig. 2.13.

Now, select an image and place it in the directory where the zip file is stored. Any picture will do the job; we usually use JPG and PNG image types.

Use the copy command in DOS, combined with the /b option, for the purpose of handling the file as a binary file.

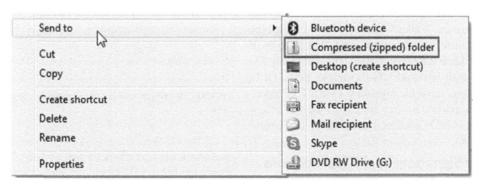

FIGURE 2.11 Accessing Windows® built-in utility for file compression.

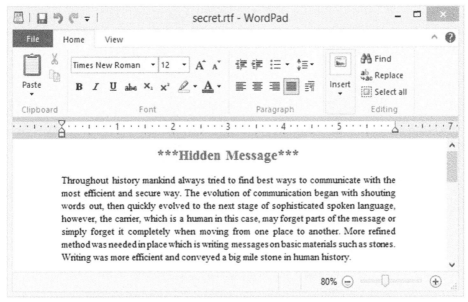

FIGURE 2.12   Create a new RTF document that contains a hidden message.

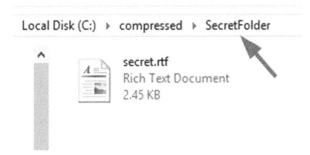

FIGURE 2.13   Put the secret file (secret.rtf) inside *SecretFolder* and compress it (Fig. 2.14).

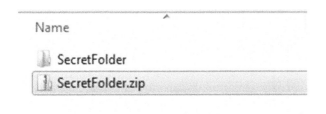

FIGURE 2.14   Zipping *SecretFolder*.

The + symbol is used to combine the two files (Fig. 2.15). Here we will combine our picture named *pix.jpg* with the compressed file we already created (*SecretFolder.zip*) and output the result with a new name, *NewPix.jpg*. The last image file will contain our archived file.

The size of our image (*pix.jpg*) before combining our RTF document was 231 KB. It grew to 232 KB after it was successfully combined with our secret folder (see Figs. 2.16 and 2.17).

In order to retrieve hidden information inside the zipped folder we need to rename the extension of our newly created picture to zip and then open it using any compressed utility we have. Alternatively we can simply right-click over the image then open it using WinRAR or 7-zip program without renaming it to view the hidden contents (Fig. 2.18).

We can achieve this trick because our zipped folder was inserted beyond the EOF marker inside jpg picture. As a result the picture is still intact, and can be viewed using any viewer available. The viewer will ignore everything beyond the EOF marker; however, the downside of this trick is that the picture size will increase after adding the zip folder to it. You need to keep your secret file to a low size in order to avoid suspicion.

We can see added information inserted into our *pix.jpg* by opening it using a hex editor. We can select from many free hex editors. The *VBinDiff* hex editor we are using here displays files in hexadecimal and ASCII (or EBCDIC). The upside of this editor is that it can display two files simultaneously in addition to highlighting the differences between them, it works well with large files (up to 4 GB), and it is free (download it from http://www.cjmweb.net/vbindiff/).

The image in Fig. 2.19 shows a screenshot (the first is a clean one (*pix.jpg*) and the second (*NewPix.jpg*) is with the added zip folder hidden inside it).

Notice how the *NewPix.jpg* has extra data after the EOF marker. The red characters (inside the box) are data hidden in the compressed folder that we combined into our picture.

FIGURE 2.15 Combine the zip folder inside the image.

FIGURE 2.16 pix.jpg original size was 231 KB.

FIGURE 2.17 NewPix.jpg size is increased because it contains our hidden zip file.

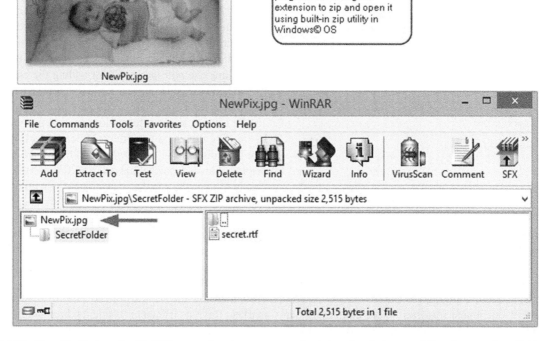

FIGURE 2.18 Open *NewPix.jpg* using WinRAR or any other zip program you already have installed on your PC to view your *SecretFolder* contents.

FIGURE 2.19   Compare two pictures (original and new picture with data hidden inside it) using VBinDiff hex editor.

HIDING DATA THROUGH FILE SPLITTING

We can hide our secret files by splitting them into many pieces. A file could be split (divided) into five parts; we can keep one part in a safe location (USB drive, for example) and the rest could be left on our PC. If an intruder has access to our PC files, he will fail to access the data without the missing part that is located in the zip drive. He also wouldn't be able to detect the contents of the split file.

There are many free tools for file splitting/joining. *GSplit* (used here; see Fig. 2.20) can split and join large files and folders (over 4 GB) using two methods: disk spanned (split into a set of files varying in size autocalculated by *GSplit* based on available free disk space and saved immediately to spannable removable disks) or blocked (split into a set of identical size split files). You may enter the size for each piece file, the number of pieces you want to obtain, or the number of lines/occurrences of a pattern by piece.

This tool can be downloaded from http://www.gdgsoft. com/gsplit/. There is a portable version so you can test and use the tool without the need to install it on your system.

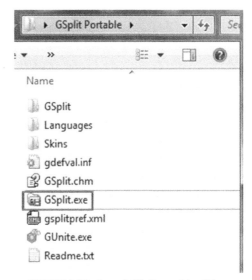

FIGURE 2.20   Launch GSplit portable edition.

In the main program window, click *Browse* to select a file to split (Fig. 2.21).

You can select any file type. If you have multiple files you wish to split, create a new folder and put all your files inside it, then compress the file using WinRAR or use the standard Windows® zip utility. The buttons on left side of the program allow you to configure the splitting/joining process. For example, click *Destination Folder* to configure where to store the split files. You can also configure the types and number of split pieces from the *Type and Size* options on the left panel.

We will split a file to show you how the process takes place:

1. Click *Browse* as we did in the last screen, and go to the *Type and Size* option on the left panel to adjust the size and number of pieces (see Fig. 2.22).
2. Click the *Split* button on the left panel and then click the large *Split* button as shown in Fig. 2.23.

FIGURE 2.21 Select which file to split.

FIGURE 2.22 Set the size of each piece.

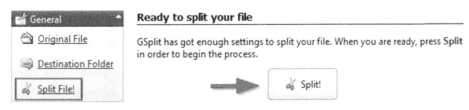

FIGURE 2.23   Begin splitting your selected file.

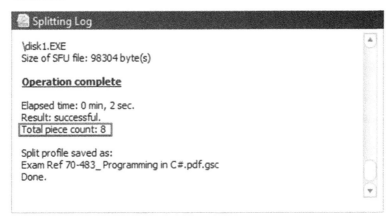

FIGURE 2.24   Viewing the splitting log.

The file will be split into pieces and stored in the destination you specified. Of course if you do not specify a destination folder, the split files will be in *C:\Users\[User Name]\Documents* by default.

In this case our file was split into eight pieces (as shown in Fig. 2.24). Each part is equally divided into 5 MB each. In order to hide this file and make it unreadable, we need to hide only one piece of the split file (Fig. 2.25). Any person who attempts to read the file will need to put together the entire eight pieces in the same sequence and within one folder.

Splitting files is a simple yet efficient way to perform data hiding; we can also securely send the file through the Internet with almost no risk of exposure. By sending one piece of the split file with another courier, we will have maximum security for our data transmission. I demonstrate splitting in this tutorial using the GSplit tool, but any similar tool can do the job (WinRAR and 7-zip, for example, can compress and split any file in a similar way).

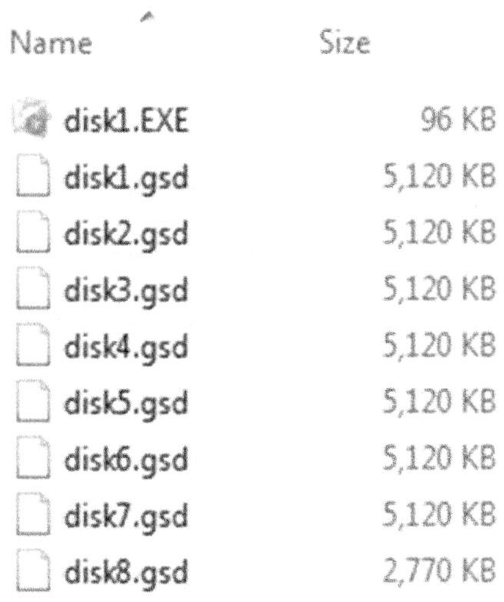

Name	Size
disk1.EXE	96 KB
disk1.gsd	5,120 KB
disk2.gsd	5,120 KB
disk3.gsd	5,120 KB
disk4.gsd	5,120 KB
disk5.gsd	5,120 KB
disk6.gsd	5,120 KB
disk7.gsd	5,120 KB
disk8.gsd	2,770 KB

FIGURE 2.25   Viewing file parts after splitting it.

HIDING DATA IN MICROSOFT® OFFICE DOCUMENTS

We can hide data in an MS Word® document using several approaches;

- Using hidden text
- Hiding data within document attributes
- Using white font
- Using OLE structured storage
- Self-encrypting an MS Office® document
- Hiding inside MS Excel® spreadsheet

FIGURE 2.30 Insert your hidden data inside MS Word® document property dialog.

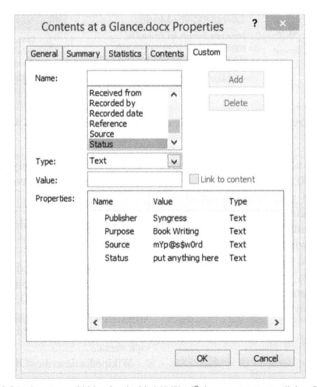

FIGURE 2.31 Insert your hidden data inside MS Word® document property dialog Custom tab.

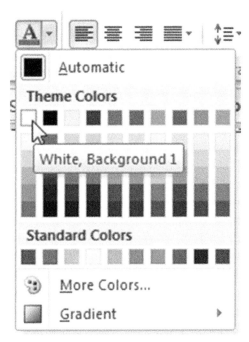

FIGURE 2.32   Make text color white in MS Word®.

FIGURE 2.33   Merging two different Office documents using a merge stream tool.

technology developed by Microsoft as part of its Windows operating system for storing hierarchical data within a single file. Structured storage is widely used in Microsoft Office applications". *Using this technology we can hide one Word® document inside an Excel® document or vice versa. This can be performed using a free tool called* merge stream *from this website http://www.ntkernel.com. The tool supports the following Windows® OS: 9x, ME, NT 4.0, 2000 and XP only.*

After you have successfully installed the tool, select two files, one MS Word® and another MS Excel®, then click *Merge* (Fig. 2.33).

A small message announcing a successful merge will appear (message shows *Merge complete* status).

Now that both documents are merged into a single file, we will need to rename the extension of the Word® file to xls since the Excel® file is now hidden inside the Word® document. Alternatively we can rename the Excel® file to doc in case you needed to select the other file. Please note this technique is supported only by MS office® suite version 2003 and earlier; newer versions of MS Office® files are not supported because they are not binary files.

Self-Encrypt MS Office® Document

We can encrypt MS Office® documents using a self-encryption facility provided with Office suite. The following steps explain how this is done (we are using MS Word® version 2010 here):

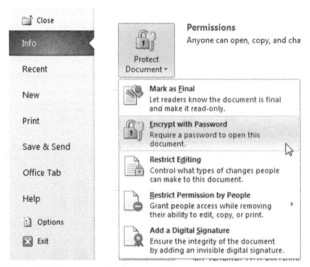

FIGURE 2.34 Select the option Encrypt with Password to protect your document.

1. Open the file you want to encrypt.
2. Go to the *File* tab in the top and select *Info* from the left menu.
3. From the *Permission* section, select *protect document* as in Fig. 2.34 (MS Word® 2013 has this feature in the same location under *Protect Document*). To access this feature in MS Word® 2007 click *Office tab* (top left corner of the screen) ≫ *Prepare* ≫ *Encrypt Document.*
4. Enter a password to protect your document. MS Word® will prompt you for the password again for verification. Refer to Chapter 5, "Data Hiding Using Encryption Techniques: Password Best Practice," on how to choose best secure passwords for your files.
5. Your document is now protected with a password. Make sure to note the password and store it inside an encrypted password storage manager (see Chapter 5 for a list of password manager tools).

If you wish to remove the password protection, repeat step 4 without inserting any password. All you need to do is to remove current password and your document will return to its original status.

The same steps could be applied to set passwords on other MS Office® applications like MS PowerPoint® and MS Excel®.

Hiding Inside MS Excel® Spreadsheet

In this exercise we will present two simple ways to hide MS Excel® spreadsheets. The first method is as follows:

1. Create a new MS Excel® workbook (we are using MS Excel® 2013 for screen captures in this exercise; text instructions are supplied for other versions of MS Excel®).

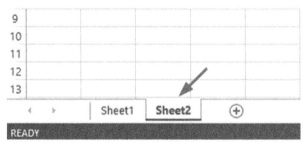

FIGURE 2.35 Add a new sheet to an Excel® workbook.

2. By default the workbook is composed of one sheet. Click the plus sign near the sheet one tab to create another sheet; select *Sheet2* as shown in Fig. 2.35.
3. From the Home tab, select *Format* ≫ *Hide & Unhide* ≫ *Hide Sheet* as shown in Fig. 2.36. We can access this feature for both MS Excel® 2007 and 2010 from the same location.
4. After implementing the *Hide Sheet* command in the previous step, Sheet2 will be hidden and not visible in the bottom of the workbook tabs. In order to unhide it again and make it visible go to *Home* ≫ *Format* ≫ *Hide & Unhide* ≫ *Unhide Sheet*. A new dialog box appears showing your hidden sheets in the document. Select the sheet you want to unhide and click *OK* as shown in Fig. 2.37.

This method is considered easy to detect by an average computer user. MS Excel® provides a more secure way for implementing a hidden sheet feature without making the hidden sheet appear when a user clicks the *Unhide Sheet* command as we did previously. This method uses Visual Basic Editor (VBE).

1. Create an additional sheet as we did in the first step. Now our workbook has three sheets (note you should keep sheet2 hidden so we can see the effects of each command on our work).

FIGURE 2.36   Hide Excel® sheet.

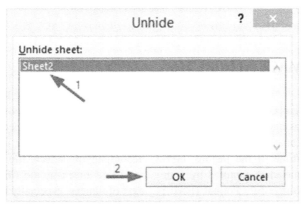

FIGURE 2.37   Hidden sheet dialog in Excel®.

2. Press ALT+F11 to access VBE.
3. From the project explorer select the sheet you want to hide, then from the Properties window select the *Visible* property. From the drop-down menu select *2 – xlSheetVery Hidden* and you are done (Fig. 2.38).

Close VBE and return to the MS Excel® main window. Try to unhide sheet3 as you did in the previous steps (*Home≫Format≫Hide & Unhide≫Unhide Sheet*). You will notice that sheet3 does not appear in the dialog box that shows hidden sheets (only sheet2 appears if it is still hidden as we did in step 3) (Fig. 2.37).

Now, in order to show sheet3, access VBE, select the sheet you want to unhide, from its property select *Visible* property, and then select *1 – xlSheetVisible* from the drop-down menu.

In Chapter 3 we will expand our discussion about hiding inside MS Office® files, and we will introduce more advanced techniques that allow us to hide our secret data inside internal documents structure stealthily with little possibility of being discovered.

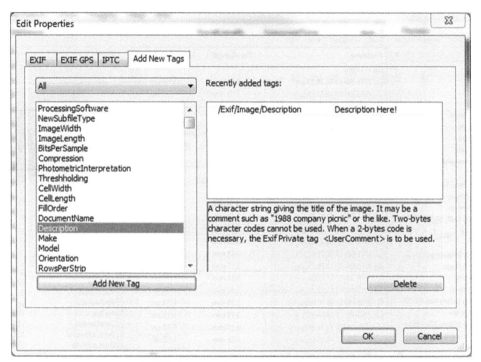

FIGURE 2.41 Add new EXIF tag to the picture.

First select the folder that contains your photos, then select the picture whose metadata you want to edit/view, and finally click *Edit EXIF/IPTC* (step 3 in Fig. 2.39).

A window featuring *Edit Properties* will appear (Fig. 2.40).

Now you can view/edit EXIF and IPTC data or completely remove the metadata from the respective fields.

You can also add new tags from the *Add New Tags* tab (Fig. 2.41).

When you are done adding/editing your image metadata fields, click *OK* and you are done. Everything you wrote inside these fields will be saved invisibly to your image.

As we said earlier, there are many more free image metadata editors [4], for example, *PhotoME* (http://www.photome.de/) and *Exiv2* (http://www.exiv2.org/). Furthermore, we have an excellent photo editor/viewer called *XnViewMP* that is provided as freeware for private or educational use (including nonprofit organizations) at the time of writing this book. You can download it from http://www.xnview.com/en/.

Another way to view and modify image metadata in Windows® without using third-party tools is by right-clicking the image and selecting *Properties*, and then selecting the *Details* tab (Fig. 2.42).

Note that standard Windows® *Details* dialog does not show all EXIF or XMP fields; however, you can still use it to hide some data from the average computer user who does not know this trick.

FIGURE 2.42 Edit picture metadata directly using the Windows® file Property.

SUMMARY

In this chapter we have explored some simple techniques used to hide and recover secret data inside images, MS Word® documents, RTF files, and compressed files. Windows® offers many possibilities for data hiding that casual users or even experts will never suspect. In the next chapter we will begin our real work by introducing different advanced techniques to hide data inside multimedia files like digital text documents, images, videos, and audio sound files.

REFERENCES

[1] File Format, Bit Order [Online]. Available from: http://www.fileformat. info/mirror/egff/ch06_04.htm (accessed 17.06.15).

[2] Hex Editor [Online]. Available from: http://www.hexworkshop.com. (accessed 17.06.15)

[3] Exif Pilot [Online]. Available from: http://www.softpedia.com/get/ Multimedia/Graphic/Digital-Photo-Tools/Exif-Pilot.shtml (accessed 18.06.15) (if any link that is pointing to any program inside this book changed after printing it, you can always search for this program inside author portal www.DarknessGate.com (to retrieve the new download link location)).

[4] List of Picture Metadata Editors [Online]. Available from: http:// en.wikipedia.org/wiki/Comparison_of_metadata_editors (accessed 18.06.15).

BIBLIOGRAPHY

[1] Understanding Image Metadata [Online]. Available from: http://www. photometadata.org/META-101-metadata-types (accessed 18.06.15).

Chapter 3

Data Hiding Using Steganographic Techniques

Chapter Outline

Introduction	**45**	Digital Image Basic Concepts	69
Text Steganography	**46**	What Is a Pixel?	69
Format-Based Steganography	46	What Is Bit Depth?	70
Line-Shift Coding	46	Monitor Resolution	70
Word-Shift Coding	46	Graphic File Types	71
Character Coding	46	Image Compression Types	71
White Space Manipulation	46	Graphics Files Format	72
Hiding Text Within Text	47	Image Steganographic Techniques	73
Random and Statistical Generation	47	Image Domain	74
Data Hiding Inside Spam Messages	48	Transform Domain	78
Linguistic-Based Methods	48	Hiding After the End-of-File Marker	79
Synonyms	48	Hiding Zip Files Inside an Image	81
Acronym	49	Hiding Inside Image Metadata	81
Change of Spelling	49	Digital Media Steganography Tools	81
Hiding Inside MS Office® Documents Based on OOXML		**Data Hiding Inside Audio Files**	**81**
File Format	49	Audio Files Basic Concepts	82
Understanding Package Relationships	51	Analog Signal	82
Data Hiding Inside OOXML Document Structure	52	Digital Signal	82
Data Hiding in the Zipped Container Comments Field	54	How Digital Sampling Works	83
Data Hiding by Reducing Image and Chart Dimensions	55	Audio File Format Types	83
Data Hiding Through Image Cropping	57	Common Audio File Types	83
Data Hiding Using OOXML Replacement Images Feature	58	Audio Steganography Types	84
Data Hiding Using XML Comments	58	Least Significant Bit Encoding Encoding	84
Data Hiding Using OOXML Markup Compatibility and		Parity Coding	85
Extensibility Feature	59	Phase Coding	88
Additional Methods for Data Hiding by Exploiting		Spread Spectrum	89
Other OOXML Features	63	Echo Hiding	89
Webpage Text Steganography	64	Data Hiding Inside Video Files	89
Hiding Data Using HTML5 Tags	64	**Data Hiding Using Other Digital Media Types**	**90**
Hiding Data in HTML/XML Files Using Tag Attributes	65	Data Hiding Inside PDF Documents	91
Hiding Data in HTML Files by Modifying Attribute		PDF Structure	91
Written State	65	Data Hiding Inside Program Binaries	94
Hiding Data in HTML by Exploiting Whitespaces		**Summary**	**95**
Using the SNOW Program	66	**References**	**95**
Hiding Secret Messages Inside Twitter Updates	67	**Bibliography**	**95**
Image Steganography	**68**		

INTRODUCTION

In today's digital age most business transactions are done electronically using networked information systems. Large volumes of digital data are preserved in digital format one way or another. Estimates show that up to 96% of all new information is created by an electronic format at the source. The majority of these documents never go for printing. Using emails as a primary communication channel for private and business use has boosted the digital revolution to a wide extent.

Electronic documents are becoming a bigger part of legal disputes. Criminals have found many ways to exploit and hide their incriminating data. Although computer forensic techniques also were developed to counter this issue, there still are many obstacles that prevent law enforcement officers from achieving complete success in this area. The large amount of digital documents that need to be investigated in some cases and the lack of training in addition to the absence of complete software solutions for automatic detection of this type of threat makes the field of investigating data hidden in digital files a challenging task.

In this chapter we are going to describe in detail how various steganographic techniques can be implemented for hiding secret data in digital files. You need to be aware that these techniques can be used by criminals to hide their incriminating data too; our approach in this book, however, is to teach people in detail how they can exploit different digital documents types, such as MS Office®, images, audio, PDF, and video files to hide their data inside them. It is crucial to know exactly how bad guys do what they do in the underground world; on the other hand, good people will also learn how to hide their personal and sensitive data in a safe location. In Chapter 6, we are going to describe how we can uncover hidden data in each method mentioned in this chapter.

This chapter will describe how steganography works behind the scene in addition to working examples using different steganography tools available online for free. We will focus on image and audio steganographic techniques because of their wide usage online and their ability to store a considerable amount of secret data. Hiding inside MS Office® documents will be covered thoroughly in a dedicated section because of the importance and the huge usage of this type of file in business organizations.

TEXT STEGANOGRAPHY

Text was the main steganographic channel used in the past to hide secret messages. In Chapter 1 we listed many old techniques to hide secret messages using text steganography like *technical* and *linguistics* steganography. In this chapter we will talk about how digital text files could be exploited to hide secret messages. As we said earlier, text steganography is generally used to store small messages and codes because of its limited usability in digital data hiding as its internal structure has a low number of redundancy and hiding messages inside digital text files can be discovered relatively easy comparable with other types of digital media.

There are many approaches in which text steganography can be achieved like changing text formatting and text size, changing some words in the overt file, generating new text that hides our secret message using a dictionary, and misspelling some words. To call a hiding technique text-based, our secret message should be covered in a character-based text file. In the second part of this section we will talk about

hiding data inside MS Office documents as we are going to acknowledge it in this book as a type of text steganography.

Mainly we have three ways in which data can be hidden inside digital text files:

1. Format-based steganography
2. Random and statistical generation
3. Linguistic-based methods

Format-Based Steganography

In this type of steganography, we exploit the physical appearance of text to disguise secret messages. Some methods are described in the following sections.

Line-Shift Coding

In this method we shift the line vertically for a fraction of an inch, up or down, so we can insert 1 bit in the space. For example we can shift the line 0.002 inch up to represent the 0 bit, and the same down to represent the 1 bit of our secret message [1].

Word-Shift Coding

This method is similar to line-shift coding. Each word is shifted horizontally to the right or left to represent a binary number (0 or 1) of the secret message. The amount of shift is usually very small to avoid making the text suspicious (about 0.02 inch). In order to decipher the secret text we need to know which word is shifted and in any direction [1].

Character Coding

Character coding (see Fig. 3.1) is also named feature encoding. This can be achieved by changing text character physical appearance; for example we can lower the height of the **d** letter column, or we can modify the horizontal line length of the **t** character, move a letter down (subscript) or up (superscript). A specialized program could be developed to make these modifications for any text automatically to obscure secret message bits; however, if we regenerate the text again (or save the file again) the secret message will get destroyed.

White Space Manipulation

Secret messages can be camouflaged in a variety of ways by using white spaces in digital text files [1]. First we need to convert our secret message into binary (0 and 1), then we can spread these bits in the cover message using a predefined method.

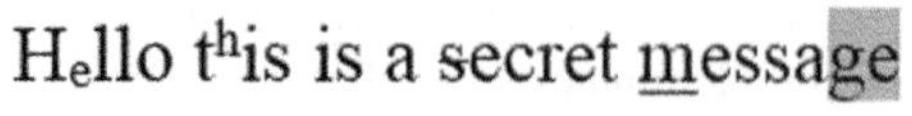

Hello this is a secret message

FIGURE 3.1 Character coding sample text.

H	e	l	l	o		t	h	i	s		i	s		a			
s	e	c	r	e	t		m	e	s	s	a	g	e	.			

FIGURE 3.2 Steganographic text after adding three spaces after the text.

TEXT	N	i	h	a	d		i	s		w	r	i	t	i	n	g		a		b	o	o	k
HIDDEN BITS						1		0									1		0				

FIGURE 3.3 Interword spacing data hiding.

For example, we can insert spaces after each full stop in the cover text: one space denotes the binary number 0 and two spaces denote the binary number 1 (see Fig. 3.2).

The steganograpic text has three spaces after the termination period (see Fig. 3.2); two spaces represent the binary number 1 and the second space represents the binary number 0 of our secret text. The advantage of this method is that it cannot be noticed by a document reader.

The same technique can be used between words in the text. We insert a single space between words to represent the binary number 0 and two consecutive spaces to represent the binary number 1 of the secret message.

For example, if we want to conceal the hex letter **A (binary value 1010)** in the text, *Nihad is writing a book*, we need to adjust the spaces between words as shown in Fig. 3.3.

Whitespace technique between words is considered easy to detect by the naked eye as any observer can immediately notice the existence of varied whitespaces between words. It also has limited ability to conceal big messages because we need large overt text in order to achieve this. In addition to this, many word processors will turn cut spaces after the termination period to only one or two spaces, which will destroy our secret message if we are hiding after termination points. Another disadvantage of whitespace techniques and line/word shifting techniques is that optical character recognition (OCR) programs will usually destroy hidden messages if used to read the overt text (assuming it is paper-based).

What is OCR:

OCR is a software program that is used to translate printed text or text images to machine-encoded characters before inserting it into computerized systems. It is widely used to convert paper documents from banks, purchase orders, or travel passports into digital data. Some OCR programs are:

1. Microsoft Office Document Imaging, which can be accessed from the Microsoft Office Tools menu. It comes installed with the MS Office Package.
2. MS Office One Note built-in OCR.
3. FreeOCR, which is a free tool for reading and converting paper documents. Download it from http://www.paperfile.net/.

The next suggested technique is disguising text within text. This tries to overcome some the drawbacks of whitespace manipulation hiding techniques.

Hiding Text Within Text

In this technique we are trying to mask secret text inside an innocent looking text file (overt text) by exploiting whitespaces that exists between words in addition to changing the font color and size of the secret message to make it disappear. This technique is simple and could be implemented using the MS Word® application as follows:

1. Prepare an MS Word® file with some text inside it; this will be our overt file.
2. Divide your secret message into words or a small group of characters. If some words are big, insert each word or character group of the hidden text inside one space that exists between overt file words.
3. Change the color of the secret text into white and reduce its size to 1 pixel (the lowest value allowed by MS Word®).

Fig. 3.4 shows a detailed demonstration of this technique.

This method will ensure that our hidden text will remain even though the user makes modifications to the document. Word processing software will not remove such text by default because it considers it as ordinary text; printing the document will not reveal hidden text either. It does not draw the attention of any user reading the document because nothing appears suspicious, however the main drawback is that computer programs searching for hiding data and text can easily detect this technique and uncover the obscured message.

Random and Statistical Generation

In this method, a secret message is hidden inside a random sequence of letters by using a predefined algorithm. Text can be spread across a large number of words, making this method hard to detect by a human observer. In statistical generation, secret message words are analyzed to determine the statistical characteristics of each one (word length, letter frequencies in each word, how many times each word gets repeated in text) in order to create another text that has similar properties as the hidden text but with a different meaning.

paper-based documents. By using this approach I select to list MS Office® steganographic techniques under this category.

Business organizations can have millions of MS Office® documents already in use. It is common to exchange Office documents through email, post it to a company website or blog, and carry it in your zip flash, smartphone, or PDA, making it very attractive to conceal secret data to and from inside organizations. Office documents can be further used to conceal malicious applications that could be used later to launch attacks or to steal sensitive data upon opening it.

Since its creation, MS Office® suite files have have two different file formats as shown in Table 3.3, which shows the extensions of the default empty file for major applications in each version of MS Office® suite since its creation.

Beginning with MS Office® 2007, Microsoft changed its file structure from binary and adopted the new XML-based file structure called OOXML (Office Open XML), which is based on the ECMA-376 standard [2]. The old binary file (with a .doc extension for MS Word® files) was exploited using different techniques to conceal data inside it. OLE structured storage was one method described in Chapter 2, but the majority of users now have started to use the new MS Office® suite based on XML, which has the .docx extension for MS Word® files. Therefore our discussion in this section will be based on how we can conceal data using the new OOXML file format.

OOXML is based on XML (Extensible Markup Language), which is used to represent text documents in a human readable language. It is a markup language similar to HTML that uses marks and tags to describe information inside the document. The main difference between HTML and XML tags is that HTML tags are predefined but XML tags are selected according to user needs. Each XML document is composed of one root element, and under it you can have as many elements as you want. Each element consists of a start and end tag in addition to an optional text element that contains the actual data of the element. For example:

<Full_Name>Nihad Hassan</Full_Name>

This line constitutes one element of an XML file and could also form one valid XML document (it still needs an XML declaration at the first line to become a valid document); element name is *Full_Name* and element text is *Nihad Hassan*.

There are many technologies that are associated with XML: XSLT for transforming XML documents into other documents formats (for example: from XML into HTML or CSV), XQuery to select specific element/s from within XML document, and XSD for defining schema for XML documents. These technologies can be used to manipulate MS Office® files based on OOXML format by any third-party tool without the need to get any permission because of the flexible open nature of the XML language.

In Chapter 2 we listed many simple ways where we can hide secret data inside MS Word® files, mainly using its formatting features and metadata fields. In this chapter we will expand our discussion on using more advanced techniques for hiding data by exploiting the new features of OOXML file structure that the modern MS Office® suite is based on. This chapter introduces the following methods for obscuring data inside the MS Office® internal file structure:

1. Data hiding inside OOXML document structure
2. Data hiding in zipped container comments field
3. Data hiding by reducing image and chart dimensions
4. Data hiding through image cropping
5. Data hiding using OOXML replacement images feature
6. Data hiding using XML comments

TABLE 3.3 MS Office Version File Format Type and Associated Extension

MS Office Version	Extension Name				Internal File Structure Format
	Word	Access	Excel	PowerPoint	
1995	DOC	MDB	XLS	PPT	OLE compound file binary format
1997	DOC	MDB	XLS	PPT	OLE compound file binary format
2000	DOC	MDB	XLS	PPT	OLE compound file binary format
XP	DOC	MDB	XLS	PPT	OLE compound file binary format
2003	DOC	MDB	XLS	PPT	OLE compound file binary format
2007	DOCX	ACCDB	XLSX	PPTX	Office open XML
2010	DOCX	ACCDB	XLSX	PPTX	Office open XML
2013	DOCX	ACCDB	XLSX	PPTX	Office open XML
2016	DOCX	ACCDB	XLSX	PPTX	Office open XML

7. Data hiding using OOXML markup compatibility and extensibility feature

8. Additional methods for data hiding by exploiting other OOXML features

Note: All hiding techniques presented in this section can be implemented on all MS Office® versions that are based on OOXML file structure like MS Office® versions 2007–2013. Some minor differences between MS Office® versions' GUI will be addressed when encountered during our examples.

In OOXML, an MS Office® file is composed of a set of XML and non-XML files (like images, video, and ODF files) contained in one zip container. This container is based on open packaging conventions (OPC), which is a technology developed by Microsoft to store different file types (XML files, images, metadata) in one container, making it represent a single entity, hence an Office document. OPC suggests a logical model for representing container files and its relationships, Microsoft uses ZIP achieve format as an implementation for OPC. We can extract zip files using free tools like 7Zip [3].

To experiment with data hiding in this section we will use an MS Word® file created with MS Office® 2013. Note that Office 2007 and 2010 versions will have the same structure; extracting any MS Word® file based on OOXML will reveal the structure shown in Fig. 3.5.

Note: We can view the internal structure of MS Office® files based on OOXML format by using a specific tool created for this purpose, Open XML Package Explorer. This tool allows you to open any document based on Office Open XML formats and view or edit the individual parts of the document. You can download it for free from http://www.codeplex.com/PackageExplorer.

---

1. **_rels**: This folder contains one XML file called *.rels*, which contains links to other XML files used to store metadata in addition to a link to the main XML file that contains the actual data of the Word file called *document.xml*.

2. **docProps**: This folder usually stores two or more XML files. The default files are *core.xml* and *app.xml*. They store metadata about the file itself and any metadata

added by the document author (like author name, comments, contact information, etc.).

3. **word**: This folder contains additional folders, and also stores many XML files. The main document in this folder is called *document.xml*. This file contains the actual text data of the Word document itself. If the document contains images, another folder will exist within this folder called *media*, to store all images in the document. Additional folders can exist inside this folder like *embeddings* and *charts* if we embed an MS Excel® chart inside our MS Word® file.

4. **[Content_Types].xml**: Every package must have one file found at its root. This XML file defines the MIME media types of all parts stored in the package. Every part that exists in the package must be listed in this file using one of the following two approaches. The first is defining default content-types based on the file extension of parts inside the package. The second involves providing overrides based on the location of a single part inside the package.

The following defines a content type for a JPG image inside the *[Content_Types].xml* file using the first approach:

<Default Extension = "jpg" ContentType = "image/jpeg"/>

Understanding Package Relationships

Every package (referring here to the unzipped container) has a relationship file that defines the relationships between other parts that constitute the package and also defines connection paths outside the package itself (resources on the Internet for example). The *_rels* folder stores the main relationship file (*.rels*) of every package. For example, the following shows an excerpt of the */_rels/.rels* file that defines the starting part of the package:

<Relationship Id = "rId1"
Type = "http://schemas.openxmlformats.org/office
Document/2006/relationships/officeDocument"
Target = "word/document.xml"/>

In addition to the main package relationship file, every part can also have its own relationship file located under the part folder in a subfolder named *_rels*. The relationship file that belongs to this part is named by appending *.rels* to the name of the part. For example, each MS Word® file will have its main content part (*document.xml*) stored under the *word* folder; within this folder is another subfolder named _rels that contains the relationship file of this part named *document.xml.rels* as shown in Fig. 3.6.

The previous introduction to OOXML was necessary in order to understand how we can exploit its features to conceal our secret data inside the internal structure of the MS Office® new file format. Now, we are ready to begin our examples of data hiding by exploiting different OOXML features.

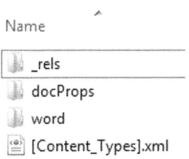

FIGURE 3.5 MS Word® document internal file structure after extracting it.

Data Hiding Inside OOXML Document Structure

As we stated before, an MS Office® file based on OOXML file format is composed of a set of XML and non-XML files. Each of these files is called a part, and all these parts are compressed in one zip container. The relationship files that exist inside each package define and organize these parts together and contain URI to external resources if needed.

In order to hide files inside this container and yet remain able to open it without error, the type of the hidden file needs to be defined in the *[Content_Types].xml* file if it is not already defined.

If we insert our hidden file inside the package without defining the type of the hidden file in the content types file, a warning message will appear when trying to open the MS Office® application—hence MS Word® file—stating that the document is corrupted. The error message will also give the user an option to fix the problem by removing the unknown parts from the document (see Figs 3.7 and 3.8).

In the coming lines we will show you how to make the necessary modification to container files in order to keep your hidden files in the package without raising any errors by the MS Office® application.

We will begin our hiding experiment by hiding two files (image and MP3), referred to as the covert message inside the MS Word® 2013 file, which plays the role of overt file or the carrier file (*MS Office® versions 2007 and 2010 support this technique by following the same steps*).

1. Unzip your MS Word® document using any zipping utility to show the internal files and folder that constitute it. Here we're using a free zipping software called 7zip [3].
2. Insert the file(s) you want to hide inside the unzipped container. We can add these files to any folder or subfolder of the container. In this case we want to hide two files—the first one is an image named *NihadHassan.jpg* and the second file is an MP3 audio file named *SimplyTheBest.mp3*. We will store both files under the *word/media* folder. MS Word® usually stores all document images and audio files in this location (see Fig. 3.9).

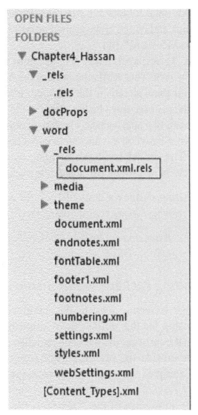

FIGURE 3.6   Part relationship file of Word subfolder.

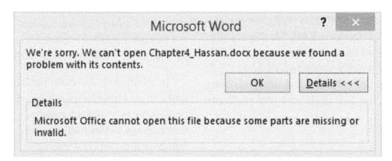

FIGURE 3.7   Error message generated by MS Word® application stating a problem with its contents after inserting an image inside its word/media folder.

FIGURE 3.8   MS Word® application gives an option to correct the damaged file by removing unknown parts from it.

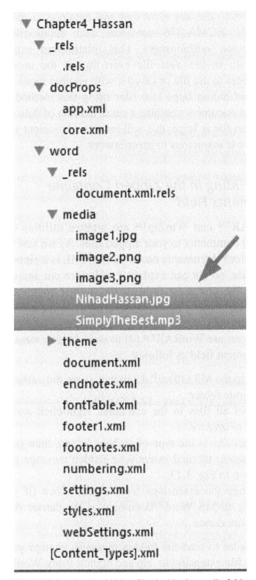

FIGURE 3.9 Storing hidden files inside the media folder.

3. We need to define the types of hidden files added to the document content types file *[Content_Types].xml*. We can find this file at the root of each unzipped MS Office® file. The MS Word® file we're using already contains many images with different extensions (like PNG, JPG). These types are already defined so there is no need to define them again. We only need to define the MP3 audio type because the document does not include such a file in its original content.

You can find the code for defining the hidden files type in *[Content_Types].xml* in Fig. 3.10.

4. We need to define the relationship entry of the inserted files in the package level relationship file that exists at *_rels/.rels*. Open this file using any text editor and add the following lines as shown in Fig. 3.11.

We added the following lines to the package relationship file (copied here if the image is not clear enough in Fig. 3.11).

<Relationship Id = "rId88"
Type = "http://schemas.openxmlformats.org/office
Document/2006/relationships/a"
Target = "word/media/NihadHassan.jpg"/>

<Relationship Id = "rId99"
Type = "http://schemas.openxmlformats.org/office
Document/2006/relationships/b"
Target = "word/media/SimplyTheBest.mp3"/>

Each relationship element entry is composed of three attributes (ID, Type, Target). Each entry should have a unique ID that is different from all other IDs that already exist in the document. The ID should be composed of either letters or letters and numbers; numbers only is not permitted in the ID.

```
[Content_Types].xml

1  <?xml version="1.0" encoding="UTF-8" standalone="yes"?>
2
3  <Types xmlns="http://schemas.openxmlformats.org/package/2006/content-types">
4      <Default Extension="png" ContentType="image/png"/>
5      <Default Extension="rels" ContentType="application/vnd.openxmlformats-package.relationships+xml"/>
6      <Default Extension="xml" ContentType="application/xml"/>
7      <Default Extension="jpg" ContentType="image/jpeg"/>
8      <Default Extension="mp3" ContentType="application/mp3"/>
```

FIGURE 3.10 Updating the [Content_Types].xml file to include new hidden file types.

```
.rels

1  <?xml version="1.0" encoding="UTF-8" standalone="yes"?>
2  <Relationships xmlns="http://schemas.openxmlformats.org/package/2006/relationships">
3      <Relationship Id="rId3" Type="http://schemas.openxmlformats.org/package/2006/relationships/extended-properties" Target="docProps/app.xml"/>
4      <Relationship Id="rId2" Type="http://schemas.openxmlformats.org/package/2006/relationships/metadata/core-properties" Target="docProps/core.xml"/>
5      <Relationship Id="rId1" Type="http://schemas.openxmlformats.org/officeDocument/2006/relationships/officeDocument" Target="word/document.xml"/>
6      <Relationship Id="rId88" Type="http://schemas.openxmlformats.org/officeDocument/2006/relationships/a" Target="word/media/NihadHassan.jpg"/>
7      <Relationship Id="rId99" Type="http://schemas.openxmlformats.org/officeDocument/2006/relationships/b" Target="word/media/SimplyTheBest.mp3"/>
8  </Relationships>
```

FIGURE 3.11 Add relationship entries for the hidden files in the package relationship file.

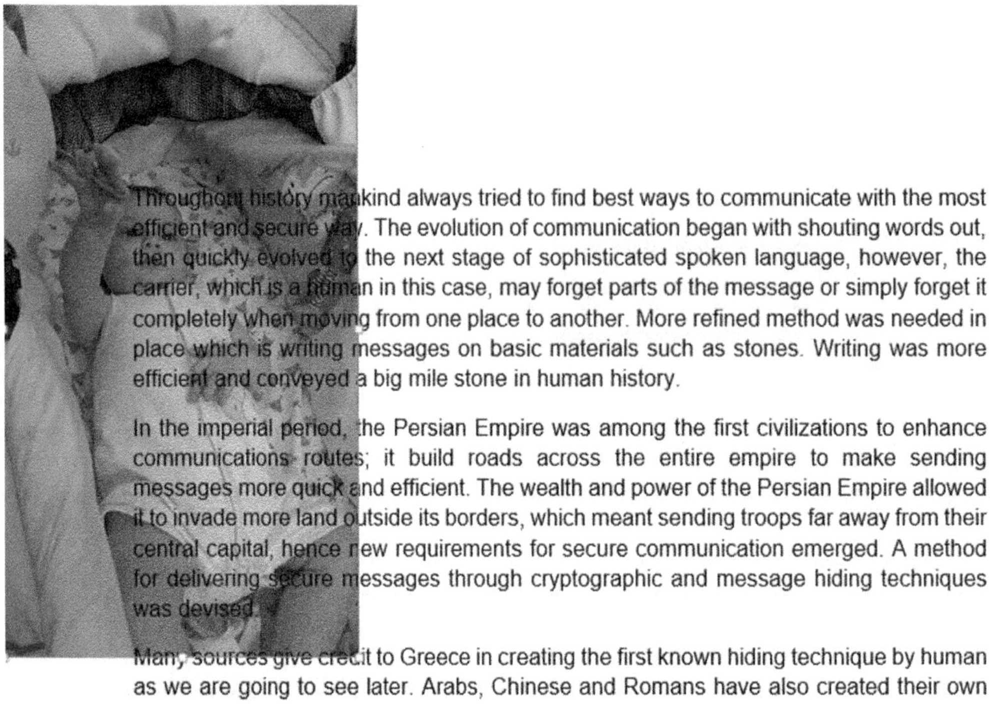

Throughout history mankind always tried to find best ways to communicate with the most efficient and secure way. The evolution of communication began with shouting words out, then quickly evolved to the next stage of sophisticated spoken language, however, the carrier, which is a human in this case, may forget parts of the message or simply forget it completely when moving from one place to another. More refined method was needed in place which is writing messages on basic materials such as stones. Writing was more efficient and conveyed a big mile stone in human history.

In the imperial period, the Persian Empire was among the first civilizations to enhance communications routes; it build roads across the entire empire to make sending messages more quick and efficient. The wealth and power of the Persian Empire allowed it to invade more land outside its borders, which meant sending troops far away from their central capital, hence new requirements for secure communication emerged. A method for delivering secure messages through cryptographic and message hiding techniques was devised.

Many sources give credit to Greece in creating the first known hiding technique by human as we are going to see later. Arabs, Chinese and Romans have also created their own

FIGURE 3.15   Move the image to the upper left corner of the page using the mouse.

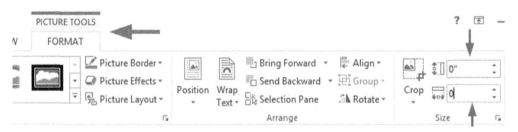

FIGURE 3.16   Set image dimension height and width to 0.

We can use the same technique to hide inside MS Excel® and MS PowerPoint® files also.)

1. Create an MS Word® document and save it as *hidden. docx*. Insert some text inside it to make it less suspicious to an outside observer.
2. Prepare the picture you want to hide. It is not necessary for the covert file to be an image; you can hide video or audio files (with MP4 or MP3 extensions, for example) by changing their extension into PNG, GIF, or JPG for easy handling of the file inside the MS document. Upon receiving the file, you can change the extension back in order to be able to open it.
3. Insert your image file into an MS Word® document using *Insert tab >> Pictures*.

Right-click over the image, select *Wrap Text >> Behind Text* (the same feature could be accessed from the same

location on MS Word® 2007 and 2010), which will make the text appear above the image.

Using the mouse, move the inserted picture to the upper left corner of the page where you want to hide the image (see Fig. 3.15). You can repeat this step in each page where you want to hide an image.

4. Click the image and go to [*Pictures Tools*] *Format* tab >> Set Shape *Height* and Shape *Width* to 0 as in Fig. 3.16.

In order to retrieve your hidden file, unzip the MS Word® document using 7-zip, go to the *word/media* sub-folder, where you will find your hidden files.

To make things more interesting, you can use a steganographic tool and hide your secret message inside the image. Then you can mask this image using the previous method that we already talk about. (We will cover image steganographic tools later in this chapter.)

The image will remain intact even if the user updates or saves the MS Office® file using another name.

Note: The inserted object that is used to hide our secret message can store metadata inside its structure; for example, in our previous example we used an image as a covert file. This image can store metadata inside its fields before inserting it inside an MS Word® file. The metadata will remain even after inserting it inside an MS Word® file (Chapter 2 shows you how to insert metadata inside images using different tools).

This technique can also be used to hide one MS Office® file inside another; for example, in Chapter 2 we showed you how to hide an MS Excel® file inside an MS Word® file using OLE structured storage (works on the old Office® format, the binary format). In a similar way we can plant an MS Excel® file inside an MS Word® file under the new OOXML file format using many ways. We will explain another method in brief using MS Word® 2013 to enrich your thinking about the wide possibilities in which we can conceal our data inside MS Office® documents based on OOXML.

1. Create a new MS Word® document, insert some text inside it, go to *Insert* tab>>*Chart*, and select a chart type to insert. Inserting a chart into an MS Word® document will automatically insert a complete MS Excel® workbook into your current document, but what you will see is only one sheet inside an MS Word® file.
2. Click the border of the newly inserted Chart, go to *Format* tab>>set the *Height* and *Width* to 0 (see Fig. 3.17).
3. The chart will turn into a single point. You can move it to the end of line as a stopping point (see Fig. 3.18).

Now our chart turned into a stopping point that will not draw any attention especially if the file was big enough and contains a large amount of text. This technique is similar to the Microdot technique used in the last century to conceal secret messages (we talked about it in Chapter 1).

In order to hide your MS Excel® file, unzip the document using the 7Zip tool, then go to the *word/embeddings* folder. Inside this folder you will find an MS Excel® file named *Microsoft_Excel_Worksheet1.xlsx*, from here you

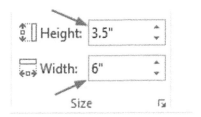

FIGURE 3.17   Reduce chart height and width.

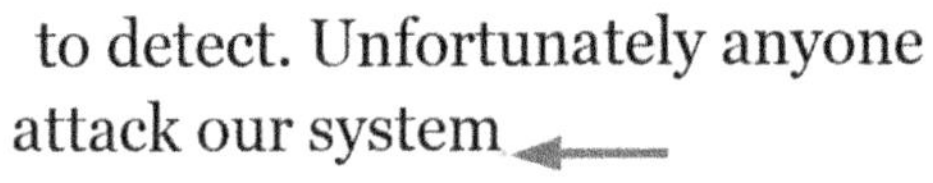

to detect. Unfortunately anyone
attack our system ⟵

FIGURE 3.18   MS Excel® chart turned into a single point after reducing its size.

can modify this file by adding your secret data or simply replacing it with another MS Excel® file that carries the same name as the original.

Zip your document and you are ready to go with your hidden MS Excel® file. If you modify the MS Word® file or change its name, the hidden file will remain intact.

Data Hiding Through Image Cropping

Similarly we can conceal our data by hiding it inside an image and cropping this image inside an MS Office® document, thus making it partly appear to a document viewer. This technique may not raise suspicion even with computer savvy users because the image already appears inside the document. However, only a part of it appears to the naked eye. Let us show you how to perform this trick.

- Create a new MS Word® document, insert some text inside it, then insert the picture you want to hide inside it using the regular insert picture function of the MS Word® application (*Insert* tab>>*Pictures*).
- Click the inserted image to activate the Format tab, and go to *Format*>>*Crop* (see Fig. 3.19).
- After clicking *Crop*, black short lines around the picture appear, allowing you to set the amount of cropping

FIGURE 3.19   Access the Crop image feature of MS Word® (applicable to MS Word® versions 2007, 2010, 2013).

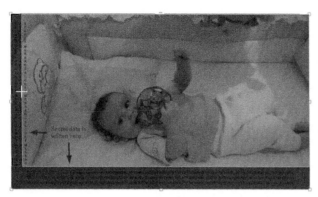

FIGURE 3.20 Cropping image by dragging its edges to hide secret text.

required. From here you can crop your image by dragging its edges to the internal side to hide your secret data written on its edges (see Fig. 3.20).

● After finishing with your image cropping, click anywhere in the file outside the image to finish the cropping action. Finally save your document and you are done!

Note that the cropped parts of the picture seem to have disappeared, but this is not true as the entire picture can be found in the unzipped container. This method is not vulnerable to saving. If a user updates the document or saves it using another name, the picture will remain intact. In order to read your secret message you need to unzip the document and go to the *word/media* folder, where you will find your complete image size without cropping.

Data Hiding Using OOXML Replacement Images Feature

This is a simple technique to hide your secret message. I will not describe it thoroughly because I think you already figured it out from the previous methods we talked about in this section.

This technique works by replacing an image inserted inside an MS Office® document with another one that contains our secret data. I will describe it briefly.

1. Create a new MS Word® document, call it *file1.docx*, and insert some text and one image inside it. This will be our overt file.

2. Create a second document and name it *file2.docx* and insert one image inside it. You should name this image with the same name as the one you want to replace it with. From this file we will take our replacement picture.

3. Now extract both files using the 7Zip utility, each one to a separate folder, and go to the second file (*file2.docx*) container and copy the inserted image from the *word/media* folder.

Take image copied from *file2.docx* and replace it with the image that belongs to *file1.docx* in *word/media* folder (see Fig. 3.21).

It is necessary to first compress the swapped image (hence *image1.jpg from file2*) before using it to replace *image1.jpg in file1*. The compression is done automatically when inserting the image using the MS Office® Insert Pictures function (accessed from *Insert* tab >> *Pictures*). This why we have used two files in this method.

Both images should have the same extensions (both JPG, for example), otherwise MS Office® will raise an error if we did not update that the content types file *[Content_Types].xml* existed at the root of unzipped container with the new file type used to replace the original image.

To further secure our secret message we can use a steganographic tool to hide our secret message and encrypt it inside the image before swapping it.

We can also implement the previous method by unzipping *file1.docx*, taking the inserted image from the *word/media* folder. We use a steganographic tool to hide our secret message inside it and return this image to its original location. Then we will zip the container again and change its extension to .docx; this trick could be achieved without using another file.

Data Hiding Using XML Comments

As we saw earlier, each MS Office® document based on OOXML is composed of several XML and non-XML files. *[Content_Types].xml* is an XML file that exists in the root of an unzipped container. XML files are text files that have a specific structure. We can insert comments inside XML files by using the following comments tag:

<!--my comments goes here-->

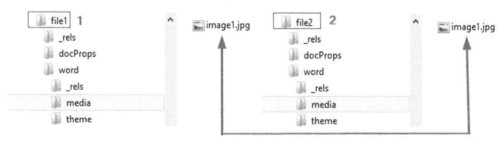

FIGURE 3.21 Swapping images between two MS Word® files.

We can insert our hidden data directly into the XML file comment field. The unzipped MS Office® container has many XML files and all could be used to store our hidden data. The MS Office® application will ignore these comments without raising any error.

An example by *Thomas Hunter* shows that we can hide secret data inside any XML document that exists within the OOXML container by encoding a secret message using Base64Encode and storing the encoded result into any XML comment field.

Base64Encode is an encoding schema that translates binary data into ASCII characters, and is commonly used to encode email attachments and to store complex data inside XML files (like other files). Base64Encode is not an encryption schema; it is mainly used to package data before transmitting it through different channels like the Internet. The unique characteristic of Base64Encode is that we can hide a complete file by encoding it using this schema; for example, encoding an image into Base64encode.

Now let us try hiding secret data by using an MS Word® document as a container:

1. Unzip your MS Word® document using any zipping utility to show the internal files and folder that constitute the file.
2. Encode your secret message or the file that you want to hide using Base64 format. There are many websites that convert text data into Base64Encode; one is http://www.opinionatedgeek.com/DotNet/Tools/Base64Encode/. In this case, we want to encode the secret message, *Nihad is writing a book*, using Base64Encode. The output is, *TmloYWQgaXMgd3JpdGluZyBhIGJvb2sNCg==*
3. Insert the encoded output into any XML file comments field. Note you cannot insert comments directly at the first line of XML file according to XML specifications.

I will use the content types XML file that exists at the root of the unzipped container [*Content_Types*].xml as a carrier of our secret message. Open this file using any text editor and insert your encoded message inside it between comment tags as shown in Fig. 3.22.

4. Save the XML file, compress container files again into a zip extension, change the .zip extension into a .docx extension and you are done.

The *Document inspecting feature* offered by MS Office® applications will fail to remove comments hidden this way; however, if the user updates the file or saves it using another name our secret message will be removed.

Data Hiding Using OOXML Markup Compatibility and Extensibility Feature

When you open an MS Word® document that was created in a version prior to MS Word® 2013, compatibility mode is turned on automatically in Word® 2013. A notification will appear next to the filename on the title bar of your MS Word® application indicating you are working in Compatibility Mode, as shown in Fig. 3.23.

Compatibility mode ensures that you will not be able to use the new features in a Word® 2013 application while you are working in a document that is created using any previous versions of MS Word® that does not support these features. This will help you maintain the format and layout of your document and use only the features that are already supported by your current document version, thus insuring you are not going to lose any changes when you return and open your document again using the old version of MSWord® that does not support the new features available in the 2013 version.

When we open a document in MS Word® 2013, it will open in compatibility mode in the following cases:

1. If it was created using Word® 2010, it will open using Word® 2010 compatibility mode.
2. If created using MS Word® 2007, it will open using MS Word® 2007 compatibility mode.

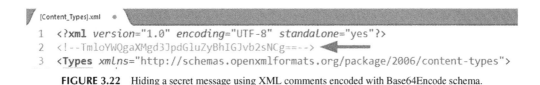

```
1  <?xml version="1.0" encoding="UTF-8" standalone="yes"?>
2  <!--TmloYWQgaXMgd3JpdGluZyBhIGJvb2sNCg==-->
3  <Types xmlns="http://schemas.openxmlformats.org/package/2006/content-types">
```

FIGURE 3.22 Hiding a secret message using XML comments encoded with Base64Encode schema.

FIGURE 3.23 Compatibility mode turned on in MS Word® 2013 after opening a file created using MS Word® 2003.

3. If created using MS Word® 1997, 2000, XP, or 2003 it will open using MS Word® 1997 or 2003 compatibility mode.

If the document is already created using MS Word® 2013, it will open normally without using compatibility mode.

Microsoft® handles the compatibility problems of its old versions of MS Office® suites by installing a compatibility pack. These packs are created for MS Office® 2003 and beyond in order to make it able to open, edit, and save newer MS Office® files created using the OOXML file format (MS Office® 2007 and later).

Backward compatibility is built into MS Office® 2013, 2010, and 2007 by default. For example, MS Word® 2013 can open a document created using MS Word® 2003 with the .doc extension without the need to install any compatibility pack. It can also create and save files using the MS Word® 2003 format, thus making it viewable in old versions of Office®. However, MS Word® 2003 is still unable to view files created with .docx extensions unless they install a compatibility pack.

Beginning with MS Office® 2007, Microsoft® changed the entire file format of its Office® suite, making it based on OOXML instead of being a binary file. OOXML is able to handle the compatibility issues by using the Markup Compatibility and Extensibility (MCE) mechanisms specified in the OOXML standard. So any file created using MS Word® 2013 can be opened, edited, and saved using MS Word® 2010 or 2007 without the need to install a compatibility pack.

What Is Markup Compatibility and Extensibility?

MCE uses a predefined approach to allow any vendor to extend his OOXML-based application with new elements created by him, and at the same time annotating these customized elements to be ignored or downgraded if other applications do not understand them (for example, applications from different vendors), thus any OOXML validator will not break when encountering these elements. So MCE in a nutshell is a set of XML elements and attributes that can be used to annotate any XML file.

Microsoft uses the MCE feature of OOXML in its newer MS Office® suites (versions 2007 and later) by using the ignorable attributes for namespaces.

To better understand this idea let us give an example.

Suppose you have an MS Word® 2013 document that employs a feature of MS Word® 2013, *Glow text* effects (we can access this feature from *Home* >> Text effects and typography (*Icon with letter A*) >> *Glow* (Fig. 3.24)), and

you want to open this file using MS Word® 2007, which does not support this feature. What will happen in this case?

MS Word® 2007 will open the file normally without launching an error, but it will show the text without any glowing effects; we will only have a normal text.

MS Word® 2007 will ignore this feature because it did not recognize it. This could be achieved because MCE has already annotated this feature code inside the file and surrounded it with ignorable attributes upon creating it using MS Word® 2013, so the OOXML processor will simply ignore its presence. This what we mean by MCE ignorable attributes.

ECMA-376 specifications describe the ignorable attribute as:

> *A whitespace-delimited list of namespace prefixes identifying a set of namespaces whose elements and attributes should be silently ignored by markup consumers that do not understand the namespace of the element or attribute in question.*

After we have a fair understanding of how MS Office® suite manages backward compatibility between different MS Office® versions, we can talk about how we are going to exploit this feature to hide our digital data. The concealment method will simply occur by defining links to our hidden files (image, audio, and video) inside internal XML files of our overt MS Office® document and then annotating these links as ignorable. These hidden files will remain in the document even if the user uses the *Inspect Document* feature to remove hidden data and personal information from the document. In the following lines we will show you how to perform and test this technique using an MS Word® 2013 document as an overt file. Our MS Word® document already contains some text in addition to one picture in JPG format.

1. Unzip the MS Word® document using any zipping utility to show the internal files and folder that constitute the file.
2. Prepare your hidden file and put it inside the *word/media* folder, which is usually used to store all images that exist inside our document. In this case we want to hide a JPG picture, so put it in this folder and name it *image2.jpg* (Fig. 3.25).

We note from Fig. 3.25 that there is already a picture named *image1.jpg* in this folder; as we said earlier we are experimenting using an MS Word® file with one image inserted inside it. MS Word® changes the image name when storing it in the *word/media* folder (*image1.jpg* was originally named *Omran.jpg*).

3. Now we need to create metadata for our hidden image just like the metadata used for any image (of type JPG) inserted using the MS Word® application. This metadata will be inserted inside the *word/document.xml* file.

This is a Glowing Text!

FIGURE 3.24 Sample Glow effects in MS Word® 2013.

My hidden file is image2.jpg and it is inserted in word/media folder

FIGURE 3.25 Insert secret image in word/media folder.

Go to the *Word* folder and open *document.xml* file using your preferred text editor and search for *image1.jpg* metadata as shown in Fig. 3.26.

Copy the code in Fig. 3.26 and paste it inside *document.xml* after the first image code block. Make sure to modify its *relationship ID* and *picture ID* entries (see Fig. 3.27).

4. Define ignorable attributes inside the *document.xml* declaration section at the top of the document along with its namespace (see Fig. 3.28). This code surrounded in the box is used to define a namespace that the MS Office® application is going to ignore because it cannot understand it. We can use any valid name to define our ignorable attributes; in our case we use the name *IgnoreAttr*.

5. Surround the hidden image code inside *document.xml* with the ignorable attribute defined in the previous step (see Fig. 3.29).

```xml
- <w:p w:rsidRDefault="00A02036" w:rsidR="00A02036">
  - <w:r>
    - <w:rPr>
        <w:noProof/>
      </w:rPr>
      <w:lastRenderedPageBreak/>
    - <w:drawing>
      - <wp:inline distR="0" distL="0" distB="0" distT="0">
          <wp:extent cy="4391025" cx="2476500"/>
          <wp:effectExtent r="0" b="9525" t="0" l="0"/>
          <wp:docPr name="Picture 1" id="1"/>
        - <wp:cNvGraphicFramePr>
            <a:graphicFrameLocks noChangeAspect="1" xmlns:a="http://schemas.openxmlformats.org/drawingml/2006/main"/>
          </wp:cNvGraphicFramePr>
        - <a:graphic xmlns:a="http://schemas.openxmlformats.org/drawingml/2006/main">
          - <a:graphicData uri="http://schemas.openxmlformats.org/drawingml/2006/picture">
            - <pic:pic xmlns:pic="http://schemas.openxmlformats.org/drawingml/2006/picture">
              - <pic:nvPicPr>
                  <pic:cNvPr name="Omran.jpg" id="1"/>
                  <pic:cNvPicPr/>
                </pic:nvPicPr>
              - <pic:blipFill>
                - <a:blip r:embed="rId4">
                  - <a:extLst>
                    - <a:ext uri="{28A0092B-C50C-407E-A947-70E740481C1C}">
                        <a14:useLocalDpi val="0" xmlns:a14="http://schemas.microsoft.com/office/drawing/2010/main"/>
                      </a:ext>
                    </a:extLst>
                  </a:blip>
                - <a:stretch>
                    <a:fillRect/>
                  </a:stretch>
                </pic:blipFill>
              - <pic:spPr>
                - <a:xfrm>
                    <a:off y="0" x="0"/>
                    <a:ext cy="4391025" cx="2476500"/>
                  </a:xfrm>
                - <a:prstGeom prst="rect">
                    <a:avLst/>
                  </a:prstGeom>
                </pic:spPr>
              </pic:pic>
            </a:graphicData>
          </a:graphic>
        </wp:inline>
      </w:drawing>
    </w:r>
</w:p>
```

FIGURE 3.26 Metadata for image1 inserted using the MS Word® 2013 application.

TABLE 3.4 Compression Algorithms Supported by MS Office® and Its Associated Characters for Hiding Our Secret Message

Algorithm	Option	Character Association
DeflateF	Ef	0
DeflateN	En	1
DeflateX	Ex	2
DeflateS	Es	3
Stored	E0	4

TABLE 3.5 Browser Support for the HTML5 Hidden Attribute

Browser Version	Chrome 6.0	Internet Explorer 11.0	Firefox 4.0	Apple Safari 5.1	Opera 11.1
Status	√	√	√	√	√

documents. The ability to exchange business data as a part of MS Office® documents offers a high level of interoperability between businesses in different domains. This method could be exploited to camouflage data by creating a hidden XML file (eg, *hidden.xml*) and storing it inside a *customXML* folder inside an unzipped MS Office® document root container. We then create a subfolder for storing the relationship file (*hidden.xml.rels*) of the *customXML* part (*customXML/_rels*). This relationship file will contain a link (relationship entry) to the secret file. In order to avoid deleting secret files, if a user uses the *Inspect Document* feature of the MS Office® application to delete custom XML parts, we should avoid creating an entry for our customXML file in the main document relationship file (hence *document.xml.rels* if we are hiding inside an MS Word® file). This method is vulnerable to saving action as custom XML files and folders will be deleted in this case.

Webpage Text Steganography

We can hide secret data inside text files based on an ASCII character encoding schema using many ways. There are many types of webpage text files like HTML, CSS, XML, and JavaScript, and we can conceal our secret message in any one of these file types. In this section we will experiment using an HTML file as an overt file to conceal our secret message using a well-known old program called SNOW. Before we begin let us first show you simple techniques that we can use to hide our data inside HTML files.

Hiding Data Using HTML5 Tags

HTML5 has introduced many new attributes—one of them is the *hidden* attribute. When applied to an element, the hidden attribute will make this element disappear from the page. It acts as the CSS property:

display:none;

To hide a specific paragraph or word we can surround it with this attribute as follows:

<p hidden>This paragraph will not appears in the browser</p>

In the same way we can hide a complete div section in the page:

<div hidden>
    See me if you can!
</div>

This attribute is not supported by all browsers. Table 3.5 shows which browser versions support it.

If you are afraid that some users may be using another browser type or the version they have is not supported you can secure yourself by adding the following property to your website CSS file to make sure that the hidden property will work with any browser and avoid uncovering your hidden message.

*[hidden] { display: none; }

This method is very simple and could be easily discovered if the user right-clicks the page and selects *View Page Source*, but it is still considered a good technique to hide your data from a known pro computer user especially when inserting your secret message inside a long webpage full of texts and images. As with many methods already discussed we can make this method far more secure by encrypting our secret message, then converting it to Base64Encoding to make it less suspicious before inserting it inside an HTML document surrounded with the hidden attribute.

Hiding Data in HTML/XML Files Using Tag Attributes

Mohit Garg (2011) suggests a method for hiding data inside HTML files by changing the order of attributes. Each HTML page can contain a large number of attributes inside its tags. The order in which attributes appear in each tag is not significant, thus will not affect the webpage display, so we can exploit this feature to conceal our data. Fig. 3.31 is an example.

The first paragraph has its attributes in this order (title, align). The second paragraph has its attributes in this order (align, title).

The first sequence donates binary number 0 of the hidden message and the second sequence donates binary number 1 of the hidden message. The same technique could be applied to XML tag attributes.

Hiding Data in HTML Files by Modifying Attribute Written State

Xin-Guang Sui and Hui Luo [5] suggested a method for embedding secret data in a webpage by switching the uppercase-lowercase states of letters in tags. This technique works as follows:

Each attribute has an uppercase letter that will hide the binary number 1, and a lowercase letter hides 0 (see Fig. 3.32 for a detailed demonstration).

This technique works on HTML files only; XML and XHTML tags are case sensitive.

```
<p title="Text steganography" align="center">Nihad website:http://www.DarknessGate.com</p>... 0
<p align="center" title="Text steganography">Rami website:http://www.mericler.net</p>... 1
```

FIGURE 3.31 Hiding data by changing the tag attribute sequence.

```
<!-- Overt File -->
<html>
    <head>
        <title>Hiding data in HTML</title>
    </head>
    <body>
        <h1>Hiding data in HTML</h1>
        <hr />
        <p>This is sample text</p>
        <hr />
        <p>Another sample text</p>
        <hr />
        <p>Last text in page</p>
    </body>
</html>
```

Ascii Text Value	Binary Value
Secret	01110011 01100101 01100011
	01110010 01100101 01110100

```
<!-- Output File -->
<hTML>
    <heAD>
        <tITle>Hiding data in HTML</TiTlT>
    </Head>
    <BOdY>
        <H1>Hiding data in HTML</H1>
        <hr />
        <P>This is sample text</p>
        <hR />
        <P>Another sample text</p>
        <hR />
        <p>Last text in page</P>
    </bODY>
</hTml>
```

FIGURE 3.32 Hiding by modifying attribute case letters: comparison between input and output files.

Hiding Data in HTML by Exploiting Whitespaces Using the SNOW Program

SNOW is a free program created by *Matthew Kwan*, available under Apache 2.0 license and can be downloaded from http://www.darkside.com.au/snow/. SNOW is used to conceal secret messages in ASCII text by appending whitespaces (spaces and tabs) to the end lines. Spaces and tabs at end lines are invisible in most text viewer programs and it will not affect text visual representation, thus making it hard to detect by any observer.

SNOW also has the ability to encrypt the secret data to be hidden with a password key. It uses *an information concealment engine* (ICE) encryption algorithm, which is a 64-bit private key block cipher designed by the author of SNOW. ICE is designed to be secure against differential and linear cryptanalysis, and has no key complementation weaknesses or weak keys. In addition, its key size can be any multiple of 64 bits, whereas the DES key is limited to 56 bits. The ICE algorithm is public domain, and source code can be downloaded from http://www.darkside.com.au/ice. There are no patents or copyrights, so its use is unrestricted.

According to its creator, SNOW runs in two modes: message concealment and message extraction.

During the concealment the following steps apply:

Message > optional compression > optional encryption > concealment in text

In the extraction we reverse the process:

Extract data from text > optional decryption > optional uncompression > message

Let us try using this tool to hide a secret message inside an HTML file.

1. Prepare your secret message. You can write it either inside a text file or if it is short you can write it directly in the program console window surrounded by quotation marks. In this case we want to hide the sentence, *Nihad is writing a book*, so we create a text document using Windows® Notepad and write the secret message inside it. Name the file *mysecretfile.txt*.
2. Prepare the overt file that you want to contain your secret message. In this case we will use an HTML file; the overt filename is *default.htm*.

To make things more secure, prepare a password to encrypt the secret message using the password *P@$$w0rd*.

3. Execute the program by opening a new command prompt, navigate to where the SNOW program is located by using the CD command, or simply press the Shift key while right-clicking the SNOW folder and select *Open command window here* to have a CMD console in the specified directory (opening the command prompt in this way is only applicable to Windows® 7 and later versions).
4. Type the command shown in Fig. 3.33 in the command prompt.

Here is a description of the SNOW concealment command shown in Fig. 3.33:

-C Compress the data if concealing, or uncompress it if extracting.
-f mysecretfile.txt The file that stores my secret message, and plays the covert file role.
-p P@$$w0rd If this is set, the data will be encrypted with this password during concealment, or decrypted during extraction.
default.htm The overt file used to embed our secret message inside it.
outputfile.htm The stego file resulted from merging our secret file (or text) inside the overt file. This file contains our secret data hidden inside it.

The output from the command prompt (see Fig. 3.33) informs us that the original message has been compressed by 40.10% and that the message used approximately 17.24% of the available space in the overt file (*default.htm*).

As we note from outputfile.htm, the inserted hidden data did not change its appearance (see Fig. 3.34).

The extraction process is easy to implement; we just need to type the following in the SNOW command prompt (see Fig. 3.35):

snow Execute the program.
-C Uncompress when extracting.
-p P@$$w0rd If this has been set during the concealment process we need to supply it during the extraction to decrypt the secret message.
outputfile.htm The file contains our secret message.

FIGURE 3.33 Using SNOW to conceal a secret message inside an HTML file.

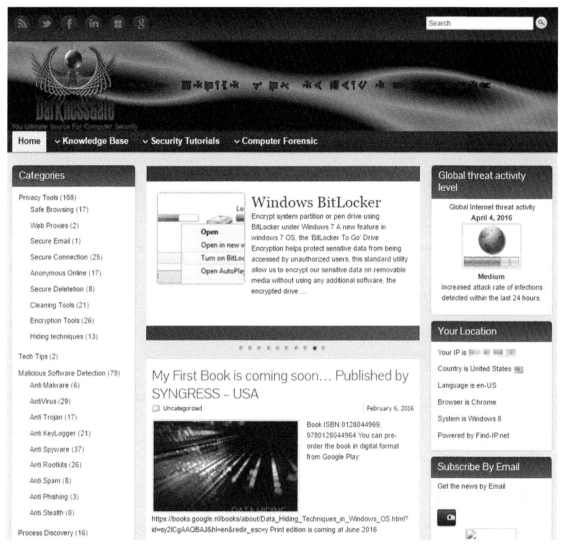

FIGURE 3.34   outputfile.htm containing our hidden message. Nothing appears suspicious and the file looks like the original.

```
D:\snwdos32>snow -C -p P@$$w0rd outputfile.htm
Nihad is writing a book! ◄━━━
D:\snwdos32>
```

FIGURE 3.35   Extraction of the secret message using SNOW.

Notice *that outputfile.htm* has increased about 1 KB in size with the addition of the secret message contained in *mysecretfile.txt*. To investigate for hidden data using this technique we can open the stego file (*outputfile.htm*) using the MS Word® application and activate the option *Show paragraph marks and other hidden formatting symbols*, which can be accessed from the *Home* tab (see Fig. 3.36). We then can see the added spaces and tabs after stopping points inside this file. It is better to use the ICE encryption supplied with this tool to make cracking secret messages very difficult to achieve.

Hiding Secret Messages Inside Twitter Updates

Launched in 2006, Twitter is considered one of the most famous social networking platforms with more than 100 million logins daily. According to Twitter's second quarter 2015 results, there are more than 316 million monthly active users. Different states show that more than 20.5% of Internet users in the United States are expected to have Twitter accounts in 2015. These numbers show the huge use of Twitter in today's digital life. Examples show that tweet updates sent by users can store hidden messages in plain sight. This is a very efficient method to exchange secret data as the huge number of tweets sent each day make analyzing it a very difficult and time-consuming process [6].

Matthew Holloway created a method for hiding messages inside Twitter updates. His technique works by

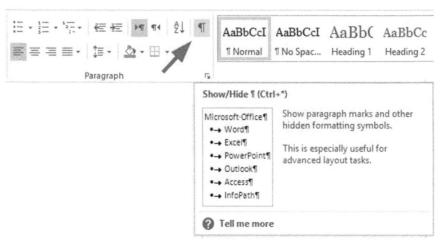

FIGURE 3.36   Activate Show hidden formatting marks in the MS Word® application to see added spaces and tabs by SNOW.

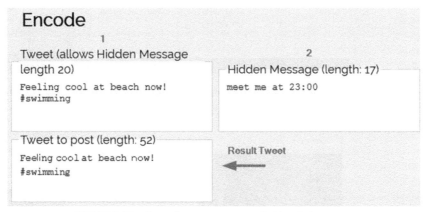

FIGURE 3.37   Concealing a secret message inside a Twitter tweet.

replacing tweet letters with similar letters that have the same appearance (Unicode homoglyphs), which are used to hide your secret message. This is not an encryption schema as anyone who may suspect the existence of the hidden message can decode and read it. Our hidden message should only contain these characters (all should be 6-bit charset):

abcdefghijklmnopqrstuvwxyz123456789'0.:/\%-_?&;

To hide your message using this method, go to http://holloway.co.nz/steg/, enter your tweet inside the first box (under the Encode section, box title *Tweet*), in the second box (*Hidden Message*) on the right enter your hidden message (maximum 20 characters including spaces). The last box named *Tweet to post* will show you the final tweet including your hidden message (see Fig. 3.37 for a demonstration).

To decode the secret message, go to the same page. In the Decode section insert the tweet you want to decode in the *Tweet* box, and the secret message will appear in the *Hidden Message* box.

In the first section of this chapter we showed you many ways in which data could be hidden within text. We also

cover MS Office® files thoroughly using many techniques because of its importance in today's world.

Text steganography is not used much compared with other digital files types because of its limited ability to store large amounts of data; however, it is still a very good place to hide small amounts of secret data. If we combine some of the text stego techniques mentioned in this section with encryption we will end up having a robust channel for exchanging secret data through public channels.

IMAGE STEGANOGRAPHY

Image steganography is defined as the science of hiding data inside image files to secure transmission of confidential information. Practically, most digital files can be used for steganography, although there are some file formats that are better than others for this because its binary structure contains a high degree of redundancy that could be used to hide secret data. The concept of redundancy in terms of object binary structure is quite simple if we explain it using an example. A digital file is represented in binary structure of 0 and 1. If we suppose that this

FIGURE 3.38 The concept of redundant data in digital files.

digital file contains my face picture, the number of bits used to display my body (the actual data) is represented in a number, and the total bits in the file are represented with another number. If we subtract the total number of bits that constitute a digital file from the number of actual data used to represent it (my face and background color), we will have the number of redundant bits shown in Fig. 3.38.

The redundant bits can be altered without affecting the visual appearance or audio sound of the digital file against the human naked eye or ear, thus making image and audio files very suitable for hiding data inside them.

As we already discussed, images can have a high degree of redundancy, which makes it very suitable for hiding data without affecting visual representation of the overt image file (the image file used to store secret messages). We can bury many types of data inside images such as text, audio, and video, including other types of images. All can be obscured inside images. What makes images also more preferable compared to other types of digital files is the wide spread of digital graphics online. Internet users exchange millions of images daily across the Internet, which makes it very ordinary for anyone to send images to their friends. Image steganography will attract less attention when used to exchange secret data through the Internet far better than encryption and secure channels, which will raise attention when used.

In this section we will talk about the most used image steganographic techniques and give examples of using different tools for performing it.

Before we begin our discussion of image steganography, we need to have a fair understanding of digital images, their types, and how they are constructed and presented on screen. It is important to understand how images can be exploited to disguise secret data within them.

Digital Image Basic Concepts

Graphic files are generally used to describe pictures generated using specialized computer programs or produced by other electronic devices such as cameras and scanners. The word digital comes from the binary numbering system that is used to represent data on computer machines, which consists of two digits, 0 and 1. The fact that digital images are stored in binary (as all digital data) make them unseen until they are opened and presented on screens.

A digital image is generally composed of a number of pixels (except some types like vector graphics as we are going to see later). Each pixel represents a dot on a screen,

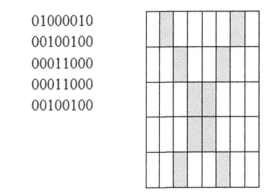

FIGURE 3.39 Black-and-white image and how it is stored in the computer (left) and displayed on the screen (right).

and the number of dots is arranged in a way that constitutes the visual image seen by the human eye on screens.

What Is a Pixel?

A pixel is a small dot on the screen that can display at least one color (either black or white) on a screen. With the advance of a graphics card, monitors were able to display more colors for each pixel.

Originally old monitors could display only two possible values, black and white (some monitors were replacing white with green or amber). The principal work of these old monitors was to show objects on screen by showing dots of lights (pixels). These old systems were only able to represent each pixel on a monitor with only 1 bit, so each pixel can only have one value, either 1 or 0 (see Fig. 3.39). For a portion of a 1-bit image represented on screen, numbers on the left represent how the image is stored on the computer disk drive using the binary numbering system.

As technology progressed, new monitors were able to display more than one color for each pixel. A colored pixel represents an RGB data value (red, green, blue). Each colored pixel has these three color representations, and each color can store 8 bits in each pixel (it can store more in some graphic formats). If we have one pixel composed of these three colors and each color contains 8 bits we call this a 24-bit color image.

Each 8 bits from RGB colors can have 256 possible values (0–255). For example, the pink color has the following RGB color value: red = 255, green = 192, blue = 203.

Image pixels are recorded in a computer file along with their location and the description of the color of each pixel to form a grid (map of bits). This file represents the final image on the screen.

The term bitmapped image comes from this map of pixels (see Table 3.6) for a portion of a 24-bit image map.

The human eye can recognize only these three colors. All other colors can be generated by making a combination of values of red, green, and blue. For example, we can generate the color *yellow* **from the RGB value combination R**=255, G=255, B=0; and the color *royal blue* **from R**=65, B=105, B=255.

Monitors display pixels on the screen with a square shape. We can magnify any image to see those pixels clearly (see Fig. 3.40).

What Is Bit Depth?

This term refers to the number of colors each pixel can display on the screen (see Table 3.7).

The best image quality widely used is based on a 24-bit RGB image (some high quality images can have more than 24 bits). Each pixel uses 3 bytes to represent color on the

screen and can have 256 shades of red, 256 shades of green, and 256 shades of blue. This equals 256×256×256≈16.7 million possible combinations of RGB colors in each pixel. This is more that a human eye can distinguish, so 24-bit or 16 million colors is often called TrueColor.

Monitor Resolution

The display resolution of a computer monitor (or any other monitor) refers to the number of pixels this monitor can display in each dimension (dimension refers to the height and width of the monitor).

Screen monitor resolution is usually calculated by multiplying width × height and using the resulted unit as pixels; for example, a monitor with 1024×768 means its width is 1024 pixels and its height is 768 pixels.

The more pixels used to produce an image, the more detailed the image will be, and the higher its resolution.

TABLE 3.6 An Excerpt From a 24-bit Image Pixel Map

R:224 G:79 B:190	R:224 G:65 B:100	R:224 G:200 B:110	R:224 G:240 B:88
R:21 G:200 B:131	R:224 G:33 B:201	R:224 G:65 B:48	R:224 G:200 B:100
R:18 G:109 B:100	R:224 G:210 B:101	R:200 G:19 B:38	R:110 G:34 B:200
R:200 G:200 B:130	R:21 G:46 B:170	R:224 G:200 B:100	R:185 G:18 B:100
R:32 G:32 B:101	R:224 G:200 B:199	R:121 G:64 B:109	R:224 G:160 B:104

TABLE 3.7 Number of Color Choices That Can Be Displayed

Bits	Number of Colors
1	2 (black and white)
2	4
4	16
8	256
16	65,536
24	16,777,216

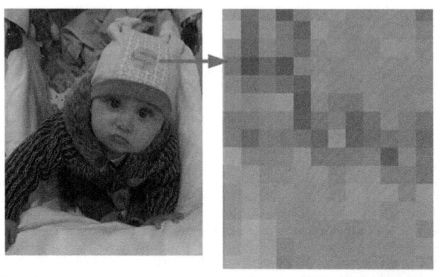

FIGURE 3.40 The picture on the right shows a magnified version of the image on the left (baby hat) showing bitmapped pixels. Each pixel is represented in a *square* shape on the screen.

TABLE 3.8 Graphic Editing Tools

No	Program Name	License	Platform	Website Address
1	Inkscape	Free	Windows®, Mac OS X, and linux	https://inkscape.org/en/
2	DrawPlus Starter Edition	Free	Microsoft Windows® 8, 7, Vista, or XP (32-bit) operating system	http://www.serif.com/free-graphic-design-software/
3	Paint.NET	Free	Windows®	http://www.getpaint.net/index.html
4	GIMP	Free	Windows®, Mac OS X and Linux	http://www.gimp.org/

Graphic File Types

Graphic file types describe the types and characteristics of the graphics files. This includes digital photograph, line art, three-dimensional images and scanned images of printed pictures.

Graphics programs are usually used to edit and create graphics files. Some of these tools are free and some are commercial. Table 3.8 shows a list of most free popular graphic editing tools.

Bitmap and Raster Graphics

Bitmap images store graphics files in a grid of pixels, hence the term bit map or a map of bits; for example, a 32×32 desktop icon means we have 32 dots in two dimensions. When these pixels are combined they constitute our visual image.

Bitmap images can be very large depending on the number of pixels used. For example, an uncompressed 1000×1000 pixel image will be at least 3 megabytes (for a 24-bit image) as bitmap images use as much color of the palette as possible.

Bitmap images are dependent on monitor resolution; if you try to resize your bitmap image you will lose some of its high quality as the decreasing action will throw away some pixels from it. Enlarging it on the other hand will also decrease its quality.

Some bitmap images formats are BMP, GIF, JPEG, PNG, TIFF, and PSD (Adobe® Photoshop).

Most scanned images are bitmap images. You can convert a bitmap image into another bitmap format (JPG or GIF, for example) by opening the bitmap image using the *Paint* program available in all Windows® OS versions. Click *File >> Save as* and select your preferred format.

There is another variation of bitmap images called *Raster images*. It uses a collection of bits just as the bitmap, but it differs from it in one way; it reads pixels row by row and is used mainly to print pictures. So when we print a bitmap image, printing software will usually convert it into a raster image before printing to simplify the printing process.

Vector Graphics

Vector graphics uses a mathematical formula to represent a drawing on the screen. This means it is not pixel-dependent as it uses lines to draw shapes, curves, and lines on the screen. A specialized graphics programs is needed to convert this formula into an image. Its size is usually smaller than images based on pixels. Vector-based images are resolution independent. This means you can enlarge or decrease the size of vector image to any degree and your image will remain sharp and clear.

Some vector images formats include AL (Adobe® Illustrator), CDR (CorelDraw®), SVG (scalable vector graphics), and WMF (Windows metafile).

Metafile Graphics

A metafile image is one that contains both bitmap and raster image components. For example, if I have a JPG image and I add a drawing above it (shapes, text) it will turn into a metafile graphic.

Metafile graphics share the same features and limitations of both vector and bitmap graphics. If we resize a metafile image, the portion of the image that has bitmap will lose some of its quality while the text part will remain clear.

Common metafile file formats include PDF (Portable Document Format) and EPS (Encapsulated PostScript).

Image Compression Types

Image data can be compressed to save memory and bandwidth. Following are the two main compression types that exist within digital images, lossy and lossless.

Lossy

This type reduces image size by degrading its quality to some extent. This technique can reduce image size more than lossless compression can. For example, a lossy algorithm might degrade the color resolution of the original image to reduce its size.

Both insertion and substitution techniques can be uncovered if an observer has the original overt file and makes a comparison between the original file and the stego file (stego file refers to the overt file including the secret message inside it). A comparison could be done using MD5 checksum. The generation technique does not suffer from this issue because the result of the generation algorithm is an original file.

Image steganographic techniques can be categorized using different approaches. As promised earlier, everything in this book will be kept as simple as possible to avoid confusing the users with scientific facts that they do not need to understand in order to hide or discover hidden data inside digital files.

We can group image steganography into two major groups:

1. Image domain (also called spatial domain)
2. Transform domain (also called frequency domain)

There are additional techniques, but the previous two techniques are considered among the most used in stego tools today. Our grouping will be based on image file types, so image domain will cover any hidden data using images files that use lossless compression algorithms like BMP and GIF. Transform domain will cover images with lossy compression such as JPEG.

Image Domain

Also known as spatial domain, in this technique hidden data is embedded directly in the intensity of image pixels while trying not to cause any visual modification of the carrier file that may raise suspicion. There are many techniques that fall under spatial domain, the most famous being the least significant bit (LSB), which substitutes secret message bits with LSB bits in the overt file.

Least Significant Bit Substitution Using Bitmap Image

In this technique the rightmost LSBs of the cover media digital data are used to conceal secret messages. Luckily the embedding procedure does not affect the original pixel value greatly. We will give an example to demonstrate this technique.

If we want to conceal a secret message inside a 24-bit BMP image, we will use the least bit of each color of the RGB to hide 1 bit of our secret message; this means each pixel can store 3 secret bits.

As we've described before, digital images are composed of a finite number of pixels (except vector formats); in our case a 24-bit image means each pixel has 3 bytes (24 bits), and each pixel can give 3 bits for hiding secret data. These 3 bits will be distributed on each byte of the pixel (bit for red, bit for green and bit for blue) (see Table 3.10).

For example, Table 3.11 shows an excerpt of digital representations of three pixels taken from a 24-bit BMP binary data.

If we want to hide the number 111, we need first to convert it into binary (01101111) and then embed each bit into the LSB of the excerpt pixels image as shown in Table 3.12.

As we note although our secret message is composed of 8 bits, we have to change only 4 bits from the pixel grid; the remaining 4 bits (underlined) remains the same. Many experiments show that in most cases we need to change only half the bits in the image in order to hide our secret message.

To perform this technique automatically, there are many image steganography tools (see Table 3.15). We selected a simple command line program that needs no installation. Its name is *Crypture* and can be downloaded from http://sourceforge.net/projects/crypture/.

Open a command prompt, change your directory to where *Crypture* resides (press and hold the Shift key and right-click the folder that contains the *Crypture* tool to open a command prompt at that directory).

Prepare a BMP image to store your hidden file; we will write our secret message inside a TXT file using Windows Notepad®.

The command that appears in Fig. 3.42 means the following:

Crypture is used to launch the program. Make sure that you download the latest version from the Internet. The latest version of this tool has the name *crypture_2*, so adjust this according to tool's current name.
Omran.bmp is the overt picture that is used to store our hidden file.
secret.txt is the TXT file that contains the secret message.

TABLE 3.10 Comparison of the Amount of Hidden Data That Could Be Embedded Using Different BMP Image Resolution

Image Resolution (24-Bit)	Total Number of Pixels	Total Number of Bits	Storage Capacity of Hidden Bits	
600 × 800	480000	11520000	1440000	≈1406 KB
400 × 500	200000	4800000	600000	≈585 KB
200 × 250	50000	1200000	150000	≈146 KB

TABLE 3.11 Excerpt of 24-Bit Image Showing Three Pixels

Pixel Number	Red	Green	Blue
Pixel 1	00110011	00011011	00011110
Pixel 2	00100100	11000110	00110011
Pixel 3	11010010	00100111	10001100

TABLE 3.12 Excerpt of 24-Bit Image Three Pixels Data After Hiding 8 Bits Inside

Pixel Number	Red	Green	Blue
Pixel 1	00110010	00011011	00011111
Pixel 2	00100100	11000111	00110011
Pixel 3	11010011	00100111	10001100

FIGURE 3.42   Using the Crypture tool to hide a secret file inside a BMP image.

FIGURE 3.43   Extracting a hidden message from BMP using the Crypture tool.

After pressing the Enter key, the program will prompt us for a password. Enter a strong password (in this case, *P@s$w0rd*) and press Enter. If everything goes well you will see a message says *Done*. This means our secret message was concealed successfully.

To extract the hidden message, we need to do the following (see Fig. 3.43).

Enter the program name to execute it, then enter the BMP image that contains your secret file. A password prompt will appear asking you to enter the password to unlock the hidden message. Enter it and press Enter. Your hidden file will be created in the same directory.

This modification will not affect on the visual representation of the carrier image, as each main color in the RGB schema can have 256 possible variations (shades). Changing 3 bits in each pixel will result in very small variations of the color; however, this variation is not recognized by the human eye (see Fig. 3.44 for a comparison between two images; on the right is the original and on the left, the second has a hidden message inside it using the *Crypture*

steganography tool). We note that the visual representation of the image after inserting our hidden data remains the same. The size of the image after inserting the secret file remains the same because we did not add any new bits to the original file in order to hide our secret message, we just substituted it with the existing bits.

The main drawback of this technique is that if an intruder discovers the algorithm he/she will be able to detect any concealed message. To counter for this, we can hide our secret message bits inside specific pixels of the overt image (this could be achieved by using a key between the sender and receiver). This method will make our system slightly more secure.

Another way to strengthen this technique is to encrypt your secret data first, convert it into binary, and then insert it using the previous method. This approach is a better guarantee for more security.

In this technique we've used a BMP 24-bit image as the overt file. This kind of image is very suitable for steganography because of the large amount of pixels that could be

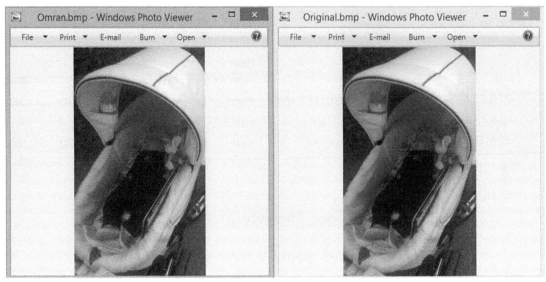

FIGURE 3.44 On the left is the BMP image with the hidden message embedded inside it. On the right is the original image. No difference appears between the two images.

exploited to hide data inside it, although using this file format is neither desirable nor common these days. The draw back here is that due to the file's large size, it takes more time to load than other file formats, especially on low Internet speeds. The other important issue with the BMP format is the infrequent usage of this format online compared to JPEG, GIF, or PNG. Exchanging pictures with large size and BMP extensions will be somehow suspicious.

The previous technique could also be implemented on JPEG 24-bit format and BMP 8-bit as well.

Least Significant Bit Using Palette-Based Images

LSB substitution was undergoing several developments so it could be implemented into palette-based images like GIF format, which is very popular online.

GIF format can only have 8-bit depth. GIF images are based on the indexed color (both PNG and TIF format can support and use indexed color). Index means the actual data in each pixel is simply a number that points back to the color in the palette, sometimes referred to as a color lookup table. For example, an index may contain the color number 111. Number 111 is the index to the palette color (in order to know what this color is, we need to check the number 111 in the palette). Its indexed color is limited to 256 colors. These 256 colors are taken from the 16.7 million colors supported by 24-bit color images. All the colors in the palette are RGB 24-bit color-based. The color of the palette is typically ordered from the most used color to the least used one to reduce the lookup time (see Table 3.13).

Palette-based images store the color palette within the image itself. As we said earlier, the color palette is composed of at most of 256 colors and each color is based on

TABLE 3.13 Number of Bits in Each Pixel and Associated Number of Colors in the Palette (Color Table)

Number of Bits in Index	Colors in Palette
1	2
2	4
3	8
4	16
5	32
6	64
7	128
8	256

the RGB color schema of a 24-bit image (3 bytes for each colored pixel). This means the color table (hence the palette) is weighted at 768 bytes (256×3) and should be stored within each image using the index schema.

The first color in the color table has an index 0, the second has 1, and so on until reaching 256, which is the maximum number supported for palette-based images.

GIF images could be used to hide data inside them using the LSB method, but extra care should be taken when working with this type of image because of its characteristics. For example, when we change the least significant bit of one pixel, this will change its index number and thus will also change its color in the palette. This may result in a completely different color, especially when the palette colors are ordered randomly.

To counter for this issue we can do the following to minimize LSB effects on palette-based images:

1. Adjust the colors' positions in the color table to become color consecutive; in this case our changes will not be noticeable to the human eye.
2. Use GIF pictures that have a small number of unique colors; in this case we can create our own palette and insert it within the image.
3. Use grayscale images. Grayscale images with 8 bits have 256 shades of gray. This will produce a very small effect when changing the color index from one position to another in the palette.

The amount of data that could be hidden using GIF images is relatively small compared with BMP and JPEG images.

There are many programs that implement GIF steganography. We will experiment using a command line tool called gifshuffle; it can be downloaded for free from http://www.darkside.com.au/gifshuffle/.

Gifshuffle is a program for concealing messages in GIF images by shuffling the color map. A shuffled image is visibly indistinguishable from the original. Gifshuffle works with all GIF images, including those with transparency and animation.

Prepare a GIF image that will be used as the cover for our secret message. If you have a JPEG image and you want to convert it into a grayscale color in a GIF format, you can do this using different graphics editing tools. In this case we have Adobe© Fireworks already installed. To convert a JPEG into a grayscale image and then save it as GIF, do the following:

- Open the image using Adobe© Fireworks.
- From the *Commands* menu >> *Creative* >> *Convert to Grayscale*.
- From the *File* menu >> *Save As* >> select GIF as the image type.

Now, let us return to the hiding process. Open a command prompt and navigate to where the GIF-SHUFFLE tool resides, and type the command prompt as shown in Fig. 3.45.

Here is a description of the command keywords:

GIFSHUF This is the name used to launch the program.
-C Compresses the data if concealed, or uncompresses it when extracted.
S Reports on the amount of space available for a hidden message in the GIF colormap. This is calculated from the number of unique colors in the image.
-m "*secret message*" The contents of this string will be concealed in the input GIF image. Note that unless a newline is somehow included in the string, a newline will not be printed when the message is extracted.
-p P@ssw0rd If this is set, the data will be encrypted with this password during concealment, or decrypted during extraction.
omran.gif This image is used as a cover for our secret message.
outputfile.gif This is the resultant stego file that contains our secret message.

In order to extract the hidden message, do the following (see Fig. 3.46):

GIFSHUF This is the name used to launch the program.
-C Compresses the data if concealed or uncompresses it if extracted.
-p P@ssw0rd *If this is set, the data will be encrypted with this password during concealment, or decrypted during extraction.*
outputfile.gif The file that contains the secret message needs to be extracted.

After typing the command press Enter. If your password is correct you will see the hidden message printed on the screen.

It should be noted that the amount of data that can be masked using the GIF image file type is relatively small. Camouflaging data inside JPEG format files is still the best choice so far, and this is what we are going to describe in our section on *transform domain*.

There are additional variations of spatial domain techniques other than LSB. They mostly work in a similar way by changing some bits in each pixel but they differ in their

```
C:\Test\ch3\GIF_DataHiding>GIFSHUF -CS -m "secret message" -p P@ssw0rd omran.gif
 outputfile.gif
Compressed by 44.64%
Message used approximately 75.00% of available space.
```

FIGURE 3.45 Hiding a secret message inside a GIF image using the GIFSHUFFLE tool.

```
C:\Test\ch3\GIF_DataHiding>GIFSHUF -C -p P@ssw0rd outputfile.gif
secret message ◄——————
```

FIGURE 3.46 Extracting a hidden message from a GIF image using the GIFSHUFFLE tool.

implementation. These techniques are still undergoing many developments and hence we may not find tools that support it online. However, we find that it is useful to mention it in order to make this book as inclusive as possible. More useful information can be found when you explore each of the following points:

1. Pixel value differencing
2. Edges-based data embedding method
3. Random pixel-embedding method
4. Mapping pixel to hidden-data method
5. Labeling or connectivity method
6. Pixel intensity-based method
7. Texture-based method
8. Histogram shifting methods

Transform Domain

In this technique, a hidden message is embedded in the frequency domain of the cover image. This is an advanced technique that supports different algorithms and transformations in order to mask secret messages. Algorithms used by this technique are:

1. Discrete cosine transform (DCT) technique
2. Discrete Fourier transform technique
3. Discrete wavelet transform technique
4. Lossless or reversible method
5. Embedding in coefficient bits

In the following sections we will discuss how we can use transform domain techniques to bury data inside a JPEG image using DCT.

Before we begin our description of the method we need first to understand how JPEG implements its compressions.

JPEG Compression

In a previous section within this chapter, we discussed each image file format type. JPEG is popular file format used heavily online because of its low size feature, comparable with its clarity and high resolution. JPEG usually uses lossy compression. This means that the original image information is lost and cannot be restored. The form of compression applied is based on DCT [8].

To compress an image into JPEG format, the RGB color representation should first be converted into a YUV color scheme. This schema takes into account the ability of human perception to see colors, allowing it to reduce the bandwidth needed to transfer chrominance components of the color, thus making the compression more efficient than using a direct RGB representation.

In YUV, Y is the luminance and describes the brightness of the pixel while the chrominance is represented with U and V and carries information about its hue. These three quantities are typically less correlated than the RGB components.

Many scientific studies and psychovisual experiments demonstrate that the human eye is more sensitive to luminance than chrominance, which means that we may neglect larger changes in the chrominance without affecting our perception of the image. This is what JPEG compression basically does. It shorthands the color data part to reduce file size.

Now comes the role of DCT algorithm—it divides the picture into blocks of 8×8 pixels. DCT now checks each block to see which one is less important for human perception; the unimportant blocks are deleted and thus image size is reduced.

JPEG Steganography

JPEG uses lossy compression algorithms, which means it cannot be used to hide data because it achieves its compression by discarding the redundant bit that exists within the image file to reduce its size. The concept of a redundant bit has been previously described thoroughly. Its major characteristic, the digital steganography, is just like all digital media; it greatly depends on it to hide the existence of the secret data without affecting the outside view of the shell media.

In JPEG the algorithm used to compress it has been exploited to hide secret messages. Indeed, JPEG uses two compression stages: the first one is lossy and the second is lossless. The DCT phase uses the lossy compression. After implementation, the next phase is the Huffman encoding stage, which compresses the data further, and uses lossless compression. We are going to hide secret data between the two stages using the LSB previously described by changing the LSB of the data before applying the Huffman encoding compression.

Hiding data inside JPEG using this method makes it very difficult to detect. The possibility of making any degradation in image quality is weak when inserting a small amount of data inside the image.

Let us now *practice* using hiding inside a JPEG image. In this example I will use a GUI tool (in case you may be bored with command line tools by now!).

JPHIDE and *JPSEEK* are programs that allow you to hide a file in a *JPEG* visual image. These programs are different from other similar tools in the market by being able to conceal a secret message using a low insertion rate (under 5%). As the insertion percentage increases the statistical nature of the *JPEG* coefficients differ from *normal* to the extent that it raises suspicion. Above 15% the effects begin to become visible to the naked eye.

These programs are available as a Windows® and DOS version ready to run. You can download both versions from the tool's official website, http://linux01.gwdg.de/~alatham/stego.html. In our experiment we will use the Windows® version, which contains both tools in one executable application.

Now, let us use this tool to hide secret messages inside a JPEG file. Launch this program after downloading it (no need for installation), prepare a JPEG image to use as an

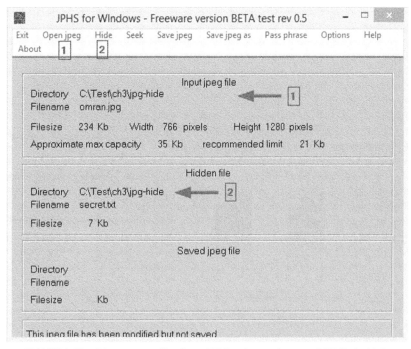

FIGURE 3.47   Select an overt file of type JPEG and conceal a secret TXT file inside it.

overt image for your secret message by clicking *Open jpeg* and selecting it, and then click *Hide* to begin the concealment process by selecting the secret file you want to hide inside this image. Here we're hiding a text document named *secret.txt*. Please note that JPHS (for Windows®) will prompt you to enter a passphrase to protect your secret payload when clicking the *Hide* button (see Fig. 3.47).

Now to finish the concealment process, click *Save jpeg as* to save the resultant stego file that contains your secret data.

In order to extract the secret message from your *JPEG* image, follow these steps:

1. Click *Open jpeg* and select your stego file.
2. Click *Seek* and enter your passphrase to unlock the file. If the entered password was correct, a pop-up window appears asking you to save the secret file to your preferred location (see Fig. 3.48).

When we compare the two images, original and stego, we notice that we cannot visually distinguish between them (see Fig. 3.49).

Hiding After the End-of-File Marker

Text files could be embedded inside an image using the Windows® command prompt only, without any tool. Experiments show that most graphics viewers will only read the digital file until it reaches the EOF marker and will ignore everything after that. Inserting data after the EOF marker will have no effect on the carrier file and it will not make it

corrupt. This feature can be exploited to bury text data inside images.

Let us show you an example:

1. Prepare an image to hide your secret data inside it and a text file that contains your secret message. We are using here a JPEG image as a carrier file named *omran.jpg* and weighted at 233 KB, and TXT file that contains our secret data and is weighted at 6.05 KB. Both are placed in the same directory.
2. Open a command prompt, change the current directory by navigating to where the TXT file and the overt image resides, and enter the information shown in Fig. 3.50.

Use the copy command in DOS with the /b option to handle the file as a binary file. The + symbol is used to combine the two files. Here we will combine our secret text file named *secret.txt* with the picture named *omran.jpg* and output the result with a new image name, *outputfiel.jpg*. The last image file is the stego image that contains our secret file inside it.

We can notice that the *outputfile.jpg* was increased by about 6.0 KB. It has now become 239 KB after adding the text inside the *secret.txt* file to it.

By hiding using this method, the image quality of the stego file will remain the same, and no visual differences will be noticed when comparing the image before and after inserting hidden data. The histogram of both images will also be identical.

To see the hidden message, all you have to do is to open *outputfile.jpg* using Windows® Notepad and you will see

FIGURE 3.48 Extract the secret file from within a JPEG image using JPHS for Windows® program.

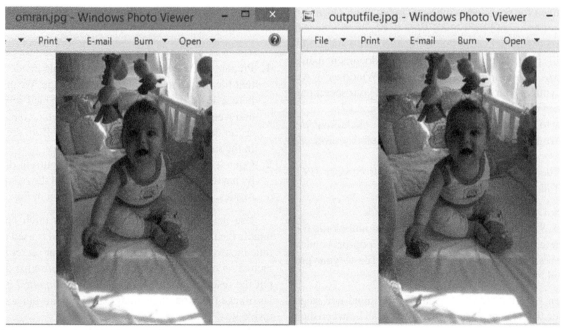

FIGURE 3.49 Comparison of a JPEG image after adding secret data inside it. The original is on the left and the right is the stego image.

FIGURE 3.50 Hide a TXT file inside a JPG image.

your hidden message after the EOF marker (see Fig. 3.51). Table 3.14 contains a list of file markers of different media files.

This technique is vulnerable to editing, resizing, and cropping, and if such modifications occur to the overt file, the secret message will get destroyed.

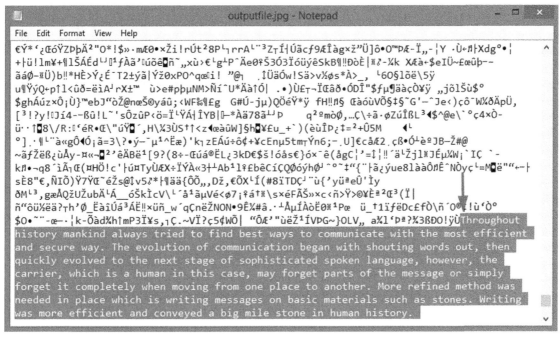

FIGURE 3.51 Viewing data hidden after an EOF marker in a JPEG image using Windows® Notepad.

TABLE 3.14 List of File Markers of Different Image File Types

File Type	Start File Marker	End of File Marker
JPEG	FF D8	FF D9
GIF	47 49	00 3B
BMP	42 4D	00 00
PNG	89 50	60 82

Hiding Zip Files Inside an Image

In Chapter 2 we practically demonstrated how we can hide a zip file inside an image file using only the Windows® command prompt without any third-party tool. This technique is similar to hiding data using the EOF marker already described, but has the same advantages and limitations in addition to some differences. For example, when hiding a zip file inside an image, the data that appears after the EOF will be unreadable when viewed with an editor like Notepad because it is compressed data. In addition to this, a zip file lets us store any type of binary data inside it before hiding the entire zip package inside the image.

Hiding Inside Image Metadata

In Chapter 2 we showed practically how we can hide data inside image metadata (EXIF, XMP, IPTC, ICC). We can access metadata properties of any image under Windows®

OS by right-clicking the image and then selecting the *Properties >> Details* tab. There are many tools that can be used to edit images metadata fields such as *XnViewMP*, *Exif Pilot*, and *PhotoME*.

Hiding in image metadata has many limitations, including:

- If the user saves the image again into another format (from JPEG to GIF), the metadata may disappear.
- If the user resizes, crops, or transforms the image in any way, metadata will be lost too.
- Metadata can only be stored in digital format. If an image got printed, its metadata will not be printed along with it.

Digital Media Steganography Tools

In Table 3.15 you will find a list of steganography tools that can be used to hide secret data in multimedia files such as images and audio and video files. Use this table as a references and return back to it as we describe audio and video steganography in the coming section. You can find a complete list of steganography tools by going to my InfoSec portal at http://www.darknessgate.com/category/digital-steganography.

DATA HIDING INSIDE AUDIO FILES

In simple terms, audio steganography is the science of hiding information inside audio signals. These secret data should be embedded without affecting the original sound perceived by the human ear. The human ear can detect noise in the range of 20 to 20,000 Hz, although many people can

TABLE 3.15 Free Image Steganography Tools

No	Program	Supported Overt Files	Support Encryption	Website Address
1	Crypture	BMP	Yes	http://sourceforge.net/projects/crypture/
2	OpenStego	Different media files	Yes	http://www.openstego.com/
3	Gifshuffle	GIF	Yes	http://www.darkside.com.au/gifshuffle/
4	wbStego4open	BMP, text files, HTML, PDF	Yes	http://home.tele2.at/wbailer/wbstego/fs_home.html
5	Our Secret	Image, audio, and video files	Yes	http://www.securekit.net/oursecret.htm
6	SilentEye	JPEG, BMP, WAVE	Yes	http://www.silenteye.org/
7	MP3stego	MP3, WMA	Yes	http://www.petitcolas.net/steganography/mp3stego/
8	Steghide UI	Different media files	Yes	http://sourceforge.net/projects/steghideui/
9	Camouflage	Different media files	Yes	http://camouflage.unfiction.com/
10	DeepSound	Audio files	Yes	http://download.cnet.com/DeepSound/3000-2092_4-75758214.html
11	FireSteg (Firefox add-on)	Image files	Yes	https://addons.mozilla.org/en-us/firefox/addon/firesteg/
12	JPHIDE and JPSEEK	Image files	Yes	http://linux01.gwdg.de/~alatham/stego.html

hear sounds in 12 Hz range too. The human ear is very sensitive to frequencies between 2000 and 5000 Hz, however some humans may have better or less sensitivity according to their age and other health characteristics like the nervous system. While the human auditory system (HAS) has a large dynamic range, it has a fairly small differential range (loud sounds drown out quiet sounds). In addition to this, the HAS is unable to perceive absolute phase. It's only a relative phase and this is where data concealment can occur according to research by Bender, Gruhl, and Morimoto [9].

Audio steganography is still undergoing many developments and different scientific research is continually being published about it. The fact that the HAS is more accurate than the human visual system makes hiding inside audio files a more challenging task.

In this section, we will briefly talk about different digital audio files and how they can be exploited to conceal secret data inside them.

Let us first give a description of how audio files are structured and the most commonly used types.

Audio Files Basic Concepts

In order to understand how digital audio files are constructed, we need to return to the basics. Let us begin with the analog signal.

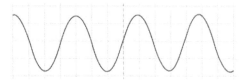

FIGURE 3.52   Sample of an analog signal.

Analog Signal

The term analog signal usually refers to electrical signals. It is a continuous signal in which each signal can vary in frequency, amplitude, or both. For example, in an analog audio signal, the instantaneous voltage of the signal varies continually with the pressure of the sound waves (see Fig. 3.52).

Digital Signal

A digital signal is a type of continuous signal (discrete signal) consisting of just two states, on (1) or off (0). In computer systems any waveform that switches between two voltage levels representing the two states of a Boolean value (0 and 1) is called a digital signal (see Fig. 3.53). Computers store digital audio as a sequence of 0's and 1's [10].

Pulse code modulation (PCM) digital schema was created in 1937 and is used to digitalize analog data. PCM has two main properties, sample rate and bit depth.

FIGURE 3.53 Sample digital wave signal.

Sample rate measures how often per second the amplitude of a waveform is taken, while the bit depth measures the possible digital values.

PCM is considered the standard form of digital audio in computers and other storage devices like CD, DVD, and portable storage. PCM's main function is to sample a waveform and turn it into digital. The sample is stored in an uncompressed format using a lossless compression, thus consuming a lot of hard disk space.

How Digital Sampling Works

Digital sampling works by creating digital samples of the originated sound; for example, when a singer sings, his voice is captured by a special software. This software takes a digital snapshot of his sound at regular intervals in time. The length of each snapshot is measured in bits and the number of snapshots per second is called the sampling rate. When we have more samples per second, the resulting recording will be more original and clear.

For example, CDs sample music at 44.1 KHz rate, which means 44,100 snapshots per second, 16 bits long (snapshot size). To calculate the bit rate you have to multiply sampling rate × sample size in bits × 2 (number of recording channels in stereo is 2):

44,100 × 16 × 2 = 1400 Kbps (kilobyte per second)

These bits constitute our digital music and can be saved similarly to any digital media file type on CD, DVD, or hard disk.

This recording is stored in a raw format; this means its size is big because we did not compress it yet. For example, if we record music for 5 min it will need about 53 MB of disk storage. This is too large to be sent over the Internet or stored on a mobile device; hence comes the role of compression. These bits can be compressed by taking away unimportant bits from the original file to save space while preserving the maximum quality of the audio recording.

Audio File Format Types

We will divide audio format types according to each file compression type.

Uncompressed Format

This type is often referred to as PCM format. It uses no compression and is relatively large. Data stored on a CD usually come uncompressed.

Lossless Compressed Format

This format applies compression to the audio files by implementing different algorithms to reduce bit size. Its compression is similar to ZIP compression. The quality of the sound remains the same as the original recording.

Lossless compression will usually produce a file that is half the original file in size.

Lossy Compressed Format

This compresses the original audio file by removing its redundant bit. The redundant bits in audio files come in a range of sounds that the human ear cannot hear. This can be achieved by using a complex compression algorithm that separates the sounds that humans can hear from the other ranges.

We can control the amount of compression using specialized programs (by lowering the number of samples per second); however, when we lower sampling rate the quality of the original sound will be degraded. In contrast we will have a smaller file size.

Common Audio File Types

In the following sections we will give a brief description about some famous audio files types.

WAV/AIFF

Both types use an uncompressed format, based on PCM schema. WAV was created as a joint effort between Microsoft and IBM. It is the default audio format for all Windows® OS versions beginning with Windows® 95. It has a .wav extension and can be played on both Windows® and MAC machines.

AIFF is a format developed by Apple Inc. and commonly used on Apple Macintosh computer systems. AIFF uses PCM schema but it supports a compressed variant of AIFF known as AIFF-C with various defined compression codecs.

Both WAV and AIFF use lossless compression and are sampled at 44,100 kHz at 16 bits. They store audio sound using a big file size (about 10 MB for each recording minute).

FLAC, ALAC, APE

These three formats are free lossless audio codec (FLAC), Apple lossless audio codec (ALAC), and monkeys audio (APE). The most commonly used one is FLAC, which is similar to MP3, but it is a lossless format. It can lower data size without losing half its quality in comparison to WAV (file with 50 MB on WAV is equal to 25 MB with FLAC format). These three format types use a lossless format.

MP3/WMA

These formats use lossy compression, meaning that we can have a small file size but with a degradation of quality. MP3

FIGURE 3.55 Extracting the hidden message from the WAV file using the Steghide GUI tool.

FIGURE 3.56 Compare waveform of WAV audio file before and after embedding secret data inside it (original is at the top).

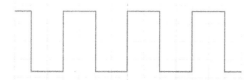

FIGURE 3.53 Sample digital wave signal.

Sample rate measures how often per second the amplitude of a waveform is taken, while the bit depth measures the possible digital values.

PCM is considered the standard form of digital audio in computers and other storage devices like CD, DVD, and portable storage. PCM's main function is to sample a waveform and turn it into digital. The sample is stored in an uncompressed format using a lossless compression, thus consuming a lot of hard disk space.

How Digital Sampling Works

Digital sampling works by creating digital samples of the originated sound; for example, when a singer sings, his voice is captured by a special software. This software takes a digital snapshot of his sound at regular intervals in time. The length of each snapshot is measured in bits and the number of snapshots per second is called the sampling rate. When we have more samples per second, the resulting recording will be more original and clear.

For example, CDs sample music at 44.1 KHz rate, which means 44,100 snapshots per second, 16 bits long (snapshot size). To calculate the bit rate you have to multiply sampling rate $\times$ sample size in bits $\times 2$ (number of recording channels in stereo is 2):

$44,100 \times 16 \times 2 = 1400\,Kbps$ (kilobyte per second)

These bits constitute our digital music and can be saved similarly to any digital media file type on CD, DVD, or hard disk.

This recording is stored in a raw format; this means its size is big because we did not compress it yet. For example, if we record music for 5 min it will need about 53 MB of disk storage. This is too large to be sent over the Internet or stored on a mobile device; hence comes the role of compression. These bits can be compressed by taking away unimportant bits from the original file to save space while preserving the maximum quality of the audio recording.

Audio File Format Types

We will divide audio format types according to each file compression type.

Uncompressed Format

This type is often referred to as PCM format. It uses no compression and is relatively large. Data stored on a CD usually come uncompressed.

Lossless Compressed Format

This format applies compression to the audio files by implementing different algorithms to reduce bit size. Its compression is similar to ZIP compression. The quality of the sound remains the same as the original recording.

Lossless compression will usually produce a file that is half the original file in size.

Lossy Compressed Format

This compresses the original audio file by removing its redundant bit. The redundant bits in audio files come in a range of sounds that the human ear cannot hear. This can be achieved by using a complex compression algorithm that separates the sounds that humans can hear from the other ranges.

We can control the amount of compression using specialized programs (by lowering the number of samples per second); however, when we lower sampling rate the quality of the original sound will be degraded. In contrast we will have a smaller file size.

Common Audio File Types

In the following sections we will give a brief description about some famous audio files types.

WAV/AIFF

Both types use an uncompressed format, based on PCM schema. WAV was created as a joint effort between Microsoft and IBM. It is the default audio format for all Windows® OS versions beginning with Windows® 95. It has a .wav extension and can be played on both Windows® and MAC machines.

AIFF is a format developed by Apple Inc. and commonly used on Apple Macintosh computer systems. AIFF uses PCM schema but it supports a compressed variant of AIFF known as AIFF-C with various defined compression codecs.

Both WAV and AIFF use lossless compression and are sampled at 44,100 kHz at 16 bits. They store audio sound using a big file size (about 10 MB for each recording minute).

FLAC, ALAC, APE

These three formats are free lossless audio codec (FLAC), Apple lossless audio codec (ALAC), and monkeys audio (APE). The most commonly used one is FLAC, which is similar to MP3, but it is a lossless format. It can lower data size without losing half its quality in comparison to WAV (file with 50 MB on WAV is equal to 25 MB with FLAC format). These three format types use a lossless format.

MP3/WMA

These formats use lossy compression, meaning that we can have a small file size but with a degradation of quality. MP3

TABLE 3.16 Hiding 8 Bits of Secret Data in 8 Samples of Audio Music Stream

Sample Audio Stream (16 Bit)	Secret Message R	Audio Stream After Hiding
1 0 1 0 1 1 0 0 1 1 0 1 0 1 1 0	0	1 0 1 0 1 1 0 0 1 1 0 1 0 1 1 **0**
0 0 1 1 0 1 0 0 1 0 1 1 0 1 1 1	1	0 0 1 1 0 1 0 0 1 0 1 1 0 1 1 **1**
1 1 1 1 1 1 0 0 0 1 0 1 0 1 0 0	1	1 1 1 1 1 1 0 0 0 1 0 1 0 1 0 **1**
0 1 0 0 1 1 0 0 1 0 0 1 0 1 0 0	1	0 1 0 0 1 1 0 0 1 0 0 1 0 1 0 **1**
1 0 0 1 1 1 0 0 1 0 0 0 0 0 1 1	0	1 0 0 1 1 1 0 0 1 0 0 0 0 0 1 **0**
0 1 1 1 1 0 0 1 1 0 1 0 0 1 0 0	0	0 1 1 1 1 0 0 1 1 0 1 0 0 1 0 0
0 0 1 0 1 1 1 0 1 0 0 1 0 1 1 1	1	0 0 1 0 1 1 1 0 1 0 0 1 0 1 1 1
1 0 0 0 0 1 0 1 1 1 0 1 0 1 0 1	0	1 0 0 0 0 1 0 1 1 1 0 1 0 1 0 **0**

is the abbreviation for MPEG-1 Level 3. It is the most used audio file format available today because it provides very good quality compared to its low size (it consumes 1 MB for each minute of recording). MP3 is very popular because any audio program can play it on almost all operating systems available today.

Windows® Media Audio (WMA), it is a file format similar to MP3 developed by Microsoft® that can compress data more than MP3. It has the WMA extension.

Audio Steganography Types

There have been many techniques for hiding information in audio files so that the embedded data in the audio file are perceptually indiscernible to the human ear. In the following sections we will list the main approaches used and give real world examples of hiding data using free audio steganography tools for the most widely used techniques.

Least Significant Bit Encoding Encoding

This is the most used technique for hiding data inside audio files. Similar to the image LSB method, we replace the LSB in some bytes inside the audio file to conceal our secret message. The big size of audio files provides a great amount of space for hiding inside it.

As we said before, each second of stereo recording is sampled at 44,100 per second for each channel, meaning that for each second there are 88,200 digital samples produced. Each of these samples is 16 bits. If we want to conceal our hidden data in these samples we can hide 1 bit of secret data in each 16-bit sample, which means that 1 s of recording can store 88,200 bits of confidential data equal to 86 KB of secret data in each second of recording. This is a huge amount of space for burying data in one file.

Changing 1 bit (the LSB) in each sample will leave minor changes in the analog signal rendering; the human ear cannot detect such an alteration easily.

As we did before with LSB images, in audio we will modify the LSB of each sample (16-bit integer values) to conceal our message. See Table 3.16 for a practical illustration.

We conclude after hiding one ASCII character (R) that we have to change the LSB of only four samples. The reaming ones already have the same bit value. Many experiments show that we need to modify only 50% of audio samples in order to hide our message. This leaves very slight changes in the audio file imperceptible to humans.

We can begin the insertion of hidden messages from the beginning of the file and go through it until its end (hidden message bits should be less than the total number of LSB available in the audio file). This is not a secure approach as anyone who knows about the existence of hidden messages and knows the technique will be able to uncover them. In addition, if the audio file has been investigated using statistical analysis techniques, the secret message will be revealed because the first part of the file that contains the hidden message will have different statistical properties than the rest of the file (assuming that the hidden message did not spread on all the samples in the overt file). Another more secure technique is to select a subset of samples from the overt audio file randomly and then insert hidden message bits inside them. Of course you need to exchange these sample locations with the receiver in order to be able to decode the message upon receiving it (in fact you can use a secret key that determines their locations within the file itself and share this key privately with the recipient).

The main disadvantage of LSBs in audio files is that if the overt audio file used to conceal our secret message gets resampled, the entire hidden message will be destroyed.

Let us now experiment using a tool for hiding data inside WAV files using the LSB method. *Steghide* is a tool created by *Stefan Hetzl* and is available at http://steghide.source-forge.net/ under a general public license (GPL). This is a command line tool, but a project called *Steghide UI* written by *Drunken* has created a user interface for it that allows the user to do everything *steghide* can do but through a GUI. You can download this tool along with its GUI from http://sourceforge.net/projects/steghideui/. In this example, we will use this tool so beginners will not get bored with our continual usage of steganography command line tools!

Prepare your overt file (audio file of type WAV) and a TXT file that contains your secret message (see Fig. 3.54).

Here is a description of each step in the *Steghide* screen capture of Fig. 3.54.

1. Cover file (also named overt file): The file inside of which we are going to hide our secret message.
2. Embed file: This file contains our secret information.
3. Output file: This is the output file after embedding our secret file (also called stego file).
4. Password: This is used to protect our hidden message.
5. Use Cover File as Output File: If we check this option, the text field in step 3 will be grayed out, and the resultant file will have the same name as the cover file.

After specifying everything, click *Embed*. If everything goes well the secret file will be embedded inside *original.wav* and outputted as *outputfile.wav*.

To extract the hidden message, go to the *Extract* tab and fill in the details (see Fig. 3.55).

1. Cover file: Select the file that contains the secret message (hence, *secret.txt*).
2. Output file: This is the extracted file that contains the secret file.
3. Password: Insert the password you've previously entered when you embedded the message.
4. Extract: Click to extract the secret file.

The embedded secret message did not affect the sound quality of the original file. After listening to both files (original and stego files) we were unable to detect any differences in sound.

Fig. 3.56 illustrates a waveform of both *original.wav* and *outputfile.wav*.

Parity Coding

Parity coding is a more robust technique for hiding data inside digital audio files. In this technique, signals are divided into regions. Each region has a parity bit that is matched with the hidden message secret bit. If a match exists, the secret bit will be encoded in this region using the same parity bit value; otherwise, the process flips the LSB of one of the samples in the region. This technique is more sophisticated than the LSB technique we talked

FIGURE 3.54 Hiding a TXT file inside a WAV file using the Steghide tool (GUI version).

FIGURE 3.55 Extracting the hidden message from the WAV file using the Steghide GUI tool.

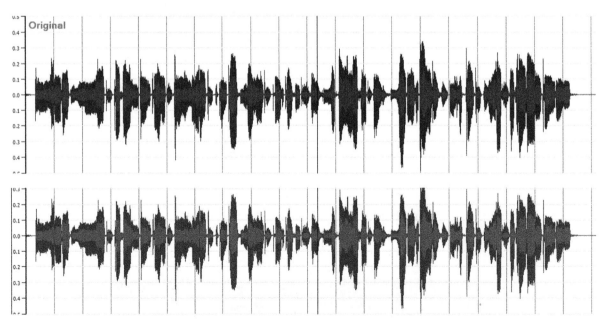

FIGURE 3.56 Compare waveform of WAV audio file before and after embedding secret data inside it (original is at the top).

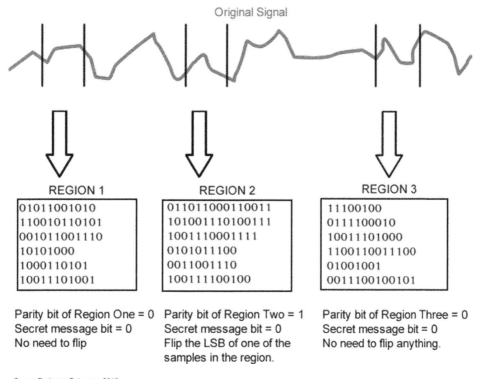

Original Signal

REGION 1

```
01011001010
110010110101
001011001110
10101000
1000110101
10011101001
```

REGION 2

```
011011000110011
101001110100111
1001110001111
0101011100
0011001110
100111100100
```

REGION 3

```
11100100
0111100010
10011101000
1100110011100
01001001
0011100100101
```

Parity bit of Region One = 0
Secret message bit = 0
No need to flip

Parity bit of Region Two = 1
Secret message bit = 0
Flip the LSB of one of the
samples in the region.

Parity bit of Region Three = 0
Secret message bit = 0
No need to flip anything.

©www.DarknessGate.com 2015

FIGURE 3.57   Demonstration of the parity coding technique to conceal data inside audio files.

©www.DarknessGate.com

```
C:\Test\ch3\MP3Stego_1_1_18\MP3Stego>encode -E secret.txt -P P@$sw0rd overtfile.wav stego_file.mp3
MP3StegoEncoder 1.1.17
See README file for copyright info
Microsoft RIFF, WAVE audio, PCM, mono 44100Hz 16bit, Length:  0: 0:20
MPEG-I layer III, mono  Psychoacoustic Model: AT&T
Bitrate=128 kbps  De-emphasis: none  CRC: off
Encoding "overtfile.wav" to "stego_file.mp3"
Hiding "secret.txt"
[Frame    791 of    791] (100.00%) Finished in  0: 0: 0
```

FIGURE 3.58   Concealing data using the MP3Stego tool.

about earlier because we have the choice to select different samples to perform LSB on it in each region (see Fig. 3.57).

The *MP3Stego tool is an implementation of the parity coding technique. It will hide information in the MP3 files during the compression process. The data is first compressed, encrypted, and then hidden inside the MP3 stream. This tool can also be used as a copyright marking system. We will experiment using this tool to hide a secret message inside an MP3 audio file. First go to* http://www.petitcolas.net/steganography/mp3stego/ to download the tool to your PC.

1. Extract the zip file that contains *MP3Stego*. You should see three folders inside it. Navigate to the *MP3Stego* folder and launch a DOS command prompt at this directory.

2. Type the information from Fig. 3.58 in the command prompt.

Here is a description of each keyword used in the command in Fig. 3.58:

encode is used to launch the *MP3Stego* tool to conceal data. You will use the decode command when you want to extract hidden data from a file.

-E is a switch that means we are encoding data (hiding it).

secret.txt contains the message we wish to hide.

-P *P@$sw0rd* is the password switch. In this case we entered *P@$sw0rd*.

overtfile.wav is the file that contains our secret message. After executing the command the file will be converted into MP3 audio file format, thus reducing its size.

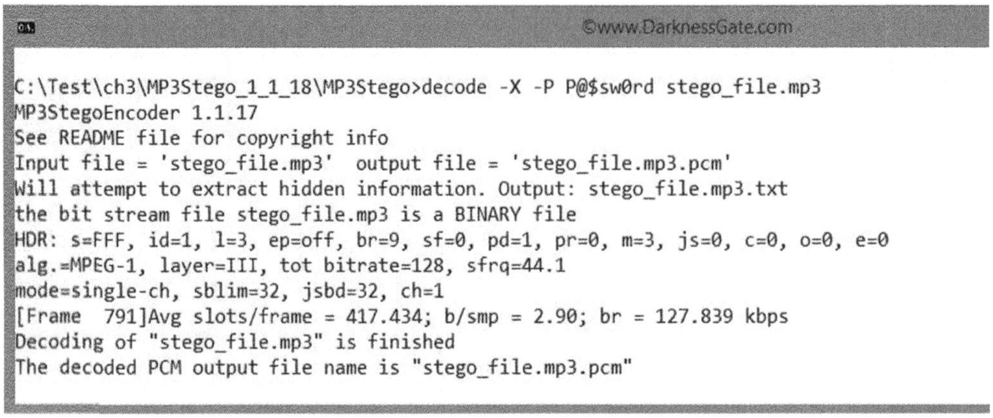

```
C:\Test\ch3\MP3Stego_1_1_18\MP3Stego>decode -X -P P@$sw0rd stego_file.mp3
MP3StegoEncoder 1.1.17
See README file for copyright info
Input file = 'stego_file.mp3'  output file = 'stego_file.mp3.pcm'
Will attempt to extract hidden information. Output: stego_file.mp3.txt
the bit stream file stego_file.mp3 is a BINARY file
HDR: s=FFF, id=1, l=3, ep=off, br=9, sf=0, pd=1, pr=0, m=3, js=0, c=0, o=0, e=0
alg.=MPEG-1, layer=III, tot bitrate=128, sfrq=44.1
mode=single-ch, sblim=32, jsbd=32, ch=1
[Frame  791]Avg slots/frame = 417.434; b/smp = 2.90; br = 127.839 kbps
Decoding of "stego_file.mp3" is finished
The decoded PCM output file name is "stego_file.mp3.pcm"
```

FIGURE 3.59 Extracting a secret message from an MP3 file using MP3Stego.

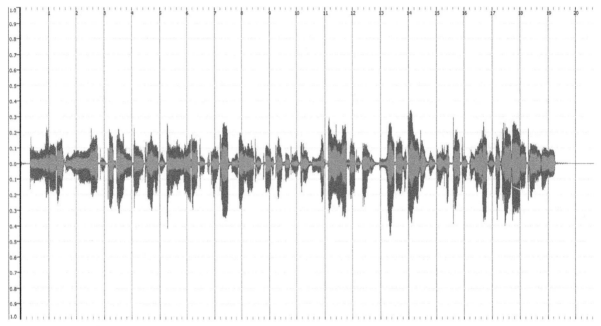

FIGURE 3.60 Waveform of the original WAV file (overtfile.wav) before concealing data inside it.

Stego_file.mp3 is the output file that will contain the *secret.txt* file inside the *overtfile.wav*.

In order to extract the hidden file, follow Fig. 3.59.
Here is a description of the decoding command (Fig. 3.59):

decode –X is used to launch the tool to extract hidden data (-X points to the extraction process).
-P *P@$sw0rd* is the password used when concealing our data. Without it we cannot extract the hidden messages.
stego_file.mp3 is the file that contains our hidden message.

After executing this command, and assuming password entered was correct, *MP3Stego* will extract two additional files in the same directory. The first one is named *stego_file.mp3.pcm* and is used to uncompress *stego_file.mp3*. The

second generated file will be our secret message file, which will carry the name *stego_file.mp3.txt*.

We have made a comparison between the sound quality of both the original file and the resulting stego file. As you will see in Fig. 3.60, we were unable to distinguish between both files, and the sound quality was the same. We notice from Figs. 3.60 and 3.61 that no major waveform adjustments have taken place after embedding secret data into the WAV file.

Phase Coding

This technique works by substituting the phase of the initial audio segment with a reference phase that represents the hidden data. In other words it encodes the secret message bit as phase shifts in the phase spectrum of a digital signal. This results in an inaudible encoding in terms of signal-to-noise ratio.

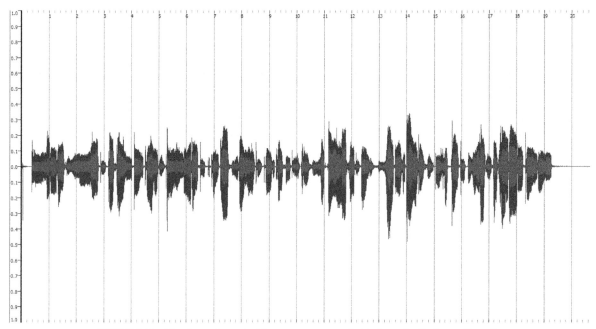

FIGURE 3.61 Waveform after embedding a secret message inside the audio file (*stego_file.mp3*).

Spread Spectrum

Spread spectrum is a form of radio frequency communication in which data is intentionally spread over a wide frequency range. This technique is used mainly for secure communications, which increases resistance to natural interference, noise, and jamming, and to prevent detection.

In the context of information hiding inside audio files, the spread spectrum method tries to spread secret data across the audio signal frequency spectrum as much as possible. There are two versions of spread spectrum, direct sequence and frequency hopping schemes [11].

Echo Hiding

In echo hiding, secret data is hidden inside a sound file by inserting an echo signal into a discrete signal. This method is far more secure and offers a high data transmission rate in addition to being more robust than the previous method, which depends on noise inducing.

Data Hiding Inside Video Files

A video file consists of a series of images, audio, and other data noting that the attributes associated with video files are similar to those associated with audio and image formats already discussed. These audio channels and pixels in addition to the new term called frame rate are specific only to video files.

Characteristics of Video Files

Whatever file format type a video file is, it should have the following characteristics:

- Container type: Contains video data in a video coding format.
- The video and audio signal: Contains the actual data of the video file.
- Codec: Used to compress and decompress the data. It interprets the video file and determines the best ways to present it on your monitor. Some video players can have their codecs preinstalled (such as *PotPlayer, which supports a large number of codecs* [12]). Some codecs are standalone installations.

Some Terms Associated With Video Files

Frame size: A video frame is composed of lines, and each line is sampled to create a number of pixels per line. The more lines we have per frame, the higher the image resolution.

Aspect ratio: This is the ratio of width to height.

Frame rate: Also known as frame frequency, it is the frequency at which an imaging device displays consecutive frames. Frame rate is expressed in frames per second.

Bitrate: This is the size of the video file per second of data. It can be expressed in kilobytes, megabytes, or gigabytes per second. The higher the bit rate, the better the video quality.

The audio sample rate: The number of audio samples per second (CD audio quality has 44,100 samples per second for each channel).

Video files have wide potential in data hiding because their large size makes concealing large volumes of data inside it feasible. Many techniques in data concealment that

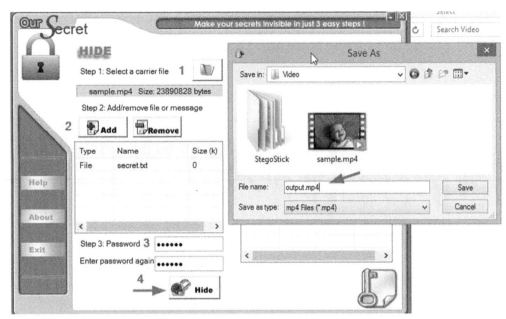

FIGURE 3.62   Hiding a secret TXT file inside an MP4 video file using the our secret steganography tool.

work on images and audio files can also be implemented on video files. As with audio files, video files have two basic types, compressed and uncompressed.

Uncompressed videos usually are produced by video cameras, or they can be generated by decompressing the video encoded in lossless compression format [13].

Compressed video files use different algorithms to reduce their size while maintaining acceptable visual quality. Without compression they will be very difficult to transmit across the Internet because of their large size.

There are two types of video compression, lossy and lossless compression.

- Lossless compression: Reduces file size by about 50%. Nothing is lost from the original video file after the decompression takes place.
- Lossy: Some data will get lost (image, audio, video data); as the compression increases, video quality decreases. Most video files available in markets (on CDs and DVDs) and on the Internet use a lossy compression algorithm. The most famous lossy compression video format is MPEGx.

Next we are going to use a tool for concealing secret data inside an MP4 video file. MP4 is a container video file that can store video and audio. It can also be used to store other data such as subtitles and images. MP4 allows streaming over the Internet but it uses a lossy compression algorithm to eliminate redundant data and thus reduce its size. It has an MP4 file extension, although it can have other extension names such as M4A and M4P [14].

Our Secret is a tool that lets you hide text files or files such as video, audio, image, and others in file. We will use

it to *practice* concealing a secret message inside an MP4 video file.

Prepare an MP4 file that will be used as a carrier, called *smaple.mp4*. Write your secret message inside a TXT file and store it as *secret.txt* (see Fig. 3.62).

In the first step we select the carrier file, which should be an MP4 file. In the second step we select a TXT file that contains our secret message. In the third step we enter a password to protect our hidden file. Finally, we click *Hide* to store the resulting stego file; in this case we named it *output.mp4*.

The process to uncover the file is straightforward one. We select the stego file along with the password entered during the concealment process.

If we check the video quality of either the original or stego file we cannot see any difference in audio or images. Audio waveform is also almost identical in both files.

Other tools for concealing data in video files are *Open-Puff* and *StegoStick Beta*. Note that many recent experiments show that most video steganography tools that are currently available for public use are easily vulnerable to different attacks. You can read more about this topic in Chapter 6 to better decide which tool is best for you.

DATA HIDING USING OTHER DIGITAL MEDIA TYPES

Until now we've shown you how to conceal data using images, text, audio, and video files; however, data could be concealed using other digital file formats. As we said before, almost any digital file can be used as a container for concealing hidden data. In this section we will begin talking about the most famous document format currently used in both private and public sectors around the globe, which is the Portable Document Format (PDF) created by Adobe® Corporation.

Data Hiding Inside PDF Documents

Adobe® makes PDF specifications available on their website for developers in order to *foster the creation of ecosystem around the PDF format* [15]. Publishing its specification online encourages software developers to create different applications that can create and read PDF documents. PDF format is considered very complex and has different types and formats to be applied. In order to understand where data can be hidden inside PDF files, a basic understanding of PDF format is needed. The sixth edition of the PDF specifications contains 1310 pages, therefore explaining it may need a book of its own. However, in this section we will briefly describe PDF structure and list the main places where data can be concealed inside it.

PDF Structure

PDF file format is a binary file composed of text and binary data mixed together. If you open it in Windows® Notepad or a similar text viewer you will see the objects that define the structure and content of the document. PDF is logically composed of four sections (see Fig. 3.63).

You can see the internal structure of any PDF file using a simple portable utility called PoDoFo that can be downloaded from http://podofo.sourceforge.net (see Fig. 3.64). Acrobat reader also offer the possibility to view the internal file structure of PDF files through *Advanced* menu >> *Browse Internal PDF Structure* in Acrobat Reader 9.0.

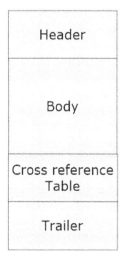

PDF File Structure

FIGURE 3.63 PDF file format structure.

There are many places where we can conceal our data inside a PDF file, as we show next.

Change Formatting

- Set the PDF font color white on a white background as we did before with MS Word® files, thus hiding it from readers' eyes.
- Reduce the size of the font to be very small.
- Exploit whitespaces between words and paragraphs to hide secret bits.

Embedding Objects Inside a PDF File

- Embed a picture inside a PDF file, which could have hidden metadata inside it. We can also use an image steganography tool to conceal our data inside this image before insertion.
- Attach files to a PDF, although they can be easily discovered by savvy users.

Advanced Techniques

- Use the wrong tag names inside PDF internal structure source code. PDF usually ignores unexpected tags, making it a suitable place to hide data.
- Insert data after the EOF marker that is similar to many digital files.
- Edit PDF source code directly by inserting your hidden text inside it. You can then mark this text object as deleted. Your secret text will be hidden after the EOF marker and it will remain there until an update or compression of the PDF file takes place.
- Exploit JavaScript inside a PDF to hide data. PDF files support adding JavaScript into the file. We can use many techniques inside JavaScript snippets to hide data such as:
  - Hiding secret letters by using the replace/restore function of JavaScript; for example, Clear text: *Nihad is writing a book!* After obfuscating it becomes ("XXXNiXXXXhXXad XXixxs XXwritxxxinxxxg xax booXXok!xx").replace(/x/g,"").
  - Encoding text as numbers; for example, encoding ASCII text as base32 and using the ().toString() function to output the result in clear text.
- Using a tool. There are few tools that support masking data inside PDF files. Next we'll use a tool called *wbStego4open* for this purpose.

WbStego4open is a tool used to conceal data inside PDF files. It is based on *wbStego4* and supports Windows® and Linux. *WbStego4open* is published under the GNU GPL.

This tool allows us to hide data in inside BMP, HTML, and PDF files. It was originally designed to embed the copyright file within the overt file for copyright purposes.

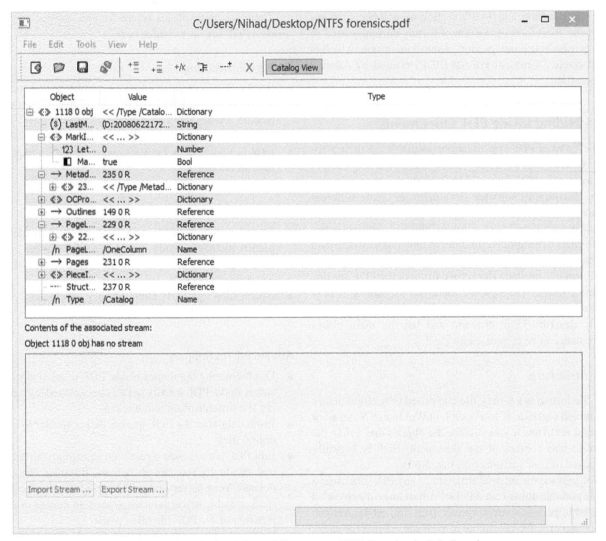

FIGURE 3.64 Viewing the internal file structure of PDF files using the PoDoFo tool.

Download the tool from http://home.tele2.at/wbailer/wbstego/fs_home.html. You will see that this is a portable application that requires no installation. Double-click on the program icon to launch the tool (see Fig. 3.65).

Click *Continue* to proceed. The next window will ask you whether you want to *encode* or *decode*. In our case we are hiding so select *encode*.

The third window asks you to select the file you want to hide (you can also select copyright info in case you want to include a hidden sign inside your file; see Fig. 3.66). In our case we have stored our secret message within a TXT file called *secret.txt*. Select it and click *Continue*.

The next window asks you to select your carrier file type (the file that will contain the hidden file). We selected our file type as *Adobe Acrobat Reader* (*.PDF*) (see Fig. 3.67).

The next window offers you the option to set password protection for your file. The last two windows of the wizard

ask you to select the location of the output file in addition to a wizard summary.

The decoding process is similar to the previous process. You initially select the output file that contains your stego file, then insert your password (if any), and select a place to output your secret file to it.

WbStego4open inserts hidden data in the PDF header in a place that will not be read by the PDF reader application. It works by changing each ASCII character of the hidden message into binary (0 and 1). It then converts each binary digit to another hex value. So the binary digit 0 becomes 20 and binary digit 1 becomes 09. We can compare both PDF files, before insertion and after (see Fig. 3.68) using a free command line utility called VBinDiff (download from http://www.cjmweb.net/vbindiff/VBinDiff-Win32).

The lower file (output.pdf) shows clearly that there are many 20 and 09 numbers. These belong to the embedded secret file.

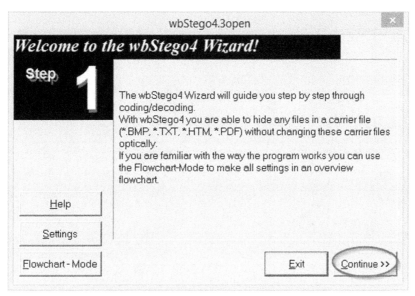

FIGURE 3.65 Launching the wbStego4 wizard.

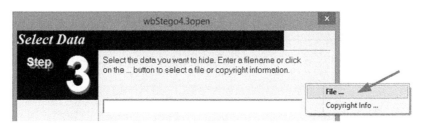

FIGURE 3.66 Choose the type of hidden file you need, File or Copyright Info.

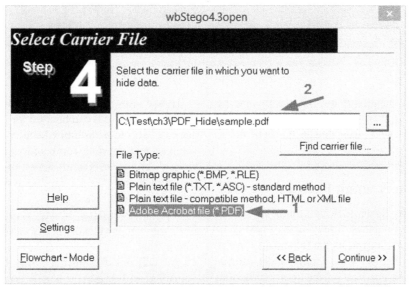

FIGURE 3.67 Select your overt file and click Continue.

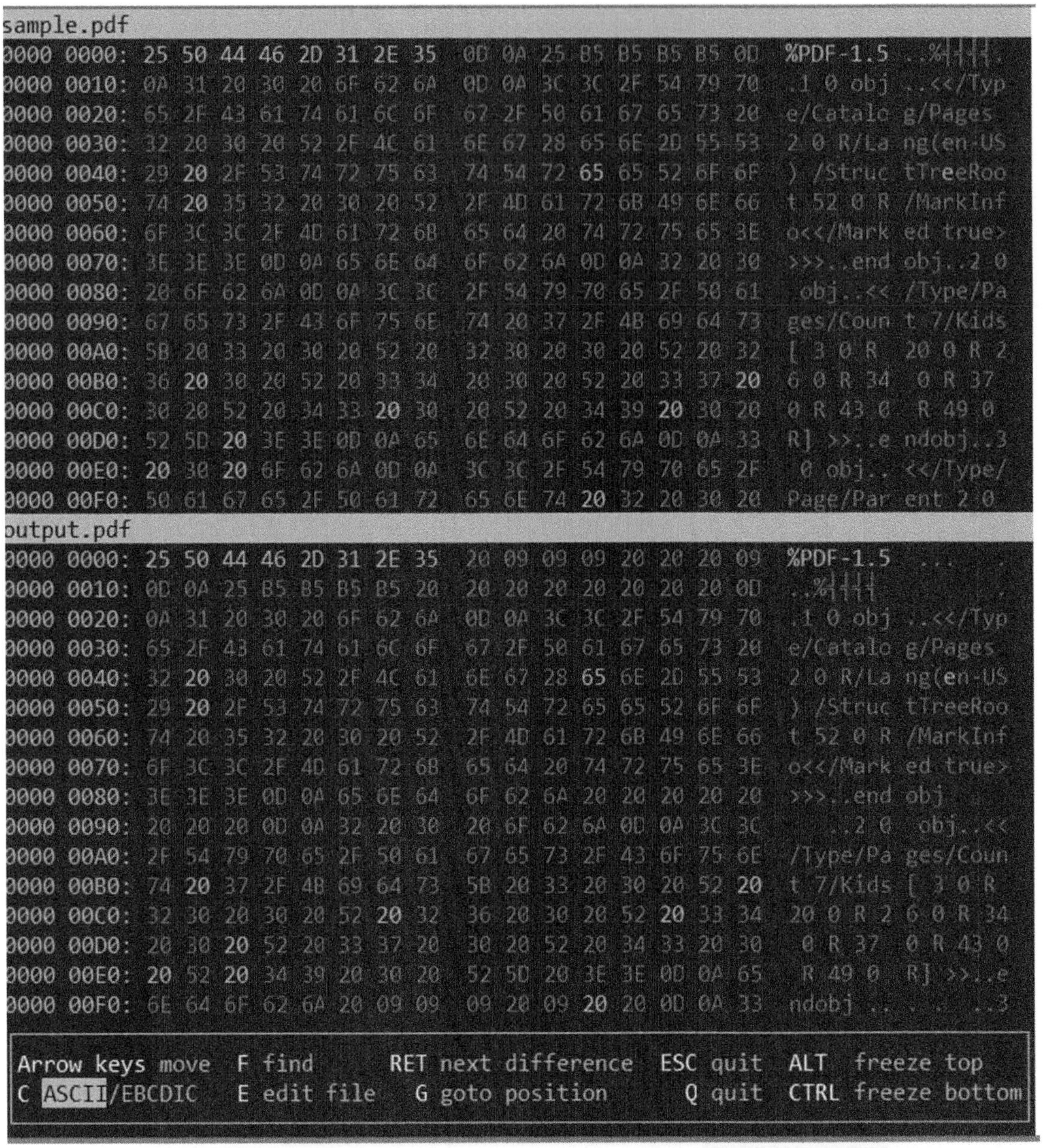

FIGURE 3.68 Compare sample.pdf to output.pdf; hidden data appears in output.pdf as 20 and 09.

Finally it is good to mention that it is better to sign the PDF file before sending it to the final recipient since the *wbStego4open* tool can work even though the PDF file is password protected.

Data Hiding Inside Program Binaries

Hydan is tool created by Rakan El-Khalil that allows users to conceal data inside Windows® applications (exe files). According to its creator, "it exploits the redundancy in the i386 instruction set by defining sets of functionally equivalent instructions. It then encodes information in machine code using the appropriate instructions from each set."

Hydan allows messages to be encrypted using a blow-fish algorithm and it can be used for file signing and water-marking. This tool has limited ability to store a considerable volume of secret data compared to image and audio files because of the structural nature of the executable files. However, it still offers a very good example of concealing data inside executable files.

Hydan is supported by Net Free BSD and Linux i386 *ELF*. You can download this tool from http://www.crazyboy.com/hydan/.

We will not demonstrate using this tool because it is Linux based; however, it is still like any other stego tool. You can check its *read me* file for a usage example.

SUMMARY

This chapter was a core chapter in the book. It introduced many techniques for concealing data inside different digital files. We've divided this chapter into three main sections. We began talking about concealing data inside text. After that we added MS Word® files as part of this section because many hiding techniques will be implemented by exploiting text features. It should be noted that MS Word® is still the most used word processing software in the world, especially on Windows®-based machines.

The next section talks about image steganography. Here we began our discussion about different image types, their formats, and how they are represented on screen. This knowledge is essential in order to understand how data concealment works inside image files.

In the third section we moved to audio and video steganography. There was a brief discussion about both file formats, types, and how they are constructed. A small demonstration on using some tools for concealing data in both types was provided. Finally we conclude this section along with the chapter by discussing how data can be concealed under different digital file formats like PDF documents and executable programs.

This chapter was rich and long at the same time. Many techniques mentioned can be combined in a sophisticated way to form very strong hiding techniques.

In Chapter 6, we will reverse everything mentioned in this chapter. The chapter will discuss in detail each hiding technique mentioned here and how it can be legally investigated and uncovered using different tools and techniques. For now, though, let us move to another core chapter that talks about obscuring data inside Windows®-based machines by exploiting its file system features.

REFERENCES

[1] Suggested whitespace manipulation data hiding techniques W. Bender, D. Gruhl, N. Morimoto, Techniques for data hiding, IBM Systems Journal 35 (3/4) (1996) 131–336.
[2] ECMA-376 standard documentation, Office Open XML File Formats [Online]. Available from: http://www.ecma-international.org/flat/publications/Standards/Ecma-376.htm (accessed 18.08.15).
[3] 7Zip program: http://www.7-zip.org/.
[4] WinRAR program: http://www.rarlab.com.
[5] X-G. Sui, H. Luo, A New Steganography Method Based on Hypertext, IEEE-2004.
[6] Twitter usage statistics [Online]. Available from: http://lorirtaylor.com/twitter-statistics-2015/ (accessed 18.08.15).
[7] Wikipedia, Image file formats [Online]. Available from: https://en.wikipedia.org/wiki/Image_file_formats (accessed 01.09.15).
[8] Wikipedia, JPEG Compression [Online]. Available from: https://en.wikipedia.org/wiki/JPEG (accessed 06.09.15).
[9] W. Bender, D. Gruhl, N. Morimoto, Techniques for data hiding, IBM Systems Journal 35 (3&4) (1996) 893–896 55.
[10] Wikipedia, The anatomy of digital signal [Online]. Available from: https://en.wikipedia.org/wiki/Digital_signal (accessed 14.09.15).
[11] Wikipedia, understanding Spread Spectrum [Online]. Available from: https://en.wikipedia.org/wiki/Spread_spectrum (accessed 02.09.15).
[12] Download PotPlayer: https://potplayer.daum.net/ (accessed 30.08.15).
[13] Wikipedia, Uncompressed video files [Online]. Available from: https://en.wikipedia.org/wiki/Uncompressed_video (accessed 22.08.15).
[14] Wikipedia, MPEG-4 file format [Online]. Available from: https://en.wikipedia.org/wiki/MPEG-4_Part_14 (accessed 08.09.15).
[15] Adobe website [Online]. Available from: www.adobe.com.

BIBLIOGRAPHY

[1] Markup Compatibility and Extensibility in New versions of MS Office [Online]. Available from: http://openxmldeveloper.org/blog/b/openxmldeveloper/archive/2012/09/21/markup-compatibility-and-extensibility.aspx (accessed 23.08.15).
[2] Markup Compatibility and Extensibility in MS Office [Online]. Available from: https://wiki.openoffice.org/wiki/OOXML/Markup_Compatibility_and_Extensibility (accessed 20.08.15).
[3] Understanding new MS Office file format based on OOXML [Online]. Available from: https://msdn.microsoft.com/en-us/library/office/ff478576.aspx (accessed 21.08.15).
[4] OOXML study [Online]. Available from: http://officeopenxml.com/anatomyofOOXML.php.
[5] Overview of the XML file formats in Office 2010 [Online]. Available from: https://technet.microsoft.com/en-us/library/cc179190.aspx (accessed 22.08.15).
[6] Analyzing Malicious Documents Cheat Sheet [Online]. Available from: https://zeltser.com/analyzing-malicious-documents (accessed 25.08.15).
[7] M. Shirali-Shahreza, Stealth steganography in SMS, in: Proc. 3rd IEEE and IFIP International Conference on Wireless and Optical Communications Networks (WOCN 06), Banglore, India, April 2006 http://dx.doi.org/10.1109/WOCN.2006.1666572.
[8] N. Provos, P. Honeyman, Hide and seek: an introduction to steganography, IEEE Security and Privacy Journal (May–June 2003) 32–44, http://dx.doi.org/10.1109/MSECP.2003.1203220.
[9] M. Garg, A novel text steganogrpahy technique based on html document, International Journal of Advanced Science and Technology 35 (October 2011).
[10] Understanding Graphic File Formats [Online]. Available from: http://webstyleguide.com/wsg3/11-graphics/5-web-graphics-formats.html (accessed 25.08.15).
[11] Graphic File Types Overview [Online]. Available from: http://sanstudio.com/tech/GraphicFileTypes.html (accessed 25.08.15).
[12] Types of Graphics File Formats [Online]. Available from: http://www.fileformat.info/mirror/egff/ch01_04.htm (accessed 26.08.15).
[13] RGB Color Chart [Online]. Available from: http://www.tayloredmktg.com/rgb/ (accessed 28.08.15).
[14] Comparison of image file formats features [Online]. Available from: http://www.aivosto.com/vbtips/imageformats.html (accessed 31.08.15).
[15] Microsoft Windows Bitmap File Format Summary [Online]. Available from: http://www.fileformat.info/format/bmp/egff.htm (accessed 31.08.15).
[16] JPEG (Transform Compression) [Online]. Available from: http://www.dspguide.com/ch27/6.htm (accessed 04.09.15).

[17] Introduction to JPEG Compression [Online]. Available from: http://www.tutorialspoint.com/dip/Introduction_to_JPEG_compression.htm (accessed 04.09.15).

[18] How digital sampling works[Online]. Available from: http://www.quepublishing.com/articles/article.aspx?p=372009 (accessed 14.09.15).

[19] Video files format overview [Online]. Available from: http://www.dpbestflow.org/Video_Format_Overview (accessed 14.09.15).

[20] PDF Tricks [Online]. Available from: https://code.google.com/p/corkami/wiki/PDFTricks (accessed 11.09.15).

Chapter 4

Data Hiding Under Windows® OS File Structure

Chapter Outline

Introduction   97
Data Hiding Using Alternate Data Stream   98
  What Is the New Technology File System?   98
  What Is an Alternate Data Stream?   98
  How Can We Use Alternate Data Streams to Hide Files?   98
  Hiding Executable Code in Alternate Data Stream Files   100
  Important Notes About Using Alternate Data Stream
  in Hiding Files   102
  How to Delete Alternate Data Stream Files   104
    Method 1   104
    Method 2   104
  Detecting Alternate Data Stream Files   104
    LADS   104
    Streams.exe From SysInternals   104
Data Hiding Using Stealth Alternate Data Stream   104
Hiding Data Inside Windows® Restoration Points   106
Hiding Data Inside Windows® Registry   109
Hiding in a File's Slack Space   112

Understanding Hard Disk Drives   112
File Allocation Table   114
  Restoring the Hidden File   115
  How Much Data Can I Hide in a File Slack Space?   117
Hidden Partitions   117
  Hidden Partitions Under Windows® OS   118
  Creating a Hidden Partition Within a USB Zip Drive   118
    Uncovering Hidden Partitions   122
Data Hiding Within Master File Table   123
Data Hiding in Disk Bad Blocks   127
Data Hiding Under Computer Hardware Level   128
  Data Hiding Inside Host Protected Area   129
    How Does Host Protected Area Work?   129
  Hiding Data in Device Configuration Overlay   130
Summary   131
References   131
Bibliography   132

INTRODUCTION

The art of data hiding is basically storing data in a place where it is not supposed to go. Current operating systems and file structures give us vast possibilities to conceal our data and make it harder to detect. Unfortunately anyone with malicious intent can also use these techniques to attack our system.

In this chapter we are going to investigate advanced methods for hiding data inside a Windows® OS file system. Most techniques mentioned in this chapter can be implemented without using third-party tools, but some require tools to perform them. We will offer detailed descriptions of how each hiding technique works in addition to detailed coverage of the exploited technology and how it is used to conceal our secret data.

In this chapter we will discuss Windows® file system types, especially the new technology file system (NTFS),

preferred for hiding data because of its support for file-level security and multiple data streams per file. Compression and auditing of files are important features of the NTFS that support large volumes and powerful storage solutions such as redundant array of independent disks (RAID). The most important features of NTFS are data integrity (transaction journal) and the ability to encrypt files and folders to protect your sensitive data.

Knowing where we can camouflage data inside Windows® OS structure is essential for both IT professionals and computer investigators. We will later explore in this chapter how an intruder can exploit hidden areas within the Windows® file structure to compromise our system and network.

Note: Most of the tasks described in this chapter require that you have administrator (access level admin) privileges to your Windows® machine.

Data Hiding Techniques in Windows OS. http://dx.doi.org/10.1016/B978-0-12-804449-0.00004-X

DATA HIDING USING ALTERNATE DATA STREAM

Before we begin our discussion on data hiding using alternate data stream (ADS) files, we will start with a brief description of the file system structure that supports this feature, NTFS. Later in this chapter we give a brief overview of other file systems supported by Windows® OS such as FAT12, FAT16, and FAT32.

What Is the New Technology File System?

NTFS is a proprietary file system developed by Microsoft Corporation for its newer Windows® operating systems, starting with Windows® NT 3.1 and Windows® 2000, including Windows® XP, Server 2003, Vista, 7, Server 2008, 8, 8.1, 10, and all their successors to date.

Formatting a volume with NTFS results in the creation of several metadata files such as the master file table ($MFT), $Bitmap, $LogFile, and others, which contain information about all the files and folders on the NTFS volume (Fig. 4.1).

NTFS supersedes the file allocation table (FAT) file system as the preferred file system for Microsoft Windows® operating systems. NTFS has several improvements over FAT and the high performance file system such as its support for metadata, compression, auditing, and the use of advanced data structures to improve performance and reliability. NTFS supports large volume size (256 TB vs. 2 TB for FAT32) and increased file size (16 TB vs. 4 GB for FAT32) in addition to powerful storage solutions such as RAID. In addition to this, additional extensions were developed, such as security access control lists and file system journaling. NTFS has the capability to encrypt or decrypt data, files, or folders and is considered the only file system on Windows® NT that allows you to assign permissions to individual files. NTFS uses a 16-bit unicode character system set to name files and folders allowing users from all over the world to use their native language to name files and folders. The main purpose for creating this new file system was maintaining the compatibility with the Macintosh hierarchical file system and to store additional data for each file called the metadata, which is what we are going to use to hide our confidential data [1,2].

What Is an Alternate Data Stream?

In NTFS, a file consists of different data streams. One stream is the primary unnamed stream that contains the visible data that we expect to see in a file after opening it. This stream is usually called the default stream and is referenced when no stream name component is specified as a part of the pathname. The second stream is the ADS. A file can have more than one ADS (Microsoft does not supply the number of allowed ADS files per a single file, but a test conducted by *Jason Fossen* suggests that the maximum is 4106 regardless of the size of the ADSs themselves [3]). For example, one stream can hold file security information such as access permission and another stream can hold other metadata about the file. For example, an MS Word file can have a number of properties like author, number of words, number of pages, date created, and so on. These alternative data streams could be accessed by referring to their names; all these streams are linked to the main default stream of one file (normal visible file).

ADS files can be appended to existing files without affecting their size or functionality. In addition to this, ADS files are not visible to Windows® Explorer or to the DIR command in CMD (unless we use the /R switch). If we append a malicious software (virus or Trojan) to an ADS file, it could be executed by using the Start command (only Windows® XP supports executing ADS binary files through this command; newer Windows® OSs require another command to handle this issue as we will see later). Once executed by the user, it can carry out silent installation of the malicious software on the victim's PC. No process will appear in the process list of Windows® task manager; the program used to open the original file (default stream) will appear in the process list but no sign of the malicious program will be visible. Furthermore, we can attach the malicious program to a legitimate process, which will make detection of the code much more difficult.

Fig. 4.2 shows four ADS files for a single file entry. Any one of the streams (Stream1 to Stream4) can hold malicious software (Trojan, rootkit, virus) or a hidden file containing our secret data appended to the default main stream (visible file **OriginalFile.docx**) without affecting its size or functionality.

How Can We Use Alternate Data Streams to Hide Files?

In order to show how we can use ADS to hide files, we will execute the following experiment (tested on Windows® XP, Windows® 7 and 8.1; screenshots in this experiment were taken using Windows® 8.1, XP, and 7). Create a new folder on the *C:* drive and call it ads. Open the command prompt window and change your working directory to *C:\ads*. Create a text file called *outerfile.txt* using DOS as shown in Fig. 4.3.

We marked the content of the file with green, *echo*, and > command DOS instructions to create a file with the specified contents. The output result will be stored in a file

NTFS Volume Main Sections

Partition boot sector	Master File Table	System Files	File Area

FIGURE 4.1 Sample formatted new technology file system volume structure.

named *outerfile.txt*. This file will be displayed in *C:\ads* as it is the current working directory as it appears in the CMD command shell window.

Now we want to create the hidden ADS file. We use the same commands to create another text file. The colon is the syntax used to create an ADS file (see Fig. 4.4). Use the *dir* command to check all files displayed inside the ads folder as shown in Fig. 4.5.

We see only one file, called *outerfile.txt*, while the other file (ADS file) is hidden.

The file hidden in the ADS cannot be seen using dir or Windows® Explorer. However, if we use the dir command combined with the /R switch we can see the hidden ADS file (see Fig. 4.6).

Notepad® can open the hidden ADS file and display its content (see Fig. 4.7).

Similarly we can copy one file and encapsulate it inside another file using the ADS command as shown in Fig. 4.8.

The Type command is used to copy the *myfile.txt* content to be included in the alternative stream of *outerfile.txt* under the name *hiddenfile.txt*.

You can make ADSs in not only files, but also directories. See Fig. 4.9 for an example.

From the screen in Fig. 4.9 you will notice that in the first line we created a directory in the *C:* root directory called *myfolder*. In the second line we changed our working directory to *C:\myfolder*. In the third line we created a hidden text file (*hidden.txt*) using the colon: and concealed it inside myfolder as a file stream, which is our working directory. Using the DIR command alone does not show the hidden stream associated with the current directory. We should use the /R switch to make it visible.

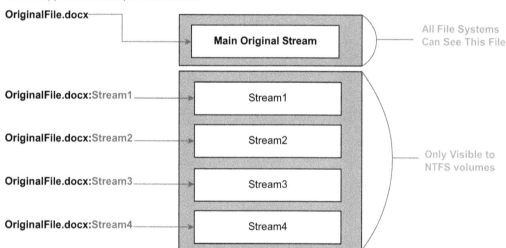

FIGURE 4.2 Default unnamed stream (MS Word file) associated with four ADS files (named streams). *Adapted from Microsoft TechNet website (Online). Available from: http://technet.microsoft.com/en-us/library/cc781134%28v=ws.10%29.aspx. Used with permission from Microsoft.*

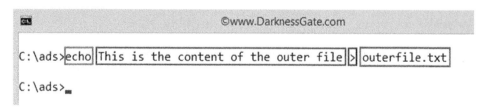

FIGURE 4.3 Creating new TXT file using command line.

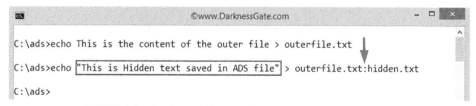

FIGURE 4.4 Creating a hidden ADS file and appending it to outerfile.txt.

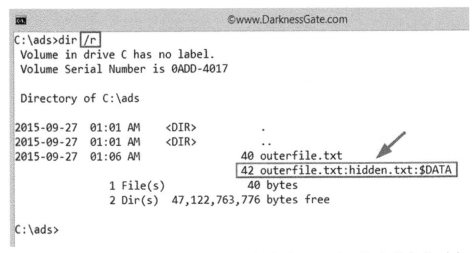

FIGURE 4.5 Listing C:\ads directory files.

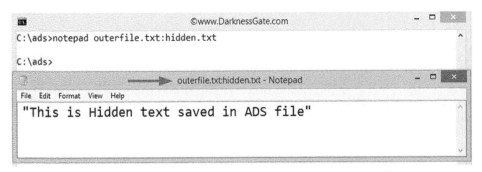

FIGURE 4.6 Alternate data stream files could be seen using the dir command combined with the /R switch.

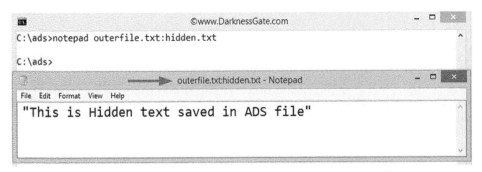

FIGURE 4.7 Opening hidden alternate data stream file using Notepad®.

Hiding Executable Code in Alternate Data Stream Files

The most interesting feature about NTFS and its associated ADS files is the ability to plant executable (binary files) inside the stream. Windows® XP supports running executable files within ADS stream files directly using the Start command. However, beginning with Windows® Vista, Microsoft® has removed this feature for security purposes. Nevertheless, we are still able to hide our binary files and execute them through using symbolic links or the WMIC command prompt in newer Windows® OS versions.

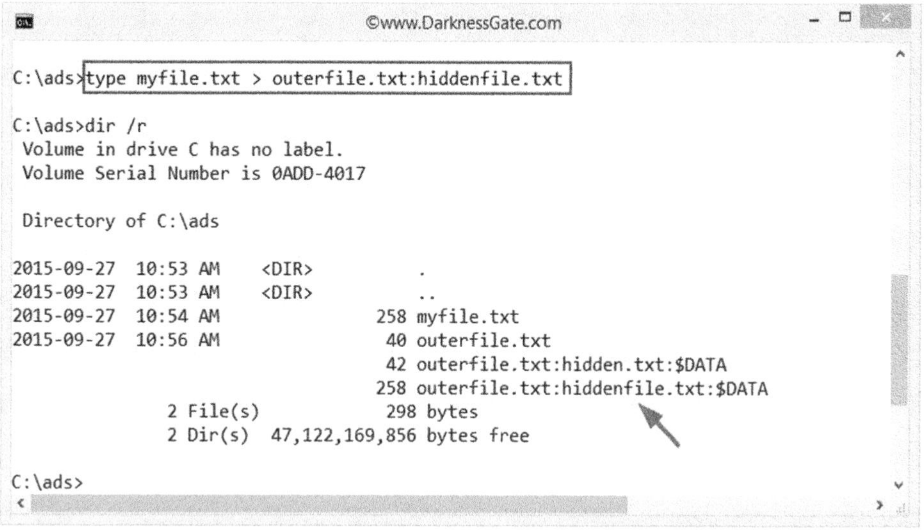

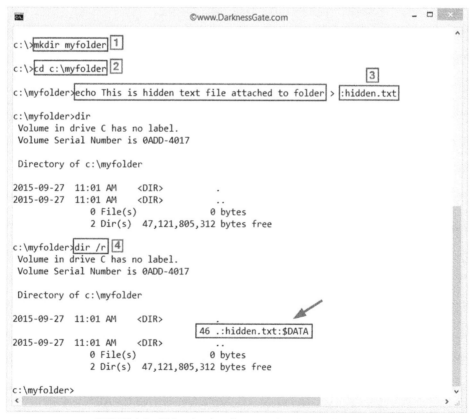

FIGURE 4.8   Hiding a file within another file using alternate data stream technique.

FIGURE 4.9   Hiding data in a directory using alternate data stream.

Let us first learn how to hide an executable file within an ADS file. We will use the standard Windows® Notepad program and hide it inside the standard Windows® calculator (see Fig. 4.10).

Now we can execute *myNotepad.exe* when it's hidden inside the file stream of *calc.exe* (see Fig. 4.11).

The visible process will appear as follows on Windows® XP Task Manager (see Fig. 4.12).

The Start command works on Windows® XP only when used to launch binary files in hidden ADS. It is not supported by Windows® Vista, 7, or later versions; however, we can still execute binary files stored inside ADSs by using

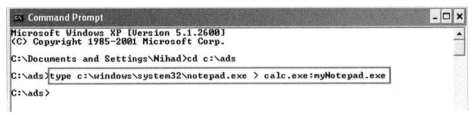

FIGURE 4.10   Hiding notepad.exe inside calc.exe under Windows® XP.

FIGURE 4.11   Running hidden notepad.exe using the Start command under Windows® XP.

FIGURE 4.12   calc.exe process in Task Manager after executing it on Windows® XP.

symbolic links or the WMIC command. The following lines describe these methods under newer Windows® OSs (Vista, 7, 8, and 10).

Let's examine a scenario where an attacker successfully compromises a remote system or simply gains physical access to the victim's PC. The attacker wants to run a password cracking tool in stealth mode without leaving any traces. The password cracking tool should be smuggled in an ADS file and executed from a USB drive formatted as NTFS. A list of saved passwords should be stored as a text file hidden inside an ADS file.

Nirsoft (http://www.nirsoft.net) developed many Windows® portable applications specialized in password recovery. One of these tools is called *MessnPass*. It specializes in recovering passwords of all major instant messenger applications. We will use this tool in our example under Windows® 7 (see Fig. 4.13).

First we stash *mspass.exe* into a hidden ADS of *outerfile.txt* file under the name *password.exe* (see Fig. 4.13). Next we create a symbolic link (*run.exe*). We are not able to execute binary files from within a hidden stream using the Start command under Windows® 7, but we are still able to execute the symbolic link (*run.exe*). It should be noted that

the *mspass.exe* tool has a specific switch to store its output into a text file (*/stext*). We will use this switch to store all recovered passwords into a text file (*P@sswordslist.txt*) and hide this file directly inside another file stream (*garden.doc*) (see Figs. 4.14 and 4.15).

If you do not like using symbolic links to run hidden executable files inside your ADS stream files, there is another method that allows you to run the ADS hidden executable directly using the WIMIC command (see Fig. 4.16).

Similarly, we can tuck away any type of security program in ADS files and execute it from within our USB flash drive. This example demonstrates the great danger of exploiting the hidden ADS feature of Window® NTFS to steal confidential data silently.

Important Notes About Using Alternate Data Stream in Hiding Files

- If we delete the main file (primary stream), the associated ADS files will be deleted too.
- We cannot set permission or any additional attributes to the ADS file, because ADS relies on the attributes associated with the primary stream file.

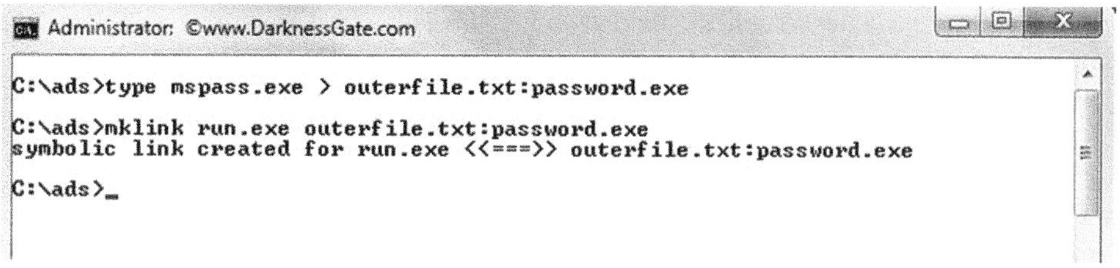

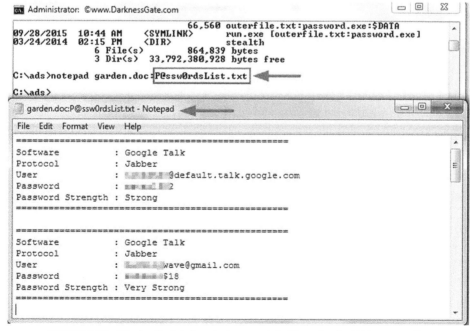

FIGURE 4.13 Hiding mspass.exe inside the ADS of a text file and creating symbolic link pointing back to it.

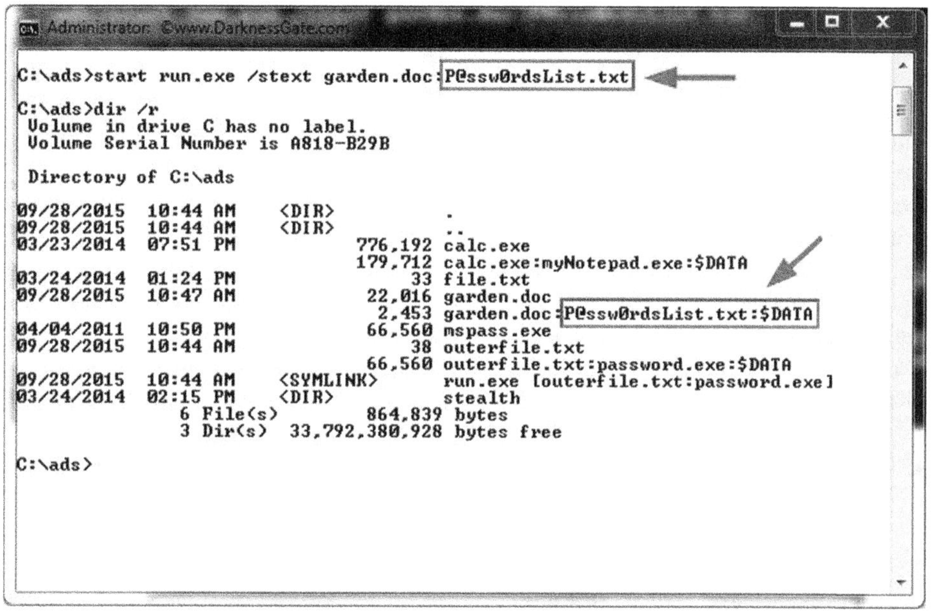

FIGURE 4.14 Executing the password cracking tool and hiding its output inside a hidden alternate data stream of garden.doc.

FIGURE 4.15 Viewing the list of cracked passwords inside garden.doc hidden stream file.

- Any new permissions or attributes (such as hidden *attrib*) to the main file (primary stream) will also affect the ADS associated files.
- ADS files can be created only on systems with NTFS file formatting. FAT file systems and other types of file systems are not supported.
- The primary stream could be any type of files like PDF, folders, MS Office® files, videos, images, executables, and so on.
- Most antivirus software does not scan Windows® ADSs for viruses or other malicious code by default. If you suspect a file contains a malicious code in its ADS file, make sure to use *Method 1* as described in the next section. The first method is the most secure one as some ADS files could be hidden from the detection tools too.
- Windows® does not provide any built-in utilities to detect the existence of ADS files.
- We can attach more than one hidden ADS file into one primary stream. In fact we can attach up to 4106 ADS files according to *Jason Fossen's* study [3].
- You can hide any type of digital files (video, audio, documents, PDF, images, etc.) inside an ADS file, which makes it a very good location to store your confidential data. The hidden files will remain attached to the main stream file as long as it is saved on NTFS formatted volume.

How to Delete Alternate Data Stream Files

In case we want to delete the ADS file and we still want to keep the main stream file we would use one of the following methods.

Method 1

Copy the main stream file to another disk that has FAT formatting. If the file is not too big we can move it to a flash memory with FAT file system and then move it again to an NTFS partition. In this case the hidden ADS stream is deleted because it will not move to the FAT partition.

A warning message appears when trying to copy a primary file stream associated with an ADS file into an FAT partition (see Fig. 4.17).

This is the best method since it can delete all ADS files, even stealth types (as we will see in the next section on stealth ADS files).

Method 2

The second method to delete the ADS file while preserving the primary stream is by copying the main file into a temporary file, then deleting the original file and renaming the temporary file again, back to its original filename.

Detecting Alternate Data Stream Files

Windows® OS does not provide any utility to detect ADS files on NTFS disks. Fortunately we have many free tools for such a job.

LADS

This program lists all ADS files of an NTFS directory. Notice the use of command in the CMD screen shown in Fig. 4.18.

The LADS program is located in the *C:* drive. We navigate to the folder where we want to check the ADSs file stream and execute the *lads.exe* tool. *LADS* can be downloaded from http://www.heysoft.de/en/software/lads.php?lang=EN.

Streams.exe From SysInternals

We can execute this tool from the command line, as shown in Fig. 4.19, to detect hidden ADSs in files located in a specific folder or drive.

In Fig. 4.19 we are testing *C:\ads* for hidden ads streams. *Streams* can be downloaded from https://technet.microsoft.com/en-us/sysinternals/bb897440.aspx.

DATA HIDING USING STEALTH ALTERNATE DATA STREAM

Microsoft uses a set of reserved names for its connected hardware devices' output operations (like printer use LTP). Microsoft also uses these names to enables software

FIGURE 4.16 Using WMIC to execute binary files inside hidden streams.

components to communicate (ie, COM). These names are CON, PRN, AUX, NUL, COM1, COM2, COM3, COM4, COM5, COM6, COM7, COM8, COM9, LPT1, LPT2, LPT3, LPT4, LPT5, LPT6, LPT7, LPT8, and LPT9 [5].

We can create more stealth ADS files undetectable using tools such as *lns.exe* (available from http://ntsecurity.nu/toolbox/lns), *Streams.exe* (available from www.sysinternals.com/utilities/streams.html), *Ad spy* (available from

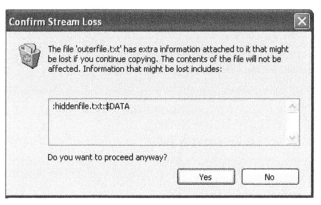

FIGURE 4.17 Warning message after moving a file with alternate data stream to a partition with file allocation table formatting.

http://www.bleepingcomputer.com/download/ads-spy/), and *sFind* (available from http://www.mcafee.com/us/downloads/free-tools/forensic-toolkit.aspx). Stealth ADS files can be created using the standard DOS commands by naming our ADS file with one of the reserved names and they will survive and remain undetectable even after using DIR and DIR/R command line switches. After testing all known ADS detection tools, only *Lads.exe* was able to detect stealth ADS files.

As shown in Fig. 4.20, attempting to create a file or directory with any of the reserved names mentioned earlier will generate an error.

Before saving any file or directory to the file system under Windows®, the OS performs a check on the validity of the name using NT-style name rules. These rules check for name and path length (255 characters maximum) in addition to checking if the pathname contains periods or any punctuation marks. In order to override the naming rules limitation we use the prefix \\?\. With file I/O, adding the \\?\ prefix to a path string instructs the Windows® APIs to disable all string parsing and to send the string that follows it straight to the file system [5].

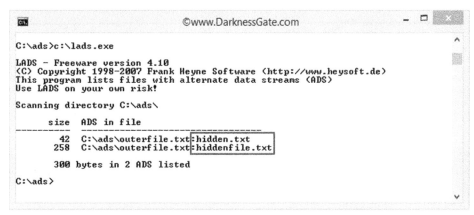

FIGURE 4.18 Using Lads.exe tool to check hidden alternate data stream files.

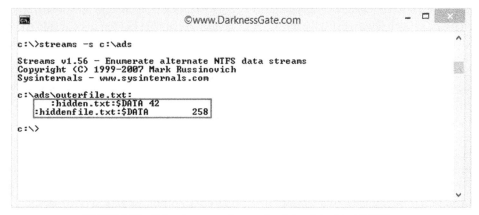

FIGURE 4.19 Using streams.exe from system internals to detect ADS files.

©www.DarknessGate.com
c:\ads\stealth>echo Invalid file name cannot be created > LPT1.txt
The system cannot find the file specified.
c:\ads\stealth>mkdir CON
The directory name is invalid.
c:\ads\stealth>dir
Volume in drive C has no label.
Volume Serial Number is 5635-8C0C
Directory of c:\ads\stealth
09/28/2015 12:38 PM <DIR> .
09/28/2015 12:38 PM <DIR> ..
09/28/2015 12:38 PM 33 file.txt
1 File(s) 33 bytes
2 Dir(s) 93,727,297,536 bytes free
c:\ads\stealth>

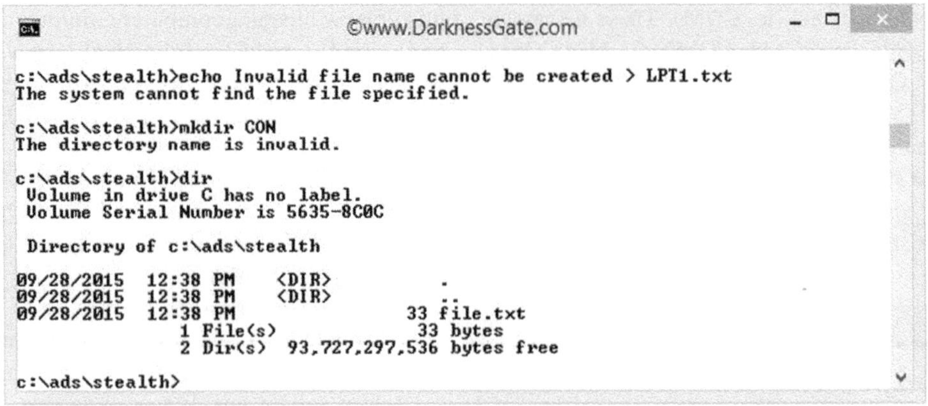

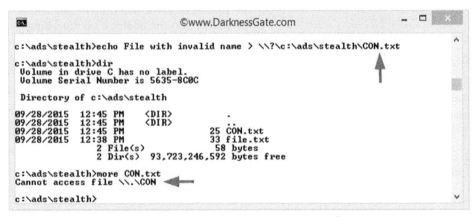

FIGURE 4.20 Error messages after attempting to name file or folder with reserved Windows® names.

©www.DarknessGate.com
c:\ads\stealth>echo File with invalid name > \\?\c:\ads\stealth\CON.txt
c:\ads\stealth>dir
Volume in drive C has no label.
Volume Serial Number is 5635-8C0C
Directory of c:\ads\stealth
09/28/2015 12:45 PM <DIR> .
09/28/2015 12:45 PM <DIR> ..
09/28/2015 12:45 PM 25 CON.txt
09/28/2015 12:38 PM 33 file.txt
2 File(s) 58 bytes
2 Dir(s) 93,723,246,592 bytes free
c:\ads\stealth>more CON.txt
Cannot access file \\.\CON
c:\ads\stealth>

FIGURE 4.21 Creating a file with reserved Windows® name.

©www.DarknessGate.com
c:\ads\stealth>more \\?\c:\ads\stealth\CON.txt
File with invalid name
c:\ads\stealth>_

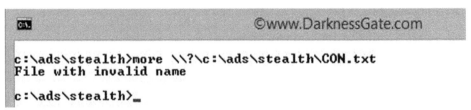

FIGURE 4.22 Reading a file with a reserved Windows® name.

We create a file with reserved Windows® name called *CON.txt*, but when trying to open it we receive the message, cannot access file (see Fig. 4.21). To read this file we need to use the prefix \\?\ again (see Fig. 4.22).

We now combine both methods, creating a file with a reserved Windows® device name and appending an ADS file to it. This creates what is called a *Stealth ADS*. This approach allows users to create completely hidden ADS files that are very difficult to detect. Most ADS detection tools and DOS commands such as DIR and DIR/R are not able to uncover the hidden streams within these files. Some antivirus software do not scan stealth ADSs, which make them an ideal place to hide your confidential information. We can also hide malicious software inside these hidden files as we did in previous sections of the book. The same technique previously described is used to launch executable hidden code inside ADS files. Here is a quick example of hiding a Windows® calculator inside a stealth ADS (see Fig. 4.23) and launching it later using the WMIC command (see Fig. 4.24).

HIDING DATA INSIDE WINDOWS® RESTORATION POINTS

Volume shadow copy service (VSS) is a service supported by Microsoft Windows® XP and all later versions of Windows®; however, not all versions of Windows® handle the GUI portion of this service in the same way (when restoring previous versions of individual files—more on this feature in Chapter 6). The screenshot in our next

FIGURE 4.23   Hiding an executable file inside a stealth alternate data stream file.

FIGURE 4.24   Running an executable file inside a stealth alternate data stream file using the WMIC command.

experiment is applicable to Windows® Vista, 7, 8, and 10. VSS coordinates the actions that are required to create a consistent snapshot copy of the data to be backed up in a specific volume at a specific point in time over regular intervals. We can access this feature through the system restore functionality, which enables us to restore our system files to a previous stable state in case of sudden system failure (eg, failed software installation, wrong uninstallation of some programs, or wrong system registry modifications). VSS technology works only on volumes formatted with NTFS, and the shadow copies created could be stored on local or external networks as needed [6,7].

The snapshots created by VSS (restore points) are taken at specific time intervals, usually after installing/uninstalling new software or performing a system update. It is difficult to predict the other cases when VSS creates a snapshot. However, there are some conditions when this happens such as when the system was idle for at least 10min while it was running on AC power (in case of a portable computer). If the two conditions were met simultaneously we can expect to have a system restore point every 2 days under Windows® Vista and between 7 and 8 days under Windows® 7. You can, of course, still create system restore points manually if you wish [8].

It is important to note that VSS is not an image of the entire drive. VSS operates on the block level (below file system level). VSS is tracking any changes made on all blocks in the storage volume. When a specific block has data written to it, VSS makes a snapshot and stores it in a hidden volume (these snapshots are read only). If a specific block hasn't changed since the last snapshot, it will not be included in the current snapshot (restore point). VSS is an incremental procedure (like the incremental backup concept of databases), which means that it will store only the modifications that happen to one file since the last snapshot.

In Windows® 8 and Windows® 10 the shadow volumes have been superseded by file history. By default file history in Windows® 8 works by taking snapshots of all the files that exist inside libraries, desktops, contacts, and favorites. This could be performed each hour (default action) or could be adjusted according to user needs (more or less). The saved version of file history can remain forever as a maximum or as a minimum for a duration of 1 month. File history backup data needs to be stored on an external USB zip drive or into a network location.

To configure VSS under Windows® 7 (also applies to Windows® 8 and 10) we can access it from *Control Panel* ≫ *System* ≫ *System protection* ≫ *System Protection* Tab, then select the drive and click the *Configure...* button.

Using the *Configure* button we can choose to activate VSS, manage allocated space, and restore points for each listed volume (Fig. 4.25).

This introduction is necessary to understand how VSS works. We now can explore the VSS snapshot potential in hiding data or other malicious software.

We can administer VSS using the VSSadmin utility that comes with Windows® Vista, 7,8, and 10, launch a DOS command and type *VSSadmin* to view command switches. We can then type *VSSadmin list volumes* to list all available NTFS volumes on our system eligible for shadow copies.

The command *VSSadmin list Shadowstorage* enables us to see the shadows and disk usage of our system's volumes. In our case we have only the *C:* volume, which has VSS enabled (see Fig. 4.26).

To list all existing shadow copies of a specified volume we need to use the following command option: *VSSadmin list Shadows/for=C:*. Here we are listing content of volume *C:* only (see Fig. 4.27). If we use the command *VSSadmin list Shadows* without parameters, it will list all volume shadows on our PC.

Here we are showing the last successful copy of our system snapshots. Fig. 4.27 shows the last successful snapshot created out of 24 operations (restore points) done previously.

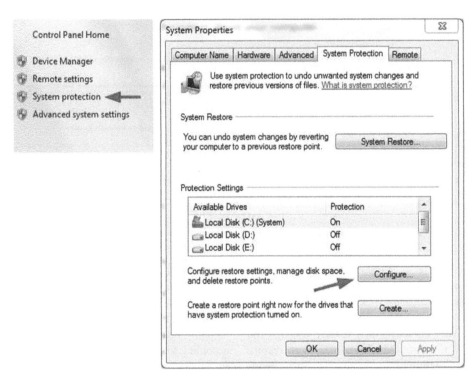

FIGURE 4.25   Configuring restore points under Windows® 7.

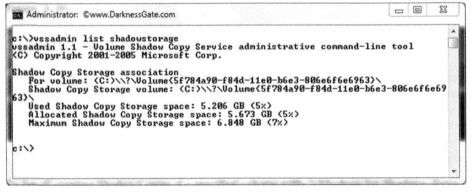

FIGURE 4.26   Listing volumes with shadow copy enabled.

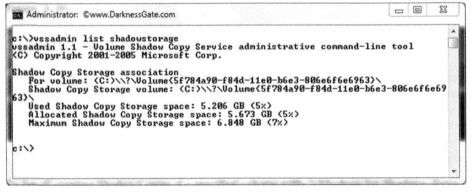

FIGURE 4.27   Screen of shadow copies available on drive C:\ showing only the last restore point, which carries the number 24.

Now we are ready to explain how we can conceal our data or malware inside one of our available restore points. Let us create a new folder on our *C:* volume and name it *TestShadow*. We will copy an executable file inside this folder (any file type will work; see Fig. 4.28).

We have only one file inside the *C:\TestShadow folder (mspass.exe)*. We now want to hide this file in one of our VSS snapshots. We therefore need to create a new restore point to save our newly created file. Go to *Control Panel≫System≫System Protection≫System Protection* Tab≫and click *Create*. A new window appears prompting us to enter a name for our *restore point*. We will call it *DarknessGateRestorePoint*, and then click *Create* (see Fig. 4.29).

Now we run the *VSSadmin list shadows* command to check that a new restoration point has been successfully created (see Fig. 4.30).

As we note from Fig. 4.30, a new restoration point is created. We now have 25 restoration points in our system.

Let us return to our folder, *C:\TestShadow*. We need to delete the executable *mspass.exe* from it (see Fig. 4.31).

Now our file *mspass.exe* has been deleted from our system; however, it is still in our newly created restoration point, which carries the name *\\?GLOBALROOT\Device\HarddiskVolumeShadowCopy25*. To access *mspass.exe* inside our restoration point, we need to create a symbolic link and save it in a separate folder (*RetrievedFiles*) in our current working directory. We also need to append a trailing slash (\) to the end of the name of the restoration point name in order to make sure it will work properly (see Fig. 4.32).

We use the *DIR* command to see the new symbolic link inside our working directory (see Fig. 4.33).

We can access our retrieved volume copy contents either directly through Explorer or by accessing it through DOS. Inside our volume copy, if we browse to the *TestShadow* folder, we can see our file *mspass.exe* listed inside (see Fig. 4.34).

After confirming that our hidden file is still inside our newly created restoration point, we can now delete the

symbolic link pointing back to our volume copy and try to execute the hidden program using the WMIC command as we did previously in our ADS section (see Fig. 4.35).

After executing the previous command, our hidden file *mspass.exe* pops up on screen confirming that our work was correct!

We note from Fig. 4.35 that we have to change the (?) sign at the beginning of the VSS name to a period (.). WMIC requires a period to work.

In summary, we found that we can hide data inside system restoration points. If this data is an executable application, we can run it using the WMIC command without creating any symbolic links. Most antivirus software do not scan volume shadow copies for malware or other security threats. It is important to remember that volume shadow copies are limited in space and time. If you store large files inside them, the system will need to delete the old restoration points to make room for newly created ones. However, if your files were small and you are a regular PC user, a restore point may last for at least 5months under Windows® 7. This is more than enough for a hacker to perform vicious acts on your system.

HIDING DATA INSIDE WINDOWS® REGISTRY

Windows® registry offers a good place for us to hide secret data with minimal possibility of being spotted. Before determining how we can hide data inside the Windows® registry let us first give a brief overview of its structure.

```
Administrator: ©www.DarknessGate.com

c:\>mkdir TestShadow

c:\>cd c:\TestShadow

c:\TestShadow>dir /r
 Volume in drive C has no label.
 Volume Serial Number is A818-B29B

 Directory of c:\TestShadow

09/29/2015  12:23 PM    <DIR>          .
09/29/2015  12:23 PM    <DIR>          ..
04/04/2011  10:50 PM            66,560 mspass.exe
               1 File(s)         66,560 bytes
               2 Dir(s)  33,777,733,632 bytes free

c:\TestShadow>
```

FIGURE 4.28 Creating a new directory on C:\TestShadow and storing mspass.exe inside it.

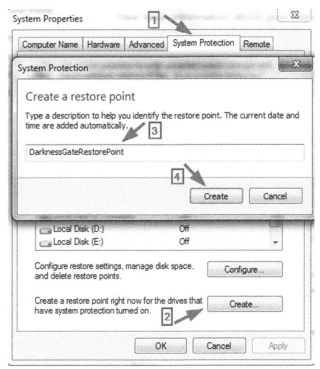

FIGURE 4.29 Create new restore point in Windows® 7.

```
Administrator: ©www.DarknessGate.com                                    □ ▣ ☒

Contents of shadow copy set ID: {4cc8e43d-74db-4c7d-bbec-d85291222c05}
     Contained 1 shadow copies at creation time: 9/29/2015 6:35:40 PM ◄─
          Shadow Copy ID: {37a878e5-3833-435c-a030-6f46afbfef72}
          Original Volume: (C:)\\?\Volume{5f784a90-f84d-11e0-b6e3-806e6f6e6963}\
          Shadow Copy Volume: \\?\GLOBALROOT\Device\HarddiskVolumeShadowCopy25  ◄─
          Originating Machine: PC14
          Service Machine: PC14
          Provider: 'Microsoft Software Shadow Copy provider 1.0'
          Type: ClientAccessibleWriters
          Attributes: Persistent, Client-accessible, No auto release, Differential, Auto recovered

c:\>
```

FIGURE 4.30 New restore point successfully created.

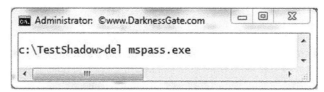

FIGURE 4.31 Delete mspass.exe using the del command option at the DOS prompt.

FIGURE 4.32 Create a symbolic link for our last created restore point.

```
Administrator: ©www.DarknessGate.com                                    □ ▣ ☒

c:\TestShadow>dir
 Volume in drive C has no label.
 Volume Serial Number is A818-B29B

 Directory of c:\TestShadow

09/29/2015  06:44 PM    <DIR>          .
09/29/2015  06:44 PM    <DIR>          ..
09/29/2015  06:44 PM    <SYMLINKD>     RetrievedFiles [\\?\GLOBALROOT\Device\HarddiskVolumeShadowCop
y25\]
               0 File(s)              0 bytes
               3 Dir(s)  33,670,328,320 bytes free

c:\TestShadow>
```

FIGURE 4.33 Create a symbolic link and point it to the last restore point.

Registry is a hierarchical database that stores system configuration settings and installed programs settings. Registry data is structured in a tree format. Each node in the tree is called a key. A registry tree can be only 512 levels deep. A registry key is a container object that plays the same role as a folder in normal Windows® naming. Registry values are noncontainer objects similar to files (cannot hold other objects). A key can contain other keys (subkeys) in addition to data values. Some installed programs under Windows® OS require only the existence of a key in the registry in order to work. Other applications may use the associated values within a key in order to function. Keys can have any number of values, and these values can be in any form. Table 4.1 lists Windows® registry value types [9,10].

The maximum size of each registry key is 64 KB (this includes its name, type, and value); when hiding our data we are going to use a key for this purpose. Some may argue that 64 KB is too small for hiding data inside it. However, this is not quite true as we can conceal more than 50 pages of pure text (ASCII) inside it, which gives plenty of space for anyone to hide valuable information.

In order to access the registry and create a key to hide data follow these steps:

1. Press the *Windows* and *R* keys simultaneously. The *run* dialog appears.
2. Write *regedit* and press *Enter* (see Fig. 4.36).
3. The Windows® registry opens. We can hide data of different formats within Windows® registry (strings

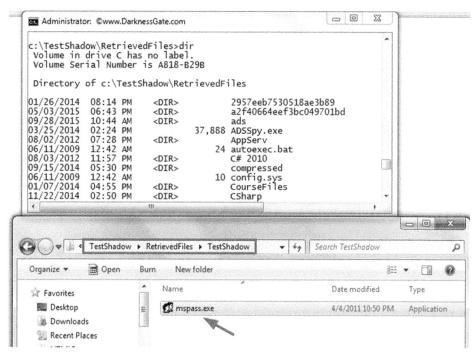

FIGURE 4.34   Accessing mspass.exe inside our last restore point.

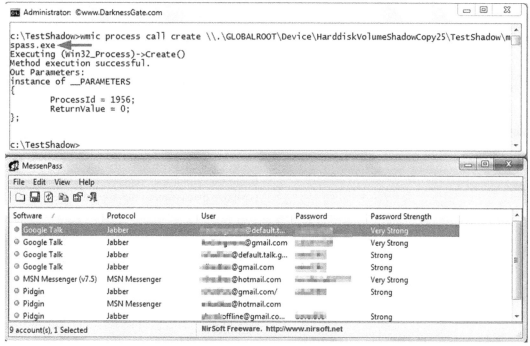

FIGURE 4.35   Executing mspass.exe from inside the last created system snapshot.

or binary data). Some registry entries are already available for storing hidden data; the best known location is *HKEY_LOCAL_MACHINE \System\ CurrentControlSet\Control\TimeZoneInformation.* This key records the difference between PC local time and the UTC time zone in addition to other functions. This key also contains two entries that can hold both

string and binary data and can be left empty since they are not used by Windows®. These entries are *StandardName* and *DaylightName*, where data can be shielded inside these entries.

4. We will create a new key and tuck away 40 pages of ASCII text inside it. Choose *HKEY_LOCAL_MACHINE\ SOFTWARE\Adobe* entry to conceal the data, navigate to

TABLE 4.1 Windows® Registry Value Types

Value	Type
REG_BINARY	Binary data in any form.
REG_DWORD	23-bit number.
REG_DWORD_LITTLE_ENDIAN	A 32-bit number in little-endian format. Windows® is designed to run on little-endian computer architectures. Therefore, this value is defined as REG_DWORD in the Windows® header files.
REG_DWORD_BIG_ENDIAN	A 32-bit number in big-endian format. Some UNIX systems support big-endian architectures.
REG_EXPAND_SZ	A null-terminated string that contains unexpanded references to environment variables (for example, %PATH%). It will be a unicode or ANSI string depending on whether you use the unicode or ANSI functions.
REG_LINK	A null-terminated unicode string that contains the target path of a symbolic link that was created by calling the RegCreateKeyEx function with REG_OPTION_CREATE_LINK.
REG_MULTI_SZ	A sequence of null-terminated strings, terminated by an empty string (\0).
REG_NONE	No defined value type.
REG_QWORD	A 64-bit number.
REG_QWORD_LITTLE_ENDIAN	A 64-bit number in little-endian format. Windows® is designed to run on little-endian computer architectures. Therefore, this value is defined as REG_QWORD in the Windows® header files.
REG_SZ	A null-terminated string. This will be either a unicode or an ANSI string, depending on whether you use the unicode or ANSI functions.

Microsoft Website, Registry Value Types (Online). Available from: http://msdn.microsoft.com/en-us/library/windows/desktop/ms724884%28v=vs.85%29.aspx.

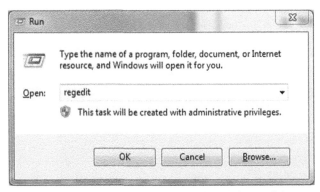

FIGURE 4.36 Access Windows registry through the Run dialog.

this entry, select it, right-click the Details pane, and then select *New » Multi-String Value* as shown in Fig. 4.37.

This will create a new key. We will give this key a name similar to what Windows® names other keys. The new key name will be **{167F5D73-87FF-4f15-8EBD-C502337D7B34}**.

Right-click the newly created key and select *Modify*.

We will insert 50 pages of ASCII text inside its value text box (see Fig. 4.38).

Since we successfully buried a large amount of data inside the Windows® registry, some may argue that this data could be easily detected. Typical machines running

a large number programs for quite some time will have thousands of registry entries, which makes searching for hidden data a challenging task for any computer forensic investigator.

In Chapter 6 we describe methods and tools to investigate the Windows® registry for hidden data, so we will postpone discussion of this topic for the moment.

HIDING IN A FILE'S SLACK SPACE

In order to understand a file's slack space, we first need to have a basic understanding of how Windows® OS handles its data on disk storage. Prepare yourself for some interesting information about this topic. Next we will show you how to stash away your secret data inside file slack space.

Understanding Hard Disk Drives

A hard disk (generally referred to as a hard disk drive) is considered the main storage location of a computer, which stores all data permanently for later use (Fig. 4.39).

We are not going to study the physical components of a hard disk since it is outside the scope of this book; however, we will describe the logical sections that are used to organize and store data on a disk drive.

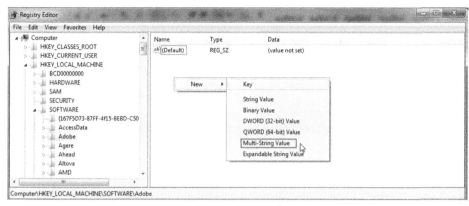

FIGURE 4.37 Adding a new key to Windows® registry to hide secret data.

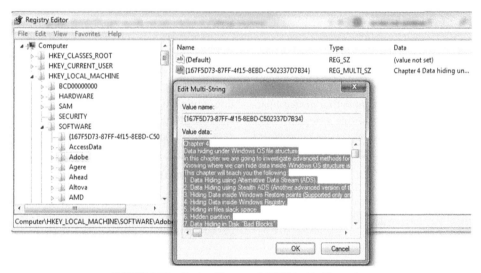

FIGURE 4.38 Storing 50 pages of ASCII text inside one key.

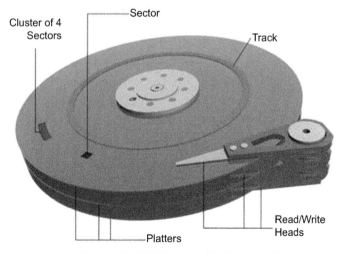

FIGURE 4.39 Hard disk schematic. *Adapted from Microsoft, Hard Disk Geometry (Online). Available from: http://technet.microsoft.com/en-us/library/dd758814%28v=sql.100%29.aspx. Used with permission from Microsoft.*

The primary physical component of a disk drive is the disk platter. A platter is a round flat metal disk that holds data physically stored in a PC. Hard disks have a number of platters, which varies between one disk and another. I have one hard disk in my laptop with 320 GB capacity and two platters. Platters store data on both sides (top and bottom surfaces). The capacity of a hard disk increases as the number of platters increase.

Each platter is divided into a number of tracks. Tracks form complete circles on each platter, which are divided in turn into an equal number of sectors.

A partition is a section on the disk (logical storage unit). As we know, a hard disk can have multiple partitions. The main purpose of disk partitioning is to treat one physical disk drive as if it were multiple disks. The advantage of this is that different file systems can be used on each partition in addition to separating operating system partitions from user file partitions [17].

There are two types of partitions:

- Primary partition
- Extended partition

Each physical hard disk can have up to four primary partitions or three primary partitions and one extended partition. A primary partition will store the master boot record files needed for booting the operating system. A hard disk can have only one extended partition, which could be further subdivided into a number of logical partitions. The number of logical partitions is limited to the number of alphabets (24 partitions), but newer file systems can support more than that.

Remember that a partition can span over multiple platters, so do not confuse yourself and think that each platter should have only one partition.

Hard disks store data in storage units called sectors; each hard disk can contain millions of sectors. A sector generally holds 512 bytes, and newer file systems can hold up to 4 KB.

All file systems that are used by Windows® organize hard disks based on cluster size (a cluster consists of a number of sectors). Cluster size represents the smallest amount of disk space that can be used to hold a file (Table 4.2).

Cluster size is dependent on the file system used and the size of partition, and it ranges from 4 to 64 sectors. This makes a single cluster able to store up to 64 KB of data using the default settings.

Each cluster can hold data from only one file at any one time. Subsequently, if we have an empty text file with 10 KB size it will occupy one cluster (assuming cluster size is 32 KB); the remaining storage size (22 KB) will stay untouched and is called slack space (see Fig. 4.40), which is where we are going to hide our secret data.

We've discussed the NTFS file system in a previous section when we discussed smuggling data inside ADSs. The following lines will give a brief overview of the other file systems supported by Windows® OS, FAT.

File Allocation Table

The FAT file system is a legacy file system designed for small disks and simple folder structures. Originally designed in 1977 for use on floppy disks, FAT was soon

TABLE 4.2 Default Cluster Sizes for New Technology File System

Volume Size	Windows® NT 3.51	Windows® NT 4.0	Windows® 7, Windows® Server 2008 R2, Windows® Server 2008, Windows® Vista, Windows® Server 2003, Windows® XP, Windows® 2000
7–512 MB	512 bytes	4 KB	4 KB
512 MB–1 GB	1 KB	4 KB	4 KB
1–2 GB	2 KB	4 KB	4 KB
2 GB–2 TB	4 KB	4 KB	4 KB
2–16 TB	Not supported*	Not supported*	4 KB
16–32 TB	Not supported*	Not supported*	8 KB
32–64 TB	Not supported*	Not supported*	16 KB
64–128 TB	Not supported*	Not supported*	32 KB
128–256 TB	Not supported*	Not supported*	64 KB
>256 TB	Not supported	Not supported	Not supported

The asterisk (*) means that it is not supported because of the limitations of the master boot record.
Microsoft, Default Cluster Sizes for NTFS (Online). Available from: http://support.microsoft.com/kb/140365.

adapted and used almost universally on hard disks. Microsoft Corporation was among the first to adopt FAT for its MS DOS operating system in 1980. Microsoft kept FAT as the default file system for all its newer operating systems up to and including Windows® NT. As the industry of disk drives matures, creating hard disks with large data capacity becomes more feasible. Capabilities of file systems have developed progressively, giving birth to three versions of the FAT file system: FAT12, FAT16, and FAT32 [12,13].

FAT file systems are still commonly found on floppy disks, USB sticks, flash and other solid-state memory cards and modules, in addition to many portable and embedded devices. Many electronic manufactures still use FAT as their standard file system for digital cameras. FAT is also utilized in the boot stage of Unified Extensible Firmware Interface-compliant computers [14].

We will not delve much into the FAT file system since newer Windows® operating systems are normally formatted using NTFS because of its robustness and advanced features. It is important to mention this information to cover all file systems supported by Windows® machines.

Now that we explained hard disk storage and how data is organized on disk, it's time to describe how to veil our secret data inside file slack space. We will use a tool called *Slacker. exe*. Slacker is a part of the Metasploit antiforensics project, which is a command line tool used to allow storage and restoration of our data stashed away inside file slack space.

Go to the Metasploit antiforensics project page [18] and download the tool box. Extract the zipped folder and you will find inside it a tool called *Slacker.exe*. (This tool is tested with Windows® XP, Vista, 7, and 8; it supports NTFS partitions only.)

Open your command prompt then change your working directory to where *Slacker.exe* resides. Type *Slacker.exe* at the command prompt and press *Enter* to launch the tool (see Fig. 4.41).

After pressing *Enter*, the *Slacker.exe* tool options page displays instructions on how to use this tool for hiding data (see Fig. 4.42).

Type the following at the command prompt and press *Enter* to shelter your first file. The following description (see Fig. 4.43) contains program instructions on how to hide your files using this tool.

Command options used to conceal our data are as follows:

slacker is the executable program.

-s instructs the program to hide in file slack space.

e:\nihad.txt is the file that we want to hide. In this case it is located in the *E:* drive.

e:\MyPicures is a directory holding jpg image files used for storing secret files in their slack space.

1 is the depth of subdirectories to search for slack space. In this case we go one level deep.

e:\image.jpg is a file to store metadata for tracking information (we cannot retrieve our hidden file without this file, so make sure it is not deleted).

mypassword is a password to retrieve the hidden file later.

-d is a program switch to determine slack space selection. You have three options here: dumb, random (−*x*), or intelligent (−*i*). Select the first one.

-n selects whether you want data to be obfuscated or not. In this case select none (−n).

We should have administrator access permission on the partition that we are going to use to hide our secret file.

After pressing Enter, if everything was typed correctly and there is enough space to store our secret file inside the *MyPictures* directory files' slack space, Fig. 4.44 appears on our tool screen.

Restoring the Hidden File

Type the following at the MS-DOS prompt. Note that we are using the same options as when we stored our file in the slack space (see Fig. 4.45).

Command options used in the retrieval process are:

slacker is the executable program.

-r tells the program to restore the file from slack space.

e:\image.jpg is the file that contains slack space tracking information (metadata).

mypassword is the password we used when we first stored our file in slack space, which was used to decrypt the metadata file.

-o tells the program to output the file to specified location. In this case we direct the program to display our

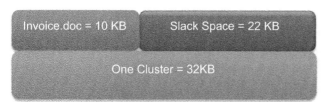

FIGURE 4.40 One cluster can hold only one file at a time.

FIGURE 4.41 Changing the working directory and launching the Slacker. exe tool.

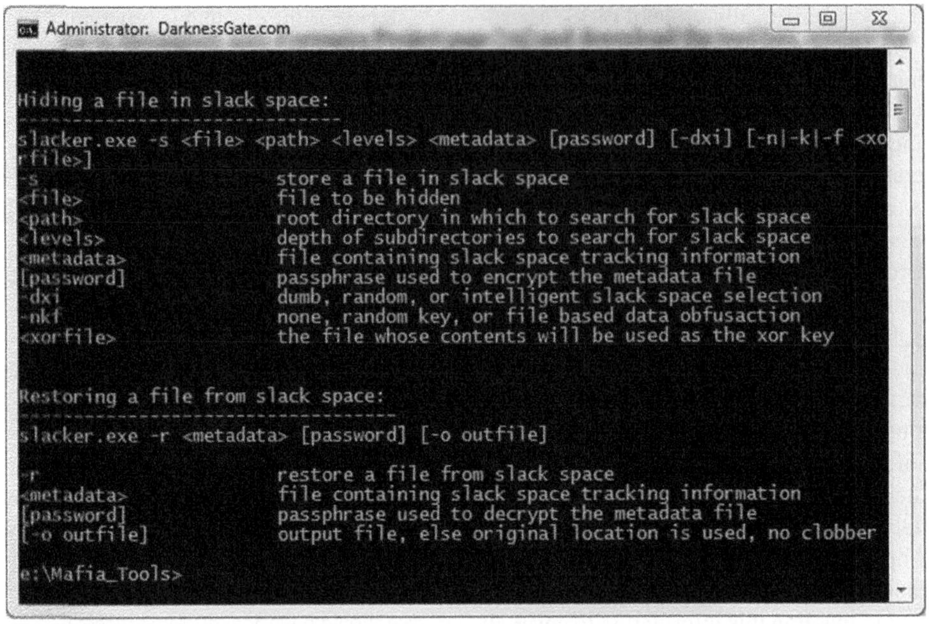

FIGURE 4.42 Slacker.exe directions page.

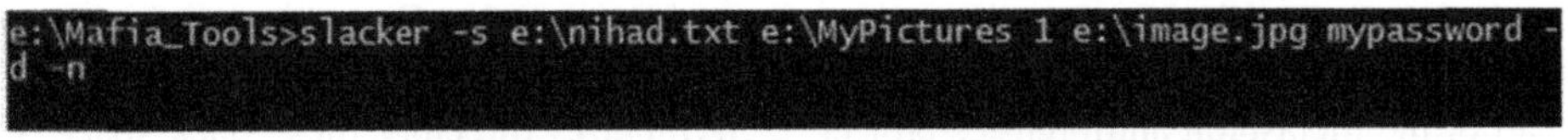

FIGURE 4.43 Hiding nihad.txt in file slack space.

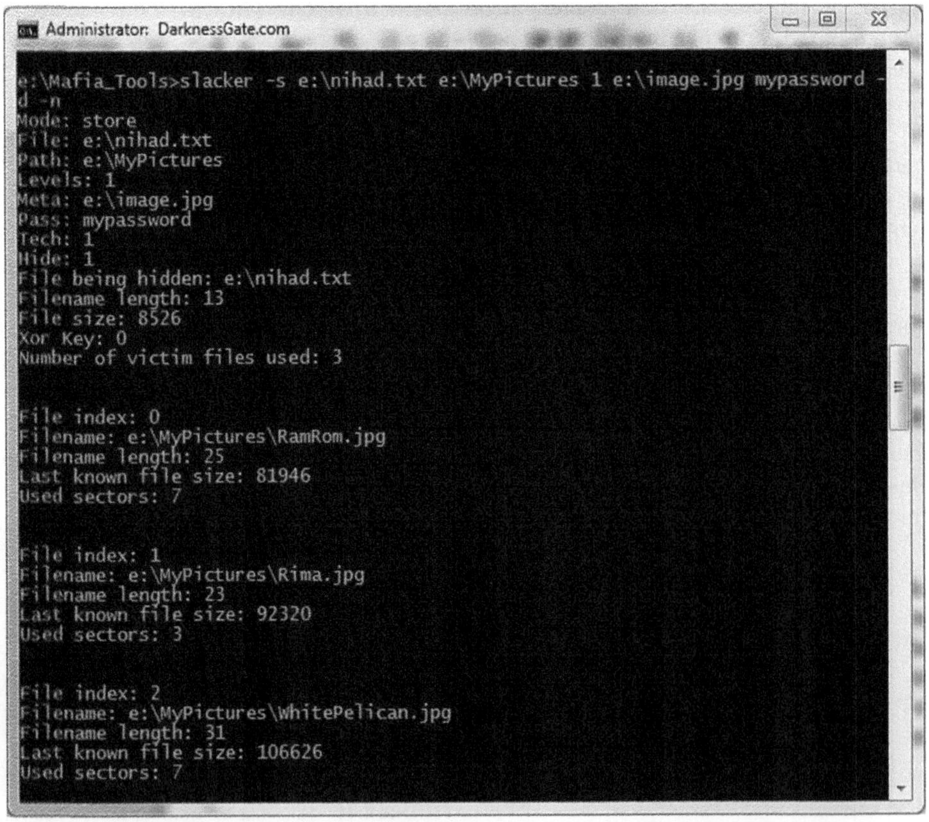

FIGURE 4.44 A success message after hiding our secret file inside slack space.

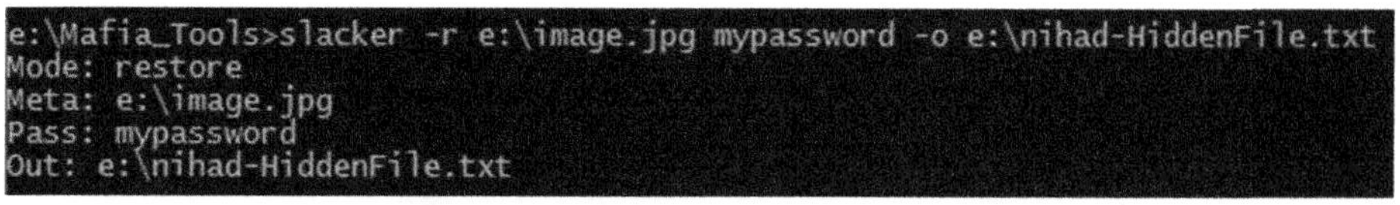

FIGURE 4.45 Restore hidden file inside slack space.

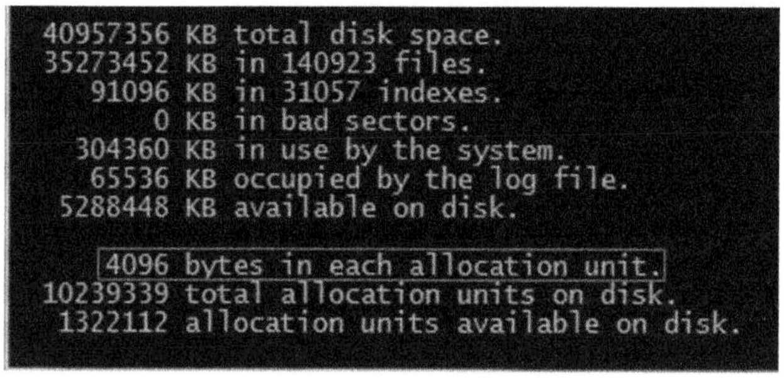

FIGURE 4.46 Knowing your operating system cluster size.

hidden file to the **E:** drive and give it the name *Nihad-HiddenFile.txt*. If you do not specify an output path it will be on same folder where the *Slacker.exe* tool resides.

How Much Data Can I Hide in a File Slack Space?

Not that much! Do not expect to bury a video file inside file slack space, as we described earlier. File slack is created by the operating system because each cluster can hold only one file at any one time. So if we have a file that spans 20.5 clusters we can still have an empty 0.5 cluster (OS reserve 21 cluster), which is where we can suppress our secret file. The size of the hidden file could be increased more by putting more files in the directory that we are using as a storage location for our slack space.

In the example we already demonstrated, we have three image files inside the *MyPictures* folder. The slack space of these three files is used to hold the secret file *Nihad.txt*. We can easily predict the amount of free slack space we can have in this folder as follows.

Let's say we have three image files inside this folder. File sizes are as follows:

RamRom.jpg	81 KB
Rima.jpg	91 KB
WhitePelican.jpg	105 KB

My PC has a cluster size of *4 KB* and sector size of *512 bytes*. This means each cluster will have eight sectors. This may be different in your machine. See the following information on how you can determine your OS cluster size.

First image (RamRom.jpg) needs 21 clusters. ($81 \div 4 = 20.25$, the operating system will reserve 21 clusters since each cluster can hold only one file. Clusters cannot be partitioned.)

21 clusters $\times 4096 = 86,016$ bytes reserved space for this image by the operating system.

Original image size $= 81,946$ bytes

We can calculate file slack space for this image as follows: $86,016 - 81,946 = \mathbf{4070}$ bytes.

4070 bytes $\div 512 = 7.9$ sectors, which means we have seven sectors slack space that could be used to store hidden data in the first image.

Second image (Rima.jpg 91 KB) needs 23 clusters, which is $91 \div 4 = 22.75 \approx 23$.

$23 \times 4096 = 94,208$ bytes

Original image size $= 92,320$ bytes

Slack space size $= 94,208 - 92,320 = 1888$ bytes

$1888 \div 512 = 3.6$ sectors, which means we have three sectors of slack space on the second image.

You can calculate the third image slack space size using the same method. The third image has seven sectors of slack space.

Now we have 17 sectors of slack space with these three images: $17 \times 512 = 8704$ bytes. This means that we can withhold a file that doesn't exceed 8704 bytes in size.

Determining the Hard Disk Cluster Size

To know your operating system cluster size follow these steps (applies to all versions of Windows®):

1. Open the MS-DOS prompt.
2. Type *chkdsk* and press *Enter*.
3. Check the number next to *bytes in each allocation unit* as shown in Fig. 4.46.
4. To know the cluster size in kilobytes divide the number 4069 by 1024 (each KB = 1024 bytes): 4096/1024 = **4 KB**.

There is also another method that could be used for the same purpose:

1. Open the MS-DOS prompt (CMD).
2. Change your working directory to C:\Windows\System32 using the CD command.
3. Type the command shown in Fig. 4.47 in your MS-DOS prompt and press Enter.
4. In the screenshot in Fig. 4.47 we highlighted details of drive *E:* sector/cluster information. You can change this to see details of all remaining partitions.

HIDDEN PARTITIONS

In this section we are going to demonstrate two techniques for creating hidden partitions under Windows® OS. The first

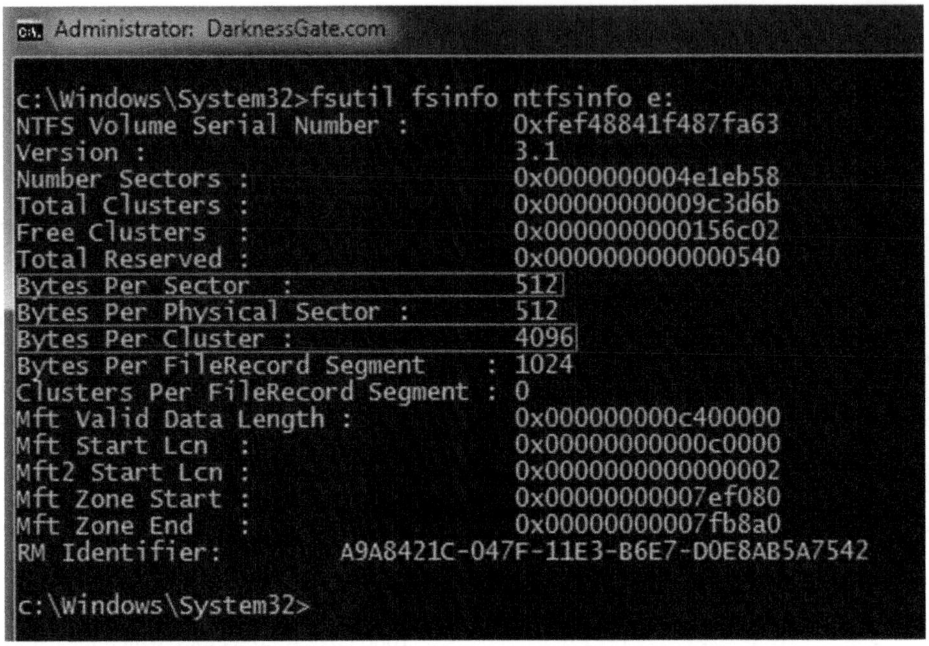

FIGURE 4.47 Determine cluster size and sector size in your Windows® machine.

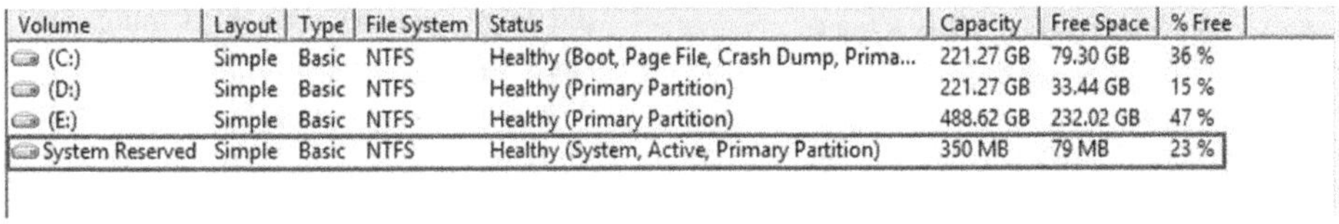

Volume	Layout	Type	File System	Status	Capacity	Free Space	% Free
(C:)	Simple	Basic	NTFS	Healthy (Boot, Page File, Crash Dump, Prima...	221.27 GB	79.30 GB	36 %
(D:)	Simple	Basic	NTFS	Healthy (Primary Partition)	221.27 GB	33.44 GB	15 %
(E:)	Simple	Basic	NTFS	Healthy (Primary Partition)	488.62 GB	232.02 GB	47 %
System Reserved	Simple	Basic	NTFS	Healthy (System, Active, Primary Partition)	350 MB	79 MB	23 %

FIGURE 4.48 Recovery volume created by Windows® 8.1 OS and used to store important recovery files for Windows®-based machines.

technique is very simple. We will use a free tool in order to hide one partition within Windows® (although we can do this manually using Windows® DOS prompt). The second technique is more secure and portable; we are going to manually create a hidden partition within a USB zip drive that will only mount (or appears) within the system in which it was created.

Hidden Partitions Under Windows® OS

In this technique we are going to use a free tool to hide one of our Windows® partitions. We will achieve this by deleting the partition letter so it will become inaccessible through *My Computer* or *Windows® Explorer*.

Windows® usually creates a hidden partition (around 70–200 MB) that stores the Recovery Environment WinRE that is of vital importance, because it allows recovery of the system if any problem is encountered at the time of startup. Many manufacturers nowadays are storing their recovery image inside a hidden partition so a user cannot alter its contents accidently. This system reserved partition has no letter assigned to it, and it does not appear in Windows® Explorer or inside My Computer. You can view this partition through the *Disk Management* console that exists within all versions of Windows® OS (see Fig. 4.48).

Now let us experiment hiding one partition using a free tool. This technique can be easily implemented by deleting the assigned letter of the drive using the disk management console; however, we found that using a free tool is better for inexperienced computer users since they can restore their hidden partition easily instead of using a DOS command.

EaseUS Partition Master Free is a free partition tool that can be downloaded from http://www.partition-tool.com/personal.htm [19]. After downloading and installing this tool on your Windows® box, right-click the partition you want to hide, then select *Hide Partition* (see Fig. 4.49). In the same way, you can click the option in the side bar of the right pane. A warning message will pop up confirming your decision to perform this operation; click *OK* and you are done.

To unhide the partition again, use the same steps and instead of selecting *Hide Partition* select *Unhide Partition*.

Creating a Hidden Partition Within a USB Zip Drive

With this technique we are going to make Windows® see our portable zip flash drive as a local drive (similar to hard disk).

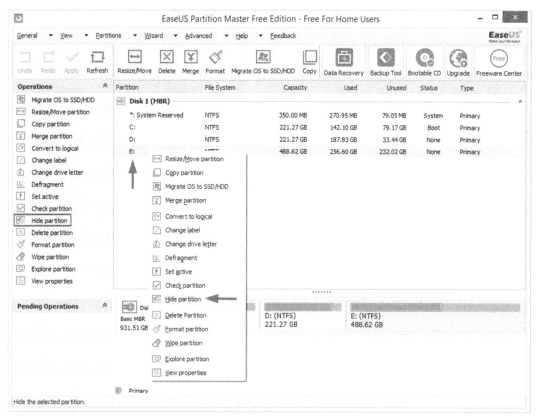

FIGURE 4.49 Hiding partition using EaseUS Partition Master Free.

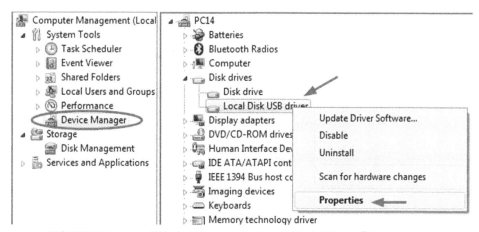

FIGURE 4.50 Access USB zip drive properties from within the Windows® device manager.

This could be achieved by installing a specific driver to make our zip drive look like a local disk. Next, we can partition it into two or more partitions, and only the first partition will appear in other Windows®-based machines. The remaining partitions will appear only on the host computer (the one used to perform this trick). This experiment is performed using a Windows® 7 (32-bit) machine.

1. Download *Cfadisk USB Local Driver* from http://www. etcwiki.org/wiki/Cfadisk_usb_driver [20]. This driver allows a user to partition and format USB drives like

regular hard drives (32-bit version). The downloaded file is a compressed zip folder; extract it and continue.
2. Plug in the USB drive into which you want to create the hidden partition into your PC. Go to *Computer Management* through *Control Panel ≫ Administrative Tools ≫ Computer Management*.

Select *Device Manager* from the left panel. From the right panel select *Disk drives*, where you should see your plugged USB drive. Right-click it and select *Properties* from the context menu (see Fig. 4.50).

3. Go to the *Details* tab. From the *Property* drop-down menu select *Device Instance Path* and copy its value (see Fig. 4.51).

Now, go to the *Cfadisk USB Local Driver* folder, open the *cfadisk.inf* file using any text editor, browse to line number 26, and paste the value already copied (device instance path) inside this file (see Fig. 4.52).

Close this file after saving it.

4. Return to *Device manager*, right-click the USB drive (as we did in step 2), and select *Update Driver Software* (see Fig. 4.53).

5. A dialog appears asking you to select the location where your software driver is located. Select the second option, *Browse my computer for driver software* (see Fig. 4.54).

Select the option *Let me pick from a list of device drivers on my computer* and click *Next* (see Fig. 4.55).

6. A new dialog will prompt you to *Select the device driver you want to install for this hardware*. Click *Have Disk…*, browse to the folder where you had extracted the USB local disk driver (step 1), select *cfadisk.inf* from it, and click *Next* to continue (see Fig. 4.56).

A warning message, *Update Driver Warning* appears (see Fig. 4.57). Ignore this warning by clicking *Yes*.

Windows® will return to launch another alarm message stating that Windows® cannot verify the publisher of this driver software. Ignore this warning and click the option *Install this driver software anyway* (see Fig. 4.58). Windows® will immediately begin installing this driver; this may take some time. Once this completes, a new dialog will appears saying *Windows has successfully updated your driver software*. Click *close* to close the dialog.

You have completed the required steps to make your USB zip drive look like a local hard disk. To create our hidden partition we need to partition our USB zip drive. Go to

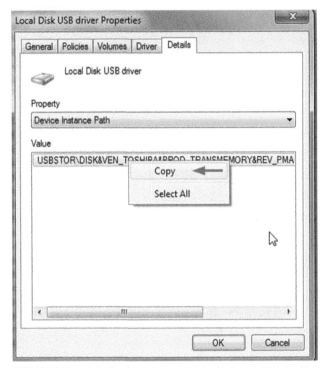

FIGURE 4.51 Copy the device instance path of selected USB zip drive into the Windows® clipboard.

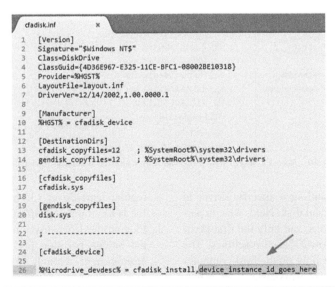

FIGURE 4.52 Updating cfadisk.inf file with my USB zip drive data.

Control Panel ≫ *Administrative Tools* ≫ *Computer Management*, select *Disk Management* from the left panel, and click your USB zip drive in the right panel to select it. In our case I will delete the USB zip partition to create two new partitions. You can do this by right-clicking it and selecting *Delete Volume* (note that deleting this volume will erase all data on the disk drive).

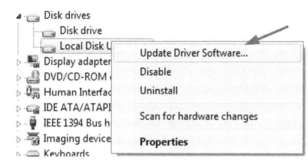

FIGURE 4.53   Update the USB zip drive driver software.

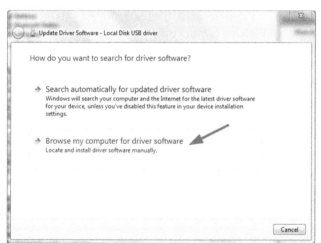

FIGURE 4.54   Specify the location where your USB drive driver's software is located.

FIGURE 4.55   Select the option to install driver software from within your PC.

FIGURE 4.56   Install USB drive software.

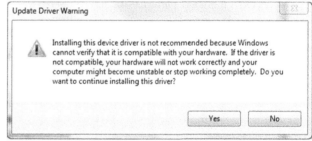

FIGURE 4.57   Warning message launched by Windows® because it could not verify drive software.

FIGURE 4.58   Error message launched by Windows® because it cannot verify the publisher of this driver.

After deleting the USB volume it becomes unallocated and you can begin creating new partitions by right-clicking the unallocated space and selecting *New Simple Volume* (see Fig. 4.59).

In this case I have created two volumes (partitions), the first one with 6500 MB volume, which I named *darkness* (my zip flash size used on this experiment is 8 GB), and the second partition size is 1120 MB, which I named *secret* (see Fig. 4.60).

The *secret* partition will always be hidden when we plug our zip flash into any PC other than the one that create it (the PC where we performed this trick).

Secret volume will always appear in the *Computer Management* console since there is no way to hide it from this location; however, this method is still very effective as most computer users will not usually check for hidden partition using the *Computer Management* console. To make the hiding process more effective using this technique, make the hidden partition small (about 2% of the entire USB zip flash size) and encrypt your data before putting it inside the hidden volume.

Uncovering Hidden Partitions

As we said earlier, there is no way to hide the partition completely from the *Computer Management* console (except HPA and DCO partitions as we will see later). You can always check for hidden partitions of any plugged USB device through this console.

Another method is by using the *DiskPart* command line utility that comes as a part of the Microsoft Windows®

family (Windows® 8, 8.1, 7, Vista, XP, and Server 2003). DiskPart is a text-mode command interpreter. This tool enables you to manage objects (disks, partitions, or volumes) by using scripts or direct input at a command prompt.

To launch this tool, open a DOS prompt, type *DiskPart*, and press *Enter*. The *DiskPart* utility will appear in a separate window (see Fig. 4.61).

In Fig. 4.61 we typed *List disk* to view a list of connected hard disks to this PC and associated numbers (in my case I have one hard disk and two attached USB zip drives). In order to view the partition of each disk you first need to select it through the *select disk = n* command, where *n* points to the disk number that appears in the first command.

After selecting the disk, type *list partition* to see list of partitions that exist within this disk; here the hidden partition of our USB zip drive (Partition 0–1147 MB) appears.

DiskPart is a powerful tool for disk management under Windows® OS. You can learn more and see a list of command line options for this tool in the link ginen in Ref. [21].

You can restore your USB zip drive to its original state by plugging it into your PC. Go to *Device Manager*, right-click it, and select *Properties*. Go to the *Driver* tab and select *Roll Back Driver*. This will uninstall the software driver you already installed and return the old driver to this drive.

Another method to restore your old USB zip drive driver software is by using a free tool called *SD Formatter* [22]. Use this tool to format your USB drive and it should returns to its original state before partitioning it.

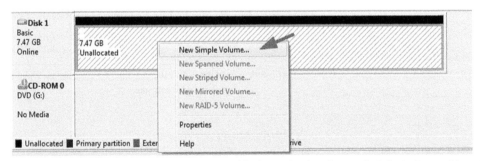

FIGURE 4.59 You can create many simple volumes, give each one a specific size, and assign a letter to it. Only the first partition will appears in other PCs running Windows®-based systems.

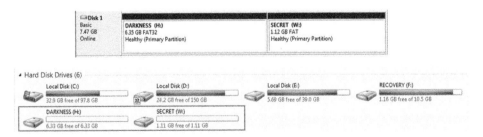

FIGURE 4.60 Our USB zip drive becomes a part of local hard disk drives. The secret partition will only appear in the PC where we have partitioned our USB drive.

DATA HIDING WITHIN MASTER FILE TABLE

The NTFS contains at its core a file called the Master File Table ($MFT). There is at least one entry for each file that exist within the NTFS volume, including the $MFT itself. $MFT can have large number of entries (we can also call them records). Small files (1024 bytes or less) could be stored entirely within the $MFT. Directory records are stored within $MFT just like file records. But instead of data, they contain index information. Small directory records can be stored entirely within the $MFT structure. Large directories are organized into trees consisting of records with links to external clusters containing directory entries (see Fig. 4.62).

In a typical volume $MFT occupies about 12.5% of the partition size; the remaining space (about 88%) is preserved for file storage. However, $MFT size could be changed according to the size of the files stored within this volume; for example, if we have large number of small files this may increase $MFT size to more than 12.5%. The same thing happens if we

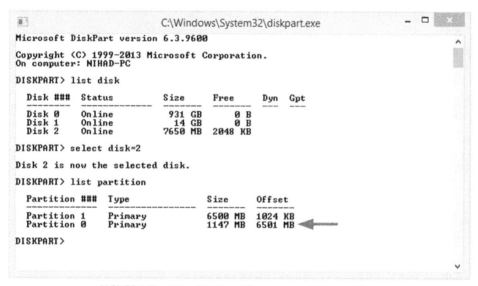

FIGURE 4.61   Using DiskPart utility to uncover hidden partitions.

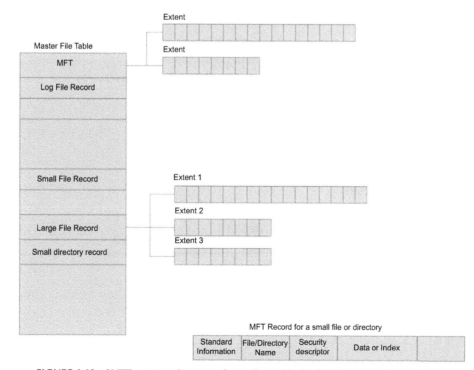

FIGURE 4.62 $MFT structure. Structure of a small record inside $MFT structure (bottom image).

have large number of large size files stored within one volume (large files may have many corresponding records).

The size of file records in $MFT is generally fixed. No matter what the size of a cluster is, all records will be 1 KB (some sources say that the size of each $MFT record is fixed at either 1024 or 2048 bytes).

The system uses $MFT records to store information about the file or directory stored within each volume; this information takes the form of attributes (eg, **size**, **date/time stamps**, and **permissions** attributes that are stored within $MFT for each file record). Since the size of each $MFT record is limited, there are different ways that NTFS can store a file's attributes:

1. Resident attributes, stored within the $MFT record.
2. Nonresident attributes, stored either in additional $MFT records or in external clusters that lie outside the $MFT. The list of clusters used is stored as clusters run in the run list of an attribute (see Fig. 4.62).

As more files are added to an NTFS volume, more records are added to the $MFT and the $MFT increases in size. When files are deleted from an NTFS volume, their $MFT entries are marked as free and become available for reuse. However, disk space that has been allocated for these entries is not reallocated, and the size of the $MFT does not decrease, leading to making it fragmented.

In order to protect the $MFT from fragmentation, NTFS reserves a portion of the disk around the $MFT that it will not allocate to other files unless disk space runs low. This area is known as the $MFT zone and it is used to keep the $MFT as contiguous as possible as it grows. Space for file and directories are also allocated from this space, but only after all the volume space outside of the $MFT zone has been allocated [23].

There is a tiny tool created by Sysinternals called **NTFSInfo**, which is used to tell you where on the disk the $MFT zone is located and what percentage of the drive is reserved for it. This tool also gives different information about disk volume. You can download it from [24].

Launch this tool using MS DOS command prompt and type *ntfsinfo* C:. Here *C:* points to drive letter and could be replaced with any volume letter (see Fig. 4.63).

FIGURE 4.63 ntfsinfo tool shows valuable information about the New Technology File System volume and its structure.

The first 16 records of the $MFT are reserved for metadata files. The metadata files define the structure of the $MFT and essentially make it a self-describing database (see Table 4.3).

The location of these files is not fixed except for the boot sector file. If the first $MFT record got corrupted for any reason, NTFS reads the second record to find the $MFT mirror file, whose first record is identical to the first record of the $MFT (see Fig. 4.64).

$MFT will always have at least 16 records. System files occupy from 0 to 11 records. $MFT records 12–15 are marked *In Use*, but are reserved for future use.

$MFT records 16–23 are marked as *Not in Use*, but are never used.

Now that we have fair knowledge about the structure and organization of $MFT, we can begin talking about how we are going to exploit $MFT to conceal data inside it.

StegoMft is a tool utilized to conceal data within $MFT https://code.google.com/p/mft2csv/wiki/StegoMft.

This tool exploits the record slack space, which is the leftover in the $MFT record after the header and attributes are defined. As we said before each record in $MFT occupies 1 KB; however, newer Windows® OS (Windows® 8, 2012, and 2010) give an option to define it higher than 1 KB.

The end marker of a record is always FFFFFFFF. Everything that comes after this mark is ignored, with exception of the fixup values (the last 2 bytes of every sector within a record), and this where we are going to conceal our data.

The amount of data that could be stored within $MFT is very limited. Many sources state that it is about 40% of its total size; however, as we said before the volume size and number of files that exist within it and its size affects this issue. When hiding using this method we should take care of the fact that hidden data could be overwritten. This happens because when a file gets deleted, $MFT entries are not immediately erased; they are simply marked as free subsequently becoming available if needed. When another new file occupies the deleted file space inside $MFT, if it takes up more space in the $MFT record than the previous one, it will destroy the space where our secret data is hidden. This fact does not mean hiding inside $MFT is an unsecure option; we can simply avoid deleting or adding files or directories to the volume where our secret data is hidden. Hiding data using this technique is considered very efficient and too difficult to track down by nonexpert investigators.

Let us return to our hiding tool. The creator of the *StegoMft* tool suggests that "In order to be able to hide any data in a record, there must be a minimum of 15 bytes of

TABLE 4.3 Master File Table Metadata Files

Record Number	Metadata	Function
0	$MFT	MFT table itself
1	$MFTMirr	Image of MFT in case the first record gets damaged
2	$LogFile	Log file, records important information that affects NTFS volume construction
3	$Volume	Volume file, contains volume label
4	$AttrDef	Attribute definition list
5	$Root	Root directory, saves index of all files and directories in root directory
6	$Bitmap	Bitmap file
7	$Boot	Boot file, stores boot commands; without it Windows® cannot start
8	$BadClus	Store bad clusters of the volume so that Windows® will not use them to store files
9	$Secure	Secure file about the volume itself
10	$UpCase	Capitalized file
11	$Extended metadata directory	Extended metadata directory
12	$Extend\$Reparse	Reparse points file
13	$Extend\$UsnJrnl	Log changing file
14	$Extend\$Quota	Quota management file
15	$Extend\$ObjId	Object ID file
16		Reserved

record slack, since the header takes 14 bytes. There is implemented a lower limit of 24 ($24 - 14 = 10$) bytes required in order to write, in order to save a little bit time. The *-check* switch accounts for the header size, so the value you get is the true number of what can be hidden with this tool. On one of my test machines, Windows® 7×64 and a volume with 592,640 records, the tool identified 280 MB of record slack in 176 s" [25].

Now we will begin practicing using this tool. I'm using a computer with Windows® 8.1 installed on it with 1 TB hard disk. Launch a command prompt (always should be run as administrator) where this tool resides. Type the following in the command prompt (see Fig. 4.65) to know the amount of available slack space that could be used to conceal data inside it for each volume in your PC.

Here in a description of the command options in Fig. 4.65.

StegoMft64 is used to launch the program. There are two versions, one for 32-bit Windows® and the second (used here) is 64 bit.

MFT Zone

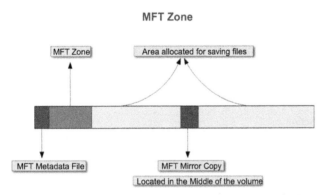

FIGURE 4.64 Master File Table zone and its location on New Technology File System volume.

-check is used to calculate the number of record slack bytes in $MFT starting at slack byte 0 on volume C:.

> c:\out.txt is used to output resulted command into a text file (out.txt) at drive *C:*.

The resultant command found 218,628 records in $MFT at volume *C:*.

Each of these records has a slack space equal to 590 bytes.

To calculate the amount of data that could be concealed within this volume we need to do the following math:

We have 218,628 records, and each one has 590 bytes of slack space (equal to 0.59 KB).
Amount of slack space in KB $= 218,628 \times 0.59 = 128,990$. 52 KB $= 125$ MB.
This means we can conceal 125 MB of secret data inside volume *C:*.

You can repeat the same process in each volume for which you need to know how much data you can conceal inside it.

Now, after we know how to calculate how much data we can hide within each NTFS volume, let us practice concealing a secret message inside it and retrieve it later.

In order to conceal a secret message inside $MFT records, launch a command prompt where *StegoMft* resides and type the following (see Fig. 4.66).

Here is a description of the command options used in Fig. 4.66:

StegoMft64.exe is used to launch the program.
-hide switches to execute the hiding function.
Secret.txt is the file that contains our secret data (in my case its size is 85.5 KB)

FIGURE 4.65 Calculating the number of $MFT record slack space available on drive C:.

D: is the volume used to conceal our secret data inside its $MFT table; it must be NTFS volume.

111 is the record number where the hiding process will begin.

33716327 is a signature used to locate the hidden data when extracted.

0 is the slack byte number 0.

Now, in order to extract the hidden data we need to enter the following command (see Fig. 4.67).

We use the same command switches as the hiding process; however, we should note to put (*-extract*) instead of (*-hide*) and select a place and name for the extracted hidden data (in our case, C:\outputfile.txt).

Finally, if we want to destroy the hidden message after extracting it, we should use the command switches in Fig. 4.68.

In Fig. 4.68, we are destroying all slack space data in volume *D:* beginning from record number 111 until 250 at slack byte 0. In Chapter 7 we will learn how to destroy data in a way that no one can ever retrieve.

As we saw, *StegoMft* is one of those rare tools that enable concealing secret messages inside $MFT of NTFS volume. Hiding data using this technique is very efficient and too difficult to crack by inexperienced computer investigators.

DATA HIDING IN DISK BAD BLOCKS

$BadClus is one of the 16 metadata files of the $MFT that exist within each NTFS volume. It resides in $MFT entry number 8. Any sector that the operating system cannot read will be marked as a bad sector and will store a reference to its location on the hard disk inside the $BadClus file. So the main role of $BadClus file is to keep track of sectors that are believed to be faulty and should not be written to by the operating system.

Two types of bad sectors are:

- Hardware bad sector: The physical presence of a sector on a disk is damaged and cannot be recovered. This type of sector cannot be corrected in most cases.
- Software bad sector: This could be made in different ways, such as when electricity is turned off suddenly from the computer during a writing process taking place on a disk. This could lead to some sectors being damaged. This type of bad sector could be recovered and repaired by performing a low level format of the hard disk or by using the check disk (CHKDSK) utility that comes with Windows® OS.

Old hard disks mainly depended on the operating system itself to discover and isolate bad sectors. Modern hard disks have the capability to perform bad sector isolation through its built-in firmware function. New hard drives are always chipped with hidden areas of reserved sectors. When a disk controller detects a bad sector, it will mark its physical address as bad in an internal table named *G-List* and will allocate a good sector from the reserved sectors to replace its logical address. This process is called remapping and it is performed transparently to the user and the OS.

In order to conceal data inside bad sectors, we need to use a low level disk editor like WinHex or Active@ Disk Editor (this is a free tool that can be downloaded from http://disk-editor.org/). A user has to edit the $BadClus to add the hidden sectors to the run list of $Bad attribute, after which,

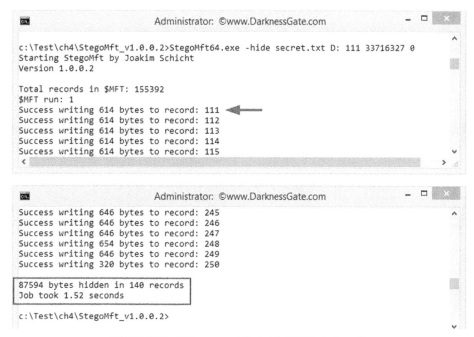

FIGURE 4.66   Hiding a secret file inside $MFT of volume D:.

the user needs to edit the $Bitmap metafile within $MFT in order to mark these sectors as unavailable through changing its allocation status to 1 (in case we are hiding) or available (in case we are extracting). Finally, we need to paste hidden data into these sectors.

The size of secret data that can be concealed using this technique is equal to the size of the partition itself! You can mark as many sectors as you want to behave as bad sectors in addressable sectors of the hard disk.

I found this technique difficult and cumbersome! Actually investigating for hidden data inside bad sectors is considered an easy task (comparable with the hiding process!) for computer investigators. I do not recommend using this method as a way to conceal your secret data as inexperienced users may cause damage to their hard disk when trying to edit it at low level as this technique suggests. However, we have mentioned this theoretically in this book because it still considered as an advanced technique for hiding data that is used by criminals to conceal what might be incriminating digital evidence. According to my research online there is no tool for performing automatic data hiding using this technique at this point.

DATA HIDING UNDER COMPUTER HARDWARE LEVEL

We can call concealing data on a hard disk directly independent from running operating systems to be considered a kind of hardware data hiding! Places on a hard disk that could be used to conceal data directly are usually reserved by computer manufacturers.

We chose to put hardware data hiding in this chapter because it's the nearest fit to it, although concealing using hardware techniques is not related to the operating system already installed on disk. Two famous techniques are described here. Trying to conceal your secret data using any of the following techniques could lead to severe damage to your hard disk and data. This is why we are describing such techniques theoretically. You need be aware that it your responsibility to make the necessary backup in case you want to apply such tests.

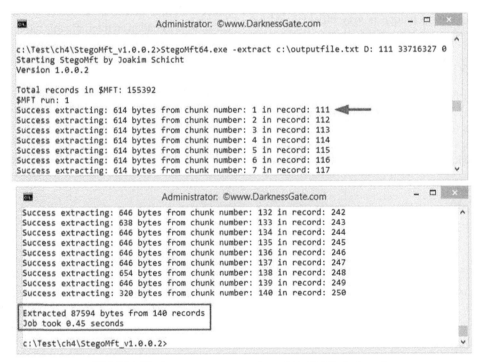

FIGURE 4.67   Extract secret message from within $MFT of volume D:

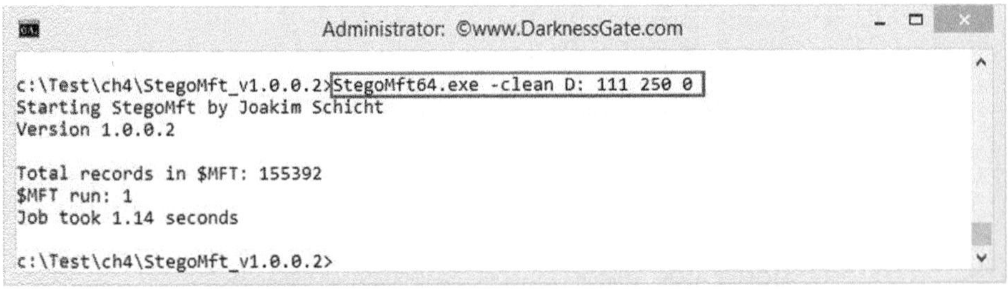

FIGURE 4.68   Destroy hidden message inside $MFT of volume D:

Data Hiding Inside Host Protected Area

Host protected area (HPA) is an area located at the end of a hard disk that is normally inaccessible to users. BIOS and operating systems are also unable to show this area to end users. HPA partition is not vulnerable to hard drive formatting, as the HPA remains untouched even after formatting the whole hard disk.

The main purpose from creating HPA is to find a way for computer manufacturers to store diagnostic utilities, recovery programs, and even recovery images of the OS itself in a region inside the hard disk that a user cannot access. HPA was first introduced in the ATA-4 standard CXV in 1998. Most hard disks currently support HPA [26].

How Does Host Protected Area Work? [26]

The IDE controller has many registers that contain data that can be queried using ATA commands. The data returned yield information about the drive attached to the controller. ATA has three commands used to create and use the HPA inside hard disks. These commands are:

- **IDENTIFY_DEVICE**: Request information about total number of user addressable sectors.
- **SET_MAX_ADDRESS**: This command changes the size of the maximum addressable user data area. The new setting is returned by IDENTIFY_DEVICE.
- **READ_NATIVE_MAX_ADDRESS**: This command returns the native device size with factory default settings.

Operating systems use the first command to find out the addressable space of a drive, thus knowing the size of the drive.

In order to create an HPA partition (Fig. 4.69), the register can be changed using the ATA command SET_MAX_ADDRESS. If the value in the register is set to less than the actual hard drive size then an HPA is created that extends from the first sector beyond the maximum addressable sector to the end of the disk. This extra space area will be hidden from the OS because the operating system only works with the value returned by the IDENTIFY_DEVICE command, making it unable to see the part of the drive that constitutes HPA space.

HPA is not accessible by OS or BIOS (initially needs to modify BIOS settings in order to allow access and then use special HPA tool for direct access). Special HPA aware tools developed to access and modify its contents can see an HPA partition because they use a special ATA command called READ_NATIVE_MAX_ADDRESS. It should be noted that this command can access the register that contains the true size of the hard drive. Under GNU/Linux they are only accessible with low level tools like dd.

As we noted from the previous explanation about HPA, concealing data using this technique is a daunting task for inexperienced computer users. Accessing it also needs special software that is strictly related to the hardware used in your PC (manufacturer related). Some generic tools that can be used to modify HPA are presented in Table 4.4.

FIGURE 4.69   Host protected area partition on a disk drive.

TABLE 4.4 List of Host Protected Area Aware Utilities

No	Program Name	URL	Description
1	Fiesta	http://sourceforge.net/projects/fiesta	This program is an easy-to-use info/backup/restore/copy tool for the host protected area (HPA) data.
2	TAFT	http://www.vidstrom.net/stools/taft/	This is an ATA (IDE) forensics tool that communicates directly with the ATA controller. It can retrieve various information about a hard disk, as well as look at and change the HPA and device configuration overlay (DCO) settings.
3	ATATool	http://www.datasynergy.co.uk/products/misc/atatool.aspx	Data Synergy ATATool can be used to display and modify ATA disk information from a Microsoft Windows® environment. The principal use of the ATA tool is to check/modify the ATA "HPA" and "DCO" features.
4	HDAT2	http://www.hdat2.com/	HDAT2 is program for test or diagnostics of ATA/ATAPI/SATA, SSD, and SCSI/USB devices.
5	DiskCheckup	http://www.passmark.com/products/diskcheckup.htm	Detect and set the size of both HPA and DCO (see next section about DCO).

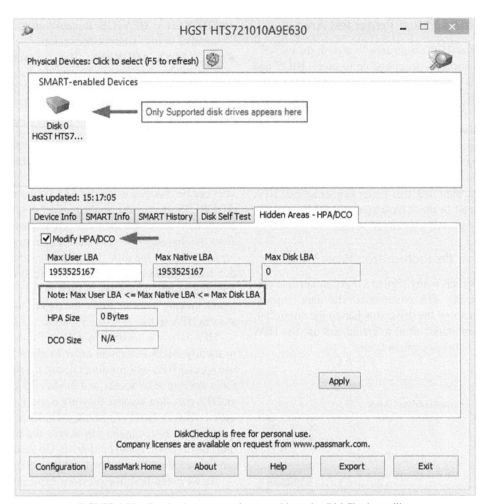

FIGURE 4.70 Creating host protected area partition using DiskCheckup utility.

DiskCheckup has the ability to detect and set the sizes of the HPA and DCO. You can see a demonstration of it in action in Fig. 4.70.

In Chapter 6 we will show you how to use special forensic tools to investigate for hidden data inside HPA.

Hiding Data in Device Configuration Overlay

The device configuration overlay (DCO) was first introduced in the ATA-6 standard. The motivation behind creating it is to allow different computer system vendors to purchase hard disks from different computer disks manufacturers and then treat all these disks as if they are the same size (the exact number of sectors). For example, a vendor can set the maximum size of a 500GB disk drive to be 320GB using the DCO technique. The remaining 180GB will be hidden from both operating system and BIOS [27].

Not all hard disk manufacturers support this feature in their disks. In our case we have a brand new hard disk drive with 1TB that does not support the DCO feature (see the bottom of Fig. 4.70 to see the text box (DCO size=N/A)).

DCO partition is stored at the end of the disk after the HPA partition (see Fig. 4.71). It can be discovered using a procedure similar to HPA. The system uses the IDENTIFY_DEVICE command to query the hard disk for information including its total size. DCO can report a false size to this command (report smaller disk size to reserve the rest of the space for its own partition). In order to check if DCO exists within the disk, the command DEVICE_CONFIGURATION_IDENTIFY should be used. The output from this command is compared with the output of IDENTIFY_DEVICE. If there is a difference between the two outputs, a DCO partition will be made. In order to remove DCO the command DEVICE_CONFIGURATION_RESET is used. This command is not reversible, meaning that after deleting the DCO we cannot return it back to the disk. This is different compared to HPA, which can be removed and returned back as needed.

HPA and DCO can both coexist in the same hard disk, but DCO should be created before HPA.

Detecting the DCO area in disks is more difficult than HPA partition. In Chapter 6 we will talk about how we can

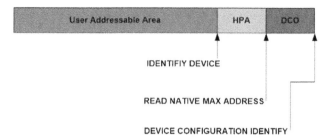

FIGURE 4.71 Device configuration overlay location inside the hard disk.

investigate and remove hidden data within both HPA and DCO partitions using specialized tools.

SUMMARY

This was a rich chapter concerning hiding inside the Windows® OS file system. We begin talking about how we can exploit a modern Windows® file system (the NTFS) to conceal our data inside it. ADS is a feature associated with NTFS that allows us to hide a large number of files inside one file stream without modifying its size. Some of these files can contain malicious software that could be used to launch sophisticated attacks against an operating system.

We also demonstrated how we can use a more advanced version of ADS, which is the stealth ADS. This is more hidden and usually not scanned by ordinary antivirus programs.

Then we talked about exploiting Windows® restore points to conceal our secret data. This technique could be used to plant malware and exploit operating systems remotely at a later time. Antivirus software usually do not scan restore points for dangerous programs.

Windows® registry could also be exploited to conceal secret data inside it. We demonstrate a simple way to perform this.

The next technique talked about concealing data using file slack space. We used a tool to perform this trick. Concealing data using this method offers a sophisticated place that is very difficult to discover by nonprofessional computer experts.

In the hidden partition section, we give two examples of how to easily make a Windows® partition become hidden. Both techniques could be performed without using any third-party tool.

Hiding inside $MFT is another advanced method, which allows us to hide a considerable amount of data inside $MFT of the NTFS volume. This is a very efficient way to conceal data used by professional computer users.

Hiding inside disk bad block is also another choice to conceal your data, although it is difficult to implement, but still considered an advanced method for concealing secret data.

The last section talked about hiding inside a hardware piece of the computer. Such techniques are not related to the operating system already installed on your machine. We theoretically talk about the two most famous techniques for implementing this, which are concealing inside HPA and DCO.

In the next chapter we are going to cover possible techniques for concealing data inside Windows®-based machines by making it unreadable. *Data hiding using encryption techniques* are going to be thoroughly covered in the next chapter using practical real world examples.

REFERENCES

[1] Microsoft TechNet, How NTFS Works [Online]. Available from: http://technet.microsoft.com/en-us/library/cc781134%28v=ws.10%29.aspx (accessed 08.10.15).

[2] Wikipedia Website, NTFS Files System [Online]. Available from: https://en.wikipedia.org/wiki/NTFS (accessed 08.10.15).

[3] Data Hiding Tactics for Windows and Unix File Systems [Online]. Available from: http://www.berghel.net/publications/data_hiding/data_hiding.php (accessed 08.10.15).

[4] Figure 4.2: Adapted from Microsoft TechNet Website [Online]. Available from: http://technet.microsoft.com/en-us/library/cc781134%28v=ws.10%29.aspx (accessed 07.10.15).

[5] MSDN Website, Naming Files, Paths, and Namespaces [Online]. Available from: http://msdn.microsoft.com/en-us/library/aa365247%28VS.85%29.aspx (accessed 09.10.15).

[6] Wikipedia Website, Shadow Copy [Online]. Available from: https://en.wikipedia.org/wiki/Shadow_Copy (accessed 26.10.15).

[7] Microsoft TechNet, Volume Shadow Copy Service [Online]. Available from: http://technet.microsoft.com/en-us/library/ee923636.aspx (accessed 26.10.15).

[8] What You Should Know About Volume Shadow Copy/System Restore in Windows® 7 & Vista (FAQ) [Online]. Available from: http://blog.szynalski.com/2009/11/23/volume-shadow-copy-system-restore (accessed 27.10.15).

[9] Microsoft, Structure of the Windows Registry [Online]. Available from: http://msdn.microsoft.com/en-us/library/windows/desktop/ms724946%28v=vs.85%29.aspx (accessed 25.10.15).

[10] Wikipedia Website, Windows® Registry [Online]. Available from: http://en.wikipedia.org/wiki/Windows_Registry (accessed 25.10.15).

[11] Microsoft, Registry Value Types [Online]. Available from: http://msdn.microsoft.com/en-us/library/windows/desktop/ms724884%28v=vs.85%29.aspx (accessed 24.10.15).

[12] Microsoft, File Allocation Table, FAT16 [Online]. Available from: http://support.microsoft.com/kb/118335/ (accessed 24.10.15).

[13] File Allocation Table General Information [Online]. Available from: http://www.ntfs.com/fat-systems.htm (accessed 25.10.15).

[14] Wikipedia Website, FAT [Online]. Available from: http://en.wikipedia.org/wiki/File_Allocation_Table (accessed 25.10.15).

[15] Microsoft, Default Cluster Sizes for NTFS [Online]. Available from: http://support.microsoft.com/kb/140365 (accessed 28.10.15).

[16] Microsoft, Hard Disk Geometry [Online]. Available from: http://technet.microsoft.com/en-us/library/dd758814%28v=sql.100%29.aspx (accessed 28.10.15).

[17] Wikipedia Website, Disk Partition [Online]. Available from: http://en.wikipedia.org/wiki/Disk_partitioning (accessed 28.10.15).

[18] Metasploit Anti-Forensics Project [Online]. Available from: http://www.bishopfox.com/resources/tools/other-free-tools/mafia/ (accessed 30.10.15).

[19] Download EaseUS Partition Master Free [Online]. Available from: http://www.partition-tool.com/personal.htm (accessed 08.10.15).

[20] Download Cfadisk USB Local Driver [Online]. Available from: http://www.etcwiki.org/wiki/Cfadisk_usb_driver (accessed 09.10.15).

[21] DiskPart List of Command Line-Options [Online]. Available from: https://technet.microsoft.com/en-us/library/cc766465(v=ws.10).aspx (accessed 11.10.15).

[22] SD Formatter Tool [Online]. Available from: https://www.sdcard.org/downloads/formatter_4/ (accessed 11.10.15).

[23] Microsoft, Master File Table [Online]. Available from: https://msdn.microsoft.com/en-us/library/windows/desktop/aa365230%28v=vs.85%29.aspx (accessed 11.10.15).

[24] Sysinternals, Download NTFSInfo v1.0 [Online]. Available from: https://technet.microsoft.com/en-us/sysinternals/bb897424.aspx (accessed 14.10.15).

[25] Hiding Inside $MFT [Online]. Available from: https://code.google.com/p/mft2csv/wiki/StegoMft (accessed 14.10.15).

[26] Wikipedia Website, Host Protected Area (HPA) [Online]. Available from: https://en.wikipedia.org/wiki/Host_protected_area (accessed 11.10.15).

[27] Wikipedia Website, Device Configuration Overlay (DCO) [Online]. Available from: https://en.wikipedia.org/wiki/Device_configuration_overlay (accessed 11.10.15).

BIBLIOGRAPHY

[1] Metadata of NTFS File System [Online]. Available from: http://www.datarecoverytools.co.uk/2009/12/10/metadata-of-ntfs-file-system/ (accessed 01.10.15).

[2] Understanding NTFS File System [Online]. Available from: http://ntfs.com/ntfs-mft.htm (accessed 01.10.15).

[3] NTFS File System Overview [Online]. Available from: http://www.c-jump.com/bcc/t256t/Week04NtfsReview/Week04NtfsReview.html (accessed 01.10.15).

[4] Structure of NTFS File System [Online]. Available from: http://www.cse.scu.edu/~tschwarz/coen252_07Fall/Lectures/NTFS.html (accessed 01.10.15).

[5] An Examination of the Windows 7 or 8 or 8.1 MBR (Master Boot Record) [Online]. Available from: http://thestarman.pcministry.com/asm/mbr/W7MBR.htm (accessed 04.10.15).

[6] Hide Data in Bad Blocks [Online]. Available from: http://www.david-verhasselt.com/hide-data-in-bad-blocks/ (accessed 05.10.15).

[7] M. Gupta, M. Hoeschele, M. Rogers, Hidden disk areas: HPA and DCO, International Journal of Digital Evidence (2006). Purdue University http://www.utica.edu/academic/institutes/ecii/publications/articles/EFE36584-D13F-2962-67BEB146864A2671.pdf (accessed 06.10.15).

Chapter 5

Data Hiding Using Encryption Techniques

Chapter Outline

Introduction   **134**
Security Awareness Corners   **134**
  Human Security   134
  Device Security   134
  Message Security   135
  Network Security   135
Anonymous Operating System   **135**
  Tails   135
    What Is the TOR Network?   135
  Ubuntu Privacy Remix   137
  Other Security Distributions   138
  Advice When Using Security Operating Systems   138
  Portable Stick Computer   140
Disk Encryption   **140**
  Encrypting Partitions Using BitLocker   141
    Data Drive Disk Encryption   142
    Windows Partition Encryption   143
  Creating Encrypted Vaults   145
    Create a Simple Encrypted Volume Using VeraCrypt   147
    How Do We Open a Normal VeraCrypt Volume?   150
    Install Virtual Machine OS Within a Hidden VeraCrypt
    Container   150
  Single File Encryption   159
    AES Crypt   159
    File Archive Encryption Using PeaZip   160
  Cloud Storage Encryption   161
    Using CryptSync for Cloud Storage Encryption   162
  Discussion of Security Level in Disk Encryption   162
    Attacking Full Disk Encryption   163
    Countermeasures Against Full Disk Encryption Attacks   165
Anonymize Your Location Online   **169**
  Using the TOR Browser   169
    TOR Browser   170
    What Is Dark Web?   170
    Warnings When Using the TOR Network   171
  Virtual Private Networks   176
  SSH Tunneling   179
  Using Proxy Server   179
    Web Proxy Types   180
    Security Risks Associated With Proxy Servers   180
  Anonymous Search Engine   180
    StartPage   180
    DUCKDUCKGO   181
    DISCONNECT SEARCH   181
  Web Browser Privacy Add-Ons   181
    Check Browser Fingerprint   181

    Mozilla Firefox Privacy Add-Ons   182
  Secure Anonymous File Sharing   183
    OnionShare   184
Encrypting Email Communications   **185**
  Email Encryption Using Gpg4Win   186
    Public and Private Key Concept in Encryption   186
    What Is a Digital Signature Concept?   186
    Create PGP Keypair Certificate   187
    Prerequisites to Send and Receive Encrypted Emails
    Using Gpg4win   188
    Encrypting Emails in MS Outlook® Using the GpG4win
    Component (GpgOL)   189
    How to Decrypt an Encrypted Message Sent to You   190
    Making Sure You Are Talking With the Correct Person   190
  Open PGP Encryption for Webmail Using the Mailvelope
  Browser Extension   190
  Secure Web Mail Providers   192
    ProtonMail   193
    GhostMail   195
Encrypt Instant Messaging, Video Calls, and VOIP Sessions   **195**
  What Are the Risks?   195
  Off-the-Record-Messaging and Pidgin   195
    Generating Our Private Key   196
    Practice Using OTR by Initiating a Secure Chat Session   197
    Authenticate the Identity of Your Contacts   197
  A Secure Video Calling Service Using Gruveo   198
  A Secure Anonymous Calling Service Using GHOST CALL   199
  Retroshare Secure Social Platform   199
  TOR Messenger   199
  Complete Anonymous IM Using Ricochet   201
Create and Maintain Secure Passwords   **201**
  Password Best Practice   201
  Password Generation Tools   202
    Norton Identity Safe Password Generator   202
    Strong Password Generator   202
    RANDOM.ORG   202
    PWGen   202
  Password-Saving Techniques   202
  Password Manager Tools   202
    KeePass   202
    Encryptr   203
    Master Password   203
Miscellaneous Security Hints and Best Practices   **203**
Summary   **204**
References   **204**
Bibliography   **205**

Data Hiding Techniques in Windows OS. http://dx.doi.org/10.1016/B978-0-12-804449-0.00005-1

INTRODUCTION

According to the initial book proposal, there should be two chapters: one devoted to *data hiding using encryption techniques* and another one devoted to best practices when communicating privately online, titled *Secret Communications Best Practices*. Hiding using encryption is the last chapter in this book that talks about obscuring your secret data, and as we talked at the beginning of this book, that using hiding techniques and combining it with encryption is considered the best practice, offering a higher level of security for our online communications if implemented correctly using a series of predefined procedures. Following this discussion we found that it would be better to combine these two chapters since communicating privately online is strongly related to using robust encryption techniques in addition to using some hiding techniques to further secure the transmitted message from any possible eavesdropper.

In this chapter you will learn how you can use different techniques to conceal your private messages (file, text, audio, video) using encryption. We will also talk about online communication encryption including encrypting emails, chats, VOIP, hard disks, cloud storage, and how to use different Windows® programs to avoid online tracking. You will also learn how to become completely anonymous online when surfing and conducting online communications.

In today's world, many parties are heavily involved in surveillance programs. The revelations by National Security Agency whistleblower *Edward Snowden* in 2013 about the mass surveillance programs conducted by the United States and other governments still cast a long shadow. Government agencies (both local governments and super power state agencies) are investing billions of dollars yearly to develop and run surveillance programs. Corporate surveillance is another dangerous type of privacy violation. Big companies monitor consumer behavior using a variety of tracking techniques to predict their actions online. These valuable data could be later passed to governments or other third parties without the user's knowledge, and these third parties can abuse the data in a way that is against the persons' interest. Search engines are also considered an important source of data about consumer behavior and attitudes. Many search engine providers (such as Google and Yahoo) save users' search keywords, helping them to predict their future actions and needs. Learning how to anonymize your online traffic and conduct encrypted online communications have become vital skills for anyone who wants to go online safely.

Encrypting a secret message along with hiding it is considered the best secure way of communicating privately because it scrambles the message and will require a key in order to decrypt the message again, in addition to being hidden while in transmission. However, as we said previously, in some situations where there is a hostile environment surrounding us, we may need a way to make our message undetectable for automated monitoring machines; this is where encryption cannot help in hiding with whom we are communicating even if the message contents remain hidden if protected with strong encryption. Having said that, it is considered illegal in some countries to use encryption software. Downloading, or using software of this sort, can be incriminating in its own right. As we mentioned in previous chapters, if the police, military, or intelligence services are among those groups from whom you are seeking to protect your information, then violating these laws can provide a pretext under which your activities might be investigated or your organization might be persecuted. It is also important to understand that many companies are limiting the possibility of using data hiding tools by their employees, and that often the use of these tools requires an administrative user account that is also restricted. Determining the best secure method of communicating online is dependent upon the situation we are currently in and the types of threats we are facing.

In the following sections we are going to show you how you can become anonymous and conceal your data while communicating online using a variety of tools and techniques. Be aware, however, that your protective measures will disappear if your PC is already compromised by malware or any kind of malicious software.

In the last section of this chapter we will give you some hints and links to free tools to protect your PC from such threats. This will be a brief section as it is outside the scope of this book.

SECURITY AWARENESS CORNERS

In order to achieve the greatest level of security and anonymity when conducting online communications, a set of techniques, tools, and human best practices should be combined to achieve this goal.

Human Security

This includes the human side of computer security, such as selecting strong passwords, and keeping your machine, operating system, and programs up to date. Avoid installing software from unknown sources, learn how phishing and scams work, and have a general knowledge about computer viruses and how your PC can get infected with them.

Device Security

This mainly includes your operating system security, such as the type of encryption used in your hard disk, what antivirus software and firewalls are installed, and how they are configured for maximum protection.

Message Security

This deals with email encryption, digital signatures, encrypting chat applications, and using communication applications that support end-to-end encryption.

Network Security

This includes encrypting transmitted data by using virtual private network (VPN) and secure socket layer (SSL). It also includes using different tools to surf the web anonymously and avoid online tracking by changing your IP and MAC address in addition to using a completely anonymous OS in extreme hostile environments.

In the following section we will describe in detail how we can achieve maximum security using different encryption techniques covering each group in our security awareness corners just described.

ANONYMOUS OPERATING SYSTEM

The first thing we need to talk about is the operating system itself. This book is about Windows®-based machines. As we all know, Windows® is not configured to be an anonymous secure OS, although we can configure it to become more secure. Being a closed code OS means it can contain many backdoors that enable third parties from spying on us. In addition to this, many sources point out that Microsoft is actively colluding with the NSA and other US intelligence agencies to offer backdoors and bypass its built-in encryption features of many of its applications (like Skype) in order to make surveillance on Windows® users easier [1]. These facts makes using an OS like Windows® not suitable at all for people performing critical tasks that requires complete online anonymity.

The best operating system that supports complete online anonymity should have a number of characteristics to assure its functionality such as:

● Its source code should be open to the public.
● A complete audit of the source code and its validity should also be constantly made to assure its safety from independent parties.
● All its applications should be configured and directed to use anonymous networks. There are many networks that support online anonymity. The best known ones are TOR and I2P networks.
● The cryptography design used in applications installed in this OS should be well documented and reviewed constantly for any vulnerability.
● It can run from within USB or CD/DVD, never stores any files on your hard disk, and has the ability to automatically wipe all your RAM memory upon closing.

Commonly, everything that is easy to use in the digital world is considered unsecure. For example, many chat applications that are used by millions every day are considered vulnerable to many threats online. Secure chat applications that support end-to-end encryption and need a key in order to work are used on small bases because they are difficult to configure by most novice users, which makes them an unfavorable choice.

Linux is a free open source operating system. Its source code can be audited by any savvy users interested in having a high level of confidence that it does not contain any backdoors or other malicious software. Public users are usually paranoid when hearing the word *Linux* because it has a reputation of being difficult to use and is command-line-based. On the contrary, many Linux distributions have a user-friendly interface just like Windows®-based machines (Ubuntu is similar to Windows® 8, Mint to Windows® XP, Kubuntu to Vista, and Zorin to Windows® 7). This makes migrating from a Windows® environment to Linux smoother for the Windows® general novice user. Most Linux distributions can be installed on virtual machines (VMs) or run from CD/DVD or USB drive.

Linux distributions do not support security and anonymity by default. The distributions we are going to talk about are specifically optimized to support anonymity and encryption by default, and these are:

1. Tails (Amnesic Incognito Live System)
2. Ubuntu Privacy Remix (UPR)

Tails

This is the operating system *Edward Snowden* used to evade the NSA. It is a live system build upon Linux Debian that aims to preserve your privacy and anonymity online. By using this operating system it is almost impossible for anyone to track you while you are online, since Tails will force all outgoing connections through the encrypted *TOR* network and blocks all nonanonymous connections (you need to follow some safety measures to assure your 100% anonymity online as we are going to see later in this chapter).

Tails comes supplied with many built-in applications that are preconfigured to provide the maximum security when it is in use. If any application tries to connect to the Internet silently, *Tails* will block it instantly. *Tails* applications includes a web browser that use a *TOR* network, instant messaging client with built-in encryption, secure email client, office suite, image and sound editors, in addition to many useful applications that are all configured with security in mind.

What Is the TOR Network?

Tails is mainly dependent on the *TOR* network to anonymize your Internet traffic, but what is TOR anyway? According to its creators, TOR is "an open and distributed network that helps defend against traffic analysis, a form of network surveillance that threatens personal freedom and privacy, confidential business activities and relationships, and state security."

TOR protects you by bouncing your communications around a network of relays run by volunteers all around the world. It prevents anyone attempting to watch your Internet connection from learning what sites you visited, and it prevents the sites you visit from learning your physical location [2].

Tails also supports another prominent anonymous network, *I2P*. *I2P* can be accessed from https://geti2p.net/, however it is better to use *Tails* with *TOR* because they are both created from the same organization and work together by default without special configuration.

Tails is a live system (like most other Linux security distributions). It runs from a USB or CD/DVD drive. It is not dependent on the operating system installed on your machine, so you can boot into *Tails* using any computer. Public computers and network routers needn't worry, because *Tails* will not engage the host machine's hard disk at all. Generally speaking, the only storage space used by *Tails* is the RAM memory; however, everything on RAM will be automatically erased when computers are shut down, so no traces will remain on host machines. This is why *Tails* is called *amnesic*. *Tails* also has the ability to change your MAC address, so if you are working, for example, in an Internet café, no one can track your MAC address back to your PC because it will change automatically many times within each working session. MAC spoofing is enabled by default in *Tails*.

Tails can be booted up on most computer systems. In order to launch the software, you first need to change your PC boot sequence from within BIOS to boot from the USB zip drive (or your DVD/CD drive if *Tails* is installed on a CD/DVD). Each PC has a different key to access the BIOS in order to change the boot sequence. The most common ones are F9 on HP; F10 on SONY; F11 on MSI; F12 on Lenovo, DELL, and ACER; and ESC on ASUS.

To boot most Windows® 8, 8.1, or 10 tablets from a USB drive, first turn the device completely off. Connect your USB stick or external drive, hold the Volume Down or "−" button, then press the power button once.

Let's try to install and boot *Tails* from a USB drive following these steps:

1. Download the latest version of *Tails* from https://tails.boum.org/download/index.en.html (size approximately 1 GB).
2. Download Universal USB installer from http://www.pendrivelinux.com/universal-usb-installer-easy-as-1-2-3/. It is a portable tool, weighs about 1 MB, and is used to install Tails on your USB stick. In case a new version is released and the download link is changed, go to http://www.darknessgate.com and search for *Universal USB installer*.

3. Insert a USB stick with at least 2 GB of free space into your PC.
4. Execute the USB installer tool. Select *Tails* in step 1. Then select the location of ISO image of *Tails* on your PC in step 2. In step 3, select your USB from the drop-down menu and check the box to format it in case it contains any data. Finally click *Create* (see Fig. 5.1). After clicking *Create* a warning message will pop up asking you to confirm your action. Click *Yes* to continue and begin installing *Tails* on your USB (note that installing *Tails* on your USB stick will erase all data on this USB, so be careful and back up your data first).
5. If everything goes well, the final window appears stating that installation is complete. Click *Close* to finish the wizard and you are done!

Now, in order to boot from *Tails*, change your PC boot sequence as we've mentioned before and make it boot from the USB drive.

If *Tails* starts successfully, the *Tails* boot menu appears (see Fig. 5.2), select *Live*, and press Enter.

Tails is based on Linux, but if you are not comfortable or never used Linux before, do not worry because this OS is preconfigured to be anonymous without user interference.

Once *Tails* starts after clicking *login* and entering your password for the current working session, you should wait some time in order for *Tails* to connect to the *TOR* network. When *Tails* gets connected it will show a green icon at the top right bar of the screen. Of course you need first to get connected to the Internet; if you are using a wireless connection click over the Wireless connection icon in the top right corner of the screen and enter your Wi-Fi password to get connected (see Fig. 5.3).

To surf the Internet you will use the *TOR* browser. This browser has limited speed but it allows you to surf anonymously. *Tails* contains a secure chat application called *Pidgin*, which allows you to chat using different chat providers like Gmail, AOL, and others. You need to set up your account first and then you can begin your secure conversation, which is completely encrypted end to end.

You can store your passwords on *Tails* using *KeePassX*, which is an open source password manager. *KeePassX* saves many different types of information like usernames, passwords, URLs, attachments, and comments in one single database. It is located under the *Applications* menu at top left bar » *Accessories*.

Tails can also be used in offline mode for higher security in case you are creating or viewing sensitive documents. To disable networking on Tails:

- When *Tails Greeter* appears (see Fig. 5.4), in the Welcome to *Tails* window, click *Yes*, then click *Forward*.
- In the Network configuration section, select the Disable all networking option.

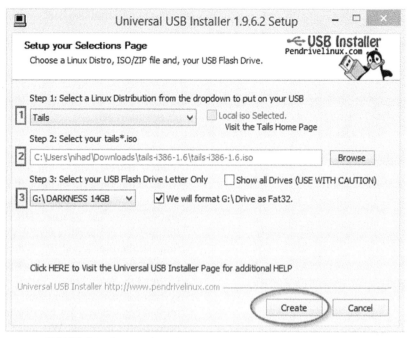

FIGURE 5.1   Set up Universal USB Installer to install Tails on a USB stick.

FIGURE 5.2   Tails boot Start menu.

Tails is the most well-known anonymous operating system used on earth. It adds a strong layer of security to our online activities if combined with the correct human security behavior.

Ubuntu Privacy Remix

This is an isolated offline operating system based on Linux Ubuntu. Its main goal is to provide an isolated working environment where sensitive data can be dealt with safely. It works by closing all connections to the outside world through removing support for LAN, WLAN, Bluetooth, and IR hardware as well as PPP from the modified kernel. Ubuntu Privacy Remix (*UPR*) is a read-only operating system since there is no install option and no access to the hard disk. *UPR* runs exclusively from a read-only CD, so the host machine

that *UPR* runs on it stays untouched. All user data are exclusively stored on encrypted removable media (Fig. 5.5).

UPR does not allow access to the local hard disk; it uses a modified kernel to alter the treatment of ATA devices during boot. This has the effect that the system completely ignores local S-/ATA hard disks, while ATAPI devices like CD/DVD drives work like usual.

UPR mounts removable media and *TrueCrypt* volumes with the *noexec* option. This prevents executing malicious programs that were imported accidentally into the *UPR* system via removable media.

Because *UPR* is a read-only operating system, program configurations and user data can't be saved permanently. This means after each reboot we need to initiate our program configurations again. *UPR* solved this issue through what it calls *Extended TrueCrypt-Volumes*. *UPR* stores all program configurations and user data of *OpenOffice*, *Evolution* (a personal information management application that provides integrated mail, calendaring, and address book functionality), and *GnuPG* within an encrypted container on a removable USB drive. Note that *UPR* relies on the *TrueCrypt* program to achieve this feature. As we all know, on May 28, 2014, a message was published on the *TrueCrypt* website claiming that *TrueCrypt* was *insecure*. Without giving any further reasons, however, an analysis done by the Open Crypto Audit Project (https://www.opencryptoaudit.org/) found that *TrueCrypt* is still considered a safe application to use for encrypting your data. Nevertheless, *UPR* teams are still working on linking the concept of *extended containers* to LUKS-based storage in next releases.

FIGURE 5.3 Tails desktop after successfully connecting to the TOR network.

FIGURE 5.4 Tails Greeter screen.

To summarize, *UPR* achieves its goal in creating a high level of security standards through implementing the following:

1. By being nonmodifiable, it is impossible to permanently install malicious software, either by network or by local hard disks.
2. Even if it were possible for malicious software to load into memory, there is no possibility of saving or sending captured data anywhere outside the system.

Keep in mind that if *UPR* has vulnerabilities, these can have security impacts during use as with any other operating system. Practically, it is too difficult to implement a 100% secure operating system for individuals if you are a target of a big intelligence agency like the NSA, as backdoors can be introduced at the software, hardware, or even algorithm level, making anything vulnerable to such sophisticated attacks.

UPR can be downloaded from https://www.privacy-cd. org/en. After downloading the ISO image you need first to burn it into a CD and then modify your PC boot sequence to boot from the CD/DVD. There are many free CD burning tools—*CDBurnerXP* is one with an excellent user interface, which can be downloaded from https://cdburnerxp.se/en/home.

Other Security Distributions

There are many other operating systems that are specialized for security and anonymity online. Two OSs that fall into the same category are:

1. **Whonix**: A free open-source OS based on Linux Debian. It uses the TOR network to anonymize your online traffic. According to its creators, "*Whonix* consists of two parts: One solely runs *TOR* and acts as a gateway, which we call *Whonix-Gateway*. The other, which we call *Whonix-Workstation*, is on a completely isolated network. Only connections through *TOR* are possible. With *Whonix*, you can use applications and run servers anonymously over the internet. DNS leaks are impossible, fortunately, not even malware with root privileges can find out the user's real IP." *Whonix* can be downloaded from https://www.whonix.org/wiki/Main_Page.

2. **Qubes OS**: A security-oriented, open-source operating system for personal computers. It uses virtualization to implement security by compartmentalization and supports both Linux and Windows® virtual environments. Beginning with version 3.0, *Qubes* introduces the hypervisor abstraction layer, which renders *Qubes* independent of its underlying virtualization system. *Qubes* works by running each program on your OS into a separate isolated island. For example, you can have a dedicated VM used only to run high-risk websites, another for using OpenOffice, and a third for making secure communications like sending emails. If one VM gets compromised the other VMs will remain unaffected. *Qubes* OS can be downloaded from https://www.qubes-os.org/downloads/.

We've found after testing many distributions that each one has its own implementation for the best security design in order to remain secure. It is too difficult to acquire 100% security or anonymity online. If a big intelligence agency like the NSA wants to break into your machine and spy on you, it will find a way in. However, these OSs we already talked about give a great level of security and anonymity, making surveillance on you very difficult and time-consuming to implement.

Advice When Using Security Operating Systems

- *TOR* alone will not protect you when you are exchanging important data online. You need to encrypt your data first before sending it through the *TOR* network.
- All security OSs are vulnerable to hardware attacks including *Tails*. For example, if an intruder inserts a hardware keylogger into your host machine, he/she will be able to intercept your communications. Not surprisingly, the same thing happens with firmware and BIOS attacks. All security OSs cannot survive such attacks, as we are going to see in a following section.

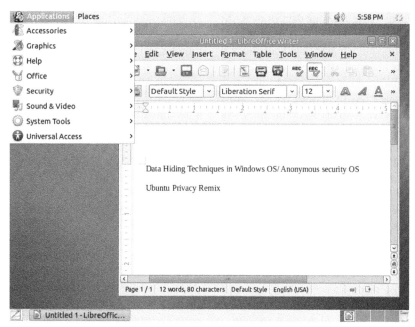

FIGURE 5.5 Desktop of Ubuntu Privacy Remix.

What are BIOS attacks? BIOS and firmware attacks are very sophisticated and usually used by intelligence agencies to attack systems silently. BIOS software work below the operating system and it is not scanned by antivirus programs. It will also survive a hard disk format. You should avoid running your portable OS on an untrusted PC to avoid uncovering all your communications [3–5].

- You should make sure that the PC you are using to install *Tails* on your USB device is not compromised, otherwise *Tails* files could be tampered by other malicious software. The same caution should be taken when burning other security OSs into a CD/DVD.
- Most anonymous operating systems rely on the *TOR* network to anonymize your traffic. ISP, however, can still detect if you are using a *TOR* network. Hiding this fact is very difficult and still is currently undergoing much research. We will cover this point in a coming section dedicated to *TOR* usage.
- *Tails* and *UPR* leave no trace on the host machine, although *Whonix* does. Be aware of this fact when selecting your anonymous OS.
- In a later section we will demonstrate how to install *Tails* inside a VM using a portable version of *VirtualBox* that is running within a secure encrypted container. Note that running *Tails* using VMs has many security implications such as:
  - Both host OS and the virtualization software can monitor your work while working on *Tails*. In case there is a keylogger already installed on your host system, it can monitor all your *Tails* traffic.
  - Some traces generated by *Tails* can be left on host hard disk, as Windows® OS usually performs paging

to boost its performance. In this process, part of RAM data is copied to the host's hard disk.
  - Some anonymity features of *Tails* may not work in such an environment; for example, *Tails* cannot change the MAC address of host machine. It cannot also anonymize host Internet traffic.

I do highly recommend using *Tails* directly from a USB stick by booting from the USB rather than using something like Portable VirtualBox. Although in some circumstances running it from within a VM may not impose any risks on the user, it all depends on the level of threats or vulnerability surrounded with each user.

- *Tails*, *UPR*, and *Whonix* (and I believe most OSs) will not clear the metadata of your documents; for example, OpenOffice and PDF creation software often store a considerable amount of data about the user and the machine used to create these files. Metadata also exists in image format, so you need to manually check for these metadata and remove them from your documents before sending them online. (We talked about different concealing techniques that depend on metadata in previous chapters. In the next two chapters we will discuss how to investigate such hidden metadata and learn how to destroy it completely.)
- To achieve a higher level of security and anonymity when using *Tails* in extremely hostile environments, you should restart *Tails* after completing each task individually. For example, if you want to publish something on a blog, do this in the first working session. Later if you want to send an email, restart *Tails* first so it will have a new identity and then send your email. This helps you separate your identity online and makes tracking you extremely difficult.

- *Tails* will automatically erase all your data from RAM upon closing it (it overwrites existing data with random data), although it is still vulnerable to cold boot attack if someone gains access to your host machine while *Tails* is still running. It should be taken into consideration that in some cases *Tails* may fail to remove all data from RAM before shutting down. Usually RAM memory will empty itself gradually within 3 min maximum, therefore attacks are rarely successful, but it should be mentioned.

   What is a cold Boot Attack? This type of attack happens where an attacker gains physical access to your PC upon shutting it down instantly and works by removing RAM memory, freezing it (eg, using compressed air cans) for a degree greater than −50°C, and then attaching it to another PC trying to recover data from it using a specific memory tool. This technique works on computers where the attacker cannot modify BIOS to boot from removable storage. Note that modern PCs like some kind of laptops are not vulnerable to this type of attack because RAM memory is soldered directly to the motherboard.

   Another method of a cold boot attack is by pressing the rest button on a PC (or powering off electricity suddenly from a PC) and trying to recover data from a previous working session through booting into another operating system that contains a specific tool for extracting remaining data including any encryption keys from RAM memory. Booting into another OS can be achieved by loading a bootable DVD/CD or a bootable USB stick. This attack relies on the data remanence property of DRAM (mostly versions DDR1 and DDR2) and SRAM to retrieve memory contents that remain readable in the seconds to minutes after power has been removed. Much research and experiments show that DDR3 is not susceptible to cold boot attacks because it loses voltage too fast to allow a computer case dismount and freeze procedure [6,7].

- Finally, always remember, neither *Tails* nor any other security OS will be valuable if you use weak passwords or you fall victim of a social engineering attack. Using secure applications is always more difficult than using commonly used ones such as Skype™ or Internet Explorer®. It is only fair to say that whatever the user decides to use, he/she should always handle basic security elements with some care.

Portable Stick Computer

The fast and continual development in the digital world is bringing new IT products to our lives every day. Major PC manufacturers have been developing the concept of the small PC . ASUS in collaboration with Google™ seems to be a pioneer in this field with their very small portable PC called **Chromebit**. This is considered among the smallest

systems a human has created for commercial usage. It measures only 12 cm long and could be attached to any TV monitor or PC through an HDMI port. **Chromebit** runs the Chrome operating system that is configured to update itself automatically. This small system can be paired with a Bluetooth keyboard and mouse in case you are attaching it to a TV monitor. It has 2 GB of RAM and 16 GB of eMMC storage, dual-band 802.11ac Wi-Fi, Bluetooth 4.0, and both USB and HDMI ports. This small system has many built-in security features like a trusted platform module (TPM) chip to safeguard internal data structures against real-world threats. It also has a notch to secure your device in public places like restaurants, airports, and exhibitions to keep your assets safe.

Intel also works to retain its share in the PC-on-a-stick market with the release of the Compute Stick (see Fig. 5.6). It's a version of a pocket PC that resembles a USB stick in size and weight. Its technical specifications include a quad-core Intel® Atom™ processor and your choice of operating systems: Windows® 8.1, Windows® 10, or Ubuntu 14.04 LTS. The Windows® version includes 2 GB memory, 32 GB of on-board storage, and comes with McAfee® Antivirus Plus for comprehensive protection from malicious software. The Ubuntu version has 1 GB memory and 8 GB of on-board storage. Both devices come with Wi-Fi and Bluetooth for connectivity, a USB port to connect peripherals, and a micro SD card slot for additional storage.

Lenovo also launched its PC stick in the summer of 2015 with similar technical specifications as Intel and ASUS. It comes with support for Windows® 8.1 and 10.

This small PC is considered an optimal choice for people who need to use a PC for their work in public places but feel suspicious about the existence of a keylogger or other monitoring tools already installed on these public PCs. They can simply plug their own PC stick to a computer or into a TV monitor that supports an HDMI port. They can work and store their files locally inside this stick, and then encrypt them and take them away with them upon finishing.

DISK ENCRYPTION

Disk encryption is a technology that protects your data by scrambling it and making it unreadable by humans. It uses special software or a hardware device in order to encipher each bit of data that exists on a disk. This protects your data from unauthorized access or a potential attacker. Full disk encryption (FDE) is increasingly required by enterprises that want to protect their mobile data. Furthermore, individuals in different business sectors are turning to FDE as an easy method to protect their sensitive data.

In this section we will show different ways to encrypt your disk in Windows® machines. Fortunately, there are many free tools for performing such a task. First, we will

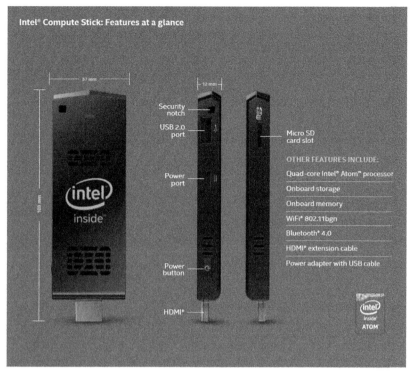

FIGURE 5.6 Intel Compute Stick, size and main technical specifications. Image from Intel.

demonstrate how to use the built-in encryption tool that already comes with some versions of Windows®, called *BitLocker*. We will also use some famous free open-source tools to encrypt your data and files that are nearly impossible to break. We will end this section by listing different attacks that can be performed against FDE and what we can do to lower such vulnerability or at least make it very hard to achieve.

Encrypting Partitions Using BitLocker

BitLocker is a new security feature that provides better data protection for your computer by encrypting all data stored on the Windows® operating system volume [8]. BitLocker is a proprietary program that belongs to Microsoft. It should be noted that, just like all Microsoft products, its source code is closed; therefore, according to our previous discussion, this can be problematic for extremely security-minded people who handle sensitive data or work in an extremely hostile environment. Generally speaking, closed source code applications cannot reveal whether there is any backdoor intentionally left to crack the application or not [9,10]. Despite this fact we are going to talk about this program and how to use it because it is already shipped with many versions of Windows® and it can still offer a sufficient level of security for most computer users who want to protect their data if their systems got stolen or unauthorized access to their personal computer took place.

BitLocker is supported by the following Windows® versions:

- Windows® 10: Professional, Enterprise, and Education editions
- Windows® 8 and 8.1: Professional and Enterprise
- Windows® 7: Ultimate and Enterprise
- Windows® Vista: Ultimate and Enterprise

In order to run BitLocker we need to have a PC with at least two partitions and a TPM. If your PC does not support TPM you can still use BitLocker but you need to store your encryption keys in a USB drive. The BIOS system (for TPM and non-TPM computers) must support the USB mass storage device class, including reading small files on a USB flash drive in the preoperating system environment.

What is a Trusted Platform Module? A TPM is a microchip that is built into a computer motherboard and used to perform security tasks such as securing hardware by integrating cryptographic keys into devices. Moreover, it communicates with the rest of the system by using a hardware bus.

TPM has the ability to generate cryptographic keys in addition to providing random number generator facility. Most computer manufacturers build computers with TPM chips, but we can find them mostly on PC models that are designed for business uses.

BitLocker uses TPM by default to store its encryption keys, making it hard to break by external software attacks and physical theft. During the startup process TPM will perform an authentication check by comparing a hash of important operating system configuration values with a snapshot taken earlier to make sure that these important files have not been tampered with. If, however, any modification occurred on your PC, it will boot in a restricted mode to deter potential attackers.

Now let us experiment with how to activate BitLocker on a machine running Windows® 8.1 Enterprise edition. I will first encrypt a nonsystem partition, in this case, the *D:* partition.

Launch BitLocker through *Control Panel > BitLocker Drive Encryption*. You can also start Windows Explorer and select the drive you want to encrypt. Right-click over it and then select *Turn on BitLocker* to begin the encryption wizard of the drive instantly.

There are two types of BitLocker available that we can activate:

1. **BitLocker drive encryption**: This option allows you to encrypt your local partitions including the Windows® partition. It works by encrypting everything that exists on your partition. After encryption is done, your Windows® machine will boot from system reserved partition (this why it is a requirement to have at least two partitions available for the system's use) and Windows® boot loader will prompt you for a password or a USB drive that contains your encryption keys if you select so during BitLocker setup to unlock your drive and launch Windows normally. (If your PC supports TPM you can also (for additional layer of security) insert a PIN to unlock the encryption keys in TPM during the boot process.)

The decryption process is transparent for the user and you can access your files as you normally would without noticing any difference.

2. **BitLocker To Go**: This is used to encrypt your removable storage drives like external hard disks and USB flash memory. You need to insert a password in order to be able to decrypt your files.

Data Drive Disk Encryption

In our case we are going to encrypt one of our data drive partitions (D drive):

1. Select the drive you want to encrypt and click *Turn on BitLocker* (see Fig. 5.7).
2. BitLocker will prompt you for a password that will be used to unlock your drive. Insert a strong password and click *Next* to continue.
3. BitLocker will ask you how you want to back up your recovery key (so you can access your disk in case you forget your password). It offers four storage locations:
   - Save to your Microsoft account
   - Save to a USB flash drive
   - Save to a file
   - Print the recovery key

   The best secure options (in my opinion!) is saving it to a USB flash drive and printing the recovery key on paper and keeping it in a safe location. In our case we will select *Save to USB*. It will prompt you to select your removable USB. Select it to store your recovery key inside it, then click *Next* to continue.

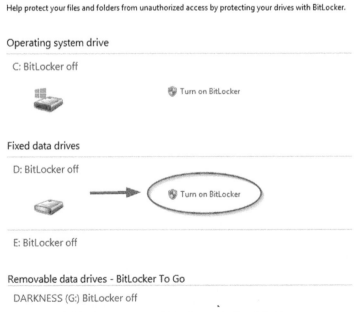

BitLocker Drive Encryption

Help protect your files and folders from unauthorized access by protecting your drives with BitLocker.

Operating system drive

C: BitLocker off

        Turn on BitLocker

Fixed data drives

D: BitLocker off

        Turn on BitLocker

E: BitLocker off

Removable data drives - BitLocker To Go

DARKNESS (G:) BitLocker off

FIGURE 5.7 Turn on BitLocker on the data disk drive.

4. BitLocker will asks you how much of your drive you want to encrypt. You have two options here:

- Encrypt used disk space only (faster and best for new PCs and drives as new drives don't contains remnants of previously edited or deleted files that need to be encrypted as well). When you add additional data, BitLocker will automatically encrypt that data.
- Encrypt the entire drive (slower but better for PCs and the drive already in use as old drives may contain deleted files and file fragments that must be encrypted as well in order to avoid recovering such files from the unencrypted part of the disk by an unauthorized person.)

For now we will select the first option; click *Next* to continue.

5. The final window in the wizard appears to ask you if you are ready to begin the encryption process. When ready, click *Start Encrypting* to begin (see Fig. 5.8). It might take some time depending on the size of your drive.

Windows Partition Encryption

If your PC does not have a TPM microchip inside it, you can still use BitLocker to encrypt the system partition. Follow these steps to achieve this (we are using Windows® 8 Enterprise edition to demonstrate this feature):

1. Click *Turn on BitLocker* beside the C: volume under Operating system drive (see Fig. 5.7).
2. If your PC does not have a TPM you will receive the message shown in Fig. 5.9.

To fix this issue and enable BitLocker on the system drive you need to edit the settings on *Local group policy*.

Please note that you should have administrator access to your machine in order to perform the following.

Click the *Windows button+R* to open the RUN dialog. Type **gpedit.msc** inside it and click *OK*. Your Local group policy editor appears. Navigate to Computer Configuration ≫ *Administrative Templates* ≫ *Windows Components* ≫ *Bit-Locker Drive Encryption* ≫ *Operating Systems Drives*. Double-click *Required additional authentication at startup*. A new dialog appears; make it *Enabled*, make sure the check box beside *Allow BitLocker without a compatible TPM* is checked, and finally click *OK* to save this new setting (see Fig. 5.10).

When done, close the *Local Group Policy Editor*. You can now use BitLocker to encrypt your system drive without having a TPM chip in your computer.

Now, return to step 1 and click *Turn on BitLocker* beside system drive C: to enable it. You will see that the first window in the setup wizard appears asking you how you want to unlock your drive at startup. In this case we will select the *Enter a Password* option (see Fig. 5.11).

In the next window you will enter the password that will be used to unlock your system drive. Enter the password and click *Next* to continue.

Now BitLocker will ask you how you want to store your recovery key in case you forget your password. You are given four options (same as the options mentioned before when encrypting the data drive). In our case we will select *Save to a USB flash drive*. A new window appears showing your connected USB sticks. Select the one you want to store your recovery key on and click *Save*. Please note saving the recovery key is very important in case your PC supports TPM or not. If your PC does have a TPM chip and you need

FIGURE 5.8   Final window of BitLocker before the encryption process begins.

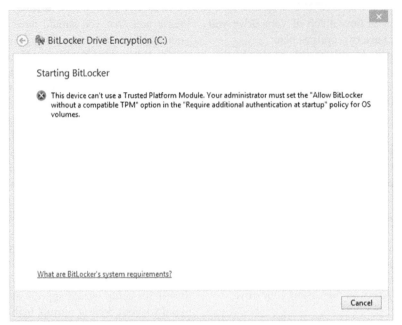

FIGURE 5.9 Error message launched by Windows when trying to enable BitLocker on a system drive that does not have TPM.

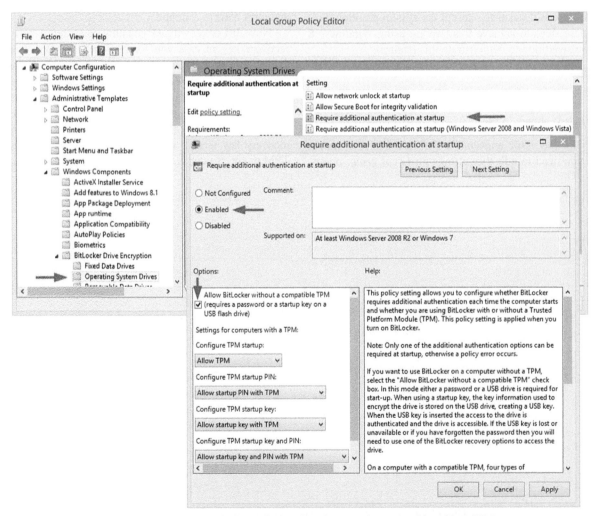

FIGURE 5.10 Change BitLocker settings to allow the encrypting system drive without TPM.

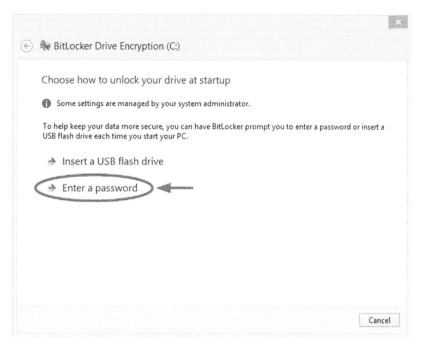

FIGURE 5.11   Select how you want to unlock your drive when Windows boots, the first step in the wizard when enabling BitLocker.

to move your hard disk to another machine, you will need this recovery key in order to decrypt your data.

The next wizard window asks whether you want to encrypt the whole drive or only the used space filled with data. In this case we will select the first option, *Encrypt used disk space only*, and click *Next* to continue.

The final wizard window appears asking if you are ready to begin encrypting your system drive (see Fig. 5.12). If everything is OK click *Continue* to proceed.

BitLocker is ready to begin encrypting your system drive; however, this will be done after you restart your PC (see Fig. 5.13).

Restart Windows®. BitLocker will ask for the unlock password. Enter your password and press *Enter* and Windows® will continue to boot normally. After booting to Windows®, BitLocker will begin encrypting your system drive. Obviously this may take some time depending on your PC hardware and the amount of used space on the drive being encrypted (see Fig. 5.14).

Congratulations, you have succeeded in your drive encryption!

If you lost your password, click *Escape* when BitLocker asks for the unlock password during the boot. You will need to insert the USB stick that contains your recovery key in order to decrypt your drive and boot normally.

You can also disable BitLocker on the selected drive through *Control panel* » *BitLocker Drive Encryption* » and then selecting *Turn off BitLocker* beside the selected drive (see Fig. 5.15). From the same location there are additional options that can be changed like Change password, Remove password, and Copy startup key.

Following the same procedures you can encrypt your removable drive by simply plugging it to your PC. You are then required to right-click over it and select *Turn on Bit-Locker*. A similar series of steps will be required as mentioned before when encrypting the data disk drive (mainly selecting a password and storing your recovery key). Avoid unplugging your USB stick during the encryption process or your data may be damaged. In order to open your USB after encrypting it you need to supply your password first (see Fig. 5.16).

As we saw, BitLocker offers an easy way to encrypt your Windows®-based PC partitions and removable storage. Encrypting your disks with BitLocker will have a very small performance degradation. If you use your PC in business and it is full of important documents you should use the safer method of BitLocker.

For security-minded people who do not trust closed software and are willing to achieve the maximum possible care to protect their data, they should use an open-source encryption tool, which is what we are going to describe in the next section. Such a tool is based on the legendary encryption program, *TrueCrypt*.

Creating Encrypted Vaults

For a long time TrueCrypt was the main encryption tool used by security professionals and many businesses and large organizations, to encrypt disk partitions in addition to creating encrypted vaults to store secret data inside them. In May of 2014, the TrueCrypt team made a breakthrough announcement on their TrueCrypt page

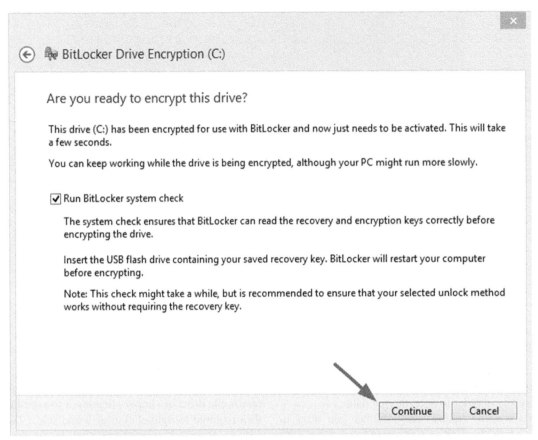

FIGURE 5.12   Final window in the wizard before BitLocker begins encrypting your data.

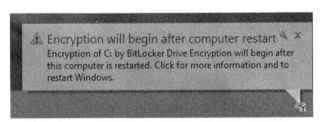

FIGURE 5.13   Disk encryption will begin after the first restart.

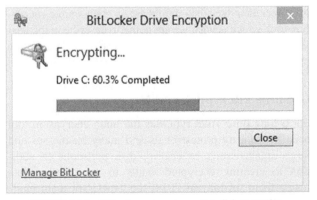

FIGURE 5.14   BitLocker processing system disk encryption.

FIGURE 5.15   Remove BitLocker protection from the selected drive.

(http://truecrypt.sourceforge.net/). They declared that TrueCrypt is not secure and advised TrueCrypt Windows® users to replace it with the Windows® built-in encryption tool we talked about earlier (BitLocker).

The sudden close of the TrueCrypt project came as a shock to the security community, who relied on this tool for many years to secure their data (*Edward Snowden* used TrueCrypt to store his leaked documents from the NSA). Rumor has it that there was pressure by government agencies in order to stop developing this tool for national security purposes.

The last known stable version of TrueCrypt is version 7.1a (supports both 32 and 64 of Windows® and Linux), available for download at Gibson Research Corporation

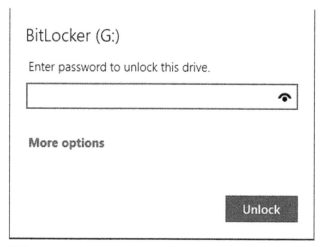

BitLocker (G:)

Enter password to unlock this drive.

More options

Unlock

FIGURE 5.16 Enter a password to unlock your BitLocker-encrypted USB drive.

through the following link: https://www.grc.com/misc/truecrypt/truecrypt.htm.

TrueCrypt was subject to audit through the *Open Crypto Audit Project*, which is a community-driven global initiative that grew out of the first comprehensive public audit and cryptanalysis of TrueCrypt (available at http://istruecryptauditedyet.com). This tool has undergone two test phases. The first phase began before support was discontinued, and passed both without discovering any major flaws in its design. Some recommendations were addressed to make this tool more secure.

There are a number of tools that have derived from TrueCrypt source code. The main ones are:

1. CipherShed: A free open-source encryption tool based on TrueCrypt. It is cross-platform, and can open encrypted containers created with the legacy program TrueCrypt. Many security researchers argue that this tool is not 100% safe because it still uses some functions from TrueCrypt that have been addressed as unsecure after performing an audit on its code. (CipherShed still uses the same key derivation technique as TrueCrypt. Open Crypto Audit Project reports this technique as being a vulnerability in TrueCrypt code.)

2. VeraCrypt: A split from TrueCrypt, which responds and solves most vulnerabilities issues raised by Open Crypto Audit Project. According to its creator Mounir Idrassi, "In the latest version, we corrected most of the security issues discovered by the Open Crypto Audit project. In the next version, we'll correct the security issue in the bootloader." VeraCrypt offers functions similar to the old TrueCrypt tool:
   a. Create virtual disks (secure containers) that can be mounted and used just like a real disk.
   b. Encrypt entire partitions (both system partition and data partition).

c. Create a hidden container that can hold a complete operating system inside it or simply contain another container.

So, following our discussion we found that VeraCrypt is currently considered the only project that is using TrueCrypt code and continually works to fix the vulnerabilities discovered by different TrueCrypt audit phases. Hence we are going to use this tool for this section as the preferred open-source tool for disk encryption.

Create a Simple Encrypted Volume Using VeraCrypt

VeraCrypt allows the creation of encrypted containers that can be used to store our secret data. These containers are portable and can be transferred with us using removable storage media. The following steps describe how to create such a simple container.

1. Download and install VeraCrypt from https://veracrypt.codeplex.com/. Initially, version 1.16 was available.
2. Launch this tool; click *Create Volume* to begin the wizard (see Fig. 5.17).
3. The volume creation wizard begins. The first window asks you to select your volume type. You will then have three options:
   a. Encrypt the file container.
   b. Encrypt a nonsystem partition/drive.
   c. Encrypt the system partition or the entire system drive.
   Make sure that *Create an encrypted file container* is selected and click *Next* to continue.
4. You need to select the volume type. You will then have two options: Standard and Hidden. Select the *Standard VeraCrypt volume* radio button and click *Next* to continue.
5. VeraCrypt will asks you where you want to store your encrypted container. Select a location and pick a name for your file. In our case we named the file *MyStore* and saved it on the E:\ drive. Click *Next* to continue.
6. Now you need to select the encryption algorithm used to encrypt your file. It is always good idea to select a good secure algorithm; however, secure algorithms usually consume more time during the encryption/decryption process. In this case we will select *Twofish* for encryption and *Whirlpool* for the hash algorithm. VeraCrypt also offers the possibility to benchmark how fast each encryption/decryption algorithm works (see Fig. 5.18). Click *Next* to continue.
7. Enter the size of your container. In this case we will create a container 200 MB in size. This container size can be the full size of the disk drive you are creating it on. Click *Next* to continue.

Encryption Algorithm Selection Criteria

Not all encryption algorithms offer the same level of security. In general we prefer to use the ones that are not developed or certified/approved by a government body like the National Institute of Standards and Technology (NIST), which is an agency of the US Department of Commerce known to work closely with the NSA.

AES has been created by the NIST. RSA on the other hand has previously been known to have a privacy affecting backdoor in some of its versions (all toolkits that use Dual Elliptic Curve Deterministic Random Bit Generator (Dual_EC_DRBG)). In addition to this issue, many journals report that RSA was colliding with NSA to offer a backdoor in its security algorithm. In 2013, The New York Times reported that documents in their possession but never released to the public "appear to confirm" that the backdoor was real, and had been deliberately inserted by the NSA as part of the NSA's Bullrun decryption program [11–13]. In December 2013, a Reuters news article alleged that in 2004, before NIST standardized Dual_EC_DRBG, NSA paid RSA Security $10 million in a secret deal to use Dual_EC_DRBG as the default in the RSA BSAFE cryptography library, which resulted in RSA Security becoming the most important distributor of the unsecure algorithm [14]. RSA responded that they "categorically deny" that they had ever knowingly colluded with the NSA to adopt an algorithm that was known to be flawed, saying "we have never kept [our] relationship [with the NSA] a secret" [15].

Twofish, published in 1998, was designed by Bruce Schneier, John Kelsey, Doug Whiting, David Wagner, Chris Hall, and Niels Ferguson. Twofish has a 128-bit block size, a key size ranging from 128 to 256 bits, and is optimized for 32-bit CPUs. According to one of its creators, Bruce Schneier, "Currently there is no successful cryptanalysis of Twofish." Twofish is unpatented, and the source code is uncopyrighted and license-free; it is free for all uses.

SHA-256 and SHA-512 hashing algorithms have been designed by the NSA and published by NIST in FIPS PUB 180-2, which makes them an unfavorable choice for us to use. The Whirlpool hash algorithm was designed by Vincent Rijmen (codesigner of the AES encryption algorithm) and Paulo S.L.M. Barreto. The size of the output of this algorithm is 512 bits. VeraCrypt uses the third (final) version of Whirlpool, which was adopted by the International Organization for Standardization (ISO) and the IEC in the ISO/IEC 10118-3:2004 international standard and is considered highly secured [16].

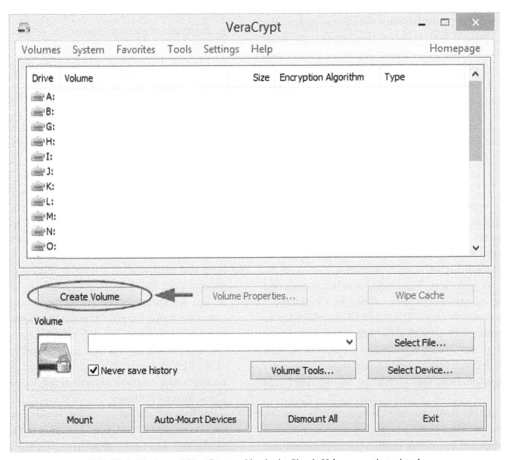

FIGURE 5.17 Launch VeraCrypt and begin the Simple Volume creation wizard.

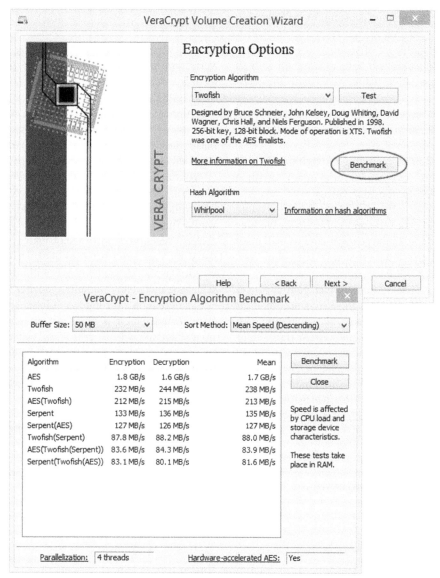

FIGURE 5.18   Select your preferred encryption algorithm to encrypt your volume with it.

8. Now the wizard will prompt you to enter a password for the required volume. You should select a very strong random password that contains a combination of upper- and lowercase letters as well as symbols and numbers. Password size should be more than 20 characters if possible. (We will give you a brief guide on selecting the best secure passwords and list some free password generation tools in a later section of this chapter.)

   You can also use a keyfile in addition to your password. A keyfile is a file whose content is combined with a password and without it you cannot unlock your container. For an additional layer of security, this keyfile can be stored on a pin-protected smart card.

   New versions of VeraCrypt let you enter a *Personal Iterations Multiplier* (PIM), which is a parameter that was introduced in VeraCrypt 1.12 and whose value controls the number of iterations used by the header key derivation function.

   The PIM is treated like a secret value that is entered by the user each time alongside any passwords. If an incorrect PIM value is specified, the mount/boot operation will fail. Using high PIM values leads to better security, thanks to the increased number of iterations, but it comes with slower mounting/booting times. With small PIM values, mounting/booting is quicker but this could affect security if a weak password is used.

   When a PIM value is not specified or if it is equal to zero, VeraCrypt will use the default values, which range between 200,000 and 327,661 iterations for system partition encryption and between 655,331 and 500,000 iterations for standard containers and other partitions.

Using a custom iteration is useful for the following reasons:

a. Adds an additional layer of security to your encryption since the attacker will have to come up with an intelligent guess before being faced with the password hurdle.

b. Increases the security level by using large PIM values to thwart future development of brute force attacks.

c. Speeds up booting or mounting through the use of a small PIM value (less than 98 for system encryption and less than 485 for the other cases).

In our case we will use a 20-character password (see Fig. 5.19) and check the option *Use PIM*. We then click *Next* to continue. In the next window we will enter the PIM. We will give it the value 600. Then click *Next* to continue (see Fig. 5.20).

9. Now the wizard will ask you to format your partition. In this case we will format it using FAT since this type is compatible with more devices and operating systems than the new technology file system (Fig. 5.21). You need also to move your mouse pointer around the window to increase the cryptographic strength of the encryption keys by introducing a truly random element (which increases security). Do this for at least 1 min. When you are ready click *Format* to create your volume using previously specified settings.

When finished, VeraCrypt will pop up a message saying, *The VeraCrypt volume has been successfully created*. You now have created a VeraCrypt simple volume.

How Do We Open a Normal VeraCrypt Volume?

Launch VeraCrypt, select a drive letter from the list in the VeraCrypt main menu. Click *Select File* and then navigate to *Select Your Encrypted Container*. Finally click *Mount* (see Fig. 5.22).

After clicking *Mount*, VeraCrypt will ask you for the *Password* to unlock this container. Enter the password and make sure to enter the PIM too, if you had already activated this option during the VeraCrypt creation wizard.

You can access your volume by double-clicking it on the VeraCrypt letter list (in this case we selected the letter *R*) or you could have simply gone to Windows explorer and you would find your decrypted container resides beside other drivers. When you finish using your container, select it in the VeraCrypt letter list then click *Dismount* (in the same location as the *Mount* button; it will be activated when you select the mounted volume in the letter list).

The creation of a hidden volume and best practices to keep it undetected is what we are going to demonstrate in next section. Please note VeraCrypt containers can also be concealed inside images or other digital media files as we have previously discussed in this book. We can also conceal it inside a stealth alternative data stream, making your container very secure.

Install Virtual Machine OS Within a Hidden VeraCrypt Container

You can add an additional layer of security if you are forced by somebody to reveal the password to an encrypted volume

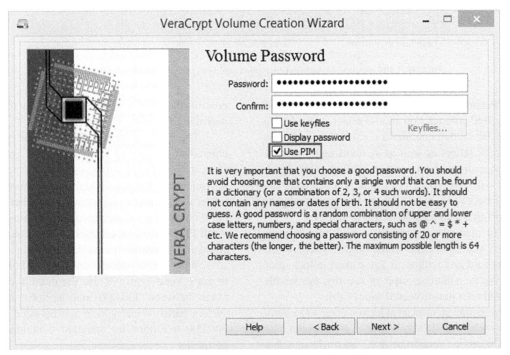

FIGURE 5.19 Insert a password for your container, at least 20 characters.

by creating another volume inside this container. VeraCrypt calls this volume *a hidden container*. Even when the outer volume is mounted, it should be impossible to prove whether there is a hidden volume within it or not (if the correct precautions [17] are taken), because free space on any VeraCrypt volume is always filled with random data when the volume is created and no part of the (dismounted) hidden volume can be distinguished from random data (see Fig. 5.23).

In this section we will show you how to create a hidden VeraCrypt container that you can use to store your secret data. Later, to make things more interesting, we will show you how to install a complete OS inside this hidden

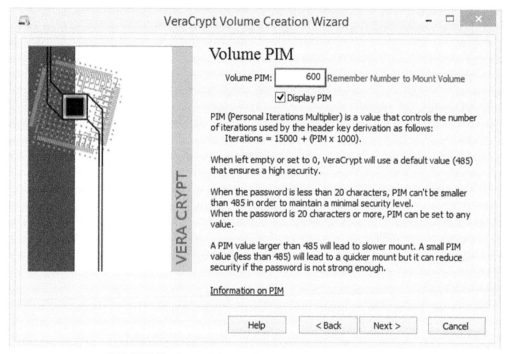

FIGURE 5.20   Insert a PIM to make your password even more secure.

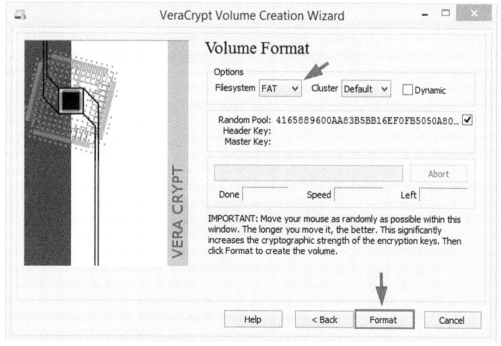

FIGURE 5.21   Format your drive using the FAT file system.

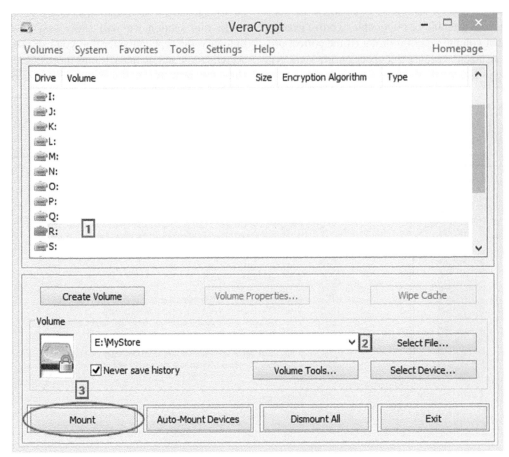

FIGURE 5.22 Mount the VeraCrypt volume.

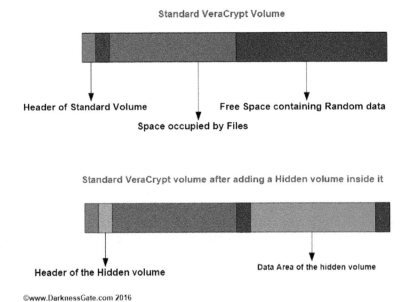

FIGURE 5.23 The layout of a standard VeraCrypt volume before and after a hidden volume was created within it.

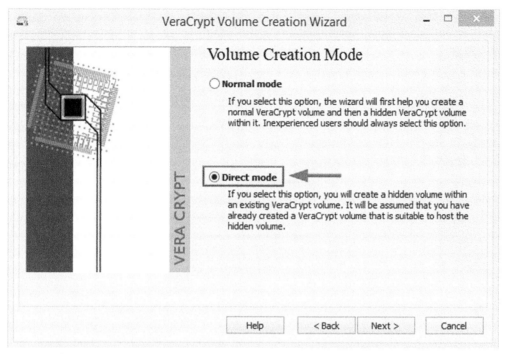

FIGURE 5.24   Select direct mode to create a hidden volume inside an existing VeraCrypt volume.

volume (we will install *Tails* in our experiment) so you can get a portable OS that resides inside a hidden encrypted container.

Create the Hidden Volume

1. Launch the VeraCrypt program by clicking *Create Volume*.
2. Select the option *Create an encrypted file container*. Click *Next* to continue.
3. Select the option *Hidden VeraCrypt* volume. Click *Next* to continue.
4. Select the option *Direct mode* if you already have a VeraCrypt container created. Alternatively select *Normal mode* if you want to create the normal VeraCrypt container and afterward create the hidden one. Here I selected *Direct mode* because I've already created a VeraCrypt volume with 15 GB in size following the same steps presented earlier (see Fig. 5.24).
5. Select the location of the VeraCrypt volume within which you will create a hidden volume and click *Next* to continue.
6. Now you need to enter the password of the normal volume (outer volume password). You should know that VeraCrypt can determine the maximum available space for the hidden volume (see Fig. 5.25). If your outer volume needs a PIM or keyfile you will also need to enter it in order to mount that volume. Click *Next* to continue.
7. The next window in the wizard will inform you that the cluster map has been scanned and the maximum possible size of the hidden volume has been determined. Click *Next* to continue.

8. Now you need to select hidden volume encryption options, which include the encryption and hash algorithms. Once more in our case we select *Twofish* as the encryption algorithm and *Whirlpool* as the hash algorithm. Please note the other algorithms are secure; however, it is best to select algorithms that are independent of any government institutions. This helps us insure that these algorithms were audited by independent parties for maximum security. Then select whether your option is an encryption or hashing algorithm finally click *Next* to continue.
9. Now VeraCrypt will prompt you for the size of the hidden volume. It will show you the maximum size allowed (see Fig. 5.26). Enter the size and select the measurement unit (MB or GB) and click *Next* to continue.
10. Enter the hidden volume password. As we previously did, select a password that is difficult to guess. Please note this password must be different from the outer volume password. Depending on which password you enter during usage, if you entered the outer volume password it will open. However, if you entered the hidden volume password you will access that instead. Click *Next* to continue.
11. VeraCrypt will prompt you with the choice of whether you want to create large files inside your hidden volume container or not. VeraCrypt is designed to ask this question in order to help you to select the best file system for your volume. Chose *No* and click *Next* to continue.
12. Now you need to select the filesystem format of your hidden volume. Select FAT as it is recommended for compatibility reasons. When finished and you are ready to create your hidden volume click *Format*.

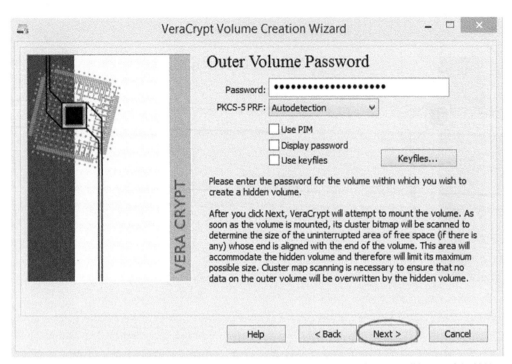

FIGURE 5.25 Enter the outer volume password in order for VeraCrypt to determine the maximum possible size of the hidden volume.

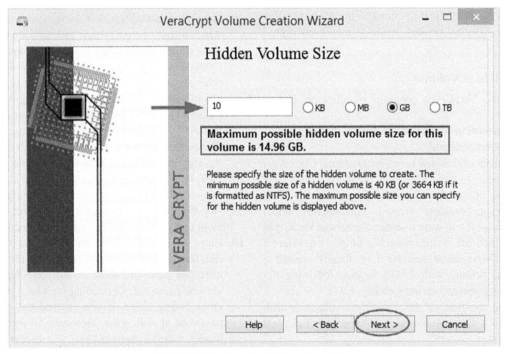

FIGURE 5.26 Insert the hidden volume size.

13. When finished with hidden volume formatting, VeraCrypt will pop up a message prompting the user for the instruction of its manual on how to protect your hidden volume data (see Fig. 5.27).

At this point we are done with creating our hidden volume. You can use this hidden container just like any disk to store your secret data. To open it you need to provide its password when mounting it and it will open as any normal volume created by VeraCrypt.

What's Next?

In the next section we will install the *Tails* operating system as a local VM using VirtualBox inside this hidden

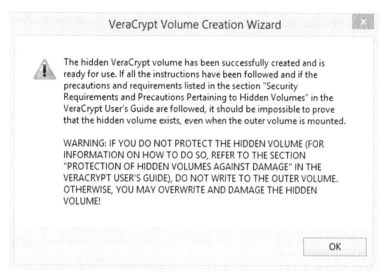

FIGURE 5.27 Final pop-up message by VeraCrypt tool after creating this hidden volume.

FIGURE 5.28 Using the Portable-VirtualBox tool to extract VirtualBox software into a portable version.

volume. To make our work more secure we will use a portable version of VirtualBox, which we will place inside the hidden volume. We can then launch it and install *Tails* on it. This gives an additional layer of security when using this OS from within that hidden volume. Please remember that you can install any OS on the VirtualBox; however, we prefer to use a Linux security distribution to lower the interactions between host and guest OS as much as possible.

Create a Portable Version of VirtualBox

VirtualBox is a powerful ×86 and AMD64/Intel64 virtualization product. It can run on Windows®, Linux,

Macintosh™, and Solaris™. You can create a portable version of VirtualBox under Windows® by performing the following steps:

1. Download and install the *Portable-VirtualBox* tool from http://www.vbox.me/. This is a free and open-source software that lets you run any operating system from a USB stick without processing an installation. It is a portable tool 1.5 MB in size. You then need to execute the installer file, then select the folder where you want to extract its contents.

2. Go to the folder and run *Portable-VirtualBox.exe*. You'll see a window similar to the one shown in Fig. 5.28.

3. If you have already downloaded the installer for VirtualBox from www.virtualbox.org click Search and navigate to the file (note that we are using Virtual Box version 5.0.10 in our example). Alternatively, click *Download the Installation Files of VirtualBox*. Portable-VirtualBox will show you the download's progress. Once the installer is downloaded, check the boxes that are appropriate and click *OK*. Portable-VirtualBox will extract the files it needs from the VirtualBox installer to the current directory.

4. The *Portable-VirtualBox* folder is your VirtualBox portable version (see Fig. 5.29). You will notice that a new folder with the name *app64* appears as a result of extracting the files of a 64-bit system (see Fig. 5.28).

You are done! You have now your VirtualBox program, which has become fully portable. You can execute it by clicking *Portable-VirtualBox.exe*. Later we will move this folder inside the VeraCrypt hidden container created in the previous section.

Install Tails Inside Hidden VeraCrypt Volume

Now we are going to begin installing *Tails* inside the hidden VeraCrypt volume. First we need to move the portable VirtualBox inside our hidden volume. We start with mounting this volume.

1. Launch the VeraCrypt program. Repeat the steps mentioned earlier in the section "How to Open Normal VeraCrypt Volume" but instead of entering the outer volume password enter the hidden volume password. If everything is OK, the hidden volume will be mounted (see Fig. 5.30).

2. Move the *Portable-VirtualBox* folder (which contains the portable version of this software) and paste it inside the hidden volume disk.

3. Launch the VirtualBox program, then select *New* to create a new VM (see Fig. 5.31).

4. The next window in the wizard will ask you to enter the OS name, its type (Windows or Linux), and its version (32 bit or 64 bit). In this case we will enter *Tails* as its name. We then type *Linux* and select the option *Other*

Linux (32 bit) in place of version, and click *Next* to continue.

5. Now select the amount of RAM to be allocated to your VM. Remember that more RAM means better performance and speed. In our case we will allow 1 GB; click *Next* to continue.

6. In the hard disk window select the option *Do not add a virtual hard drive*. Click *Create* to proceed. Click *Continue* in the warning dialog about creating a VM without a hard drive (see Fig. 5.32).

7. If *Tails* did not appear instantly on the left pane of VirtualBox, you may need to restart your VirtualBox. Now we need to configure the VM to start from an ISO image following these steps:

a. Select the new VM in the left pane.

b. Select *Machine ≫ Settings*.

c. Select *Storage* in the left pane.

d. Select *Empty* below *Contoller IDE* in the *Storage Tree* selection list in the right pane, then click the *CD* icon on the right of the window. You will have to select *Choose virtual Optical Disk File......* to browse for the ISO image from where you want to start Tails. Finally, check the *Live CD/DVD* option (see Fig. 5.33) and click *OK* to close the window. In our case the *Tails* ISO image resides inside a hidden volume. *Tails* can be downloaded from https://tails.boum.org/download/index.en.html; please make sure to download the Tails ISO image form its own website to avoid downloading a tampered image. It is always better to check your downloaded file after finishing against SHA256 checksum provided in the same download pages.

Now to start the new VM (Tails), select the VM from the left pane and click *Start* on the upper bar.

If everything goes well *Tails* will get started within the VirtualBox (see Fig. 5.34).

After finishing with using your VM OS, make sure to shut it down and dismount your hidden volume through VeraCrypt program interface.

There is a range of alternative OS you can install instead of *Tails*. Other types of Linux or even Windows® will work

FIGURE 5.29 Contents of the portable version of Virtual Box software extracted for ×64-base system.

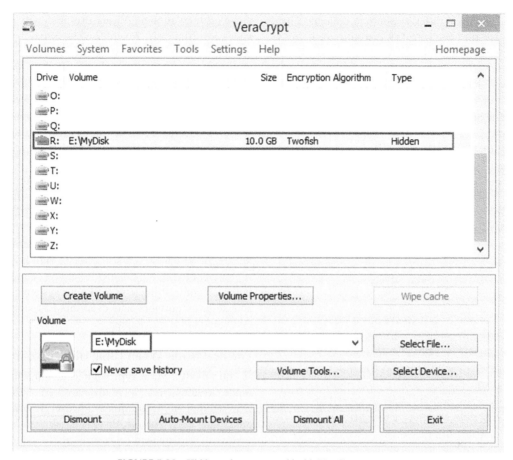

FIGURE 5.30   Hidden volume mounted inside VeraCrypt program.

FIGURE 5.31   Launch VirtualBox. Click New to create a new VM.

just the same. You need to follow the same steps with minor modifications. The main differences are in creating a hard disk (virtual disk file) for your OS that you are going to install inside the Portable VirtualBox (see step 6). In this case we've used *Tails* and let it boot up using the ISO image (for security reasons). If you install Windows® instead, you would need to create a virtual disk and store this virtual disk on your hidden VeraCrypt volume, while all other steps remain the same.

During its first run, the VirtualBox requires system drivers that need to be installed on the host system that is running it. These drivers will be installed automatically on those systems if they don't exist, which means that the system is not 100% portable as that is a requirement for it to run properly. When *Portable-VirtualBox* starts, it checks to

see if the drivers are installed. If they are not it will install them prior to running VirtualBox and will remove them afterward. Similarly, *Portable-VirtualBox* checks to see if the services are running. If not, it will start them and then stop them when it exits.

Even though running *Tails* using portable VirtualBox from within a hidden volume is considered more secure and has almost no interactions with host OS, running this OS specifically using a VM can have various security implications because people who use *Tails* are pursuing the maximum security and anonymity online. You are advised to read the previous section titled "**Advice When Using Security Operating Systems**," which contains various security consideration and best practices when using *Tails* and similar security distributions.

Considering all previous issues about running a portable version of VirtualBox, it still offers a high level of security if you want to run a hidden OS that you can take anywhere with you while still keeping all your system configurations and settings portable and everything is stored inside an encrypted hidden container.

Practical Notes When Using Hidden Volume

If you mount a VeraCrypt volume within which there is a hidden volume, you may read data stored on the (outer) volume without any restrictions. However, if you need to save data to the outer volume, there is a risk that the hidden volume will get damaged (overwritten). To avoid such a case follow these steps:

1. Mount the outer volume by entering its password, then click *Mount Options…* before clicking *OK* (see Fig. 5.35).

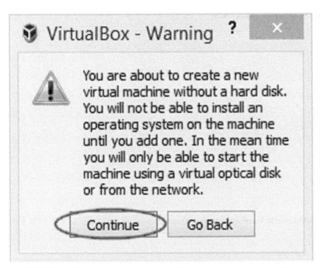

FIGURE 5.32 Configure your new VM to start without a hard disk.

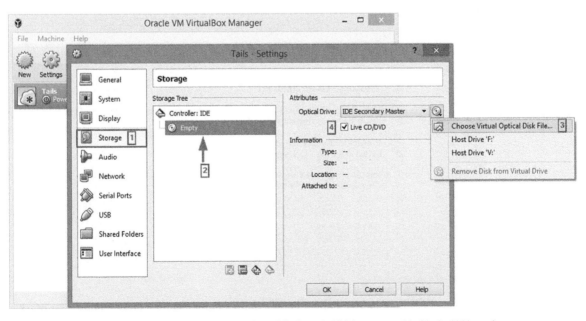

FIGURE 5.33 Configure your new VM to boot Tails from the ISO image stored inside the hidden volume.

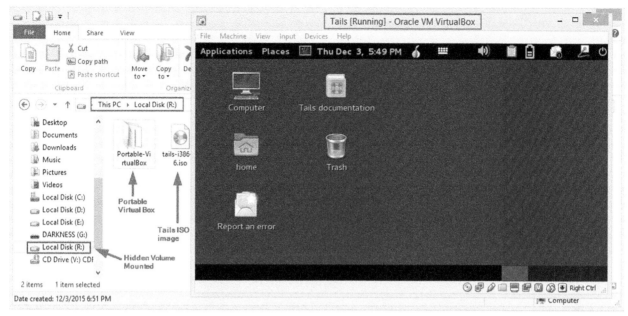

FIGURE 5.34   Tails launched inside VirtualBox, which is already stored inside the hidden volume.

FIGURE 5.35   Access Mount options of the hidden volume.

In the *Mount Options* dialog window, enable the option *Protect hidden volume against damage caused by writing to outer volume*. In the *Password to hidden volume* input field, type the password for the hidden volume. Click *OK* and, in the main password entry dialog, click *OK* (see Fig. 5.36).

When hidden volume protection is enabled, VeraCrypt will not mount the hidden volume. It only decrypts its header (in RAM) and retrieves information about the size of the hidden volume (from the decrypted header). Next, the outer volume is mounted and any attempt to save data to the area of the hidden volume will be rejected (until the outer volume is dismounted).

If the protection was successful the pop-up window in Fig. 5.37 appears.

If you need to mount an outer volume and you know that you will not need to save any data to it, then the most comfortable way of protecting the hidden volume against any damage is to mount the outer volume as read-only. You can activate this option from *Mount » Password* dialog » *Mount options …»* and check the option *Mount Volume as read-only*.

Single File Encryption

Sometimes we may want to have a simple solution to encrypt files using only a password, so we can do this fast and maybe email our encrypted files instantly through email or store it in our USB stick to take it with us. There are many tools that can perform such functions; we mention two here because of their simplicity and robustness in addition to being open source.

AES Crypt

This is an open-source encryption software that uses an AES encryption algorithm to encrypt single files. It adds a context menu item in the Windows file system context menu and can be downloaded from https://www.aescrypt. com/download. Encrypting a file with this Windows® application is very simple. You start by right-clicking on the file you wish to encrypt. Then select the *AES Encrypt* option and enter a desired password (see Fig. 5.38). *AES Crypt* will produce an encrypted file with the same name as the original file but with an *aes* extension. Decrypting a file has a similar process. You need to right-click the encrypted file and select *AES Decrypt*. Enter the correct password and the encrypted file appears in the same folder/directory.

This tool is handy for a quick encryption of a single file, and is suitable for encrypting files before moving them into a USB drive. You can also use it to send encrypted files through email; however, we prefer to use a complete encryption solution like (Gpg4win) that uses private key encryption and digital signature for secure email transactions as we are going to see in the next section.

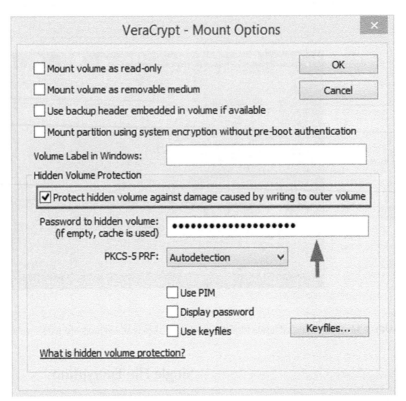

FIGURE 5.36 Activate the option Protect hidden volume against damage caused by writing to outer volume.

FIGURE 5.37 Success message after protecting the hidden volume area against a write from the outer volume.

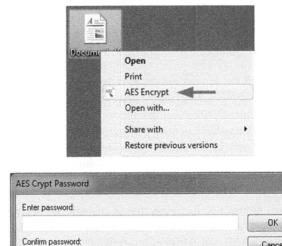

File Archive Encryption Using PeaZip

PeaZip free archive and file compressor is an open-source WinRar, WinZip alternative tool for Windows® and Linux. It can perform many functions such as extracting, creating, and converting files. It can also split/join and provide strong encryption to files. In addition to this, it has an encrypted password manager, secure data delete, find duplicate files, compute hash, export scripts to automate backup, and restore tasks. You can download it from http://www.peazip.org.

To password protect your archive, open PeaZip and click *Add* in the application's toolbar. You can then drag

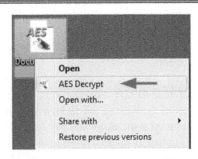

FIGURE 5.38 Encrypt a single file using AES Encrypt.

and drop files you want to include in the archive into the program window. The bottom program window allows you to select your preferred archive type (ZIP, TAR). Additionally, you can specify the output file name and select whether you want to split this archive into many parts. Additional options exist as we can see in Fig. 5.39. Using this window, you can encrypt your archive by clicking *Enter password/ keyfile*. PeaZip also uses the AES256 encryption algorithm, which you can use two-factor authentication with, password and keyfile.

In order to extract a password-protected archive open it with PeaZip, then use the Extract button in the application's toolbar. Otherwise, use *Extract* entries in the system context menu for direct extraction without browsing the encrypted container.

PeaZip also provides an **encrypted password manager** in *Tools» Password manager* from the main menu. In this way a master password can be used to encrypt passwords the user wants to save. The password manager file is unique for each user on the system using PeaZip, so multiple users can keep multiple separated password lists.

Cloud Storage Encryption

In brief, cloud storage is a set of computers with large hard disk capacity that resides somewhere on the Internet used to store your files. Many people may find it more convenient to store their data on the cloud. This allows you to back up, sync, and access your data across multiple devices as long as they have Internet capability from anywhere on earth. However, storing

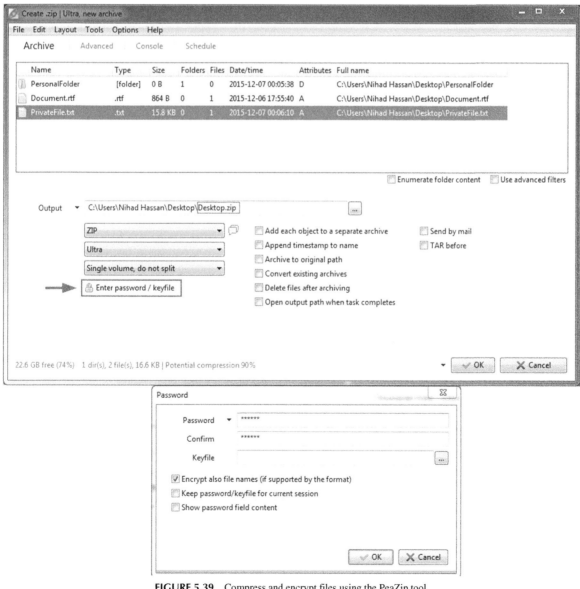

FIGURE 5.39 Compress and encrypt files using the PeaZip tool.

such data virtually has many security considerations such as the risks that your information may be accessible to others or to the cloud provider itself. After the celebrities scandal, which took place in 2014 where thousands of celebrities' pictures were leaked from an iCloud provider [18], people become suspicious when storing their private data using such services. It should be noted, however, that this is not completely true. The following simple security measures can safeguard your files in the cloud even if your cloud storage account gets compromised.

Let us first introduce average computer users to the most famous cloud storage providers:

- Dropbox (https://www.dropbox.com)
- Amazon Cloud Drive (https://www.amazon.com/cloud-driv)
- Google Drive (https://www.google.com/drive)
- Microsoft OneDrive (https://onedrive.live.com/about/en-us)

To protect your personal data when using such services, all you need to do is encrypt your files locally before uploading them to the cloud. This of course may limit your ability to share files with your friends or colleagues as they will need passwords in order to decrypt your files. This is so far considered the only safe solution you have in order to keep everything secure in such a virtual environment.

You can use any encryption tool to encrypt your data before uploading them to the cloud. We already talked about the VeraCrypt container, which can be used to store your files and then upload the entire container content to the cloud. Using this technique may not be suitable in some cases; for example, let us assume you store your files in the cloud using a VeraCrypt container that is 5 GB. If you want to view one picture stored inside this container, you will have to download the entire container after you mount it, as described previously, in order to extract one file. As you can see this is not the most practical solution.

There are other tools that are designed for the cloud storage model, as they are designed to streamline encryption of files you are going to upload to the cloud automatically one by one, avoiding the size problem we discussed previously. Selecting the best encryption tool is not as straightforward as some people may think. There are a number of criteria we've used in order to select the best secure cloud storage encryption tools:

- It should use a robust encryption algorithm that must always undergo audit by different parties in the tech community.
- It must be an open-source program to insure it contains no backdoors.
- It should not require you to create an account before you can use it.
- Preferably it should not store your files on its internal servers, as some tools may require this (even temporarily). The objective here is to limit spreading your personal files across many servers.

- It is designed with cloud storage in mind, and can integrate smoothly with famous cloud providers in addition to being maintained and updated regularly.

Using CryptSync for Cloud Storage Encryption

CryptSync is a small utility that synchronizes two folders while encrypting the contents in one folder. That means one of the two folders has all files unencrypted (the files you work with) and the other folder has all the files encrypted. The encrypted folder can be your local Dropbox folder, for example.

The synchronization works both ways: a change in one folder gets synchronized to the other folder. If a file is added or modified in the unencrypted folder, it gets encrypted. However, if a file is added or modified in the encrypted folder, it gets decrypted to the other folder.

The encryption is done using 7-Zip, which also compresses them at the same time. That means you not only get encryption but also compression for free, which reduces the storage space you use in the cloud.

To use this tool, follow these steps:

1. Download it from http://stefanstools.sourceforge.net/CryptSync.html. Install the application on your PC (supports all Windows® editions after Windows® XP).
2. Launch the tool and click *New pair....*
3. Enter your paired folder location. You can also set some additional options for the paired folders (see Figs. 5.40 and 5.41).

Note: If you select the option *Encrypt filenames* make sure to use filenames for both files and folders that are no longer than 120 characters. Encrypting those names will approximately double their length, so keep in mind that Windows has a limit of 255 characters per file or folder name.

4. Click *OK* to return to the main program window. At this point, you can select *Run In Background* to make synchronization transparent. Alternatively you can view its progress by selecting *Sync files and exit.*

There is another open source cloud encryption program worth mentioning that uses AES encryption called *Cryptomator*, which can be downloaded from https://cryptomator.org.

Discussion of Security Level in Disk Encryption

Implementing a full disk encryption is considered an important protective measure to keep your data secure, but we cannot consider encrypting the whole disk as being a 100% secure solution for all our security needs. Naturally, many sophisticated attacks can still attempt to steal encryption keys used in full disk encryption, which is what we are going to address in this section. We will also

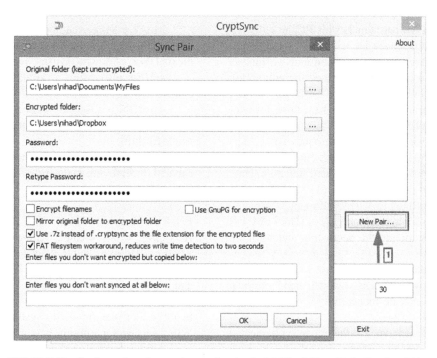

FIGURE 5.40 Configure CryptSync tool to synchronize the MyFiles folder with the Dropbox folder.

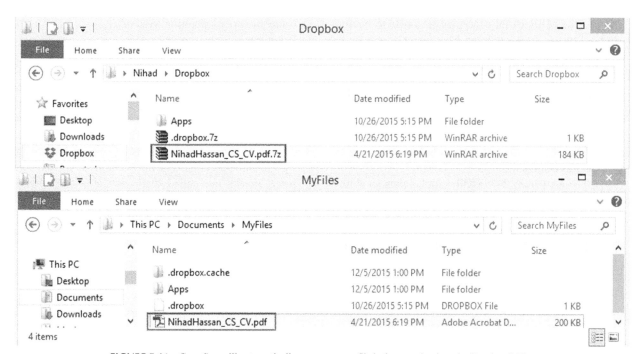

FIGURE 5.41 CryptSyn will automatically encrypt every file before moving it to the Dropbox folder.

mention countermeasure steps in order to mitigate such kinds of attacks.

Attacking Full Disk Encryption

Possible attacks against full disk encryption includes but may not be limited to the following:

1. *Evil Maid* Attacks on Encrypted Hard Drives
   This sort of attack takes place when an attacker gains physical access to the machine. The attacker will boot it into a separate volume or from a USB stick if possible, after which he or she will install a modified bootloader onto the system, and will finally shut down the entire system.

When the PC owner launches his PC, he will boot from the hacked bootloader. He will type his encryption key in order to unlock his drive and continue working as usual. The hacked bootloader can send the encryption keys silently through the Internet to the attacker or it can save it in some location inside PC's hard drive for later access by the attacker [19].

Most full disk encryption techniques are vulnerable to this method; however, conducting this attack against BitLocker, which is activated on computers that have a trusted platform module (TPM) installed, is considered very difficult to achieve although not impossible according to some researchers [20]. The TPM will detect any modification to the bootloader and warn the user about it.

Evil Maid attacks fall under the Bootkit category of malicious software attacks, but still need physical access in order to execute successfully.

2. Bootkit and Rootkit Attacks
Bootkit is considered one of the most sophisticated attacks against computer systems. It works by masking itself as the master boot record (MBR) or volume boot record (VBR) and executes its code before the OS's launch. It has the ability to paypass full disk encryption as the MBR is not encrypted (in order to be able to boot into OS). Bootkit can have direct access to the Windows® kernel, giving it unrestricted access to all Windows® functions as the OS itself.

Detecting Bootkit is very difficult because all its components reside outside of the standard file systems. More advanced Bootkits have the ability to hide the fact that the MBR itself has not been compromised by returning a legitimate copy of the MBR when an attempt to read has been made.

The Kaspersky **TDSSKiller** tool claims an ability to detect most commonly known Bootkits and Rootkits. It can be download from https://usa.kaspersky.com/downloads/TDSSKiller.

Rootkit, on the other hand, tries to gain administrative access to your computer. It is different from viruses and worms because it tries to scan the target system for vulnerabilities (like open network port, weak password, unpatched system), and the attacker can use any of these vulnerabilities to access the system stealthy. It can install keylogger or make some modifications to the OS itself without you noticing. Identifying Rootkit is very difficult as the more advanced types of Rootkits can use the polymorphism techniques to rewrite core assembly code of its internal engine, making antivirus/rootkits that uses signature-based defenses useless.

There is much software that tries to scan and find such malware but a few of them can achieve a higher success rate in removing them. In most cases removing Rootkit is only possible by wiping the disk and installing the OS again.

McAfee *Stinger* can be used to detect some kinds of rootkits and can be downloaded from http://www.mcafee.com/us/downloads/free-tools/stinger.aspx.

GMER also offers a similar detection function against major rootkits (http://www.gmer.net).

aswMBR is a Rootkit scanner that scans for MBR/VBR/SRV Rootkits (http://public.avast.com/~gmerek/aswMBR.htm).

It is always a good idea to have more than one tool capable of removing malware as not all antirootkits can detect all threats.

3. Stoned Boot Attack
Peter Kleissner developed a new Bootkit called Stoned. According to its creator, "Stoned Bootkit is a new Windows Bootkit which attacks all Windows versions from 2000 up to 7. It is loaded before Windows starts and is memory resident up to the Windows kernel. Thus Stoned gains access to the entire system. It has exciting features like integrated file system drivers, automatic Windows pwning, plugins, boot applications and more."

More information about this Bootkit and its source code can be found at http://www.stoned-vienna.com/.

4. Cold Boot Attack
This was discussed earlier in the section "Advice When Using Security Operating Systems."

5. Brute-Force Sign-In Attacks
This is a form of offline attack that attempts to discover the secret password by trying millions of different passwords until finding the correct one. In theory this kind of attack can occur against almost all encrypted data types. It can be executed against preboot authentication and against the recovery key in case of full disk encryption. Such attacks can also occur against the OS sign-in authentication. The most common type of brute-force attacks are called dictionary attacks or hybrid brute-force attacks. This attack starts with dictionary words since most people will use words that are easy to remember and not completely random.

There are many tools that can automate this attack. The most common ones are:

a. John the Ripper: http://www.openwall.com/john
b. Rainbow Crack: http://project-rainbowcrack.com
c. Cain and Able: http://www.oxid.it/cain.html

Some virus scanners may detect such tools as malware, so make sure to add the password cracking tool to the exclusion list first or disable your antivirus software when using such tools.

Additional password recovery tools can be found on the InfoSec portal: http://www.darknessgate.com/category/forensic/password-cracking/.

6. Direct Memory Access
Direct memory access (DMA) is a feature of computer systems that allows some hardware devices (either internal or external) to communicate directly with another computer system's RAM memory and transfer data

from it without processing it using the CPU. Most input/output data from computers must be processed by the CPU but some does not require processing or can be transferred to another hardware device to perform its task. It must be noted that DMA is used in such cases to save processing time, which can also increase computer throughput as the data will be transferred directly without processing through the CPU [21].

The DMA feature can be exploited to crack the encryption keys of any full disk encryption solution you are using since DMA ports do not use authentication and access control to protect the contents of RAM memory. Not all PC ports allow DMA attacks. Fortunately, USB ports do not allow such attacks. Ports vulnerable to this kind of attack include FireWire, Thunderbolt, PCMCIA, PCI, PCI-X, and PCI Express.

This kind of attack requires some technical skill by the attacker. You can perform it by connecting your device (for example, your laptop), which is running specialized software (used to find the encryption keys), to the target PC using the Thunderbolt port. After connecting your device, you will scan the target PC memory using the password cracking tool already installed to find the encryption keys.

Giving a full description on how each attack's technique works needs a book of its own, but we tried here to draw your attention to possible attacks that you may encounter even though your disk is fully encrypted.

As we noted earlier, full disk encryption attacks are similar to some attacks that can take place against the OS itself (whether it is installed on disk or bootable from a USB drive). Any of the previous attacks can be performed to crack most encryption solutions used by the user to protect data. Here is a list of possible countermeasures.

Countermeasures Against Full Disk Encryption Attacks

1. Most hardware attacks (Evil Maid, hardware keylogger) rely on the hacker's ability to physically access the target PC at least twice without the owner's knowledge. Protective measures include:
   a. Use preboot authentication by setting a password for the BOIS. With preboot authentication, users must provide some form of credential before unlocking encrypted volumes and starting Windows®. Typically they authenticate themselves using a PIN or a USB flash drive as a key [21].
   b. Try to use unified extensible firmware interface (UEFI)-certified devices. Microsoft begins to promote the usage of UEFI as a replacement for BIOS. According to Microsoft, "The UEFI is a programmable boot environment introduced as a replacement for BIOS. Like BIOS, PCs start UEFI before any

other software. It initializes devices, and UEFI then starts the operating system's bootloader. As part of its introduction into the pre–operating system environment, UEFI serves a number of purposes, but one of the key benefits is to protect newer devices against Bootkits attacks through the use of its Secure Boot feature. Recent implementations of UEFI (starting with version 2.3.1, which is in all Windows® 8–certified devices) can verify the digital signatures of the device's firmware before running it. Because only the PC's hardware manufacturer have access to the digital certificate required to create a valid firmware signature, UEFI can prevent firmware-based Bootkit. Thus, UEFI is the first link in the chain of trust" [22,23].
   c. For security-paranoid people who travel a lot and need to carry sensitive documents with them, an *Evil Maid* attack can be countered against full disk encryption by installing the boot partition and bootloader into a portable USB stick and carrying this USB with you. In this way even though an attacker gains physical access to your PC and tries to install a hacked bootloader, he/she cannot hack your encryption keys because you will still boot from your USB bootloader, which is not tempered with any malicious software. Plop Boot Manager gives you the ability to boot from a USB stick drive. You can download it from https://www.plop.at/en/bootmanagers.html.

2. Install the latest version of Windows® OS and keep it up to date. Windows® 8.1 supports four features to help prevent rootkits and bootkits from loading during the startup process; however, some of these features require Windows® 8.1 certified PCs [24] (Fig. 5.42).
   a. Secure boot: PCs that support UEFI firmware and have a TPM microchip can be configured to load only a trusted OS bootloader.
   b. Trusted boot: Windows® checks the integrity of each startup file before loading it.
   c. Early launch antimalware: Tests all drivers before they load and prevents unapproved drivers from loading.
   d. Measured boot: The PC's firmware logs the boot process. Windows® can send this log to a trusted server that can assess the PC's health.

3. Disable hyberfil.sys and Pagefile.sys: *hyberfil.sys* is responsible for the hibernate mode of Windows® OS. It usually resides at system drive (C:\ drive in our case) and it is a hidden operating system file. When hibernate mode is enabled, it is used to store the current memory state of Windows®. When selecting to hibernate your PC, Windows® will completely write RAM memory to the hard drive and then turn off the PC. The hibernate file will usually store the encryption keys of any encryption technologies you may use. If an attacker gains access to your machine while it is unattended for a short time,

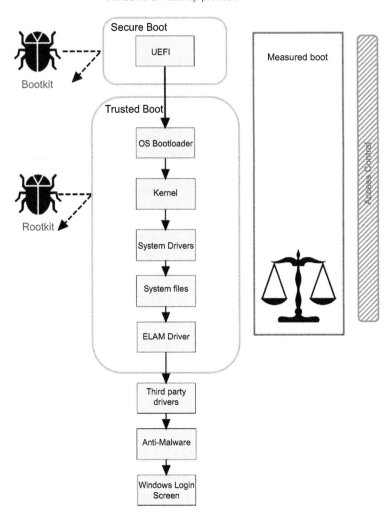

FIGURE 5.42 Windows 8.1 startup process. *Microsoft TechNet, Secure the Windows 8.1 boot process, [Online]. Available from: https://technet.micro-soft.com/en-us/windows/dn168167.aspx. Used with permission from Microsoft.*

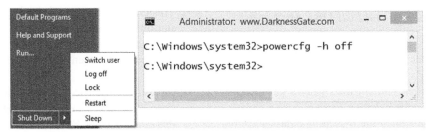

FIGURE 5.43 Disable hibernate mode under Windows® 10, 8, 7, or Vista.

he/she can easily copy this file to a USB stick and then using a specialized software he/she can extract your current encryption keys from this file. This will gain him/her full access to your machine later. For this reason it is better to remove this file completely and disable the hibernate mode on your PC. The following steps show how to disable it under a Windows® 10, 8, 7, or Vista machine:

a. Open a command prompt (using administrator privilege).

b. Type *powercfg –h off* and press Enter (see Fig. 5.43).

  You will notice that the hibernate option has been removed from the *Shut Down* menu. You can enable and activate hibernate mode again by using the command *Powercfg –h on.*

Pagefile.sys (also called virtual memory) is a file created by Windows® to compensate for the shortage capacity of RAM memory. It usually resides in *C:\ pagefile.sys* by default. Normally Windows® sets the initial virtual memory paging file equal to the amount of RAM you have installed. This feature works by allowing Windows® to use hard disk space as memory when your machine RAM begins to fill up. Parts of RAM files are moved from it into the virtual memory to free up more space. Now when the operating system needs to process any of the files that are already sent to virtual memory it cannot do this directly. It will therefore need to send additional files to virtual memory in order to free up more space in order to be able to retrieve the files it wants to process from virtual memory into RAM again. This process is called swapping or paging and it is transparent to the user.

Swapping is considered a security risk for many reasons. For example, if you have a file encrypted or stored inside an encrypted container, when you want to read this file first you need to decrypt it. This decrypted file may still exist in the pagefile long after the user logs off. For this reason it is better to disable paging in Windows® for maximum protection.

It is better to have a PC with more than 4 GB of RAM before disabling paging. Computers with lower RAM memory may become unstable after turning off the paging feature.

To disable paging on a computer running Windows® 8.1 (also applies to Windows® 7) follow these steps:

a. *Control Panel≫System≫Advanced system settings≫Advanced* tab≫from the *Performance* section and choose *Settings…≫Advanced* tab≫Virtual memory section.

b. Click *Change…* (see Fig. 5.44).

From here you can select the drive you want to disable paging file on it by checking the option *No paging file* and then clicking *Set*.

Your page file should be turned off now and the file named Pagefile.sys should be automatically deleted.

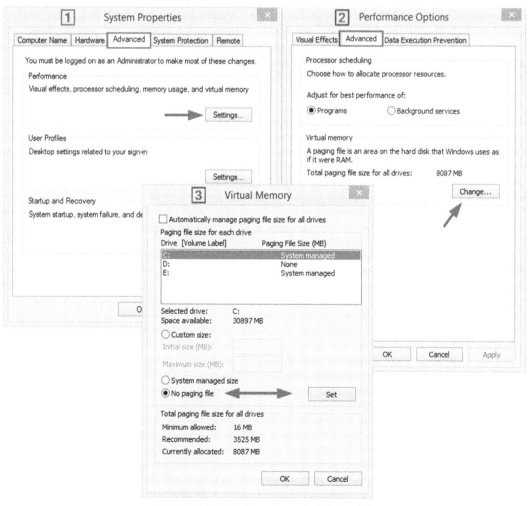

FIGURE 5.44   Disable paging under Windows® 8.

4. DMA exploits uses of DMA ports on your PC to have direct access to computer physical memory. To mitigate such attacks you can:

a. Disable DMA ports within BIOS or UEFI.

b. Implement physical security measures through preventing physical connections to such ports within your organization without prior permission.

c. Install the latest version of Windows® (+8.1) and keep it up to date. Starting from Windows® version 8.1, Windows® begins to reject access to DMA access memory by external devices until after the Windows® OS is in control to parse DMA requests.

5. Mitigations against cold boot attacks: Many researches show that using RAM of type DDR3 and beyond is far more secure than the previous versions (we covered this in the section, "*Advice When Using Security Operating Systems*").

Technical tip: If you do not know the type of RAM memory already installed on your PC, you can download a free system information tool called CPU-Z, which is a portable application, from http://www.cpuid.com/softwares/cpu-z.html. Execute the software and go to the memory tab to see your RAM type (see Fig. 5.45).

6. Do not store sensitive data on an encrypted system volume. If you must store such files on this volume, encrypt it using another passphrase that is different from the volume password to achieve the maximum level of security (if your PC has DDR3 RAM or beyond no need to perform this check, but it is still a good practice to stay near your PC for 3 min after turning it off to make sure that RAM is 100% cleared). The following warning is quoted from *VeraCrypt* documentation on this issue:

To summarize, VeraCrypt cannot and does not ensure that RAM contains no sensitive data (eg passwords, master keys, or decrypted data). Therefore, after each session in which you work with a VeraCrypt volume or in which an encrypted operating system is running, you must shut down (or, if the hibernation file is encrypted, hibernate) the computer and then leave it powered off for at least several minutes (the longer, the better) before turning it on again. This is required to clear the RAM [25].

7. It is always a good practice to provide multilevel authentication when encrypting your disk drive by using a PIN or keyfile stored in an external USB stick in addition to providing an encryption key (or TPM key if you are encrypting your files using BitLocker) before launching Windows®.

8. Attacks using brute-force techniques can be mitigated by using long random and complex passwords. In addition most encryption solutions offer a limited number of error password trials before blocking your system for a

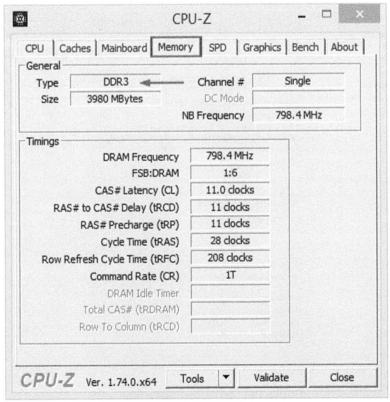

FIGURE 5.45 Knowing various information about your system parts using the CPU-Z tool.

specific period of time. Such attacks can also be mitigated using two-factor authentication.

9. Use long passwords to protect your encrypted volumes and OS; use at least 20 characters containing random letters, numbers, and symbols. Use automatic password generations tools to automate password creation, making it random and very difficult to crack. We will cover how to create random secure passwords in a coming section.

ANONYMIZE YOUR LOCATION ONLINE

Data encryption and data hiding techniques help you secure your transmitted data, but do not conceal the identity of the person sending the communication over. In some cases hiding your identity online is as important as hiding your transmitted data. Fortunately, with cryptographic anonymity tools, an eavesdropper may not even know where to find your communications in order to snoop it.

Security guru *Bruce Schneier* talks about the importance of anonymizing your online traffic to better secure yourself online. He advises users to use TOR to hide their identity online. In his article, "How to Remain Secure Against the NSA" [26], *Bruce* talks about how the NSA snoops on people on a worldwide basis by analyzing network traffic:

The primary way the NSA eavesdrops on Internet communications is in the network. That's where their capabilities best scale. They have invested in enormous programs to automatically collect and analyze network traffic. Anything that requires them to attack individual endpoint computers is significantly more costly and risky for them, and they will do those things carefully and sparingly.

Bruce assures the importance of using robust encryption anonymity tools by saying, "The less obvious you are, the safer you are."

There are different ways to obscure your identity online; in this section we will list most secure techniques and tools to anonymize and conceal your online traffic.

Using the TOR Browser

TOR is a system designed for true online anonymity. The software was originally named *The Onion Router* and was developed in the mid-1990s by US Naval Research Laboratory employees to protect US intelligence communications online. After many years and different development stages TOR become a free anonymizing tool used worldwide by many different user groups. At the time of writing this book, TOR has more than 2,000,000 users [27].

TOR is basically composed of two parts:

1. The software that runs the TOR client on our PC.
2. A network of volunteer computers that direct your traffic, anonymously through the Internet.

Onion routing is implemented by encrypting the *application layer* of the protocol stack. TOR encrypts both data and destination IP addresses before sending them through a virtual circuit that consists of many nodes (no less than three nodes in any given time). Each node decrypts part of the data, to reveal only the next node in the circuit in order to direct the remaining encrypted data to it. The next node performs the same function until the message reaches the final node, which is also named exit relay. The exit relay will decrypt the data without revealing the source IP address then sends it to its final destination (see Fig. 5.46).

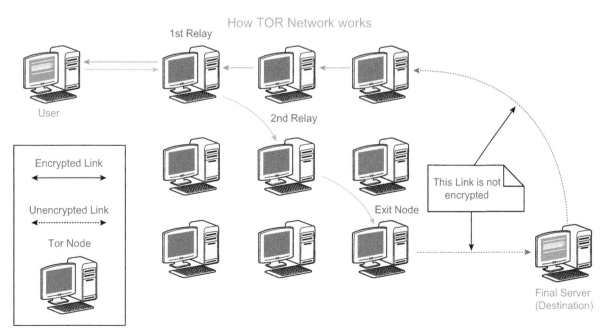

FIGURE 5.46 How traffic goes through a TOR network.

The term node generally refers to a computer or a server that operates as part of the TOR network. Sometimes people name it *relay* or *router* instead of *node* but all three names are interchangeable.

When using TOR your IP address will become hidden and your connection will seem to originate from the TOR exit relay. The number of TOR relays are increasing steadily. At the time of writing this book, there are about 7000 relays operated by individuals and organizations worldwide [28]. As the number of relays increase, TOR becomes faster and more secure.

There are three kinds of TOR relays that can be operated by any user who wishes to become part of TOR network:

1. Middle relays
2. Exit relays
3. Bridges

TOR assures that your Internet traffic will run through at least three relays before reaching its final destination. The first two relays are the middle relays. They receive traffic and forward it to other relays, middle relays, in their turn, and show their presence to the rest of TOR network so TOR users can connect to them. Individual volunteers usually run this kind of relay because they are not liable for any illegal activities that may pass through them as the traffic between middle relays is internally within the TOR network. Keep in mind that the middle relay's IP address will not show to the outside TOR network publicly.

An exit relay is the final node before your data leaves the TOR network for its final destination. Individuals are encouraged not to run an exit relay at home or use a home Internet connection. Exit relay is the one where its IP address will appear as the source IP address publicly. If law enforcement becomes interested in the traffic passing through your exit relay, it's possible that officers will seize your computer and you can get into big trouble.

The third kind of TOR relays are bridges. These relays are not publicly listed as part of the TOR network. It is used as a censorship circumvention in countries where the TOR's public IP address is regularly blocked, such as China, Iran, and Syria. A bridge is generally safe to run in your home, in conjunction with other services, or on a computer with your personal files [29].

As we saw previously, by using TOR, it becomes almost impossible to trace a user's online activity, whether it is website visits, online transactions, or instant messaging. The main users of the TOR project are:

1. Normal Internet users who seeks privacy online
2. Journalists and human rights activists
3. Law enforcement officers, intelligence agencies, and militaries

4. Some business organizations who seek maximum privacy for their online communications
5. IT professionals and security researchers

Unfortunately, TOR is also used by criminals and terrorist organizations to access the dark web and to hide and anonymize their online communications. We will briefly discuss the dark web in the next section.

TOR Browser

Now, after we have defined the TOR network and shown you how it works to anonymize its traffic, we need to tell you how to use it to anonymize your online activities. Using TOR network is very simple. All you need to do is download the TOR browser, which includes everything you need to access and use the TOR network.

The TOR browser is a hardened, security-focused version of Firefox that pushes all of your Web traffic through TOR's anonymizing network. It supports all major OSs (Windows®, Linux, and Mac), can be used without installation, and can run from within a USB stick. You can download it from https://www.torproject.org/projects/torbrowser.html.en.

After the download completes, extract the file contents to a specific folder or directly into your USB drive. Launch the TOR browser by clicking on the *Start TOR Browser* icon. Once TOR is ready, the TOR browser will automatically open (see Fig. 5.47). Only web pages visited through the TOR browser will be sent via TOR. Other web browsers such as Internet Explorer™ and Opera™ are not affected.

After finishing with using the TOR browser make sure to close it properly by clicking the (✗) in the top right corner. TOR is preconfigured to forget and delete all your browsing history upon closing.

What Is Dark Web?

We said previously that TOR is sometimes used by criminals to access the dark web, so what does this means? Dark web is a set of websites that are publicly available, but hide their identity and the servers that run them using anonymous networks like TOR and I2P. Knowing who is responsible for such websites is very difficult [30].

To visit a website on the dark web you need first to connect to it through the same anonymous network it uses. For example, a website that is anonymous using TOR can only be accessed by users who use the TOR network (through the TOR browser). Websites on the dark web will not be listed on a search engine. You need to type the website URL address directly in order to access it. These sites do not utilize the common website address extensions like .com or .org. Instead, they use the Onion web address extension (for TOR-based websites) and.i2p for I2P anonymizing networks.

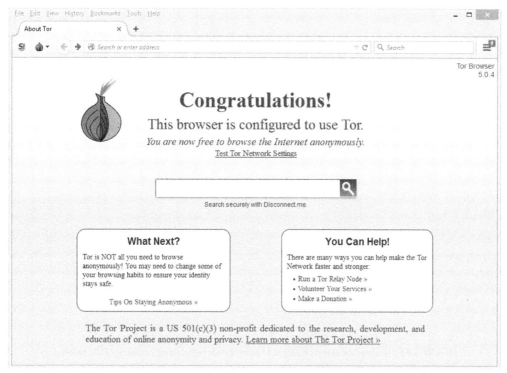

FIGURE 5.47 Launching the TOR browser to anonymize your location online.

Websites that run along the dark web generally deal will illegal content, like promoting drugs, weapons, false passports, and the like, although there are a few innocent websites that are anonymous in this mode to avoid security review and monitoring imposed by some third-world nations. Recent research estimates the number of active websites in the dark web can be between 30,000 and 40,000 [31].

If you want to discover the dark web, you can launch your *TOR Browser* and type the following URL: http://grams7enu-fi7jmdl.onion. This will open the Grams search engine, which specializes in searching inside the dark web (see Fig. 5.48).

Some websites offer search facilities to search inside the dark web contents without using the TOR browser (you still need to use the TOR browser bundle to access many of these hidden services). Examples of such websites include:

1. Onion Link | http://onion.link
2. Ahmia | https://ahmia.fi

Dark web is beyond the scope of this book, although it is worth mentioning in order to introduce users who do not know about the existence of such a cyberspace on the Internet. In addition, dark web is the **hidden** Internet and a book about data hiding cannot ignore it!

Warnings When Using the TOR Network

- TOR alone will not protect you when you are exchanging important data online. You need to encrypt your data first

before sending it through the TOR network. Otherwise an attacker can intercept your communication on TOR exit relays (the link between TOR exit relays and final destination is not encrypted) (see Fig. 5.46).
- If you are using the TOR network to anonymize your traffic, your ISP can still detect you are using the TOR network, and hiding this fact is very difficult and is still undergoing much research. However, you can still try to conceal your TOR to a great level using the following techniques:
  - **Use TOR bridges**: Bridges are the entry points to the TOR network. By connecting to nonpublicity bridges you can almost hide the fact you are using TOR and avoid any censorship against using TOR if imposed by your ISP, but remember this does not guarantee the fact that you are not using TOR. To use a bridge follow these steps:
    - Go to https://bridges.torproject.org/bridges, where you will see a list of three bridges. Enter the captcha first to access the secure area (see Fig. 5.49).
    - To enter bridges into the TOR browser, launch TOR and before TOR gets connected, click *Open Settings* (see Fig. 5.50).
    - A TOR network settings window appears; click *Configure*.
    - TOR asks you whether your ISP is blocking or otherwise censor connections to the TOR network; select *YES* (see Fig. 5.51) and click *Next* to continue.

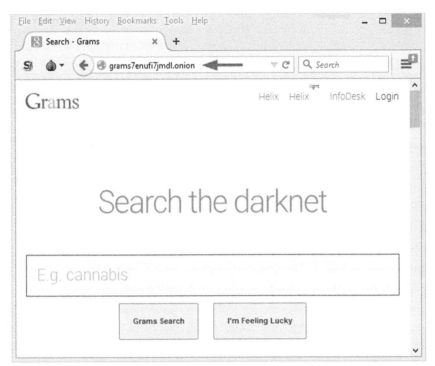

FIGURE 5.48 Access Grams search engine to browse dark web contents using the TOR browser.

FIGURE 5.49 TOR bridges.

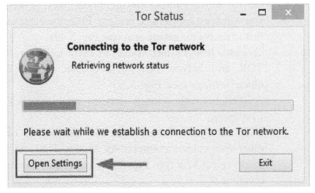

FIGURE 5.50 Access TOR browser settings to access TOR network settings.

- In next wizard window, select the option *Enter custom bridges*, copy the bridges you have from step 1 (see Fig. 5.49), and paste it in the text box (see Fig. 5.52).
- The next wizard asks you if this computer needs a proxy to access the Internet. In our case we do not need one (and this will be in most cases), so click *NO* and click *Connect* (see Fig. 5.53). In case you sit behind a proxy server, select the checkbox *YES*, enter your proxy settings, and finally click *Connect*.
- If everything goes well, the TOR browser will open using your customized bridges.

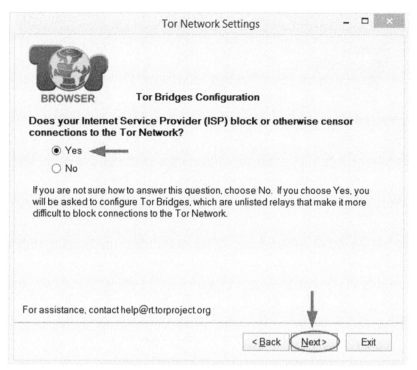

FIGURE 5.51 TOR Bridge configuration wizard.

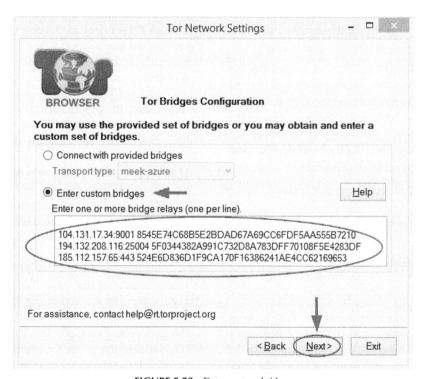

FIGURE 5.52 Enter custom bridges.

TOR bridges are a good way to prevent your ISP from knowing that you are connecting to TOR; however, this method may not always work, as some ISPs may use a deep packet inspection (DPI) technique to deeply analyze Internet traffic to examine whether it contains TOR traffic and try to block it. Some controlled ISPs may carry out such an inspection; in fact, China and Iran have repeatedly conducted such actions to block TOR in the past.

A DPI is a form of computer network packet filtering that examines the data and header part of a packet as it passes through an inspection point (router, proxy server). The filter searches for specific criteria or certain protocols, which

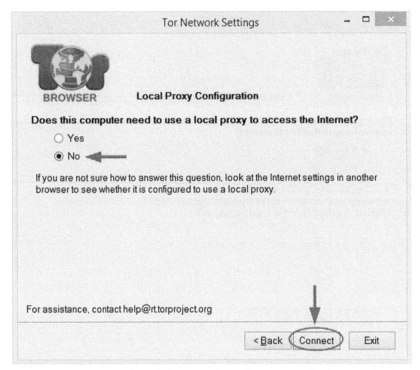

FIGURE 5.53 Final wizard window before connecting to the TOR network using customized bridges.

is noncompliant, in order to decide whether the packet can pass or should be routed to another destination [32].

1. **Using Pluggable Transport**: To work around the DPI censorship technique, TOR introduced pluggable transports, which work by transforming the TOR traffic flow between the client and the bridge. This way, censors that monitor traffic between the client and the bridge will see innocently camouflaged-looking transported packages instead of the real TOR traffic [33].

TOR has many pluggable transports; the most common ones are:

- Obts4
- Flashproxy
- Format-transforming encryption
- ScrambleSuit
- Meek

To use a pluggable transport launch the TOR browser, click *More settings ≫ Configure ≫ Yes*. You will then see the message, *Does your Internet Service Provider (ISP) block or otherwise censor connections to the Tor Network*? Select the option *Connect with provided bridges*.

From the *Transport type* drop-down menu, select your preferred pluggable transport, then click *Next*. The final wizard window will ask, Does this computer need to use a local proxy to access the Internet? Select *No* and click *Connect*. If you are sitting behind a proxy, select *Yes* and enter the proxy details and finally click *Connect* (see Fig. 5.54).

2. **Using VPN services**, in this case we connect to our VPN service and then connect to the TOR network using the anonymizing techniques just mentioned (for additional security) to hide the presence of the TOR browser connection to the TOR network.
3. **Avoid installing unsecure plug-ins to your TOR browser**. Applications such as Flash and QuickTime have a tendency to compromise your anonymity by leaving a trace of your actual non-TOR IP address. You should not use your TOR browser as if you are using an ordinary Firefox browser by installing and activating different add-ons and themes. If you need to view a website with flash contents, view it using your regular browser and leave TOR for hiding your important communications.
4. You can increase the level of privacy and avoid sophisticated attacks against your TOR browser by **modifying the security settings of the TOR browser**. You can access these settings from the TOR onion icon beside the address bar (see Fig. 5.55). The default low setting is fine for everyday privacy protection; however, you can increase it to achieve the maximum protection possible online (setting it too high may make some websites display incorrectly).
5. **Avoid man-in-the-middle attacks**. A man-in-the-middle attack (Fig. 5.56) is a form of active eavesdropping in which the attacker makes independent connections with the victims and relays messages between them, making them believe that they are talking directly to each other

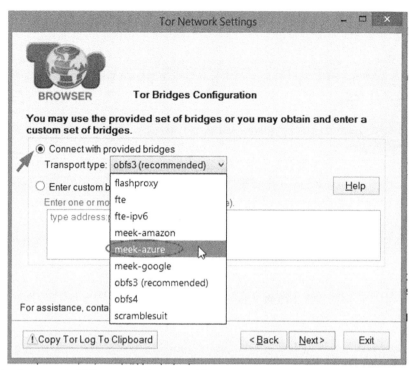

FIGURE 5.54 Connect to the TOR network using a pluggable transport to prevent the ISP from knowing you are using TOR.

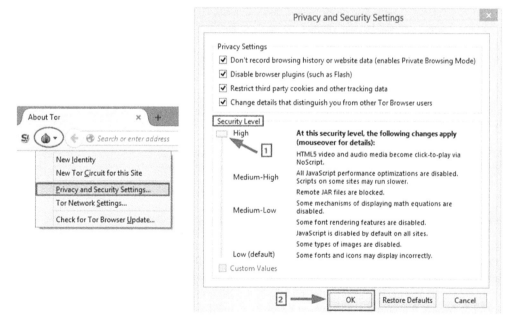

FIGURE 5.55 Update privacy and security level in the TOR browser to achieve the maximum security possible.

over a private connection, when in fact the entire conversation is controlled by the attacker [34].

The main defense against man-in-the-middle attacks is by using end-to-end encryption. TOR uses HTTPS *Everywhere*, a Firefox extension that forces the use of HTTPS encryption with major websites that support it. However, you should still watch the browser URL bar to ensure that the website to which you provided sensitive information has https://in the URL.

The TOR browser, just like any Internet browser, uses certificates to verify the identity of the server when communicating over HTTPS. These certificates are verified by reputable third-party authority companies such as VeriSign™. If your

MITM can happen at TOR exit relay
User
Server
Original Connection
Man-In-Middle-Attack
Attacker

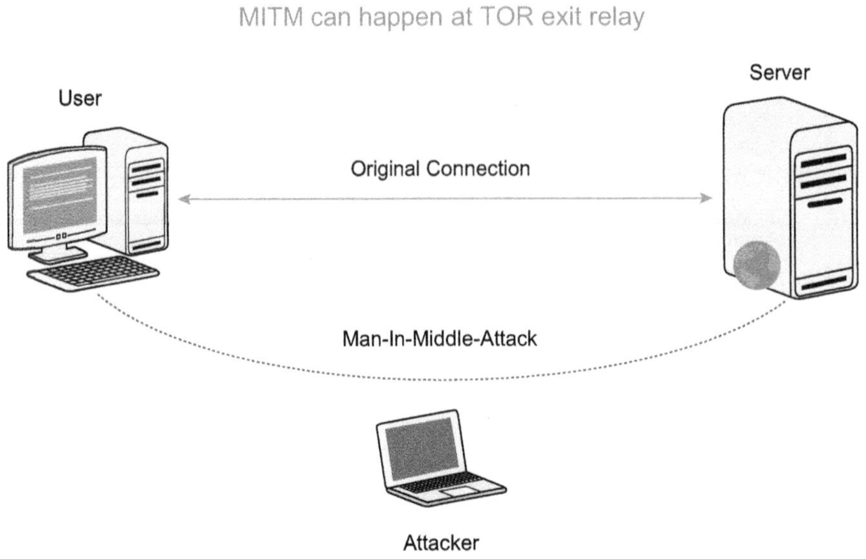

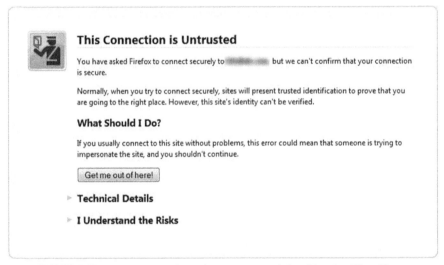

FIGURE 5.56 Man-in-the-middle attack.

This Connection is Untrusted
You have asked Firefox to connect securely to but we can't confirm that your connection is secure.
Normally, when you try to connect securely, sites will present trusted identification to prove that you are going to the right place. However, this site's identity can't be verified.
What Should I Do?
If you usually connect to this site without problems, this error could mean that someone is trying to impersonate the site, and you shouldn't continue.
Get me out of here!
Technical Details
I Understand the Risks

FIGURE 5.57 Error message when trying to access a website with an invalid certificate.

browser does not recognize the authority of any certificate sent from a particular server, it will display a warning message indicating that this certificate is not trusted (see Fig. 5.57).

If you get a security exception message such as the one in Fig. 5.57 you might be the victim of a man-in-the-middle attack and should not bypass the warning unless you have another trusted way of checking the certificate's fingerprint with the people running the service.

6. **Do not open documents downloaded through TOR while you are online**. The TOR browser will launch an alarm when you try to open documents that are handled by outside applications. For example, if you download a PDF file and then open it directly, you may risk your system accessing sources outside the TOR network through the application that opens it (in this case, Adobe® Acrobat), which will reveal your true IP address. This is the most serious warning that may reveal your identity while using TOR.

TOR is a continuously developing project, and just like all Internet projects, it has weaknesses and strengths. Bear in mind that, when using an anonymizing tool, you need to educate yourself about possible online dangers and how to mitigate them. You should always return to the *TOR project website* and check the latest warnings and any new features deployed.

Virtual Private Networks

A VPN is a network that can use the Internet to provide secure connections between one or more devices for data exchange (Fig. 5.58). A VPN can open a secure tunnel between different devices and the data that passes through

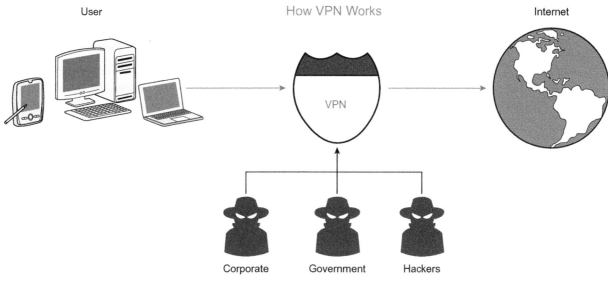

FIGURE 5.58 How VPN works.

the tunnel can be encrypted. Most often, VPNs are used to connect a company's main office with its satellite offices or its field agents. In some cases, people choose to connect their personal devices to a VPN service provider to secure their own connections (with the same kind of tunneling and encryption) to the general Internet, saving their banking details, credit card numbers, passwords, and other sensitive data from being intercepted. VPN also affords the user an anonymous IP address, making them appear as if in another location so they can avoid censorships, share files with other people anonymously, and more.

There are many companies that offer VPN services; most of them offer paid service, but you can still find free VPN providers, although they may not be as reliable as the paid ones.

I'm not going to describe how VPN infrastructure works in detail, since this section is to guide you through how to select the best VPN company for better anonymity. The following are some VPN provider criteria to help you select the best one:

1. The provider should operate from outside the United States, United Kingdom, Australia, Canada, and New Zealand jurisdictions. These countries, also known as the five eyes countries, form an intelligence alliance to intercept online traffic, so using VPN servers based in these countries may not be a secure option if you want to use your VPN for mission-critical tasks.

   This list of states involved in mass surveillance programs is noninclusive; countries like Russia, China, Iran, and all more restrictive countries (like the Arab states) also maintain their own surveillance programs. The best nation for respecting user privacy at the present is Switzerland. Other nations who respect user privacy and have formulated special laws for this issue are Iceland, Norway, and Netherlands; we encourage Internet users who seek

maximum privacy to utilize services provided by companies located in these nations.

2. Supports OpenVPN software, an open-source software, so we can make sure no backdoor existed in the VPN client software.
3. Separates file sharing from web browsing, meaning each one has its own server.
4. Accepts Bitcoin, cash through intermediary agents, cash cards, and other anonymous methods of payment without revealing your true identity.
5. Requires little personal information to set up your account; for example, username and a password is enough to set up a VPN account.
6. Does not store your connection log.. Some providers keep a info logs about your VPN usage (IP address you log from and connection length) for a week or 10 days, but a VPN with no log is still the most secure option.
7. Finally, and most importantly, read the *terms of service* and *privacy policy* of the VPN provider very carefully, and make sure you understand the amount of data each provider stores about your connection and personal details required. If you suspect that the information is biased in any way do not register with this provider. It is also useful to read user reviews about the VPN provider where you plan to register; use your preferred search engine for this task.

We select a free VPN provider to demonstrate how we can connect and use such services (although each provider may have its own setup instructions usually detailed on its website).

VPNBook is a free VPN service that can be used to unblock any website online. It uses strong encryption AES-256 to connect to VPN servers; *VPNBook* sets no bandwidth limit. Another bonus is that it does not store any of your Internet browsing traffic. All that is logged is your IP address and time the connection was live. As part of its housekeeping, connection logs are automatically removed every week. Not surprisingly, *VPNBook* puts its free euro VPN servers in countries where there are no government laws that require the mandatory data retention and snooping on users. Finally, *VPNBook* uses the OpenVPN software to connect and utilizes this service for its own use.

To set up VPNBook on Windows® 7:

1. Download OpenVPN Windows Client from the following link: http://openvpn.net/index.php/opensource/downloads.html (there are two versions for 32 and 64 bit).
2. Install and launch the OpenVPN client.

3. Download one of the VPNBook OpenVPN certificate bundles from here: https://www.vpnbook.com/(OpenVPN tab) (see Fig. 5.59).
4. Unzip the bundle and copy OpenVPN profiles to C:\ Program Files\OpenVPN\config (see Fig. 5.60).
5. Right-click the OpenVPN client icon and select one of its profiles. Next, click *Connect* (see Fig. 5.61).
6. OpenVPN will prompt you for a username and password. Enter the username/password from http://vpnbook.com/freevpn (see Fig. 5.59 for the password/username location).

If everything goes well, you should connect to the selected VPN server of your choice. You can now safely say that all your online communications will be directed through an encrypted tunnel. *VPNBook* changes its

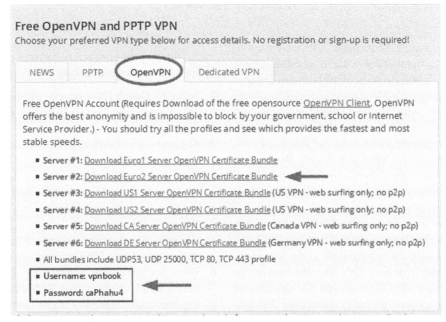

FIGURE 5.59 Download one of the VPNBook OpenVPN certificates bundles.

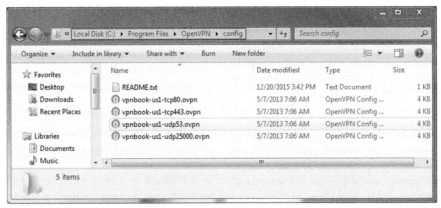

FIGURE 5.60 Copy OpenVPN profiles to C:\Program Files\OpenVPN\config.

password once every week, so you are advised to visit its website regularly to update your password.

SSH Tunneling

Both SSH and VPN do similar work in encrypting your online traffic, however, they are different in the way they implement this on your PC.

VPN works on the Transport layer of the OSI model while SSH works on the application layer, therefore, when using VPN on your machine all your Internet traffic for all applications will be directed through the VPN tunnel. In SSH the situation is slightly different. When using SSH you need to make a direct connection with the SSH server, then you need to manually configure the applications (email

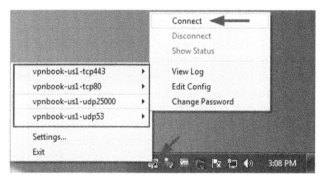

FIGURE 5.61 Connect using one of the profiles available within each bundle.

client, web browser, chat program, etc.) in order to route their much needed traffic through an SSH connection.

VPN is considered easy to use by the average computer users and offers a good amount of security in addition to its ability to disguise traffic, unlike SSH, which is difficult to configure by the average computer user and has fewer providers than VPN. Also, the fact that SSH doesn't encrypt all Internet traffic makes it favorable in some cases when you need to use two different connections at the same time (eg, encrypt your web browsing while keeping your email client to use the available Internet connection without encryption). We suggest using VPN over SSH for most of your tunnel encryption needs.

PuTTY is a famous SSH client, which is an open-source software developed for Windows® OS. You can download it from www.chiark.greenend.org.uk/~sgtatham/putty if you wish to use the SSH secure connection. Unfortunately, you still need to have a free SSH account in order to encrypt your connection.

Using Proxy Server

A proxy server is a computer that functions as an intermediary between your web browser and the Internet (Fig. 5.62). A web proxy is a kind of proxy that provides a quick way to change your IP address when surfing the Internet thus helping you avoid censorship restrictions in countries that restrict access to some Internet resources for different

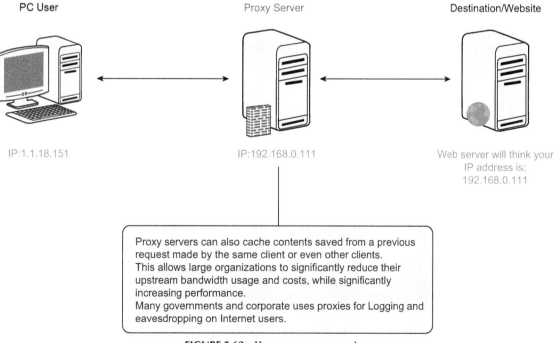

FIGURE 5.62 How a proxy server works.

reasons. When using a web proxy server the IP of this proxy will not appear to the public as your real IP address, thus helping you anonymize your traffic. There are many types of proxy servers, but what we care about here are the web proxy types that help us anonymize and/or encrypt our traffic. The best web proxies are the ones that offer SSL to encrypt the connection between the user and the proxy.

Web Proxy Types

1. Accessible through a web interface, you enter to the proxy website, enter the website you want to visit anonymously in the form, and click Submit. The proxy will fetch the page for you. This kind of proxy may not work on all websites because of modern design techniques employed by many websites, so it is better to use the other types if you encounter many broken links and empty pages. Examples of such a proxy are https://hide. me/en/proxy and http://free-proxy-list.net/web-proxy. html.
2. HTTP proxies require a piece of software to run on your machine in order to change your web browser settings (it can come in the form of a browser extension). This kind of proxy can only be used to access web contents. *Ultrasurf* is an example of this type.
3. SOCKS proxy also may require a piece of software to run on your machine or can be entered directly into the application settings, whereas the HTTP proxy can only be used for surfing. You can use a SOCKS proxy to send email, transfer files, chat online, play games, as well as surf websites. https://www.socks-proxy.net/ has a list of SOCKS proxies that is updated daily.

Security Risks Associated With Proxy Servers

- When using a proxy server, all your PC traffic will pass through this proxy. Bear in mind that if you are transmitting important data such as passwords or credit card details, you may impose security risk, as your proxy server can intercept all communications between your PC and the Internet.
- Most free proxy servers have annoying ads on the web pages you are viewing. Although this might sound harmless at first, these ads can carry viruses and Trojans within them. These malwares can be easily downloaded to your machine as a result of a single click on one of these ads, causing real damage to your files and stored data.
- Some proxy servers are controlled by government intelligence; for example, many third world countries use proxies to allow their users' access to government censored websites such as Facebook™, in order to monitor their online activities and then arrest them if necessary.

- A proxy server is usually slower than VPN or the standard Internet, as thousands of users may be using it simultaneously.

I do not recommend using a proxy server unless you trust the provider of that service and it is located outside the countries that collect information about their users. Make sure that the proxy used offers a secure connection between your PC and the proxy. You should also read carefully the privacy agreement and terms of service before using such services to assure that the proxy provider will not keep records of your online activities.

Anonymous Search Engine

Most Internet users (or even all) use search engines like Google™ and Yahoo™ to search the Internet. Search engines have the ability to track user's search activities with ease. Personal information can be revealed through searches by the user's computer, account, and certainly the IP addresses associated with the search terms used. Search engine providers can store large amounts of information about user preferences, starting with health concerns to sexual orientation or political interest. The search engine can also retain other information such as user location and time spent using the search engine. This can be very dangerous information if fell into the wrong hands. It can lead to a serious breach of privacy for companies and individuals around the world. In order to counter such risks we can use anonymous and secure search engines that do not keep any information about their users.

Google™ is still considered the best search engine in the market because of its advanced search algorithm features that are developed continuously to increase its efficiency and accuracy. Google™ servers are mainly based in the United States and therefore follow US jurisdiction and regulations, which a user cannot rely on to keep their private data secure from mass surveillance programs and corporate advertisement campaigns that seek to buy such data to target search engine users with specific ads. Currently Google™ holds first position in the market share of search engine users despite privacy concerns. In the following section we will introduce some secure search engines that can be used to fetch Google™ results and present it to the end user anonymously without keeping any private data about that user.

StartPage

StartPage introduces itself as *the world's most private search engine*. This search engine intelligently connects the user securely to its portal through SSL, allowing him/her to search as if he/she is using Google™. StartPage will take user queries and fetch the results back from Google™ and present it to the user. This process is transparent and fast.

FIGURE 5.63 StartPage proxy service allows you to get through censorship and anonymize your online traffic.

StartPage meets its promise by keeping the identity of the user anonymous; however, it takes matters further by not keeping any records of:

- Your IP address
- Visit log
- Session cookies, which your browser usually leaves in order to track your online movements.

StartPage also offers a unique service, which is allowing the user to access any website through the built-in proxy server associated with it. For example, if the TOR website is forbidden in your country, you can search for it using Start-Page and then click the *Proxy* link in order to direct your connection through the StartPage web proxy (see Fig. 5.63). This feature helps you anonymize your cyber activities and prevents websites from planting any cookies on your browser because they can only see the StartPage IP address, not yours.

Note: The StartPage proxy service will disable JavaScript and filling text forms for security reasons, so some websites may not view correctly.

The *StartPage* website is found at http://startpage.com/. You need to conduct a top-secret Internet search to test it. We recommend using the StartPage search engine from within the TOR browser for better results.

DUCKDUCKGO

This is another search engine that stores no information about its users (does not store the IP address, log visits, or plant cookies in your browser); however, this engine will not fetch its results from Google because it has his own searching algorithms. You can try it here: http://duckduckgo.com.

DISCONNECT SEARCH

DISCONNECT allows you to select your preferred search engine provider allowing the necessary private browsing you are after. Paid VPN services are provided with this search engine. Keep in mind to review our previous criteria when selecting the best secure VPN provider. DISCONNECT is available from https://search.disconnect.me/.

Web Browser Privacy Add-Ons

There are large numbers of security and privacy extensions that help us add an additional layer of security when we are surfing online. Such extensions are mainly targeted for Mozilla Firefox® and Google™ Chrome. It provides you with protection of your connection and avoids website tracking. You will find a list of the most reputable privacy extensions later, which you can use to harden your browser. Let us first examine what information about our machines our browser would reveal when we are using the default configuration.

Check Browser Fingerprint

Browser fingerprint shows you the amount of detail your browser reveals to the public about your machine. At the beginning of the Internet era, the IP address and the HTTP cookies were the only reliable digital fingerprints that affected the online privacy and web browser identity. Soon after, the privacy invaders began looking for ways to increase user-tracking reliability to identify users from the general flow. They started to collect more and more user-sensitive information. You will find online services that give you a full report about your web browser digital fingerprint. Use this report to compare your browser privacy before and after installing the suggested Firefox browser add-on.

BrowserLeaks.com (https://www.browserleaks.com)

Here you will find the gallery of web browser security testing tools that tell you what exactly personal identifiable data may be leaked without any permissions when you surf the Internet (see Fig. 5.64).

FIGURE 5.64 BrowserLeaks.com offers different security testing tools to access your web browser digital fingerprint.

Panopticlick (https://panopticlick.eff.org)

Panopticlick is a research project created by the Electronic Frontier Foundation (https://www.eff.org/) designed to better uncover the tools and techniques of online trackers and test the efficacy of privacy add-ons (see Fig. 5.65).

In the next section we will show you how to modify your browser fingerprint to mislead tracking techniques used by many websites and advertisers.

Mozilla Firefox Privacy Add-Ons

In this section we will only talk about the Mozilla Firefox® browser. You may, of course, argue that there are other browsers in the market such as Internet Explorer™, Opera™, and Google™ Chrome to name a few, but Firefox® is considered the only true open source browser among the most commonly used web browsers on the Internet. Remember, always try to use open source programs since it is not only better and safer but most certainly more secure than standard closed source software.

In this section we will talk about the most famous security and privacy add-ons used globally for Firefox® browser. The list of add-ons has been compiled following strict selection criteria (the developer or organization who creates the extension, its license type, number of downloads, number of active users, user feedback, and finally its usability to better protect users online).

HTTPS Everywhere

According to its creator, "HTTPS Everywhere extension used in a Firefox®, Chrome, and Opera browsers that encrypt your communications with many major websites, making your browsing more secure."

This extension is produced as a collaboration between the TOR Project and the Electronic Frontier Foundation. Many sites on the web offer limited support for encryption over HTTPS, but make it difficult to use. For instance, they may retreat to using unencrypted HTTP, or fill encrypted pages with links that go back to some unencrypted site previously visited. The HTTPS Everywhere extension fixes these problems by using clever technology to rewrite requests to these sites to HTTPS. It can do its job without any user intervention.

HTTP Everywhere can be downloaded from https://www.eff.org/https-everywhere.

Disconnect

Disconnect is an add-on that blocks web trackers from gathering your personal information. It claims its ability to load pages 27% faster in addition to stopping tracking that comes from more than 2000 third-party sites.

You can download it from https://addons.mozilla.org/en-US/firefox/addon/disconnect/.

Privacy Badger

This is an ad blocker extension created by EFF. According to its creator, "Privacy Badger is a browser add-on that stops advertisers and other third-party trackers from secretly tracking where you go and what pages you look at on the web. If were a victim of cyber tracking by an advertiser across multiple websites without your permission, Privacy Badger automatically blocks that advertiser from loading any more content in your local browser. To the advertiser, it's like you suddenly disappeared" (see Fig. 5.66).

You can download this extension from https://www.eff.org/privacybadger.

Self-Destructing Cookies

According to its creator, "Self-Destructing Cookies automatically removes cookies when they are no longer used by open browser tabs. With the cookies, lingering sessions, as well as information used to spy on you, will be expunged. Websites will only be permitted to identify you while you actually use them and cannot stalk you across the entire web. This is the

FIGURE 5.65   Panopticlick tracking sample test report (this is a brief view; click Show full results for fingerprinting for a full report).

closest you will get to cookieless browsing without breaking every second site or tedious micromanaging."

This add-on can be downloaded from https://addons. mozilla.org/en-US/firefox/addon/self-destructing-cookies/.

uBlock Origin

This is a lightweight and efficient blocker, which is certainly easy on memory and CPU footprint. The extension has no monetization strategy and most importantly development is volunteered. It supports the following browsers: Firefox®, Safari®, Opera®, and Chromium®.

This add-on can be downloaded from https://addons. mozilla.org/en-US/firefox/addon/ublock-origin/. It has very good user review and stood at more than 600,000 downloads at the time of writing.

Random Agent Spoofer

Random Agent Spoofer (Fig. 5.67) is a privacy enhancing Firefox® add-on. It hides your browser's real profile by rotating it (changing it many times) at any user-defined time interval, and includes many extra privacy-enhancing options.

Be careful when selecting the *Random* option; some websites may be viewed incorrectly because the add-on may change your browser profile to *Mobile*. It might be better in this case to select the *Random (Desktop)* option, which can avoid such problems.

This add-on can be downloaded from https://addons. mozilla.org/en-US/firefox/addon/random-agent-spoofer/.

Secure Anonymous File Sharing

There are numerous sites that offer file sharing capabilities, however, none of them offer the capability to fully anonymize sending or receiving parties. Experienced users can configure their machine and online sharing account to be more anonymous, however, they cannot conceal the presence of such connection from a third-party observer (at least for the sharing service provider). In the following section, we will talk about OnionShare, which depends on the TOR network to perform its job. By using the TOR service to share your files, you can upload any file size and share it with another user without leaving any traces at all.

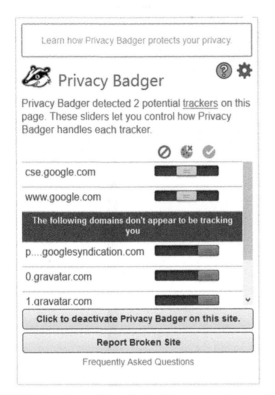

FIGURE 5.66 Privacy Badger blocks different types of web tracking.

OnionShare

According to its creators, "OnionShare lets you share files securely and anonymously of any size. It works by starting a web server, making it accessible as a TOR hidden service, and generating an unguessable URL to access and download the files. It doesn't require setting up a server on the internet somewhere or using a third party file sharing service. You host the file on your own computer and use a TOR hidden service to make it temporarily accessible over the internet. The other user just needs to use the TOR Browser to download the file from you."

In order to send a file using OnionShare follow these steps:

1. Download *OnionShare* from https://onionshare.org/. Install the application using simple steps,
2. Launch *OnionShare*, select the file you want to share by clicking *Add Files* (see Fig. 5.68).
3. Launch your TOR browser. When your TOR browser successfully connects to the Internet, click the *Start Sharing* button in the *OnionShare* program (see Fig. 5.68).
4. When *OnionShare* successfully creates a hidden TOR service for your shared file(s) (also known as a temporary website hosted on a TOR network) it will give you a URL to this file (see Fig. 5.69). The location of shared file(s) will remain on your PC. Then all you need to do next is to give the recipient the URL to that website so he/she can download your shared file (see Fig. 5.70).

You must leave your *OnionShare* and TOR browser running during the sharing process as they play the role of the web server on your PC. When the recipient finishes

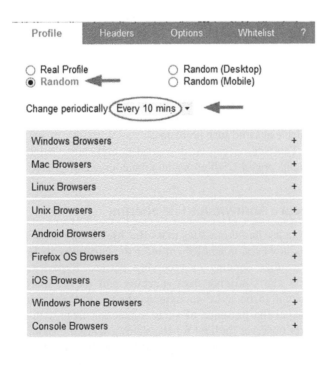

FIGURE 5.67 Random Agent Spoofer interface.

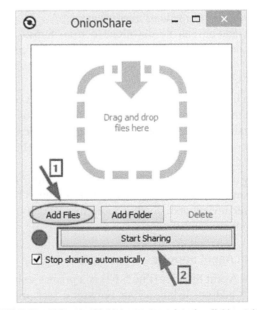

FIGURE 5.68 Select the file(s) you want to share by clicking Add Files. You can also select files by dragging and dropping them in the empty panel.

FIGURE 5.69 OnionShare provides a URL for your shared files, sends it to the recipient, and keeps it confidential.

downloading the shared file(s), *OnionShare* will stop the sharing process automatically on the sender side.

Keep in mind that you need to keep your shared file URL confidential. Anyone who owns this URL can download your shared file(s) through the TOR browser.

OnionShare is not vulnerable to sniffing attacks (when an eavesdropper monitors traffic on a TOR exit node) because connections between TOR hidden services and the TOR browser are end-to-end encrypted. No network attackers can eavesdrop on the shared files while the recipient

is downloading them. Despite this fact, we advise you to encrypt files before sharing them using the *OnionShare* program for maximum security.

We suggest sending a shared file URL (and its password if encrypted) by encrypted instant messaging (as Pidgin IM configured with OTR extension) or by sending it in an encrypted email using Gpg4Win (as we are going to see in the next section).

OnionShare can work from within the *Tails* OS for paranoid security users working in hostile environments.

ENCRYPTING EMAIL COMMUNICATIONS

Hundreds of top-secret NSA documents provided by whistleblower *Edward Snowden* already uncovered that spying projects like PRISM [35] and MUSCULAR [36,37] have direct access into Google™ and Yahoo™ internal networks to access our emails and cloud storage accounts. The NSA also developed many tactics to defeat the SSL encryption, so unsecured email can easily be monitored and even altered as it travels through the Internet.

Email is the most used digital communication on the Internet; individuals and organizations usually send most of their work through emails, and important documents, pictures, and the like are mostly sent through email. Knowing how to encrypt and secure your email communication is vital for any Internet user.

Encrypting your email may sound daunting, but it's actually quite simple. In the following section we will use a famous encryption program called *Gpg4Win* for encrypting your emails using a Windows® Outlook email client, and we will also show you how to encrypt your webmail using a JavaScript implementation of the OpenPGP standard called *OpenPGP.js*. During this section we will give you a list of email providers

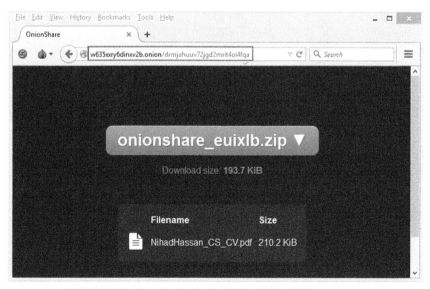

FIGURE 5.70 Download a file shared using the OnionShare program.

(other than Gmail, Yahoo, and AOL) that offer unique privacy and security features for their users free of charge.

Email Encryption Using Gpg4Win

Gpg4win enables users to securely transport emails and files with the help of encryption and digital signatures. Encryption protects the contents against an unwanted party reading it. Digital signatures make sure that it was not modified and comes from a specific sender. *Gpg4win* supports both relevant cryptography standards, *OpenPGP* and *S/MIME (X.509)*, and it is the official GNU Privacy Guard (GnuPG) distribution for Windows®. GnuPG is free and open source software for both commercial and personal use.

You can download *Gpg4Win* from https://www.gpg-4win.org/download.html; at the time of writing the book, *version 2.3.0 (Released: 2015-11-25)* was available.

The following section touches base on symmetrical and asymmetrical encryption, although we will not discuss them since both were been discussed clearly in Chapter 1. We will nevertheless briefly define both techniques.

Public and Private Key Concept in Encryption

1. **Secret key cryptography** (symmetrical encryption): Both the sender and receiver must use the same key to encrypt and decrypt messages being sent. This imposes a security risk as we need to deliver the key to the recipient of the message in a secure way to make him/her able to decrypt the message. If an intruder gets hold of the key somehow, he/she will be able to decrypt the secret message and thus compromise the whole operation.

2. **Public key cryptography** (asymmetrical encryption): In this method we use two keys, one for encryption and the second for decryption. A user will use his/her friend's public key to encrypt the message. The receiver will use a private key (which should be kept secret) in order to decrypt this message when needed. The public key is used to encrypt plain text or to verify a digital signature, whereas the private key is used to decrypt cipher text or to create a digital signature. Messages encrypted with the public key can only be decrypted using the associated private key pair.

What Is a Digital Signature Concept?

The digital signature is a method used to make sure that the person who sends us an encrypted message is the same person whom he/she pretends to be. This could be achieved (from the sender side) by encrypting the message using a private key (sender private key) and then encrypting the result again using the receiver's public key. When the receiver receives the message, he/she needs to decrypt it using his/her private key, and then decrypt the result again using the sender's public key. The receiver can then read the message and also make sure it is originated from a genuine sender.

Gpg4win implements the digital signature concept by using Secure/Multipurpose Internet Mail Extension (S/MIME—X509) as in Fig. 5.71. Your key must be authenticated by an accredited organization before it can be used. The certificate of this organization in turn was authenticated by a higher-ranking organization and so on, until we arrive

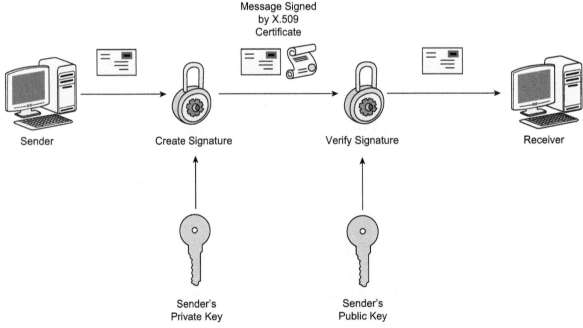

FIGURE 5.71 Digital signature using the X.509 certificate.

at the so-called root certificate. This hierarchical chain of trust usually has three links:

- The root certificate
- The certificate of the issuer of the certificate (the certificate authority (CA))
- Your own user certificate

A second alternative and noncompatible notarization method is the *OpenPGP* standard. It does not build a trust hierarchy, but rather assembles a *Web of trust*. The web of trust represents the basic structure of the nonhierarchical Internet and its users. For example, if User B trusts User A, then User B could also trust the public key of User C, who does not know if this key has been authenticated by User A.

Therefore *OpenPGP* offers the option of exchanging encrypted data and emails without authentication by a higher-ranking agency. It is quite sufficient if you trust the email address and associated certificate of the person you are communicating with.

Gpg4win allows for the convenient and parallel use of both methods when signing encrypting messages.

Create PGP Keypair Certificate

Now, after we have introduced a brief reminder of these important concepts in modern cryptography systems, it is time to begin encryption using *Gpg4Win*. We will explain this process using a series of steps:

1. Install the program using simple steps. Note that during installation a pop-up message will appear asking you whether you want *Claws mail* to be your default email program. In this case we are using MS Outlook® as our default email client, so click *No* to continue or *Yes* if you do not have an email client already installed and you want to use *Claws mail*.
2. After finishing with the program installation, we first need to create a certificate for our use. This certificate will hold our keypair (private and public keys). This definition applies to both *OpenPGP* as well as *S/MIME* (*S/MIME certificates correspond with a standard described as X.509*). *Kleopatra* is the primary key-management program in the *Gpg4win* suite. Open the *Kleopatra* program using either the Windows start menu or the program icon on the desktop. The main *Kleopatra*

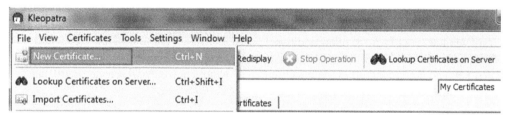

FIGURE 5.72 Create a new certificate using Kleopatra.

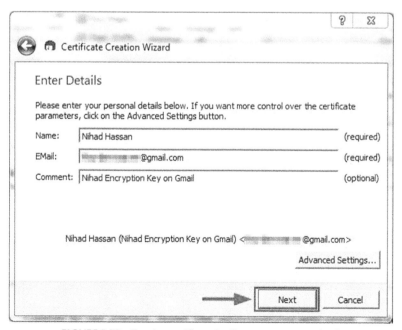

FIGURE 5.73 Entering certificate details; comments are optional.

program interface appears. Select *File* Menu and choose the option *New Certificate* (see Fig. 5.72).

3. A pop-up window will appear asking you which type of certificate you want to select; the differences and common features of the two formats have been previously discussed. In this case, we will select the first option, which goes as follows: *Create a personal OpenPGP key pair* and click *Next* to continue.

4. The next dialog asks you to enter your name, email, and comment; all this information will be made visible to the public. Enter the information and click *Next* to continue (see Fig. 5.73).

5. The next screen shows a summary of the entered data. If everything is correct click the *Create Key* button. A pop-up window will appear next asking you to enter a passphrase for securing your key (use strong passwords with both upper- and lowercase letters, numbers, symbols, at least 20 characters).

6. If everything is *OK*, the final window will appear confirming that the keypair was successfully created (see Fig. 5.74) and you will be presented with your fingerprint, which is a 40-digit number and is unique worldwide. Fortunately, you do not need to remember or write down the fingerprint; you can also display it later in Kleopatra's certificate details.

The last wizard window (see Fig. 5.74) offers additional options. The first option allows you to make a backup of the newly created key and the second allows you to send your certificate by email to someone else using your default email client (with your new public certificate in the attachment). The last option allows you to upload your certificate to *Directory Service* so anyone can see it and use it to send you encrypted files/emails. In our case, we will select the first option and make a backup of our newly created certificate and save it on our USB stick and store it in a safe location. The file extension of the backup key will be .asc or .gpg.

7. Now, click *Finish* in the main window to finish the key creation wizard. A new key with the name you specified will appear in *the Kleopatra main window* under the *My Certificates* tab. If you want to change certificate expiry date or passphrase you can do this by double-clicking on this certificate to view its complete details and make appropriate adjustments.

Please note that each certificate can be associated with more than one ID. To add additional IDs (emails), right-click on your key and select *Add User-ID....*

Prerequisites to Send and Receive Encrypted Emails Using Gpg4win

In order to send encrypted emails, you need to send your public key to the person that you are going to communicate with. To do this follow these steps:

1. Open the *Kleopatra* program.
2. Right-click on your selected certificate and click *Export Certificates....*

FIGURE 5.74 Summary of newly created certificate.

3. Give your exported certificate a meaningful name and save it with an *.asc* extension. You can open this file using Windows® Notepad to view its contents.

4. To send your public key certificate, you can open your preferred email client and copy the entire certificate file (opened using Notepad) and paste it in the email, or you can simply send it as an attachment (this is the best method).

5. Before sending and receiving messages, we need to make sure that we have the public key certificate of the person we are corresponding with and that it is already imported in our *Kleopatra* program:

    a. Open the *Kleopatra* program and click *Import Certificates* (see Fig. 5.75).

    b. Select the certificate/file you want to import (public key certificate) and click *Open*. If the import was successful, a success message will appear telling you the result.

    c. Click *OK* to exit the current window. The newly imported certificate will appear in the main Kleopatra program under the *Imported Certificates* tap.

FIGURE 5.75 Click Import Certificates to import new certificates to the Kleopatra program.

Encrypting Emails in MS Outlook® Using the GpG4win Component (GpgOL)

There is an MS Outlook® plug-in for encrypting and decrypting emails automatically from within the MS Outlook® email client called *GpgOL*. It supports nearly all available versions of MS Outlook® starting from 2003, 2007, 2010, and 2013 to 2016 (for all: 32-bit only).

To send encrypted emails using MS Outlook® follow these steps:

1. Compose a new email in MS Outlook® and address it to the person you are writing to (we are using MS Outlook® 2010).

2. Click the *GpgOL* tab in the message bar and click *Encrypt* (see Fig. 5.76).

3. After clicking the *Encrypt* button, select the certificate dialog that will prompt you for choosing your encryption certificate and the signing type (OpenPGP OR X.509). We've selected to encrypt our email using the *OpenPGP* method. In our case, we are sending email using the email account we used to create our certificate so it appears by default. The receiver's public key certificate is also appearing since we already imported it to our *Kleopatra* program (see Fig. 5.77). Click *OK* to continue, and the entire message will be encrypted,

4. Finally, click *Send* on the message and we are done!

Remember: I used the receiver's public key certificate to encrypt the message.

Note that *GpgOL tap* in the message bar (new message window in MS Outlook®) contains additional security buttons:

FIGURE 5.76 Create a new email using MS Outlook® 2010 and encrypting it using the GpG4win add -in.

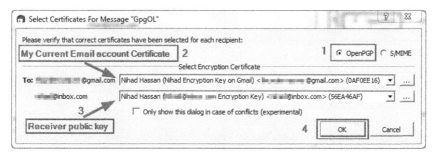

FIGURE 5.77 Select signing type and encryption certificate.

1. **Sign**: Digitally signs your email by using your private key.
2. **Encrypted File**: Attaches files to the current message, it will also encrypt them using the same method we already used for email encryption.
3. **Verify**: Verifies the attached signature with the received message.
4. **Decrypt**: Decrypts the received message using a sender public key.

How to Decrypt an Encrypted Message Sent to You

You should use your private key certificate to decrypt a message sent to you.

When receiving an encrypted message, follow these steps to decrypt it:

1. Open the email using MS Outlook®.
2. Go to the *GpgOL* tab in the message ribbon and click *Decrypt*.
3. A new dialog box will appear asking you to enter your private key passphrase in order to decrypt the message. Click *OK* after entering your full passphrase to see your decrypted email message.

Making Sure You Are Talking With the Correct Person

If we are going to communicate with people for the first time we must make sure that the public certificate does in fact belong to them. We will need to check the fingerprint of their certificate for the identity check. The following steps describe how this is done.

1. Select the *Imported Certificates* tab in the *Kleopatra* program and double-click any of the available certificates to view its details.
2. Communicate with the owner of this certificate by email, phone, or any other secure method and ask him/her to send you his/her fingerprint. Match the fingerprint with the version you have on your *Kleopatra* program. If both fingerprints match, this means the certificate is authentic, otherwise it is not.

We have demonstrated how to use *Gpg4win* to encrypt and decrypt messages using *Outlook*® 2010. The most important thing in this section was to create your key pair using *Kleopatra* program. Note that the same key can be used in many applications to send and receive encrypted emails. You can see from this link, https://enigmail.wiki/Quick_start, how you can use Mozilla Thunderbird® to send and receive encrypted emails using the OpenPGP standard. If you want to send your emails anonymously, *Thunderbird* offers an extension called *TorBirdy*, which configures *Thunderbird* to make connections over the TOR anonymity network. TorBirdy can be downloaded from https://addons.mozilla.org/en-us/thunderbird/addon/torbirdy/.

Open PGP Encryption for Webmail Using the Mailvelope Browser Extension

Mailvelope is an open source software used to send and receive encrypted emails using the *OpenPGP* standard. It does not require installing any software on your machine as it works on any standard web browser. It typically has its own extensions, one for *Google*™ *Chrome* and the second for *Mozilla Firefox*®. *Mailvelope* is based on *OpenPGP.js*, a JavaScript implementation of the *Open-PGP* standard.

In this experiment we are going to install *Mailvelope* on *Mozilla Firefox*® and use it to send and receive encrypted messages.

1. Install the *Mailvelope* extension from https://www.mailvelope.com/en/, where you can download either the *Firefox*® or *Chrome*® version according to your browser. Both extensions are the same with respect to their application.
2. Launch the extension control panel from the *Firefox*® top-right bar. Next click the Add-on icon and click *Options* (see Fig. 5.78).
3. Now we need to import the keys we've already created using *Gpg4win* in the previous section into the *Mailvelope* add-on. Public and private keys, as well as

FIGURE 5.78 Access the Mailvelope options panel.

encrypted messages in *OpenPGP*, are all encoded in a defined text format that allows them to be exchanged or stored as text files.

In the previous *Gpg4win* section we showed you how to export your public key from the *Kleopatra* program. In order to use this add-on for both encrypting and decrypting work, however, we need to have the key pair (both public and private key). To obtain your private key, open the *Kleopatra* program, click the *My Certificates* tab, right-click your certificate, and select *Export Secret Key....* Select where you want it saved, give it a name, check *ASCII armor*, and click *OK* (see Fig. 5.79).

If you forget how to export your public key you can do this simply by selecting your certificate, right-clicking it, and selecting *Export Certificates...*, or you can simply press *Ctrl+E* in the *Kleopatra* program.

With this, we now have our keypair. Go to the *Mailvelope* add-on control panel and click *Key Management* » *Import keys* (see Fig. 5.80). At this stage, you can either import your keys by opening each one using Windows® Notepad and perform copy/paste inside the textbox, or by importing the whole file by clicking *Select a key text file to import* (you should import each key alone). The system will recognize linked keys and store them as one keypair.

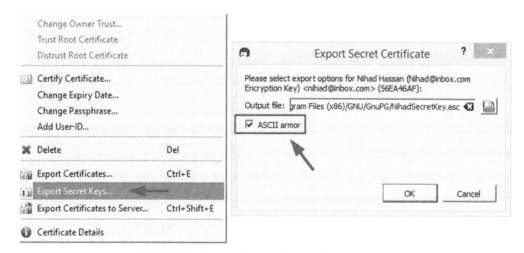

FIGURE 5.79 Export private key from the Kleopatra program.

FIGURE 5.80 Import keypair into Mailvelope.

Now, it's time to begin encrypting. *Mailvelope* supports recognition of most famous email providers, but if your email is not listed you can simply access your webmail. Click the *Mailvelope* icon on the *Firefox/Chrome* bar and click *Add*. This will add your current opened webmail to the list of approved mail providers (see Fig. 5.81). Make sure to check the *Activated* option also.

Click *Compose* email in your web mail to open a new empty message. The *Mailvelope* icon should appear on the right. Click it to access the extension panel where you can write your message and encrypt/sign it (see Fig. 5.82).

When you click *Encrypt*, a dialog box will appear showing your imported public certificates. You should first import your receiver's public certificate before you can send this email (as previously described in the *Gpg4win* section). After clicking *Encrypt* and selecting the recipient public key certificate, your message will get scrambled. The *Encrypt* button will disappear, and another button labeled *Transfer* appears. If you click this new button it will take you back to your webmail compose window to send your message as usual.

On the recipient side, the receiver clicks the message, where a pop-up window will appear. The receiver will need to enter his/her private key passphrase and the message will get decrypted instantly (see Fig. 5.83).

Both parties (sender and receiver) should have installed the Mailvelope add-on in order to communicate securely using this method. In case you have not created your keypair already (using *Gpg4win* program as in our experiment), you can use the *Mailvelope* add-on for this purpose. All you need to do is to access this feature from *Key Management≫Generate Key*, and you can enter your name, email, and passphrase in order to create your keypair certificate as mentioned in the previous section on the *Kleopatra* program.

Mailvelope is a very efficient web implementation of *the OpenPGP standard*. You can use it within the TOR browser to send and receive encrypted email anonymously. It should be noted that both can work without installation (from a USB stick, for example).

Secure Web Mail Providers

Most Internet users have an email account on either Google™, Hotmail™, Yahoo™, or AOL™. These giant companies are famous for providing free email service with a considerable amount of storage. They also have a good reputation for being able to operate with very limited down time. Some of them also offer cloud storage as a part of their email service (Hotmail® has Microsoft OneDrive® and Gmail™ has Drive). Most of these companies operate from within the United States, and some of them have servers in Europe (the United Kingdom and Germany, for example) but they honor US jurisdiction with regard to handling private user data.

As we mentioned earlier, top secret documents that were leaked by former NSA whistleblower *Edward Snowden* show that the NSA was able to access private email

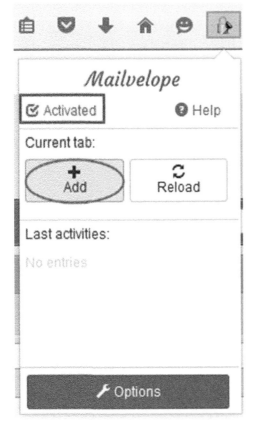

FIGURE 5.81 Add your webmail provider to the list of approved mail providers in order to let the Mailvelope icon appear when composing new email.

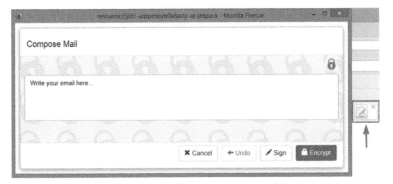

FIGURE 5.82 Access the Mailvelope panel to encrypt/sign your email.

accounts on some big email providers without any difficulty. This clearly shows that sending and receiving unencrypted emails using some email providers is highly likely to be monitored easily by any third party with the required resources to perform this task.

We already discussed how we can use any webmail provider to send and receive encrypted emails using the *Mailvelope* add-on, but there are some email providers that offer built-in security features not offered by the giant providers. In the following sections we will talk about two secure web email providers you can use to exchange secure emails without installing any add-on from your side.

ProtonMail

ProtonMail (https://protonmail.com) is a secure email provider based in *Switzerland*. It has many security features, which makes it the most secure, free web email service currently available for public use. Its security features include:

- The body and attachments of all messages exchanged with other *ProtonMail* users are fully encrypted. *ProtonMail* also saves the message in an encrypted format, making them impossible to read, even by its own administrators.
- The *ProtonMail* segregated authentication and decryption system means logging into a *ProtonMail* private email account requires two passwords. The first password is used to verify the identity of the user, after which the encrypted data can be retrieved. The second password is a decryption password used to decrypt data on your device so *ProtonMail* has no access to the decrypted data, or the decryption password.

- It uses secure implementations of AES, RSA, along with OpenPGP. In addition to this all cryptographic libraries used in *ProtonMail* are open source to guarantee no backdoors exists to breach the system.
- It does not store your data in the cloud, it has its own servers, which are all based in *Switzerland* in a very secure physical location.
- *ProtonMail* is more anonymous than the other providers, as system administrators do not store logging information about the user such as IP address, nor do they serve advertisements to the user simply because the user's location is unknown. Furthermore personal information is not required upon registration.
- It has a message expiration feature, meaning that when you send an email to another *ProtonMail* user, you can determine how much time the email will stay in your friend's inbox before it is automatically deleted forever (see Fig. 5.84). Keep in mind that this feature will only work with encrypted messages.
- The connection between the user's computer and *ProtonMail* servers is protected using SSL secure connection. The provider of this certificate (certificate authority) is *SwissSign*, a subsidiary of Swiss Post (a public institution owned by the Swiss Confederation and not under the control of US or EU governmental agencies).
- It is Swiss based! All user data is protected by the Swiss Federal Data Protection Act (DPA) and the Swiss Federal Data Protection Ordinance (DPO), which offer some of the strongest privacy protection in the world for both individuals and corporations. As ProtonMail is outside of US and EU jurisdictions, only a court order

FIGURE 5.83 Enter your secret key passphrase to decrypt the received message.

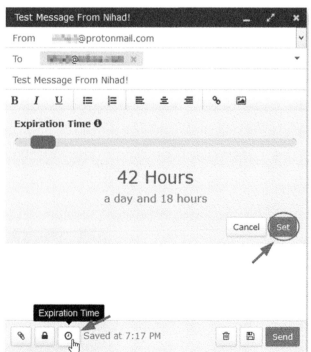

FIGURE 5.84 Set the expiration time when sending an email to another ProtonMail user.

from the Cantonal Court of Geneva or the Swiss Federal Supreme Court can force them to release the extremely limited user information they have about their users.

ProtonMail can be used to send emails to other non-*ProtonMail* users such as Yahoo™, Gmail™, Hotmail™, and AOL™ to name a few; however, the following applies in terms of encryption status:

ProtonMail **TO** ProtonMail (end-to-end encryption)
Gmail™/Yahoo™/Hotmail™ **TO** ProtonMail (not end-to-end encrypted, stored encrypted)
ProtonMail **TO** Gmail™/Yahoo™/Hotmail™ (not end-to-end encrypted by default, can be encrypted)

ProtonMail supports sending an encrypted communication to non-*ProtonMail* users via symmetric encryption (see Fig. 5.85). When you send an encrypted message to non-*ProtonMail* users, they receive a link that loads the encrypted message into their browser, which they can decrypt using a passphrase that you have shared with them (see Fig. 5.86).

At the time of writing, *ProtonMail* was requiring new users to wait for a while before they can have their email account ready because of the pressure on their service. The wait time is not that big; for me, it was only 11 days. This company assures its users that it will always remain a free service, although they plan to launch paid subscriptions with more storage space. Currently the free account storage is 500 MB.

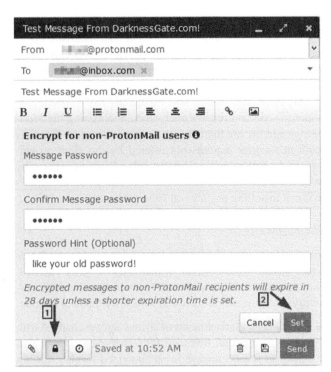

FIGURE 5.85 Send encrypted email to a non-ProtonMail user by protecting this email with a password.

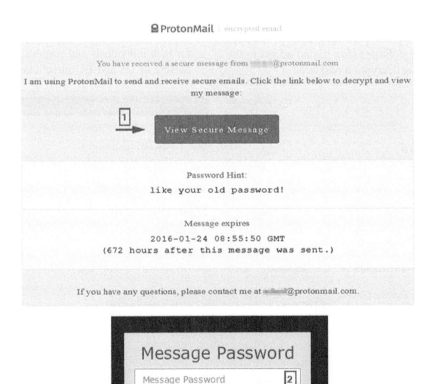

FIGURE 5.86 Decrypt a message sent to a non-ProtonMail user by entering a shared password between you and the sender.

GhostMail

GhostMail (https://www.ghostmail.com) is another secure email provider that offers free and secure email, chat, and storage. It also offers many unique security features like encrypted chat (for its users), encrypted cloud storage (currently each account allows for 1 GB of storage), self-destruct emails, two-factor authentication, and much more. It is also based in *Switzerland* and uses Swiss SSL-based certificate authority for maximum protection.

ENCRYPT INSTANT MESSAGING, VIDEO CALLS, AND VOIP SESSIONS

More and more Internet users choose to use Internet applications to communicate instead of a regular phone. Many Internet applications give the user the ability to use the same phone number he/she owns in different places around the world. For example, Viber™ is the famous VOIP provider, which allows you to send free messages as well as make free calls to other Viber users in any country using one phone number! Thus, you can still use the same number (eg, your phone in England) to communicate with any person wherever you are now on earth. There are many other providers that offer similar services to Viber™, and most of them are free of charge—you only need an Internet connection and an active phone number in order to receive the activation code and you are ready to go.

What Are the Risks?

This simplicity in international calls encourages large numbers of users, enterprises, and even nonprofit organizations to use such methods to communicate worldwide as a cost-effective means of communication. This imposes great security risks to end users, since these Internet communication providers can become a rich source of information for mass surveillance programs run by state government agencies. Most of these providers keep a log of your calls, your contacts, phone number lists, and information about your location, the device you are using to communicate, in addition to the IP address used for each call. In addition to all these concerns, most of these companies operate from countries where mass surveillance programs are actively working to monitor all Internet traffic; for example, Viber™ foundation began in Israel and still, according to its founder, maintains a research and development center in Israel [38]. Skype™ on the other hand, which is a famous VOIP service owned by Microsoft, has been accused of having strong relationships with surveillance programs run by the NSA [39].

In this section we are going to avoid the dangers of using unsecure voice Internet communications services. Instead we will list a number of open source tools that can be used to perform similar functions privately and securely. We will begin with Pidgin IM and Off-the-Record (OTR) security plugins used for securing Internet chat. We will describe this in some detail because it needs a little bit of work to configure properly. Other security tools will be described briefly they are already described well with examples on each tool's website.

Off-the-Record-Messaging and Pidgin

According to its creators, OTR messaging allows you to have private conversations over instant messaging by providing:

- **Encryption**: No one else can read your instant messages.
- **Authentication**: You are assured that the correspondent is who you think it is.
- **Deniability**: The messages you send do not have digital signatures that are checkable by a third party. Anyone can forge messages after a conversation to make them look like they came from you. However, during a conversation, your correspondent is assured the messages he/she sees are authentic and unmodified.
- **Perfect forward secrecy**: If you lose control of your private keys, no previous conversation is compromised.

In order to use OTR, we need first to install the Pidgin IM client on our system. Download Pidgin IM from https://www.pidgin.im/download/windows/.

Now, let us show you how we can use it to have secure encrypted chat sessions.

1. Install *Pidgin* using simple steps.
2. Install the *OTR* plugin for our *Pidgin IM*, which will perform the encryption for your chat. Go to https://otr.cypherpunks.ca and download the latest Windows® version available, and install it as any other Windows® program.
3. Now we need to integrate the *OTR* plugin to our *Pidgin IM* client. Open *Pidgin IM*, and go to the *Tools* menu, select *Plugins*, search for *Off-the-Record Messaging*, enable it by checking the checkbox on the left of the plugin, and finally click *Configure Plugin* to generate your private keys (see Fig. 5.87).
4. Basically, there are three steps needed in order to configure **OTR** properly to effectively enable private and secure **IM** sessions.
   a. Generate a unique private key associated with your account and display its fingerprint.
   b. Initiate a secure messaging session with another party currently online with the same software currently installed on his/her PC (Pidgin and OTR).
   c. Authenticate the identity of your Pidgin buddy. (Note: In Pidgin, a buddy is anyone you correspond with during IM sessions.) This process of verifying a buddy's identity is referred to as *authentication* in **Pidgin**. This is very important because we need to know that the person we are communicating with is who he/she pretends to be and not someone else who is trying to impersonate him/her.

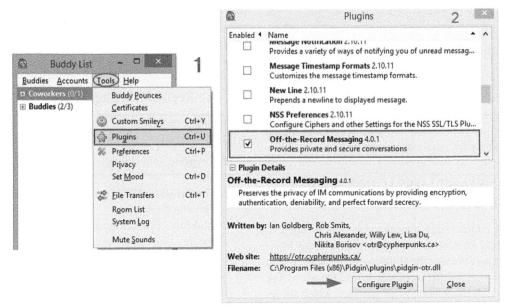

FIGURE 5.87 Enable the OTR plugin in the Pidgin IM program.

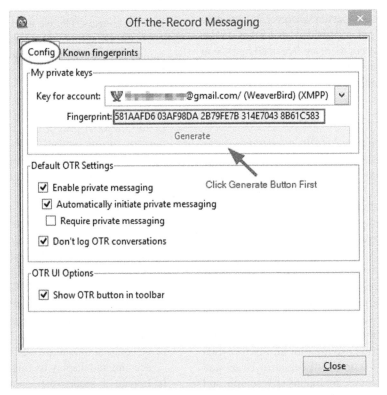

FIGURE 5.88 Generate your OTR private key to conduct a secure chat.

Generating Our Private Key

After clicking *Configure Plugin* in step 3, an OTR configuration window appears. Go to the *Config* tab and click the long button labeled *Generate* to have your private key (see Fig. 5.88).

The OTR configuration window is divided into the *Config* and the *Known fingerprints* tabs. The *Known fingerprints* tab contains a list of fingerprints of the keys of your contacts. You need to possess a key for any buddy with whom you wish to chat privately. Any person who wants to communicate privately with you should follow the same steps in order to have a private key and associated fingerprint.

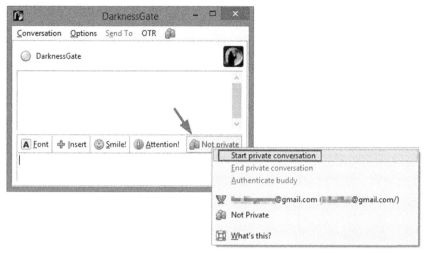

FIGURE 5.89   The pop-up menu with the Start private conversation item selected.

Practice Using OTR by Initiating a Secure Chat Session

Select an online person you want to speak with privately, and make sure that you both have *Pidgin IM* and *OTR* already installed. The chat window displays an *OTR* button named *Not private* to warn you that you are conducting an unsecure chat. click on this button and select the option *Start private conversation* (see Fig. 5.89).

Your *Pidgin IM* will try to connect to your buddy, but since this is the first time you are connecting with this buddy privately, OTR will launch warning messages asking you both to authenticate each other (see Fig. 5.90). The *Not private* label will turn into *Unverified*.

Now the connection between you and your buddy becomes encrypted, but wait—you cannot trust this connection because you need first to assure that this person is your real buddy. Whenever we communicate with a friend through *OTR*, we need to authenticate this friend first; once this done, there is no need to repeat this process since *OTR* will recognize him/her automatically, unless the user has changed PCs or is communicating through another account. In both those cases we need to repeat the authentication process we are going to describe now.

Authenticate the Identity of Your Contacts

OTR offers three authentication types:

1. Question and answer
2. Shared secret
3. Manual fingerprint verification

Let us start authenticating using the first choice, *Question and answer*. Note that we need to be in *Unverified* or *Private* state with the buddy we are communicating with for this method to work. From within the opened chat window, select OTR from the top menu and then select *Authenticate buddy* (see Fig. 5.91).

FIGURE 5.90   The Pidgin IM window displaying the unverified button.

This will activate the *Authenticate buddy* window, prompting you to select an authentication method (see Fig. 5.92).

Depending on the user authentication method, you need to exchange this private secret between you and your buddy in order to authenticate it (using phone calls, face to face, encrypted email, or any secure medium). For example, if you select to authenticate using *Shared secret* you will enter the secret and click *Authenticate*. On your buddy side a pop-up window appears asking him/her to enter the *secret* you already wrote on your *Authenticate Buddy* window (see Fig. 5.93).

After completing this process successfully, we notice that in our chat window the OTR button has changed to *Private* (see Fig. 5.94).

Notice that when you Select *Tools* menu ≫ *Plugins* ≫ *Off the Record Messaging* ≫ *Configure Plugin*, the Known

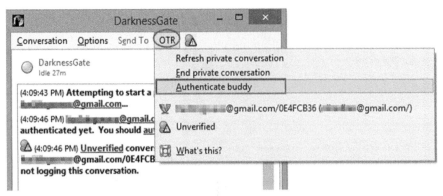

FIGURE 5.91 Begin the authentication process with your correspondent.

FIGURE 5.92 The Authenticate buddy screen with the drop-down list revealed.

FIGURE 5.93 The Authenticate buddy window appears on my buddy side.

FIGURE 5.94 OTR button status shows Private label.

fingerprints tab now displays your buddy's account, and a message that his/her identity has been verified (see Fig. 5.95).

This is it! We are done, and you can have a private, encrypted chat with your friends using *Pidgin IM* and *OTR*. The next time you need to chat with the same buddy, you do not need to repeat all of these steps. All you need to do is request a secure connection and your friend needs to accept your request.

A Secure Video Calling Service Using Gruveo

Gruveo (https://www.gruveo.com) is a secure video calling service. It is easy and does not require any registration in order to use it. All you have to do is share a code between you and the person you are communicating with and you are ready to go.

Gruveo offers an SSL connection to secure its communication. It also tries to perform peer-to-peer direct connection to make data flaws between participants' devices directly. It is an anonymous service that records no log for

FIGURE 5.95 The OTR messaging screen displaying the Known Fingerprints tab.

its users. *Gruveo* requires no installation and it runs from within your web browser.

A Secure Anonymous Calling Service Using GHOST CALL

This is a secure anonymous calling service that uses *Linphone* to make VOIP Internet communications. *Linphone* is an open source SIP phone, available on mobile, desktop environments and on web browsers. *Ghost Call* recommends using ZRTP media encryption, which allows for both *Diffie Hellman* key exchange and audible key matching. This verifies that your call is encrypted from end to end.

GHOST CALL numbers are free and you can use this service to contact other *GHOST CALL* members only. In order to have your free number all you have to do is to fill a captsha in the *GHOST CALL* website and they will provide you with the needed information to configure your client to use this service (see Fig. 5.96).

At the time of writing, *GHOST CALL* was keeping the connection log for one day for experimental purposes as it was still in the Beta release. They did confirm that soon they will stop saving any logs about their users. You can configure the *GHOST CALL* client to connect over the TOR network, so no one can record your originated IP address. The *GHOST CALL* website is https://ghost-call.io.

Retroshare Secure Social Platform

Retroshare is a decentralized open source system used to connect people using a secure encrypted connection. It has many unique features that make it a secure social media platform:

1. Encrypted chat with other users
2. Voice and video encrypted calls
3. Sending and receiving encrypted emails (only available to other members of the network)
4. Sharing files with anonymous tunnels
5. Creating and posting content to forums
6. Configuration of *Retroshare* clients to connect through the TOR network for maximum anonymity online

FIGURE 5.96 Register for a free GHOST CALL account.

Download *Retroshare* from http://retroshare.source-forge.net/, and install it using simple steps described online.

Once you run the program, it will show you a window prompting you to create your profile in addition to supplying one password to create your cryptography keypair (see Fig. 5.97).

To configure Retroshare to use TOR, go to *Options* [at top bar] ≫ *Network* [from the left menu] ≫ *Tor Configuration*.

TOR Messenger

The TOR Project launched its first beta version of *TOR Messenger*. Its *long-in-the-works*, open source instant messenger client is based on *Instantbird* IM client. TOR Messenger is a cross-platform chat program that aims to be secure by default and sends all of its traffic over TOR. It supports a wide variety of transport networks, including Jabber (XMPP), IRC, Google Talk™, Facebook™ Chat, Twitter™, Yahoo™, and others. It enables OTR messaging automatically (we already described how to use OTR with *Pidgin IM*). It has an easy-to-use graphical user interface

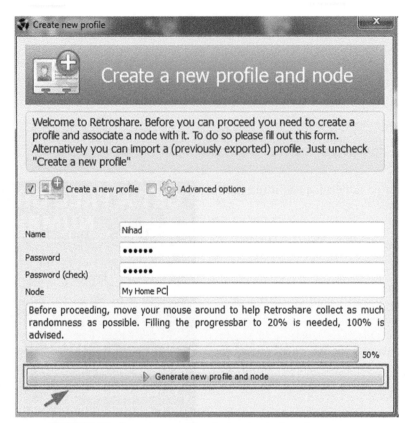

FIGURE 5.97 Create a new profile to begin using the Retroshare program.

localized into multiple languages. *TOR Messenger* can be downloaded from https://blog.torproject.org/blog/tor-messenger-beta-chat-over-tor-easily.

TOR messenger directs your connection through the TOR network, thus your route and originated IP address are completely anonymous. It also encrypts the connection end-to-end between all parties involved in the chat session. *TOR messenger* still uses the traditional client-server model used by most IM providers such as Google™ and Facebook™, meaning that your metadata can be logged by the server you are currently using (if you are chatting using *Google Talk* your connection metadata will be saved on the *Google talk server*), however, your route to reach the chatting server will remain anonymous.

Do not use Google™ or Facebook™ accounts with the *TOR messenger* as TOR changes IP addresses frequently, where these services rely on security mechanisms that cannot work easily with this continual change of the IP address. I have tried to use Google™ Talk, but I failed to connect as Google accounts usually stop any visits that come from unusual locations and warns the user with an email. It considers such actions as such suspicious logging and an attempt to hack your account.

To counter for this issue, it is you use recommended a Jabber/XMPP account or connect to an IRC network that is TOR-friendly like OFTC (http://www.oftc.net) or Darenet (https://www.darenet.org). There are many free services

that offer free Jabber/XMPP accounts such as https://rows.io/. You can create the account directly from within *TOR Messenger*, which is sometimes referred to as in-band registration so you can do it right from the Messenger without having to fill in any forms.

To create a Jabber/XMPP account using *TOR Messenger* directly, go to *the Tools menu ≫ Accounts*, then select your account type (XMPP in this case) and enter your username and domain (rows.io in this case) and click *Next*. The next window in the wizard will prompt you to choose a password for this account. Enter a password and click *Next*, which will then take you to the final wizard window, which will ask you to select a *Local alias*. You can leave it blank for the moment. Click *Next* to continue and in the final window, click *Finish* to connect to your new account (see Fig. 5.98).

TOR Messenger offers strong security capabilities in addition to its inherent anonymity from the TOR network without the need to make manual configuration as we did before when we used an OTR plug-in to make *Pidgin IM* encrypt our chat. At the time of writing this chapter, *TOR messenger* was at beta release so we have expected some bugs when using it; even so, this tool remains a great addition to your privacy toolbox, and once matured into a stable release, we think it will become the first choice for users in this category.

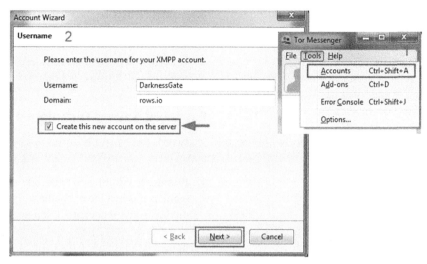

FIGURE 5.98 Create a new Jabber/XMPP-capable account directly on TOR Messenger.

Complete Anonymous IM Using Ricochet

Ricochet uses a different approach to protect your privacy that doesn't trust anyone. Unlike *TOR Messenger*, *Ricochet* uses the TOR network to reach your contacts without relying on messaging servers (for example, Yahoo™ or Google™ Talk server). It creates a hidden service, which is used to rendezvous with your contacts without revealing your location or IP address.

Instead of a username, you get a unique address that looks like *ricochet:ahyb4ghkd2bwaqxb.*

Other Ricochet users can use this address to send a contact request, asking to be added to your contacts list. You can see when your contacts are online, and send them messages. Your list of contacts is only known to your computer; it is never exposed for servers or network traffic monitoring.

Everything is encrypted end-to-end, so only the intended recipient can decrypt it, and it is anonymized, so nobody knows where it's going and where it came from.

Download Ricochet from https://ricochet.im/. Once installed and run for the first time, it will ask you how to connect to the TOR network (Fig. 5.99). Select your option and you are ready to go chatting.

CREATE AND MAINTAIN SECURE PASSWORDS

Many computer users do not give much thought to the complexity of their passwords. They still prefer to use similar passwords across many websites/accounts. These passwords are usually easy to remember and they tend not to change them frequently. Such practices when handling passwords is very dangerous and can lead to serious problems if an attacker stole your password and gained access to your confidential data such as your bank account or medical

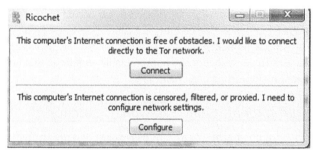

FIGURE 5.99 Select how to connect to the TOR network.

records. In this section we will see the best practices, tools, and methods to create, save, and secure your passwords to protect your online assets and digital identity.

Password Best Practice

Here are a few tips for creating strong passwords:

1. Must be at least 20 characters in length
2. Contains lowercase letters
3. Contains uppercase letters
4. Contains numbers
5. Contains symbols like { + _ - * & ^ % $ # @ ! ~ ' " ; : / | , < > ? }
6. Does not include your date of birth
7. Does not include your name, either the first name, last name, or middle name
8. Does not include any of your family member names
9. Is not your girlfriend's or boyfriend's name
10. Does not include a sequence of letters like **abcdefgh** or a sequence of numbers like **123456**
11. Does not include places, names, cites, countries, street names, and so on
12. Is not found in a dictionary (like school, tree, hotel, swim, etc.)

13. Is not a common name (like famous movie names, famous actors, political leaders, and famous people worldwide, etc.)
14. Is not like your old passwords
15. Do not use a free online service or any automated tool to generate your most important passwords like a bank account password or your medical health record online
16. Change your password regularly
17. Don't store your password or passphrase within web applications (like web browsers).

Password Generation Tools

There are many free services and tools that offer secure password generation services, although such services are very secure and produce passwords that are almost impossible to crack. We recommend not using such services for your top-secret password (like bank account or your PC encryption passphrase); in this case we recommend following our guide for creating a secure password created by using a human brain (your brain in this case), which remains the best secure and unpredictable technique that no automated machine can crack.

Norton Identity Safe Password Generator

This tool creates highly secure passwords that are difficult to crack or guess. Just select the criteria for the passwords you need, and click *Generate Password(s)* (https://identitysafe.norton.com/password-generator).

Strong Password Generator

This offers a free service for generating secure passwords. The new generated password is generated on the user's browser and does not travel across the Internet to reach the user's computer (http://strongpasswordgenerator.com).

RANDOM.ORG

The passwords generated by this service are transmitted to your browser securely (via SSL) and are not stored on the RANDOM.ORG server. The randomness comes from atmospheric noise, which for many purposes is better than the pseudo-random number algorithms typically used in computer programs (https://www.random.org/passwords).

PWGen

PWGen is a professional password generator capable of generating large amounts of cryptographically-secure passwords: *classical* passwords, pronounceable passwords, pattern-based passwords, and passphrases consisting of words from word lists. It uses a *random pool* technique based on strong cryptography to generate random data from indeterminate user inputs (keystrokes, mouse handling) and volatile system parameters. *PWGen* provides lots of options to customize passwords to the users' various needs.

You can download this software from http://pwgen-win.sourceforge.net/downloads.html.

Password-Saving Techniques

Passwords are generally saved in one of the following formats:

1. **Plaintext**: With this method, the system stores the password as it is in a file or database. For obvious reasons this method is not secure at all. If a hacker got hold of the file or database where passwords are saved he/she will pretty much take complete ownership of your system.
2. **Hash**: This is the most secure manner of saving passwords. In this scenario the system modifies the plaintext password and converts it to a hash using a complex algorithm. This hash is then stored in a file or database. The hash is a one-way formula as there is no way to retrieve the password again from its hash, thus making it an excellent security tool.
3. **Encryption**: This method uses the same technique as plaintext, but it adds an important security aspect in encrypting the stored plain text password with a secret key. Only the person with the right key can decrypt the password. This method is not that secure because all passwords in the system are vulnerable to exposure to anyone who has access to this master key.

Password Manager Tools

Creating strong passwords is a necessary procedure in order to stay safe online. Unfortunately complex passwords are difficult to remember; besides, you need to create a separate password for each account. For example, if you have 10 login passwords for different Internet accounts, memorizing becomes very difficult, especially if you are changing them every 3 months. Fortunately there is a solution for this problem as for many others.

Password manager helps you to organize your passwords according to each Internet service used. You can set complex passwords for each account and retrieve them easily when needed. In the following section we will give you a list of the best password managers you can choose from. This list is selected according to strict security standards as we did before with other privacy programs.

KeePass

KeePass is a free open source password manager. You can put all of your passwords in one database, which is locked with one master key or a keyfile. So you have only to remember one single master password to unlock the whole database. The databases are encrypted using secure encryption algorithms like (AES, Rijndael) and the Twofish algorithm.

KeePass can be downloaded from http://keepass.info. It is supported by Windows®, Mac, Linux, iOS, Android, and BSD.

Encryptr

A password manager and e-wallet that is free, open source, zero-knowledge, and cloud-based.

Zero knowledge means *Encryptr* know nothing about the encrypted data you store on its servers. This unique design means that nothing leaves your computer until after it is encrypted and is never decrypted until it is unlocked with your password on your computer. It's not just *end-to-end encryption*; it's a zero-knowledge system. Your private password is never transmitted to or stored on *Encryptr* servers, thus making decrypting your stored data on *Encryptr* servers impossible.

You can download Encryptr from https://spideroak.com/solutions/encryptr. It supports Windows®, Mac, Linux, and Android.

Master Password

This application uses a different approach to secure your passwords. It is based on an ingenious password generation algorithm that guarantees your passwords can never be lost. While password managers generally save your passwords in an encrypted vault or upload them to the cloud for safekeeping, unfortunately, they make you dependent on syncing, backups, or Internet access. *Master Password* has none of these downsides. Its passwords aren't stored, they are generated on-demand from your name, the site, and your master password.

Master Password is based on a stateless algorithm that frees it from the reliance on storage of secrets. Since your generated passwords aren't saved to your device, there is no risk you'll be forced to divulge them to aggressive peers. And since these passwords don't need to be backed up or synchronized between devices over the network, there is no risk of them getting intercepted.

Download *Master Password* from https://ssl.masterpasswordapp.com. Again it is supported by Windows®, Mac, Linux, iOS, Android, Web.

MISCELLANEOUS SECURITY HINTS AND BEST PRACTICES

In this section we will give general advice on the best methods to secure your Windows® PC to avoid being hacked or your communication getting intercepted. As we said at the beginning of this chapter, whatever steps you take to secure your online communications, if your PC is already compromised with a malware or keylogger, all your security measures will be useless. Some security measures to protect your Windows® PC include:

1. **Install antivirus**: We recommended installing a paid version. Although there are many free antivirus programs, they lack some important features provided by the paid ones.
2. **Install antimalware**: Windows® requires an antimalware in addition to antivirus software as this OS is vulnerable to such threats more than the rest of OSs. *Spybot*: *Search* and *Destroy* is a free malware solution that is free for personal users. You can download it from https://www.safer-networking.org/mirrors16/. Windows also has a built-in program for malware removal called Windows Defender.
3. **Install a firewall solution**: If you already installed an antivirus software associated with firewall make sure to configure it properly to monitor both incoming and outgoing traffic. If your antivirus does not contain a firewall consider installing a free one like *Comodo Personal Firewall* from https://personalfirewall.comodo.com.

For people who operate in hostile environments where there is close monitoring of their online activities, they should consider using two PCs for their work. The first PC is completely isolated from the Internet (it is preferable to remove its Wi-Fi and network card or disable it from BIOS). This PC can be used to create sensitive documents and encrypt them. It can also be used to decrypt sensitive files received. Documents come and go out of this isolated machine through the USB stick drive only. The second PC can be connected online and can be used to send and receive documents already encrypted using the first PC. The second PC must also have an antivirus and antimalware already installed in addition to a firewall configured with a strict security policy. If this PC (the one connected to the Internet) got infected with a keylogger, it will not be able to break your security as this keylogger will not be able to know anything about your encryption keys because no encryption/decryption will actually take place here.

In case you are traveling and cannot afford to have two PCs to securely isolate your work, you can use a VM. A VM allows you to install another OS system on top of your host machine. In case the VM operating system get infected with a virus it will not affect the host machine. Also, the VM OS can also be entirely encrypted and can also be hidden and portable as we already described earlier in this chapter. Be very careful to encrypt your traffic using VPN when using public Wi-Fi networks. Also make sure to use disposal email (or temporary email that does not contain your previous email messages) when using such networks. For critical missions encrypt your data and send it using the Tails OS, which is considered an indispensable tool for protecting your data and anonymizing your identity online.

Finally, it is important to take special care of the greatest security risk that you may always face, your online habits and social life. Security on the Internet cannot be isolated from your day-to-day life; it is essential to avoid posting private details about anything related to your life or job to social networking websites like Facebook™ and Twitter™. You should educate yourself and your family members who share your life and continually keep updated on information about computer security risks. You do not have to be an expert in this domain, but it is essential to at least understand the risks that you may face online and learn how to mitigate them, which is what this chapter is all about!

SUMMARY

In this chapter we showed you wide arrays of techniques for making your online communications more secure. We also showed you how you can harden your computer and use different anonymity cryptographic tools to anonymize and conceal your identity online.

What we conclude after this long chapter is that using such security tools will increase your privacy online to a large extent. It will also make spying on you or discovering your identity more time-consuming and require lots of resources, but after all you can't consider yourself anonymous when you are online. Even with privacy tools such as TOR and VPN, these tools can protect you from the mass surveillance programs deployed by superpower intelligence services. They can also fully protect you (following advice mentioned during this chapter) from most techniques deployed by third-world countries with less freedom who use different methods to monitor and limit access to Internet resources. However, these security tools cannot protect you if you are specifically targeted by a big intelligence agency. Those people will certainly find a way to break your security walls and access your private data using a combination of online and offline cracking techniques.

As we mentioned before, using security tools is more difficult than regular programs and this is what makes most Internet users avoid using it. However, if you want to protect your work and personal life you need to practice using them and adopt them with all your online communications. Day after day, you will get used to using them and they will become part of your online activities.

This chapter can be read alone; in fact, you can consider it a minibook dedicated to teaching you practical tricks and guidelines for online risks and steps to protect yourself against cyberattacks.

REFERENCES

[1] Microsoft and the NSA, [Online]. Available from: http://techrights. org/wiki/index.php/Microsoft_and_the_NSA (accessed 12.12.15).

[2] What is TOR Network, [Online]. Available from: https://www.tor-project.org (accessed 12.12.15).

[3] Wired, Hacking BIOS Chips, [Online]. Available from: http://www. wired.com/2015/03/researchers-uncover-way-hack-bios-undermine-secure-operating-systems (accessed 12.12.15).

[4] ThreatPost, New BIOS Implant, Vulnerability Discovery Tool to Debut at CanSecWest, [Online]. Available from: https://threatpost. com/new-bios-implant-vulnerability-discovery-tool-to-debut-at-cansecwest/111710/ (accessed 12.12.15).

[5] The Register, Noobs can pwn World's Most Popular BIOSes in Two Minutes, [Online]. Available from: http://www.theregister.co.uk/2015/03/19/cansecwest_talk_bioses_hack/ (accessed 12.12.15).

[6] Cold Boot Attacks on Encryption Keys, [Online]. Available from: http://static.usenix.org/event/sec08/tech/full_papers/halderman/halderman.pdf (accessed 12.12.15).

[7] Wikipedia website, cold boot attacks, [Online]. Available from: https://en.wikipedia.org/wiki/Cold_boot_attack (accessed 12.12.15).

[8] Microsoft TechNet, BitLocker Drive Encryption Overview, [Online]. Available from: https://technet.microsoft.com/en-us/library/cc732774. aspx (accessed 12.12.15).

[9] Techrights, Cryptome Reveals How Microsoft Gives the FBI and the NSA Back Doors to Crack Encryption, [Online]. Available from: http://techrights.org/2014/11/04/cryptome-reveals-that-microsoft-backdoors-os (accessed 12.12.15).

[10] Mashable, Did the FBI Lean On Microsoft for Access to Its Encryption Software? [Online]. Available from: http://mashable.com/2013/09/11/fbi-microsoft-bitlocker-backdoor/#wVPLuMxCn8qP (accessed 12.12.15).

[11] Wikipedia website, Bullrun (decryption program), [Online]. Available from: https://en.wikipedia.org/wiki/Bullrun_%28decryption_program%29 (accessed 12.12.15).

[12] The guardian, Revealed: how US and UK spy agencies defeat internet privacy and security, [Online]. Available from: http://www.theguardian. com/world/2013/sep/05/nsa-gchq-encryption-codes-security (accessed 11.04.16).

[13] Siliconangle, Bullrun: The NSA Backdoor Anti-Encryption Bug Program That Breaks Most Encryption on the Internet, [Online]. Available from: http://siliconangle.com/blog/2013/09/06/bullrun-the-nsa-backdoor-anti-encryption-bug-program-that-breaks-most-encryption-on-the-internet/ (accessed 11.04.16).

[14] Reuters, Exclusive: Secret Contract Tied NSA and Security Industry Pioneer, [Online]. Available from: http://www.reuters.com/article/us-usa-security-rsa-idUSBRE9BJ1C220131220 (accessed 11.04.16).

[15] RSA, RSA Response to Media Claims Regarding NSA Relationship, [Online]. Available from: https://blogs.rsa.com/rsa-response (accessed 11.04.16).

[16] VeraCrypt documentation, Hash algorithms, [Online]. Available from: https://veracrypt.codeplex.com/wikipage?title=Hash%20Algorithms (accessed 11.04.16).

[17] VeraCrypt documentation, Security Requirements and Precautions Pertaining to Hidden Volumes, [Online]. Available from: https://veracrypt.codeplex.com/wikipage?title=Security%20Requirements%20for%20Hidden%20Volumes (accessed 11.04.16).

[18] The Guardian, Naked Celebrity Hack: Security Experts Focus on iCloud Backup Theory, [Online]. Available from: http://www.theguardian.com/technology/2014/sep/01/naked-celebrity-hack-icloud-backup-jennifer-lawrence (accessed 12.12.15).

[19] Schneier, "Evil Maid" Attacks on Encrypted Hard Drives, [Online]. Available from: https://www.schneier.com/blog/archives/2009/10/evil_maid_attac.html (accessed 12.12.15).

[20] Attacking the BitLocker Boot Process, [Online]. Available from: http://testlab.sit.fraunhofer.de/downloads/Publications/Attacking_ the_BitLocker_Boot_Process_Trust2009.pdf (accessed 12.12.15).

[21] Microsoft TechNet, Types of Attacks for Volume Encryption Keys, [Online]. Available from: https://technet.microsoft.com/en-us/ library/dn632182.aspx (accessed 12.12.15).

[22] Wikipedia website, Unified Extensible Firmware Interface, [Online]. Available from: https://en.wikipedia.org/wiki/Unified_Extensible_ Firmware_Interface (accessed 12.12.15).

[23] Microsoft TechNet, BitLocker Countermeasures, [Online]. Available from: https://technet.microsoft.com/en-us/library/dn632176.aspx (accessed 12.12.15).

[24] Microsoft TechNet, Secure the Windows 8.1 boot process, [Online]. Available from: https://technet.microsoft.com/en-us/windows/ dn168167.aspx (accessed 12.12.15).

[25] Vera Crypt documentation, Unencrypted Data in RAM, [Online]. Available from: https://veracrypt.codeplex.com/wikipage?title= Unencrypted%20Data%20in%20RAM (accessed 12.12.15).

[26] Schneier on Security, How to Remain Secure Against the NSA, [Online]. Available from: https://www.schneier.com/blog/ archives/2013/09/how_to_remain_s.html (accessed 01.01.16).

[27] Tor Metrics, [Online]. Available from: https://metrics.torproject.org (accessed 01.01.16).

[28] Tor Network Status, [Online]. Available from: https://torstatus.blut-magie.de (accessed 04.01.16).

[29] Tor Project, the Legal FAQ for Tor Relay Operators, [Online]. Available from: https://www.torproject.org/eff/tor-legal-faq.html.en (accessed 04.01.16).

[30] PC Advisor, What is the Dark Web? How to access the Dark Web. What's the difference between the Dark Web and the Deep Web? [Online]. Available from: http://www.pcadvisor.co.uk/how-to/inter-net/what-is-dark-web-how-access-dark-web-deep-joc-3593569 (accessed 04.01.16).

[31] Wired, Darpa Is Developing a Search Engine for the Dark Web, [Online]. Available from: http://www.wired.com/2015/02/darpa-memex-dark-web/ (accessed 04.01.16).

[32] Wikipedia Website, Deep Packet Inspection, [Online]. Available from: https://en.wikipedia.org/wiki/Deep_packet_inspection (accessed 04.01.16).

[33] TOR Project, Tor: Pluggable Transports, [Online]. Available from: https://www.torproject.org/docs/pluggable-transports.html (accessed 04.01.16).

[34] Tails Documentation, Warnings When Using TOR, [Online]. Available from: https://tails.boum.org/doc/about/warning/index.en.html (accessed 04.01.16).

[35] The verge, Everything You Need to Know About PRISM, [Online]. Available from: http://www.theverge.com/2013/7/17/4517480/nsa-spying-prism-surveillance-cheat-sheet (accessed 04.01.16).

[36] Wikipedia Website, MUSCULAR (Surveillance Program), [Online]. Available from: https://en.wikipedia.org/wiki/MUSCULAR_ %28surveillance_program%29 (accessed 04.01.16).

[37] Washington Post, NSA Infiltrates Links to Yahoo, Google Data Centers Worldwide, Snowden Documents Say, [Online]. Available from: https://www.washingtonpost.com/world/national-security/nsa-infiltrates-links-to-yahoo-google-data-centers-worldwide-snowden-documents-say/2013/10/30/e51d661e-4166-11e3-8b74-d89d714ca4dd_story. html (accessed 04.01.16).

[38] The Guardian, Viber Founder: 'People Should Be Concerned About Privacy', [Online]. Available from: http://www.theguardian.com/ technology/2013/aug/30/viber-founder-talmon-marco-privacy (accessed 12.04.16).

[39] The Guardian, Microsoft Handed the NSA Access to Encrypted Messages, [Online]. Available from: http://www.theguardian.com/ world/2013/jul/11/microsoft-nsa-collaboration-user-data (accessed 12.04.16).

BIBLIOGRAPHY

[1] Howstuffworks, How Cloud Storage Works, [Online]. Available from: http://computer.howstuffworks.com/cloud-computing/cloud-storage. htm (accessed 13.12.15).

[2] Techtarget, Evil maid attack definition, [Online]. Available from: http://searchsecurity.techtarget.com/definition/evil-maid-attack (accessed 13.12.15).

[3] The Intercept, Microsoft Gives Details About Its Controversial Disk Encryption, [Online]. Available from: https://theintercept. com/2015/06/04/microsoft-disk-encryption/ (accessed 13.12.15).

[4] Hurricane Labs, Attacking and Defending Full Disk Encryption, [Online]. Available from: https://hurricanelabs.com/blog/attacking-defending-full-disk-encryption-blog/ (accessed 13.12.15).

Chapter 6

Data Hiding Forensics

Chapter Outline

Introduction	**207**
Understanding Computer Forensics	**208**
Computer Forensic Process	208
Seizure	208
Acquisition	208
Analysis	209
Reporting	209
Differences Between Computer Forensics and Other	
Computing Domains	209
The Need for Digital Evidence	209
Steganalysis	**210**
Steganalysis Methods	210
Destroying Hidden Data	211
Steganalysis of Digital Media Files	**211**
Text Document Steganalysis	211
Open Space Technique Forensics	211
Linguistic Method Forensics	211
OOXML Format Document Forensics	212
Webpages Text Documents Steganalysis	213
Image Forensics	214
Visual Detection	216
Signature Analysis	216
Statistical Analysis	217
Audio Forensics	219
Video Forensics	219
Digital Files Metadata Forensic	222
File System Metadata	222
Digital Images Metadata	223
Audio/Video Metadata	223
Document Metadata	226
Windows Forensics	**227**
Capture Volatile Memory	228
DumpIt	228
Belkasoft	230
FTK® Imager	231
Capture Disk Drive	231

Using FTK® Imager to Acquire Disk Drive	232
Deleted Files Recovery	233
Acquiring Disk Drive Images Using ProDiscover Basic	234
Analyzing the Digital Evidence for Deleted Files and	
Other Artifacts	235
Windows Registry Analysis	239
Windows Registry Startup Location	239
Checking Installed Programs	239
Connected USB Devices	242
Mostly Recently Used List	243
UserAssist Forensics	245
Internet Programs Investigation	245
Forensic Analysis of Windows Prefetch Files	249
Windows Minidump Files Forensics	250
Windows Thumbnail Forensics	250
File Signature Analysis	252
File Attributes Analysis	252
Discover Hidden Partitions	252
Detect Alternative Data Streams	255
Investigating Windows Volume Shadow Copy	255
Virtual Memory Analysis	257
Windows Password Cracking	259
Password Hashes Extraction	259
Ophcrack	262
Offline Windows Password and Registry	
Editor: Bootdisk/CD	262
Trinity Rescue Kit	262
Host Protected Area and Device Configuration Relay	
Forensic	262
Examining Encrypted Files	262
TCHunt	262
Cracking TrueCrypt Encrypted Volume Passwords	263
Password Cracking Techniques for Encrypted Files	264
Summary	**264**
References	**265**
Bibliography	**265**

INTRODUCTION

Digital forensics is a branch of forensic science that uses scientific knowledge for collecting, analyzing, and presenting evidence for use in a court of law. The term "digital forensics" is widely used as a synonym for "computer forensics," but has expanded to cover investigating all devices that are capable of storing digital data such as mobile phones, cameras, and magnetic media like CDs and DVDs for offline storage [1].

Conducting a computer forensic investigation requires implementing rigorous standards to stand up to cross-examination in courts. This includes procedures to acquire both static and live data. It can also mean analyzing data using court

Data Hiding Techniques in Windows OS. http://dx.doi.org/10.1016/B978-0-12-804449-0.00006-3

accepted tools as well as searching through digital media to seek evidence and finally present all findings to the court in official reports. If these procedures were implemented in the wrong way, we risk destroying digital evidence, making it inadmissible in a court of law.

Computer forensics is considered a new discipline in the computing domain; many organizations have attempted to standardize and address computer forensic investigation procedures. The National Institute of Standards and Technology published a report, *"Guide to Integrating Forensic Techniques into Incident Response"* [2], which addresses most issues related to conducting investigations in a lawful and legal way.

The US Department of Justice also published a report, *"Forensic Examination of Digital Evidence: A Guide for Law Enforcement"* [3], which describes procedures and best practices for conducting computer investigations. The Association of Chief Police Officers, which leads the development of policing practices in the United Kingdom, has also published a guideline, *"ACPO Good Practice Guide for Digital Evidence,"* to ensure the authenticity and integrity of evidence during computer forensic investigations. Although voluntary, this guide is widely accepted in British courts [4,5].

In this chapter, we will try to give you a brief introduction to the science of computer forensics. Later, we will move to investigate the main areas within the Windows® OS and digital media files where data can be concealed. It should be noted that the digital forensic science is not just concerned with data hiding techniques. There are other important issues like network and email investigation, attached devices investigation, and finding other clues for law violation within computer files. The focus of this book is on data hiding techniques, so this chapter will mainly limit its forensic works to this topic only since covering the main areas of Windows® forensics needs a book of its own and cannot be described in one chapter.

UNDERSTANDING COMPUTER FORENSICS

This section talks in brief about the primary process of computer forensic investigation. It also identifies the concept of digital evidence in addition to showing the difference between computer forensic science and other similar disciplines in computer science arenas.

Computer Forensic Process

For digital evidence to be legally admissible in court, investigators must follow proper legal procedures when recovering and analyzing data from computer systems. There are many approaches to conducting computer forensic investigations; however, all approaches divide work into the main stages shown in Fig. 6.1.

Seizure

In this first stage, the actual physical evidence will be seized first and transferred in a proper way to a safe location. The physical evidence can be a portable hard disk, laptop, mobile phone, PDA, or even a desktop PC. During the initial stage, evidence should be examined by a well-trained law enforcement technician to ensure the preservation of the evidence. Running computers should be handled with special care; in some cases an investigator may want to seize a computer while it still runs. The old-school practice was to unplug the PC/laptop and then seize it in a special antistatic case. However, modern forensic practices focus on the importance of acquiring RAM memory while the PC is still running. For obvious reason, this technique is also called live acquisition. RAM memory can contain a wealth of information like cryptographic keys used to unlock the disk drive or encrypted containers. Fragments of files and even full documents extracted from encrypted containers, Internet activities, and IM chat logs can also be extracted from RAM memory. In this chapter we will see some tools that perform this operation securely with minimum tampering of existing evidence.

Acquisition

This stage mainly deals with the hard disk itself. In this stage a computer forensic investigator will conduct a duplication of the suspect disk drive. This duplication is also referred to as a bit-to-bit image. The final output is a complete image of the seized disk drive. Analysis will be performed on the digital copy later. Investigators usually use hard drive duplicators or software imaging tools like the DD command in Linux to duplicate disks. Note that the suspect disk drive should be write-protected when conducting the duplication process to avoid tampering with the evidence. In case the PC you are going to seize was still turned on, you need to perform live

FIGURE 6.1 Main computer forensic processes.

acquisition of RAM memory first as we mentioned in the seizure stage earlier.

Analysis

This stage is performed on a copy of images acquired during the previous stage (this includes both RAM image and disk drive image). Investigators use a set of tools to search for interesting leads within the acquired image. Deleted files, IM chat logs, and deleted emails can all be recovered using specialized tool like *Pro Discover® Basic, EnCase®, ILOOKIX,* and *Forensic Toolkit* (FTK)®, and some tools have the ability to access the Host Protected Area and unallocated disk space to search for hidden data.

During this stage forensic tools use hash signatures to identify notable files or to exclude known ones. Acquired data is hashed and compared to precompiled lists such as the Reference Data Set (RDS) from the National Software Reference Library, which tries to collect software from various sources and incorporate file profiles computed from this software into an RDS of information. The RDS can be used to review files on the seized computers by matching file profiles in the RDS. This will help alleviate much of the effort involved in determining which files are important as evidence on computers or system files that have been seized as part of criminal investigations. You can download a single 7GB ISO image containing all data from http://www.nsrl.nist.gov/Downloads.htm [6,7].

Incriminating evidence will be recovered and analyzed to reach conclusions related to the case in hand. All these facts will be presented later in a formal report as we will see in the next stage.

Reporting

In this stage, the examiner produces a structured report about his/her findings. Such a report is usually prepared for nontechnical people (either law enforcement in public investigations or companies in private investigations). Writing style, terminology, and the way facts are presented should be taken into consideration when writing the report.

Evidence should be presented along with the report, mostly in digital format.

Differences Between Computer Forensics and Other Computing Domains

Computer forensics is considered a standalone domain, although it has some overlap with other computing domains such as data recovery and computer security.

Computer security aims to protect systems and data according to a specific security policy set by individuals or organizations, whereas computer forensics tries to explain how security policies became violated. One of the aims of computer security is to protect user data and assure privacy by using encryption and hiding techniques whereas computer forensics tries to recover passwords, access encrypted files, discover hidden data, and recover deleted files and wiped disks for evidence.

Data recovery involves recovering data from computers that were deleted by mistake or lost because of power failure or hardware crash. The user usually knows what he/she is looking for when conducting data recovery; however, in computer forensics an investigator is searching for hidden data and intentionally deleted files for the purpose of using them as evidence during a trial.

Data recovery has many things to share with computer forensics as it uses many of its techniques to restore data that has been lost, but the main difference between both is the final outcome of the process and the way to achieve it. The ultimate goal of computer forensics is to acquire data in a lawful way so that it could be submitted to a court of law.

The Need for Digital Evidence

According to a study report by Digital Universe [8], the amount of digital data produced by humans and machines will exceed 44 zettabytes by the year 2020 (1 zettabyte = 1 billion terabytes). People are increasingly accessing the Internet, using it on a daily basis to perform different activities like posting on social networking websites like Facebook™ and YouTube™, sending emails, and browsing the Internet. Most of these activities will produce traces and remain present on users' PCs and mobile devices for many years to come. As most computer users are nonprofessionals, they believe that deletion of a file will erase it completely and forever from their hard disk—this is quite wrong. Information stored on disks can be repaired even after formatting the disks many times over. Some tools can be applied to further wipe disk space to make it irrecoverable (discussed in Chapter 7). However, even with these modern tools it is possible to deduct traces, allowing computer forensic investigators to obtain essential evidence to help them solve criminal cases and prevent other crimes using computer forensic techniques.

Computer forensics involves acquiring digital evidence from computers, mobile telephones, and other storage devices systematically, to be used in court during a trial. Digital evidence may vary and include the following and more:

1. Audio and video files
2. Digital images
3. Electronic documents and databases
4. Browser data (bookmarks and favorites, browser history, cookies)
5. Instant messenger history
6. GPS tracking information history
7. ATM transaction logs

8. Previous backups and restore points under Windows® machines
9. Email messages and attachments (both online and client emails as MS Outlook® or Thunderbird)
10. Log files, system files, configuration files
11. Hidden files and encrypted files (including protected zipped folders)
12. Virtual machines

We can summarize digital evidence as any kind of file or data that is presented in digital format and can be used during a trial. These files are stacked away on hard disks (both interior and external), mobile phones, CDs, DVDs, PDAs, or USB zip drives in a binary format. As we already discussed in previous chapters of this book, most of the digital files can be used to conceal data inside them.

For now we have finished our discussion about computer forensics in general. The rest of this chapter is devoted to describing how we can use different techniques and tools to investigate data concealed inside the Windows® file system and other digital media files.

STEGANALYSIS

Steganalysis is the science of detecting the presence of hidden data in cover media files. It is a relatively new research discipline and is still undergoing continual development and research.

The security of a steganography system is defined by its strength to defeat detection. Steganalysis on the other hand reverses the process. Its main goal is to identify suspected information streams, determine whether or not they have hidden messages encoded into them, and then try to recover hidden data if possible.

Steganalysis is concerned with deciphering the contents of the hidden message (also called the payload). In some cases, this may not be possible as the payload can be encrypted and needs a cryptanalysis to render the message readable. If decrypting the payload was impossible, destroying it is also considered a part of steganalysis work.

Many steganalysis cases involve two stages; the first determines that there is a hidden message and knowing its steganography embedding technique in order to extract it and the second examines whether the hidden message is encrypted (Fig. 6.2). A cryptanalysis needs to be done in order to decrypt its contents. If decrypting the secret message was unsuccessful, try to destroy it to prevent its transmission.

Steganalysis Methods

Steganalysis can be done using a variety of techniques depending on the information already in hand. Here is a list of possible attacks on hidden information:

1. **Stego-only attack**: In this case we have only the stego object available for analysis. For example, we have only the image that we suspect contains the concealed message without the original one.
2. **Known cover attacks**: Both the stego object and the original cover file is available. This simplifies our investigation of the hidden data as we can compare both files to see the difference.
3. **Known message attack**: The concealed message and the stego object are both known. The stego object can be further analyzed for patterns that correspond to the hidden information, helping us to decipher it.
4. **Known stego attack**: Here both the steganography algorithm used to conceal the secret message/file is known and we already have the stego object and an original file.
5. **Chosen stego attack**: The stego object and the steganography algorithm used to conceal data are both known.
6. **Chosen message attack**: In this case a steganalysis expert tries to know which tool/steganography algorithm is used by using many steganographic tools to conceal an experiment message, then compares the stego object with the one he/she wants to decipher in order to determine the usage of a specific steganography tool or algorithm.

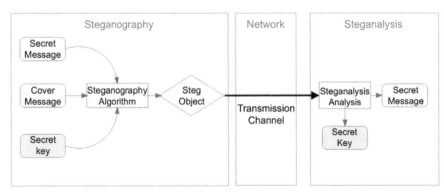

FIGURE 6.2 Steganalysis and steganography main process.

Destroying Hidden Data

In some cases, the steganalysis expert may be interested in destroying the hidden message instead of wasting time trying to decipher it. Hidden data can be removed partially or completely depending on the type of embedding and type of information contained in the cover file. In this chapter, we'll introduce many ways to destroy hidden data concealed in digital media files.

STEGANALYSIS OF DIGITAL MEDIA FILES

In Chapters 2 and 3 we listed many ways in which digital data can be concealed using media files. In this chapter, however, we'll reverse the method and show you how each steganographic technique mentioned before can be detected.

Text Document Steganalysis

Text steganography is a subpart of steganography that conceals a secret message behind the other cover text. The concealment can be done either through changing text format properties or changing how text is read (as in linguistic techniques). During previous discussions of this technique, we covered data concealment within MS Office® files as a part of text steganographic methods. Following we will list each concealment technique and how we can reveal a secret messages hidden inside it. Of course our search in text steganography will only cover digital files; paper channel is not described in this book.

Open Space Technique Forensics

In digital text documents, open space hiding techniques include all types of formatting techniques that can be applied to text in order to conceal secret data.

To investigate hidden data using this technique, we need to apply the following:

1. Select all text inside the text document (**CTRL+A** in MS Office®) and change the font type to *Arial* or *Times New Roman.*
2. Select all text in the document and change the font color to black. If the document is using a black background, change the font color to green.
3. Select all text inside the document and make the font size larger than 16 pixels.
4. Check spaces between words; spaces at the end of the line before or after the period can indicate the existence of hidden bits.
5. Use a text reader (Adobe® Acrobat has one by default). The text reader will read all text contained in a digital document, even though it is hidden text.
6. Reveal *hidden text* property in MS Word® files as described in Chapter 2.

7. Check all links inside digital documents. Data can be hidden inside URL links. The links can be created without being underlined. You can find links on a page by viewing the source and searching for HREF=. Alternatively, you can also use the Tab key to highlight all the clickable items on the page.
8. Check document comments for any hidden data.
9. Check other objects inside the document for hidden data. For example, images, video, and audio files can be used to conceal data before embedding them in text documents. We'll talk more about this next.

Linguistic Method Forensics

Linguistic data hiding techniques exploit text semantic and syntactic properties to hide data inside it. This book covers the following linguistic text techniques:

- Misspellings
- Jargon code
- Null cipher
- Grille cipher
- Synonyms
- Acronym
- Word misspelling

Linguistic techniques can be revealed by using human analysis of the text. Such a technique is not used much these days as it can conceal a small amount of data in the carrier file and it is relatively easy to discover by a common human observer. However, it is still used successfully to cheat automated monitoring tools that search for specific keywords that exist within text to capture.

We can use automated tools or specialized websites in order to simplify our investigation of the concealed data using text linguistic steganography. Some of these websites are:

Acronyms List (http://www.acronymslist.com) lists more than 40,000 acronyms and abbreviations in different specialized categories. You're able to browse in alphabetical order or by selecting the category that fits your search. Find out the meanings of acronyms, abbreviations, initials, lingo, jargon, or slang and what they stand for.
Thesaurus (http://www.thesaurus.com) is a database that keeps track of thousands of synonyms and antonyms. It also gives you word origin, history, and example sentences.
txtn.us (http://txtn.us/anti-monitoringPag) has many tools for changing word spelling to conceal data and avoid detection. You can use this website to check how any suspected words can be written by changing their spelling to avoid detection (see Fig. 6.3).

The *Jargon code* hiding technique (which is a language that is only meaningful for a group of people) can be detected

Input text

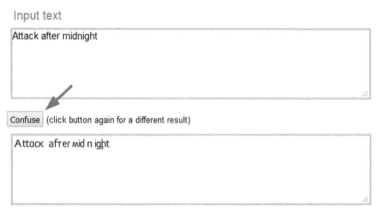

Attack after midnight

Confuse (click button again for a different result)

Attack afrer mid n ight

FIGURE 6.3 Change word misspellings using an automated tool to avoid detection.

by analyzing suspicious word meanings using the following websites:

Urbandictionary: https://www.urbandictionary.com
Wiktionary: https://en.wiktionary.org/wiki/Wiktionary: Main_Page
Word Spy: http://www.wordspy.com

OOXML Format Document Forensics

Chapter 3 gives a detailed technical description of OOXML format files and how data can be concealed inside them using different approaches. In this section we will talk about how we can investigate data hiding inside OOXML-based files. If you want to review the OOXML data hiding section again, go to the section, "*Data Hiding Inside OOXML Document Structure*" in Chapter 3.

Forensics of OOXML Document Structure

When examining the main relationship file in the unzipped package (once MS Office extracts its compressed files) it can be located inside the **_rels** folder in a file named **.rels**. Additionally, every part can also have its own relationship file located under the part folder in a subfolder named **_rels**. The relationship file that belongs to this part is named by appending .rels to the name of the part. All these relationship files must be checked for any unknown relationship type not stated in the OOXML specification: http://www.ecma-international.org/publications/standards/Ecma-376.htm.

As we all know, each relationship element entry is composed of three attributes: ID, Type, and Target. Each entry should have a unique ID, which must be different from the rest of the other IDs that exist in the document. The target attribute contains the path to the file beginning with its root folder.

The type of each entry has the following format: *http://schemas.openxmlformats.org/officeDocument/2006/relationships/SSS*.

The last letters in the type (**SSS**) are not defined within the ECMA specification of OOXML. This means that relationship entries are pointing to a hidden file. Follow these pointers to locate the hidden file.

This hiding technique is the most commonly used to conceal data inside MS Office® documents because it can resist the *inspect document* feature. It must be noted that you can also change the document name, update its contents, and rename it without losing your hidden files.

Forensics of Data Hidden in a Zipped Container Comments Field

WinRAR® and WinZip® are archived utilities that offer the possibility of adding comments to your zipped files. As we already know, MS Office® documents, which are based on OOXML, are zipped container files. Data can be hidden by storing our secret messages in the comment field of the zipped container. To check for hidden data using this method, do the following:

- Right-click the MS Office® document and select *Open with…*.
- Select *WinRAR Archive*.
- The hidden message should appear in the comment field to the right side of the window.

This exercise assumes WinRAR® is already installed on your Windows® machine.

Forensics of Data Hidden by Reducing Image and Chart Dimensions

This hiding technique works by inserting OLE objects (image, audio, video, other MS Office® files like Excel) that will be used as a carrier for our hidden data in the MS Office® file. Then we need to reduce their size to the maximum (0 PX), making them disappear from the overt file. To investigate data hidden using this method follow these steps:

- Unzip the MS Office® document to reveal its content structure.
- Check the *word\media* folder for hidden images (MS Office® usually stores images in this folder).

- Check the *word\embeddings* folder for any hidden MS Office® files (like Excel) stored here.
- Keep in mind that each hidden file discovered, whether it is an image or other MS Office file, can have its own metadata, which in turn can be used to store hidden information. You will find more information on metadata in this chapter.

Forensics of Data Hidden Through Image Cropping

Image cropping allows us to insert an image in an MS Office® file and crop its edges to conceal data in this area. Discovering hidden data using this method is easy. Go to the *word/media* folder and check all images that exist in thumbnail view, and open any suspected image using your preferred image viewer in a full view to see concealed data on the edges.

Forensics of Data Hidden Using OOXML Exchanging Images Feature

This hiding technique works by replacing one image with another one with the same name that contains the hidden data. Our exercises show that it is impossible to prove that this image has been replaced with another one that contains secret data. Detecting this technique requires using a steganalysis tool in order to prove whether there is any hidden data inside this image or not. More on this in a coming section.

Forensics of Data Hidden Using XML Comments

Comments can be inserted inside all XML files that exist inside an unzipped MS Office® document package. XML comments follow the exact same syntax as HTML comments. To investigate for hidden data inside comments, first unzip the MS Office document, then open each XML file inside the package and read the comments inside it. You can also use a search facility (CTRL + F), which exists within most text viewers, to search for specific keywords quickly if the file is big. Sometimes the hidden data can be encoded using base64 format. There are many websites that convert text data into Base64Encode and vice versa; one of them is http://www.opinionatedgeek.com/DotNet/Tools/Base64Encode.

Forensics of Data Hidden Using the OOXML Markup Compatibility and Extensibility Feature

This is the most sophisticated concealment technique as it satisfies all related requirements imposed by the OOXML standard and it is difficult to draw attention. In order to discover data hidden in this way we need to follow these steps:

1. Unzip the suspected MS Word® document to view its internal structure.
2. Open the main document, *document.xml*, using your preferred text editor.
3. Go to the declaration section at the top of the document and check the ***mc:Ignorable*** namespace values. For each ignorable attribute value found, search for its corresponding tag inside *document.xml*. This should lead you to the hidden file inside the unzipped package by searching inside ***word/_rels/document.xml.rels***, which contains an entry of the hidden file (Fig. 6.4).

Webpages Text Documents Steganalysis

Data can be easily concealed inside webpages (HTML pages). Following are some methods to discover it quickly.

```
File  Edit  Selection  Find  View  Goto  Tools  Project  Preferences  Help

  document.xml          x

 1  <?xml version="1.0" encoding="UTF-8" standalone="yes"?>
 2  <w:document xmlns:wpc="http://schemas.microsoft.com/office/word/2010/wordprocessingCanvas"
 3              xmlns:mc="http://schemas.openxmlformats.org/markup-compatibility/2006"
 4              xmlns:o="urn:schemas-microsoft-com:office:office"
 5              xmlns:r="http://schemas.openxmlformats.org/officeDocument/2006/relationships"
 6              xmlns:m="http://schemas.openxmlformats.org/officeDocument/2006/math"
 7              xmlns:v="urn:schemas-microsoft-com:vml"
 8              xmlns:wp14="http://schemas.microsoft.com/office/word/2010/wordprocessingDrawing"
 9              xmlns:wp="http://schemas.openxmlformats.org/drawingml/2006/wordprocessingDrawing"
10              xmlns:w10="urn:schemas-microsoft-com:office:word"
11              xmlns:w="http://schemas.openxmlformats.org/wordprocessingml/2006/main"
12              xmlns:w14="http://schemas.microsoft.com/office/word/2010/wordml"
13              xmlns:w15="http://schemas.microsoft.com/office/word/2012/wordml"
14              xmlns:wpg="http://schemas.microsoft.com/office/word/2010/wordprocessingGroup"
15              xmlns:wpi="http://schemas.microsoft.com/office/word/2010/wordprocessingInk"
16              xmlns:wne="http://schemas.microsoft.com/office/word/2006/wordml"
17              xmlns:wps="http://schemas.microsoft.com/office/word/2010/wordprocessingShape"
18              xmlns:p1="http://schemas.openxmlformats.org/MyExtension/p1"
19              mc:Ignorable="w14 w15 wp14 p1">  ◄——
```

FIGURE 6.4 Detect concealed data using Ignorable attributes.

Forensics of Data Hidden Using the HTML5 Tags

Data can be concealed using the HTML5 attribute *hidden*. Some old browsers may not support this attribute so the following CSS property can be used instead:

*[hidden] { display: none; }

To detect data concealed in this way:

- Open a webpage and view its source code (right-click the page and select *View Page Source*; we're using Firefox here).
- Search for the word *hidden*. If found, read the element contents.
- Check the CSS file attached to the current webpage and search for the property *display: none*. Check the class name beside it (in our example it is called *hidden*) and search for all its instances inside the webpage HTML source code.

Forensics of Data Hidden by Exploiting XML/HTML Tag Attributes

Attribute order can be changed in XML/HTML files to conceal data inside them. Such a technique is rarely used because of its limited ability to store considerable amounts of hidden data. You can check HTML source code files for uncommon distribution of similar attributes between successive elements and try to determine whether this is used to conceal data.

Forensics of Data Hidden by Modifying HTML Attribute Written State

In this technique, data is concealed by switching the uppercase–lowercase states of letters in tags. For example, each attribute has an uppercase letter that will hide the binary number 1, and a lowercase letter (ordinary case) that hides 0.

Discovering such a technique is easy. View HTML source code and check for any attribute written in this way. Finding one attribute written using both upper- and lowercase letters may denote using this technique to conceal data.

Forensics of Data Hidden in HTML by Exploiting Whitespaces

In Chapter 3 we introduced the *SNOW* tool, which is used to conceal secret messages in ASCII text by appending whitespaces (spaces and tabs) at the end of lines.

SNOW works by writing data 3 bits at a time, coding for 0 to 7 spaces. Any messages not a multiple of 3 bits will be padded by zeroes. During extraction, an extra 1 or 2 bits at the end will be ignored.

Discovering data concealed using this tool is simple using any *HEX* editor. *SNOW* relies on appending spaces and tabs at the end of lines because it is invisible when displayed in almost all text viewing programs. To demonstrate how these spaces will appear, see Fig. 6.5. I am using a free hex comparison utility to compare two HTML files. Before and after

concealing data inside them, extra points that appear in *output.html* (see Fig. 6.5) denote hidden data.

VBinDiff can be downloaded from http://www.cjmweb.net/vbindiff.

Image Forensics

Digital images are still the most used medium for concealing data digitally. Digital images commonly exchanged between Internet users make it less suspicious when concealing data inside them. In Chapter 3, we showed you different techniques and tools to conceal data inside digital images. Now we'll reverse the process and see how we can detect and/or destroy data buried inside such images.

Data can be concealed inside images using different approaches; nevertheless, investigators usually begin their search for concealed data from the opposite side. First, they should investigate Windows® to check for any clues about the use of steganography tools that have been used to conceal incriminating data. When they find such clues, they begin investigating digital image files to see which one may contain concealed data.

There are hundreds of steganography software programs available right now; many of them are free and even open source. Computer forensic investigators need to be familiar with the names of most popular steganography tools. They should also have a fair understanding of where data can be concealed in digital files in addition to the techniques used to achieve this.

Investigating Windows® OS can reveal a great amount of detail about the previous use of the PC. Searching inside the suspect's Internet history, cookies, list of installed programs and most accessed programs, email messages, Prefetch files, and others can reveal whether this user has used stego tools or not. The existence of a large number of digital images, audio and video files, in addition to files duplicated using different formats, can also increase this possibility. The level of technical experience of the suspect will also help investigators determine his/her ability to conceal data. For example, installing a hex editor, programming tools, disk wiping tools, and portable applications can raise suspicions about the existence of secret data concealed without using a steganography tool (for example, using an *alternative data stream* as we saw in Chapter 4).

The Windows forensic process, which is related to discovering concealed data, will be covered thoroughly in this chapter; the focus of the first part of this chapter, however, will be on steganalysis of digital media files.

Data concealed in digital images can be detected using the following main approaches:

1. Visual detection
2. Signature-based analysis
3. Statistical analysis

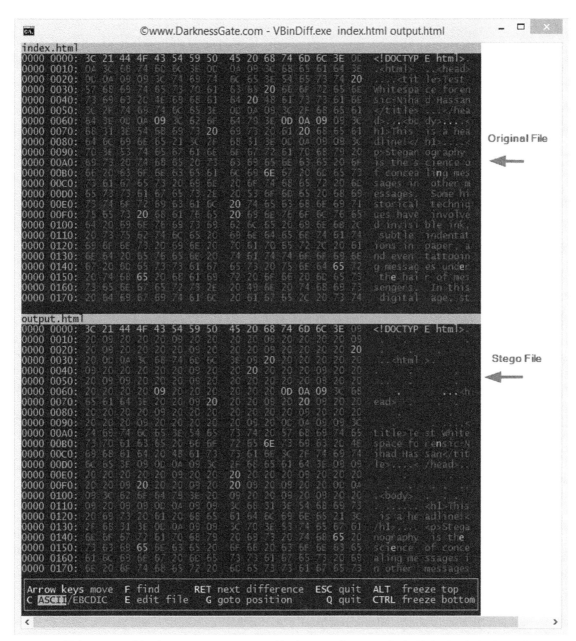

FIGURE 6.5 Modifications appended to an HTML file after concealing a TXT file inside it using the SNOW tool.

We will describe each technique using simple technical terms and give examples of sample tools. Understanding the algorithms behind each detection technique is beyond the scope of this book.

Signature-based steganalysis gives a good detection rate for simple uncompressed files but is ineffective in the case of compressed files. Statistical analysis, on the other hand, does not require the existence of the original file in order to compare it with the stego object (original file after adding the secret data inside it). This is why this technique is also known as a stego-only technique.

We can investigate for data hidden inside images by performing a simple analysis of the carrier file when we have both the original and the suspected stego files. This kind of analysis is usually referred as **structural detection**. For example, when we have two files, the original and the stego file, we can perform a comparison between both files to determine which one contains hidden data. The comparison process will focus on file size and the creation date (see Fig. 6.6).

From Fig. 6.6 we can clearly see that there are differences in size and the creation date of the two similar images. This should draw our attention to the existence of the concealed data in *image2.jpg* because it's bigger in size than *image1.jpg* and has different creation time.

The previous method is not always feasible. Advanced stenography tools can conceal data without changing the size

```
                    ©www.DarknessGate.com          - □ ×
C:\work\Ch6>dir
 Volume in drive C has no label.
 Volume Serial Number is 5635-8C0C

 Directory of C:\work\Ch6

02/18/2016  04:52 PM    <DIR>          .
02/18/2016  04:52 PM    <DIR>          ..
09/04/2015  10:36 PM           238,796 image1.jpg
09/05/2015  12:12 PM           239,024 image2.jpg
               2 File(s)        477,820 bytes
               2 Dir(s)  132,323,282,944 bytes free
<                                              >
```

FIGURE 6.6 Comparing two files: the original and stego images show different size and creation date.

or date of creation. To counter for this, calculate the hash of both files and compare them (see Fig. 6.7).

If the original image is not available for comparison and we only have the suspected stego image, we can check for hidden data using signature analysis technique. This technique is simple and is similar to how most antivirus programs work. It scans any suspected image for a signature left by a steganography tool. This signature is usually created by the steganography tool when it alters the media properties of the carrier file in order to insert secret message bits. This signature is sufficient to imply the existence of a hidden message and distinguishes the tool used to embed the message.

Visual Detection

This relies on the human eye in order to discover anomalies in the observed image. Many steganography techniques, including least significant bit (LSB)- and discrete cosine transform (DCT)-based methods, leave noticeable distortions in homogeneous areas of the image. Furthermore, some embedding algorithms may change some of the original colors contained in images as they appear to the human eye. In the last case we are suggesting that we already have both the original image file and the stego image to make such a comparison.

Usually, visual detection will not give reliable results as most recent versions of steganography tools will not alter the image in a way that makes it appear as modified to the naked eye. In addition to this, such attacks are only applicable to certain types of images that use special domain embedding techniques to conceal secret data.

Signature Analysis

Steganalysis tools that detect concealed messages based on signature analysis are sometimes called steganalysis scanners. Such scanners can be used as a part of a whole intrusion detection system solution installed on an organization's network gateway to detect concealed messages crossing through the company network. The carrier of such messages can be either media files or the network protocol itself (like hiding data in a TCP/IP header).

Backbone Security has released a *steganography application fingerprint database (SAFDB)* that contains 1050 steganography applications' signature. SAFDB is the world's largest commercially available hash set, exclusive to digital steganography applications. The database is widely used by US and international government and law enforcement agencies to detect digital steganography applications on seized digital media and within inbound and outbound network traffic streams. You can find it at https://www.backbonesecurity.com/Database1050Applications.aspx.

There are many steganalysis scanner tools, both free and paid. The commercial tools have a wide database of steganography tool signatures, making it more powerful to detect data concealed using vast arrays of steganography tools.

StegSpy

StegSpy (http://www.spy-hunter.com/stegspydownload.htm) is a free portable signature analysis tool run on old Windows® machines (XP-), which can detect messages hidden using the following steganography tools:

- Hiderman
- JPHideandSeek
- Masker
- JPegX

FIGURE 6.7 Comparing two images to check for hidden data by calculating the MD5 of each one to reveal any differences.

- Invisible Secrets

StegSpy, just as most freeware steganalysis programs, has a limited set of signatures that limits its ability to discover concealed data in comparison to commercial tools.

Statistical Analysis

Another way to detect concealed data in images is by using a statistical analysis technique. This technique relies on the fact that the embedded secret message bits appeared more random than the original bits already replaced with the target image. The statistical analysis technique can be broadly classified as follows:

1. **Specific statistical analysis** (also known as a chi-square attack): This technique assumes previous knowledge of the embedding technique used to conceal the secret data in order to compare it with certain image statistics to guess whether there is any hidden data.
2. **Universal statistical analysis**: This technique requires no previous knowledge of the embedding algorithm used by the steganography tool.

There are few free tools that use statistical analysis technique to detect hidden data. The best known is StegExpose, described next.

StegExpose

StegExpose is a steganalysis tool specialized in detecting LSB steganography in lossless images such as PNG and BMP. It has a command line interface and is designed for analyzing images in bulk (see Fig. 6.8).

Here is a description of StegExpose command line switches:

Java – jar is used to run the Java program from the command line. You must have Java runtime already installed on your machine in order to execute this tool.
StegExpose.jar is the tool name.
imagesFolder contains the images that need to be analyzed. In our case we have 18 images in this folder. The tool has successfully detected five images as being suspicious and possibly containing concealed data.

StegExpose can be downloaded from https://github.com/b3dk7/StegExpose.

Stegdetect

Niels Provos, who is considered a pioneer in the steganalysis field, has published many important papers about using statistical analysis steganalysis techniques. He created a famous tool for detecting concealed data in images called Stegdetect. The current research project website is http://niels.xtdnet.nl/stego and you can download the most current version of his tool (Linux only) from https://github.com/abeluck/stegdetect.

This book is about the Windows® OS, so all tools mentioned should run on Windows® machines. There is an old version of Stegdetect published on the developer's old website, currently offline (http://www.outguess.org/download.php), that runs on Windows® OS and comes in two versions: command line and GUI version. Although the website is currently down, you can still download the binary version for Windows® from *Gary C. Kessler* page at: http://www.garykessler.net/download/stegdetect-0.4.zip. The Windows® version is named *Stegdetect 0.4–Windows Binary*.

Stegdetect is an automated tool for detecting steganographic content in images. It is capable of detecting several different steganographic methods to embed hidden information in JPEG images. Currently, this tool can detect the following steganography programs: jsteg, jphide (Unix and Windows®), invisible secrets, outguess 01.3b, F5 (header analysis), appendX, and camouflage.

Here is a description of command line switches:

stegdetect launches the tool.
-tjopi the character **t** alone will set the types of test run on the image. **j** tests for data concealed using jsteg tool, **o** tests for the outguess tool, **p** tests for the **jphide** tool, and finally **i** tests for data concealed using the invisible secrets program.
-s 10.0 changes the sensitivity of the detection algorithms; the higher the number the more sensitive the test will become. The default is 1. In this case the maximum is set, which is 10.0.

```
C:\work\StegExpose-master>java -jar StegExpose.jar imagesFolder  ⬅
Omran.bmp is suspicious. Approximate amount of hidden data is 654134 bytes.
Original.bmp is suspicious. Approximate amount of hidden data is 817190 bytes.
stego_6666458261_e455d262b5_z.png is suspicious. Approximate amount of hidden data is 114785 bytes.
stego_6672108499_85c582a7f9.png is suspicious. Approximate amount of hidden data is 137047 bytes.
stego_6672542201_532f70bffe.png is suspicious. Approximate amount of hidden data is 67141 bytes.

C:\work\StegExpose-master>
```

FIGURE 6.8 Execute the StegExpose tool to detect concealed messages inside a folder that contains 18 images. The tool successfully detected five suspected images.

*.jpg searches the current directory for all images with a .jpg extension.

When the tool suspects the existence of hidden data inside any image, it will draw stars next to it (see Fig. 6.9)—the higher the number of stars, the more likely that there is concealed data inside the detected image. In our running sample test, *Stegdetect* indicates the possibility of hidden data using the *jphide* steganography tool; the level of confidence was two stars.

Stegdetect has a GUI version that is easy for Windows® users to use called XSteg, which can be found in the same downloaded folder of the Windows® binary version (named Stegdetect 0.4). We ran it using Windows® 8.1 OS without any problem (see Fig. 6.10) for a scan conducted against the same directory used in the command line version.

During our tests, *Stegdetect* was not able to detect all files that contained concealed data. For example, in Fig. 6.10, *Stegdetect* couldn't identify the existence of hidden data in an image name (*output.jpg*), despite the fact that

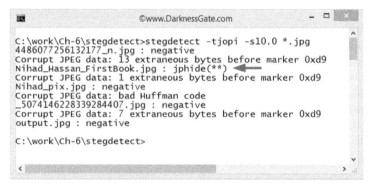

FIGURE 6.9 Using the Stegdetect tool to find concealed data within JPG files.

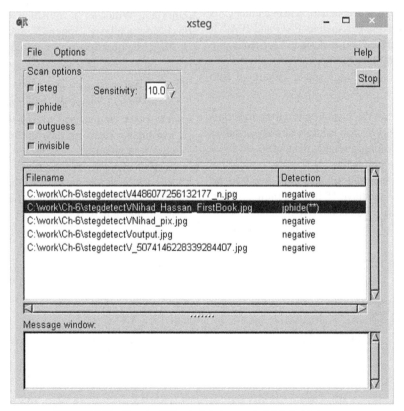

FIGURE 6.10 Running XSteg to detect concealed data inside images.

this image contained hidden data using the *camouflage* tool. This fact should not underestimate the power of this tool. JPG files have complex structure and it is too difficult to investigate hidden data in such an image type; nevertheless, *Stegdetect* still does a good job with JPEG steganalysis.

As mentioned previously, destroying secret messages is also considered part of a steganalysis operation. For instance, one of the easiest ways to defeat LSB steganography techniques is to convert the original BMP file to the JPEG format. When using a lossy compression method most of the LSBs will be removed as redundant bits. Subsequently removing them will result in destroying the secret message. Note that the destruction attacks against concealed data can be used whether a secret message is actually detected or not.

Audio Forensics

In recent years audio steganography becomes more appealing as more tools have been developed for this purpose. Just as with image steganography, audio steganography is also accomplished by the execution of several techniques. Going back to Chapter 3, we briefly talked about each one of these tools and have given practical examples on hiding data in MP3 and WAV audio files. What makes audio steganography more successful than images is that few steganalysis tools exist to detect data hidden in audio files and are mostly commercial tools.

The most used technique to conceal data within audio files is using the LSB. This technique works by selecting a subset of the LSB of host audio samples and substituting our secret message bits with it. To decode the secret message again, you need to use a secret key, which points to all samples of the stego file that were used during the embedding process. As the number of LSBs used during the concealment process increases, the probability of making the secret message detectable to statistical analysis increases. In addition to this, there is a limit to the depth of the used LSB layer on each sample of host audio that can be used for data concealment. For example, in 16-bit audio samples we can use only four layers (or less); otherwise, a noticeable degradation in audio sound will be heard by the normal human ear.

The basic idea behind detecting data hidden in WAV files using LSBs is to compare both the original and stego files using the structural analysis technique previously mentioned. In most cases, we will only have the stego file. In order to determine whether there is any hidden data in a WAV file, we need to extract the LSB of all samples and analyze it to determine whether it contains information or not. LSB of WAV file samples will usually contain artifacts of music or simply random noise, not readable information. This will be our main clue to further analyze extracted data LSB audio samples.

Data concealed in audio files can be further strengthened against steganalysis by encrypting the secret message

and then storing it inside an image (as we did before in the image steganography section). That image will be embedded into the audio. Notice that data confidentiality is therefore increasing and extraction is almost impossible, which explains the reason for its military application.

Data concealed using LSB in audio files can be destroyed by changing all LSB audio sample bits to zero. This will effectively render the secret message unreadable and will not affect the audio sound even if there is no hidden data in the file.

Through our Internet search, we couldn't find any free, reliable steganalysis tool for audio files. Having said that, many experimental tools are presented in academic research papers as a proof of concept, but they are still not available for public use.

Video Forensics

As we've already seen in Chapter 3, a video file consists of a series of images, audio, and other data. This fact allows us to exploit it to conceal data using the same techniques used in images and audio files.

Unlike image steganography, there are a few tools that can be used to conceal data inside video files. In fact, video steganography is still highly dependent on academic research with few practical tools published for public use.

Steganalysis of video files can be accomplished using similar techniques to audio and images. For example, signature analysis can reveal whether a particular stego tool has been used to conceal data. This method will not only uncover the tool used, but also the embedding algorithm used to conceal the data. Signature analysis can be accomplished using automated tools or manually by using hex editors if we already know the tool signature.

Statistical analysis, on the other hand, tries to examine the statistical properties of the overt file and matches it with a predefined statistical pattern that can apply to different steganography tools in order to guess the embedding algorithm used to conceal the data.

Both statistical and signature steganalysis techniques can be combined to achieve the greatest possible ability to discover hidden data inside video files.

Currently (according to our research) there is no free program specialized in detecting concealed data in video files. Current research is conducted mainly by universities in the form of research papers. Some of these papers suggest demo tools or programming scripts as a proof of concept for detecting hidden contents, but nothing is published in the form of a complete toolkit that can be used by the public.

In Table 6.1 you will see the most known video steganography programs currently available for public use online. This table also includes the embedding algorithm used by each tool to conceal data.

TABLE 6.1 List of Video Steganography Tools

Program	Embedding Algorithm	License	Download Link
OurSecret	EOF data injunction	Free	http://www.securekit.net/oursecret.htm
StegoStick	EOF data injunction	Free	https://sourceforge.net/projects/stegostick
OmniHide Pro	EOF data injunction	Paid	http://omnihide.com
Masker	EOF data injunction	Paid	http://www.softpedia.com/get/Security/Encrypting/Masker.shtml
BDV DataHider	EOF data injunction	Paid	http://www.bdvnotepad.com/products/bdv-datahider
OpenPuff	File metadata	Free	http://embeddedsw.net/OpenPuff_Steganography_Home.html
MSU	DCT algorithm	Free	http://www.compression.ru/video/stego_video/index_en.html

MSU (Moscow State University) *Stego Video* is considered among the first video steganography tools published for public use. It has been successfully attacked based on the analysis of the distribution characteristics of the embedded data used by *MSU* tool. The detection algorithm is implemented by utilizing the difference of block artifact distribution between natural frames and stego frames. According to its creators, this detection algorithm can reliably detect data hidden using the *MSU* tool in real-time mode. This study was conducted by Jia Wu et al. (2010) [9].

In Chapter 3, we demonstrated using a tool called *OurSecret* to conceal data inside video files. Research conducted by Adonis (aka NtWaK0, 2007) [10] shows that *OurSecret* program versions 1.7.1 and 1.8 embed password information in the carrier file, which allows remote attackers to bypass authentication requirements and decrypt embedded steganography by replacing the last 20 bytes of the JPEG image with alternate password information. This vulnerability is only applicable to JPEG carrier files. Detailed steps on how to crack the *OurSecret* program is presented by the person who discovered this design bug in the SecurityFocus website [11].

Next, we are going to introduce another vulnerability that is going to make the *OurSecret* program (current versions) useless for concealing any data.

Based on the vulnerability discovered by *Adonis in 2007, Sloan and Hernandez-Castro in 2015* [12] discovered another critical vulnerability in this software: They found that it is possible to extract the full embedded hidden contents from a video modified by *OurSecret* by replacing the password used to protect the hidden contents. This can be achieved by replacing the user-provided password with another 16-byte hexadecimal string that represents the null password state when no password is provided as a part of the hidden process. An attacker can simply copy the null password and paste it using any hex editor instead of the user-defined password. The

attacker can then simply open the program and extract the hidden contents as if there is no password set to protect hidden contents.

We've created the following example to confirm the *Sloan and Hernandez-Castro* finding. *OurSecret* stores its secret key at the final 26 bytes of the stego file. If we conceal a secret message using this tool without protecting it with a password, the last 26 bytes of the stego file will appear as in Fig. 6.11.

We are using a freeware hex editor called HxD; you can download it from https://mh-nexus.de/en/hxd.

Now, let us conceal a secret message and enter a password to protect its hidden contents using the *OurSecret* tool. Open the stego file using your preferred hex editor and navigate to the last 26 bytes of the file (see Fig. 6.12).

As noted in Fig. 6.12, the highlighted part shows that the 16-byte user-defined password can be cracked by replacing the 16 bytes with the null password string, **6C 3C 39 6C 30 6B 6C 31 30 6E 38 38 6A 3A 38 3C**, and then saving the file and opening it using *OurSecret* to extract hidden contents without entering any password.

Sloan and Hernandez-Castro (2015) also discovered another major flaw in the *OurSecret* tool. They found that each file (includes all file formats and encoding options) modified using this tool to store hidden contents adds a 40-byte string (see Fig. 6.13). This signature appears after the final byte of an unmodified file (the virgin carrier file). Therefore, whenever you find this 40-byte signature inside any suspicious stego file, you can instantly know the embedding technique and the program used to conceal the data, armed with these facts. You can easily implement the previous steganalysis technique to extract the hidden payload.

Sloan and Hernandez-Castro (2015) have conducted a complete study regarding the steganalysis of other video steganography programs (*OmniHide Pro, Masker, StegoStick, and BDV DataHider*). It is strongly recommended you download and read this paper because it covers major current tools available for public use and suggests detection scripts

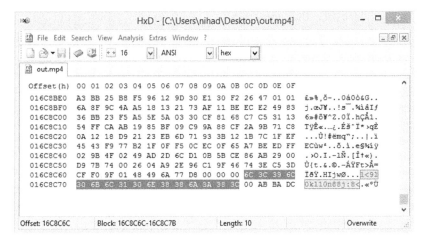

FIGURE 6.11   The location of the password and its value when no user-defined password is entered during the hiding process.

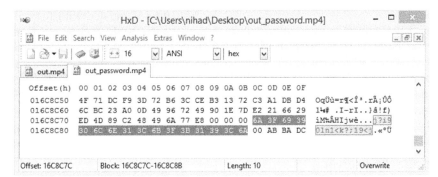

FIGURE 6.12   The highlighted part shows the user-defined password when a password is set to protect hidden contents.

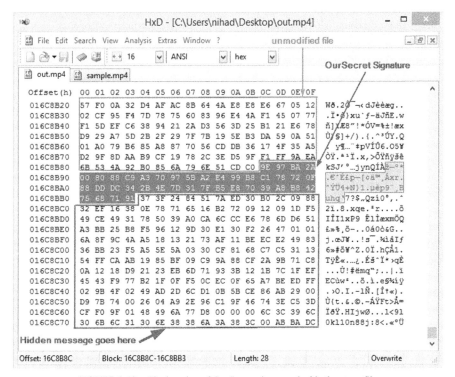

FIGURE 6.13   The location of OurSecret signature inside the stego file.

to automate the finding of any hidden data. The paper can be found at this link: https://peerj.com/articles/cs-7.

Another study conducted by Thomas Sloan and Julio Hernandez-Castro (2015) presents a technique to detect concealed data within the famous steganography tool OpenPuff. Entitled, *Steganalysis of OpenPuff Through Atomic Concatenation of MP4 Flags*, the paper can be found at https://www.researchgate.net/publication/273331420_Steganalysis_of_OpenPuff_through_atomic_concatenation_of_MP4_flags.

To conclude, most video steganography tools that employ EOF injunction techniques to conceal secret data are considered easy to investigate for hidden data, and according to the *Sloan and Hernandez-Castro (2015)* study, many of these tools leave other clues on their usage like signature or additional blank spaces in the stego file, making it easy to detect by investigating file structure using any hex viewer.

Steganalysis of digital media files, especially audio and video files, still undergoes much research and development with very few tools available for public use to help detect concealed data in these files. Sometimes, the ability to destroy hidden data can be the only available choice for investigators when they cannot prove the existence of concealed data and/or cannot extract it.

Digital Files Metadata Forensic

In a nutshell, metadata is data that describes other data or gives information about this data. So, for example, letters or characters in a text are data. The number of letters in a text and author name is the metadata. Most digital files save metadata inside their structure; however, metadata is not visible at first sight when someone opens the file in application software. Also, when we print file contents (for example, of a document) on paper most metadata will be lost.

During this book, we've talked many times about metadata and how we can exploit it to conceal secret data. In fact, metadata can be presented in most digital media files. It is enough to know where metadata exists within famous digital files in order to detect whether it contains secret data buried inside it or not. In this section, we'll recap this topic covering all major media files. In the next chapter, however, we will teach you how to destroy metadata using different techniques to assure your privacy and prevent using a metadata concealment technique to steal confidential data from your company.

Metadata can be presented on computers in the following forms:

- File system metadata (eg, associated user, access time, permissions, attributes, etc.)
- Digital images metadata (covered thoroughly in Chapter 2), which includes EXIF, EXIF GPS, IPTC, and other imaging

software that allows you to add additional tags depending on need without affecting image quality or visual appearance

- Audio and video files, which can also have embedded metadata
- Document metadata, especially MS Office documents (covered thoroughly in Chapters 2 and 3) and PDF files

File System Metadata

Windows® XP File Explorer allows us to edit the metadata (author name, comments, keywords) of any file type or folder (see Fig. 6.14). In Vista and later Windows® versions, this has been possible only for certain types of files, such as MS Office® documents, JPEG images, and MP3 audio files.

Metadata associated with files in Windows® OS can store a considerable amount of secret data. We can use a free tool to add such metadata in newer Windows® versions and also investigate secret data hidden in metadata fields. A tool called *File Metadata*, which is available for download free of charge at https://filemeta.codeplex.com, supports all Windows® newer versions.

This tool comes supplied with a file association manager, to manage the registry settings that turn on (and off)

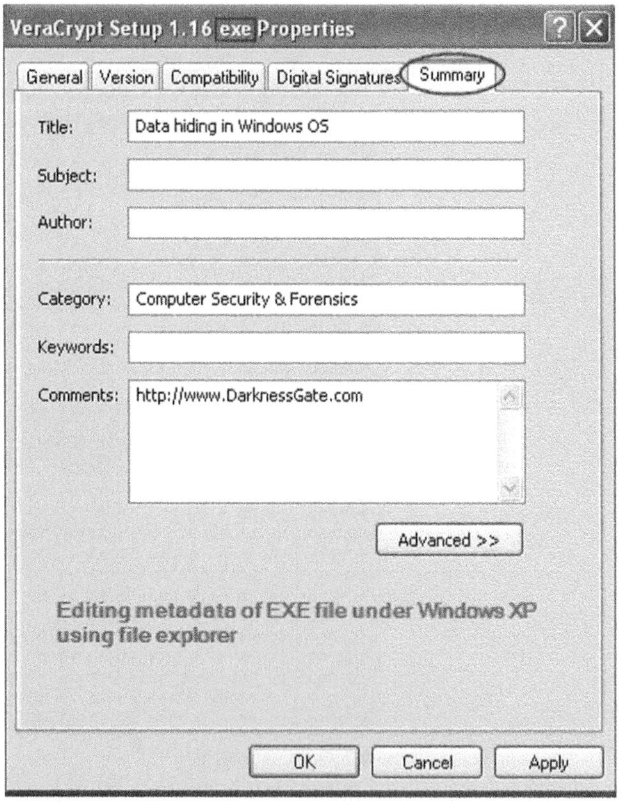

FIGURE 6.14 Windows XP file explorer allows editing metadata of any file type.

file metadata support per file extension and tells Explorer to allow you to see and edit the metadata for a file type. By default, file metadata will not appear for any additional extensions—you need to turn support on explicitly per extension.

In order to view/edit the metadata of any file from within File Explorer in both Windows® 8 and 10, you first need to activate *Details pane* from the *View* menu. The Details pane will appear to the right of the Explorer window (see Fig. 6.15).

As we already mentioned, Windows® Vista and above, by default, do not allow editing metadata of all files directly in File Explorer, except for some file types. Having said that, to make this possible for all files, install *File Metadata*. To launch the tool, go to *File Extension* and select the extension you want to enable metadata editing to. Then click *Add File Meta Data Handler* and finally click *Restart Explorer* to apply changes to the registry. In this case we will select to update the **.PDF** extension file handler (see Fig. 6.16).

Now, return back and select any PDF file and check its metadata in the *Details pane*. You will see that you can now edit its metadata attributes (see Fig. 6.17). This tool will also read some metadata written under XP, hidden by a Windows® upgrade.

Digital Images Metadata

In Chapter 2, we have covered *hiding data in image metadata* thoroughly and described other metadata types such as IPTC and XMP, which is associated with most digital image types and can be used to conceal data. We do not have much information to add because the information presented in Chapter 2 is enough for this book's scope. However, we will remind you again of some free tools that can be used to investigate and extract metadata in digital images.

1. **Exif Pilot**: Free EXIF editor that allows you view/edit EXIF, EXIF GPS, IPTC, and XMP data. You can also add new tags, and import/export EXIF and IPTC from/to XML files. http://www.colorpilot.com/exif.html
2. **PhotoME**: Metadata viewer and editor for digital images. http://www.photome.de
3. **XnViewMP**: Metadata viewer and multimedia viewer, browser, and converter. http://www.xnview.com/en/xnview

Audio/Video Metadata

Audio files can have a number of metadata tags. The most common are ID3 tags, which provide the title, artist, year, genre, and other information when you're listening to music.

ID3 tags are the audio file data standard for MP3 files in active use by software and hardware developers around the world. ID3 tags are supported in software such as iTunes, Windows Media Player®, Winamp, VLC, and hardware players like the iPod, Creative Zen,

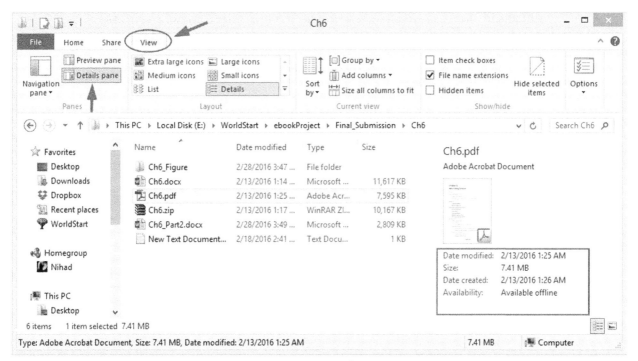

FIGURE 6.15 Showing the Details pane in Windows® 8 and 10 to view files/folders metadata.

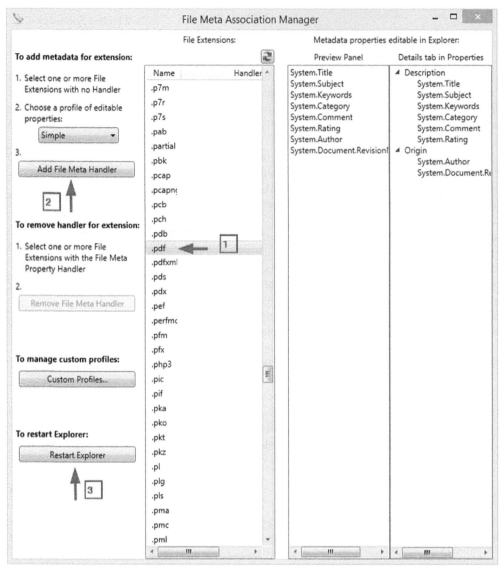

FIGURE 6.16 Activate the metadata view/edit for all files of PDF type for the current Windows® machine.

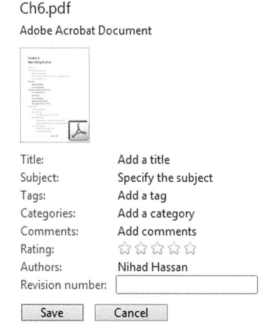

FIGURE 6.17 Edit/view metadata information of a PDF file after activating its extension handler.

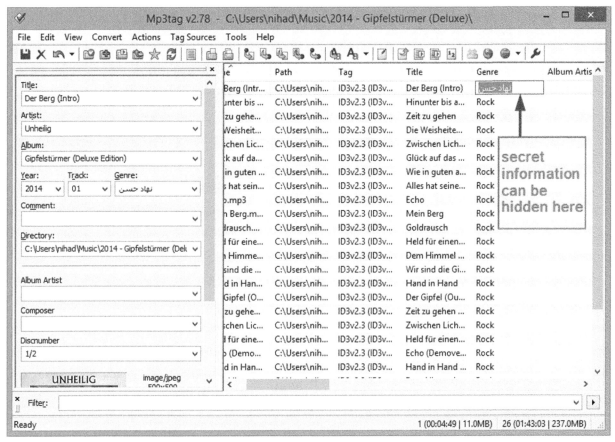

FIGURE 6.18 Investigating for hidden data inside audio metadata files (MP3 files) using the Mp3tag program.

Samsung Galaxy, and Sony Walkman. More information about this tag format can be found on its official website: http://id3.org.

There are many ways in which we can edit audio file's metadata. In this case we are using a free metadata editor called Mp3tag (see Fig. 6.18), which is a powerful and easy-to-use tool to edit metadata of audio files. This supports batch tag-editing of ID3v1, ID3v2.3, ID3v2.4, iTunes MP4, WMA, Vorbis Comments, and APE Tags for multiple files at once covering a variety of audio formats. You can download this tool for free from http://www.mp3tag.de/en.

Another tool that supports tag editing on additional audio file formats is *TagScanner*, which is a powerful tool for viewing and editing metadata information. It can edit tags of most modern audio formats and supports ID3v1/v2, Vorbis comments, APEv2, WMA, and MP4(iTunes) tags, MP3, OGG, FLAC, WMA, MPEG-4, Opus, Musepack, Monkey's Audio, AAC, OptimFROG, SPEEX, WavPack, TrueAudio, WAV, AIFF, and Direct Stream Digital files. It also supports embedded lyrics and cover art. This tool can export all tag information to HTML, XML, CSV, or any user-defined format (see Fig. 6.19). You can download this tool from http://www.xdlab.ru/en/index.htm.

Video files can also have their own metadata, and mainly contain two types of metadata:

1. **Source metadata**: This kind of data is created automatically by the camera or the editing software you use, like camera version, date/time of the shot, GPS coordinates of shooting location, camera settings, video recording duration, and any technical information produced by your various devices when you have acquired this video.

2. **Human-authored video metadata**: This kind of data is added by humans for different purposes. For example, a webmaster can add specific data related to his website/product to increase search engine visibility of his video.

Most of the video metadata is the automatically created metadata. From a computer forensic perspective, investigators are more concerned with source metadata, which reveals information about the technical details of the camera and date/time of the shot; however, in data hiding cases, human-created metadata is more important.

Video metadata can be investigated using many tools. A free one, called *MediaInfo*, can be downloaded from https://mediaarea.net/en/MediaInfo. This tool has the ability to extract metadata of various video files like

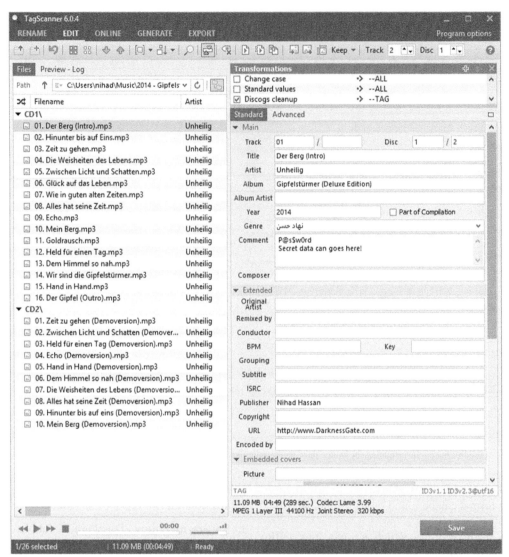

FIGURE 6.19 Using TagScanner to view/edit MP3 file tags, this tool also supports editing MP4 video file tags.

MPEG-1/2 Video, H.263, MPEG-4 Visual (including DivX, XviD), H.264/AVC, and Dirac. It also has the ability to view/edit metadata of various audio files (see Fig. 6.20).

Document Metadata

Digital documents, especially PDF and MS Office files, are widely used in business and academic areas. When creating a document using MS Word, Excel, or Power-Point it will save to this document a host of additional data within the file. Such data is often saved to your file without your knowledge (see Fig. 6.21). Such metadata fields can be used to conceal secret data inside it.

For MS Office® 2010, 2013, and 2016, you can check document metadata by going to *File » Info*. The

properties panel will be on the right side as shown in Fig. 6.21. In MS Office® 2007 you need to click *Microsoft Office Button » Prepare » Properties*.

You can automate your search for metadata inside different files using specialized tools. One of these tools is *Meta-Clean*, which is a powerful tool to read, search, remove, and edit document metadata of MS Office (Word, Excel, PowerPoint, and Visio) and OpenOffice (word processors, spreadsheets, and presentations), and PDF and multimedia files (image, audio, and video). This is a commercial application, but still offers a trial version. We found this tool very effective and easy to use while investigating different file types for their metadata (see Fig. 6.22).

If you want a dedicated metadata viewer for PDF files you can try to use this free program: Free *PDF Metadata Editor 4dots*. This program allows you to batch edit PDF

FIGURE 6.20 Viewing metadata of MP4 video files using the MediaInfo program.

properties of many PDF documents; that is, set metadata such as author, title, subject, and keywords with a single mouse click. You can also batch set unlimited user-defined custom PDF metadata (see Fig. 6.23).

In this section, we present some tools that can be used to view/edit metadata of various media files. Later in this chapter you will learn how to use specialized computer forensic software (like ProDiscover® Basic)

to bulk search for specific keyword(s) inside metadata of different file types.

WINDOWS FORENSICS

In this section, we will talk about how we can use different tools/techniques to investigate hidden data inside Windows® OS-based machines.

Capture Volatile Memory

Volatile memory analysis has become a significant part of the digital investigation because there is digital evidence that resides only in physical memory (RAM) and nothing is written to the hard disk that indicates its presence. Data is considered volatile when it is going to be lost when a machine is powered off or rebooted. Such data will also get overwritten during the normal machine use (eg, when closing a specific application on a PC the reserved data space will disappear from RAM memory allowing other applications to use its space for operation). Network devices like routers, switches, and firewalls can

also have volatile data represented in its log. The process of capturing data from memory is known as dumping, and acquiring it differs according to each operating system type. In this book we focus only on computers running Windows® OS.

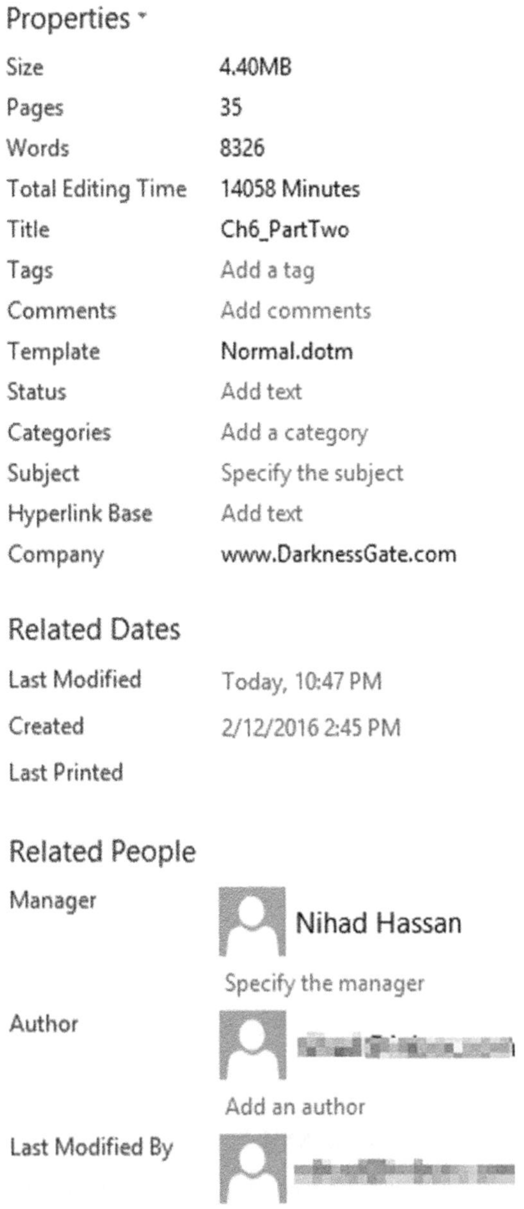

Capturing a RAM memory will give computer forensic investigators a wealth of information such as passwords to encrypted volumes like *TrueCrypt, VeraCrypt, BitLocker*, and *PGP Disk encryption*; running tasks; terminated and cashed processes; the login information for webmail (Gmail™, AOL™); and IM chat and social network services like Facebook™ and YouTube™. File sharing services such as Dropbox™, Flickr™, and SkyDrive™ login information can also be found in RAM dumps.

The analysis of RAM dumps needs specialized tools since unlike a hard disk image, data are not stored in a structured way in the RAM memory image. In this section, we will show how you can capture the RAM memory using different tools.

Before we move on, you should note the capturing tool used to acquire the RAM memory will leave traces on the suspect machine. Computer forensic software vendors claim that their tools will leave a very small footprint on the acquired system; this means some data may be overwritten as a result of acquiring live memory. These changes should be well documented in order to avoid destroying your legal evidence. Live acquisition will usually make the following modifications to any Windows® machine:

- Registry changes
- Memory entries
- May write a very small amount of data to a disk drive

This section is beyond the scope of this book. A well-trained technician should perform this task and must have the proper authorization from the appropriate corporate authority before proceeding.

Now let's try creating a RAM dump using different tools. Later, this dump can be analyzed to extract important information from it, which can reveal concealed data and other clues of encryption software used. We will begin using a simple, portable utility created by MoonSols called *DumpIt*.

DumpIt

1. Download this tool from http://www.moonsols.com /2011/07/18/moonsols-dumpit-goes-mainstream/. You can save this tool on your USB zip drive, so in case you want to perform a live acquisition on a particular PC all you need to do is double-click on this tool to begin capturing the RAM. (Make sure when using *DumpIt* from within a USB drive that it is large enough to hold the file that is created. If you want to capture a 6 GB RAM

Properties ▾

Size	4.40MB
Pages	35
Words	8326
Total Editing Time	14058 Minutes
Title	Ch6_PartTwo
Tags	Add a tag
Comments	Add comments
Template	Normal.dotm
Status	Add text
Categories	Add a category
Subject	Specify the subject
Hyperlink Base	Add text
Company	www.DarknessGate.com

Related Dates

Last Modified	Today, 10:47 PM
Created	2/12/2016 2:45 PM
Last Printed	

Related People

Manager   Nihad Hassan

Specify the manager

Author

Add an author

Last Modified By

FIGURE 6.21   Microsoft Word properties panel showing some document metadata.

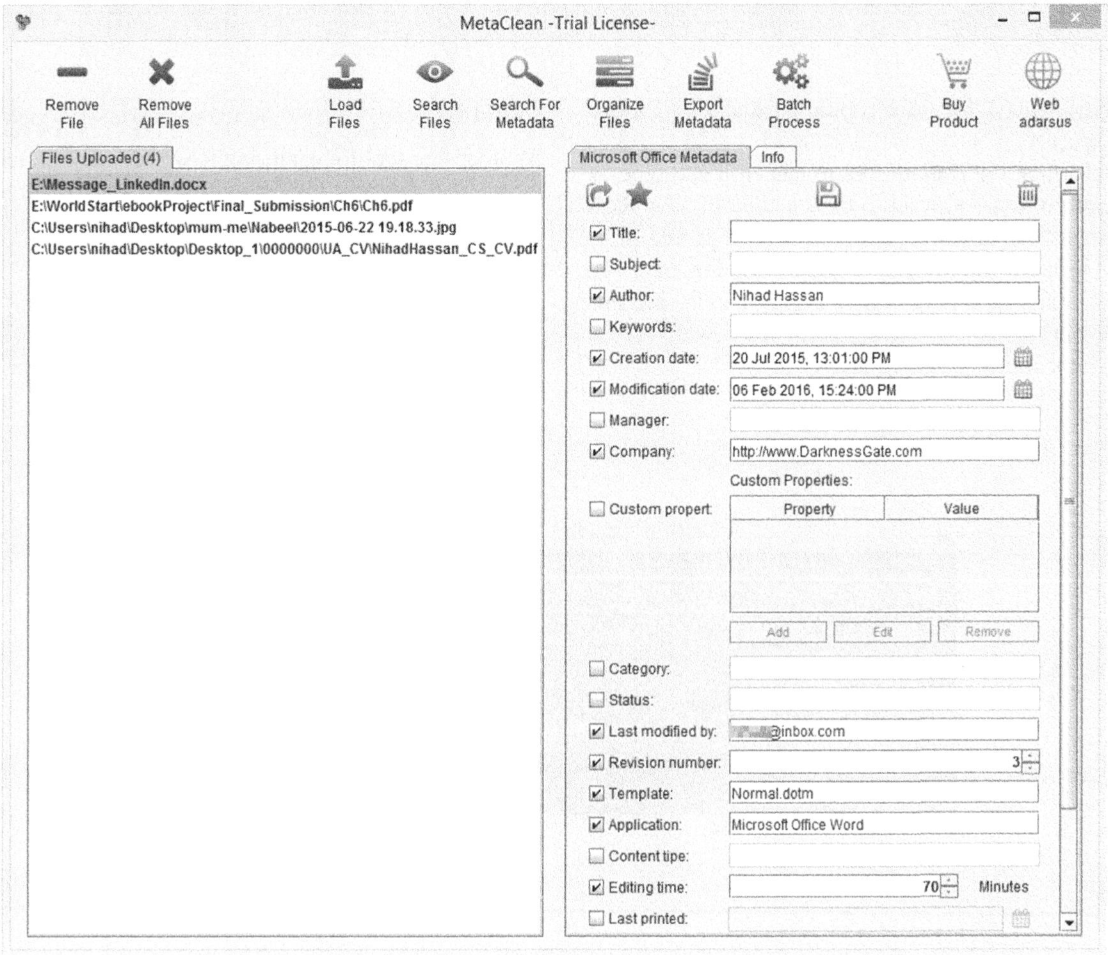

FIGURE 6.22 Using MetaClean to view the metadata of different file types; you can also update and save new metadata.

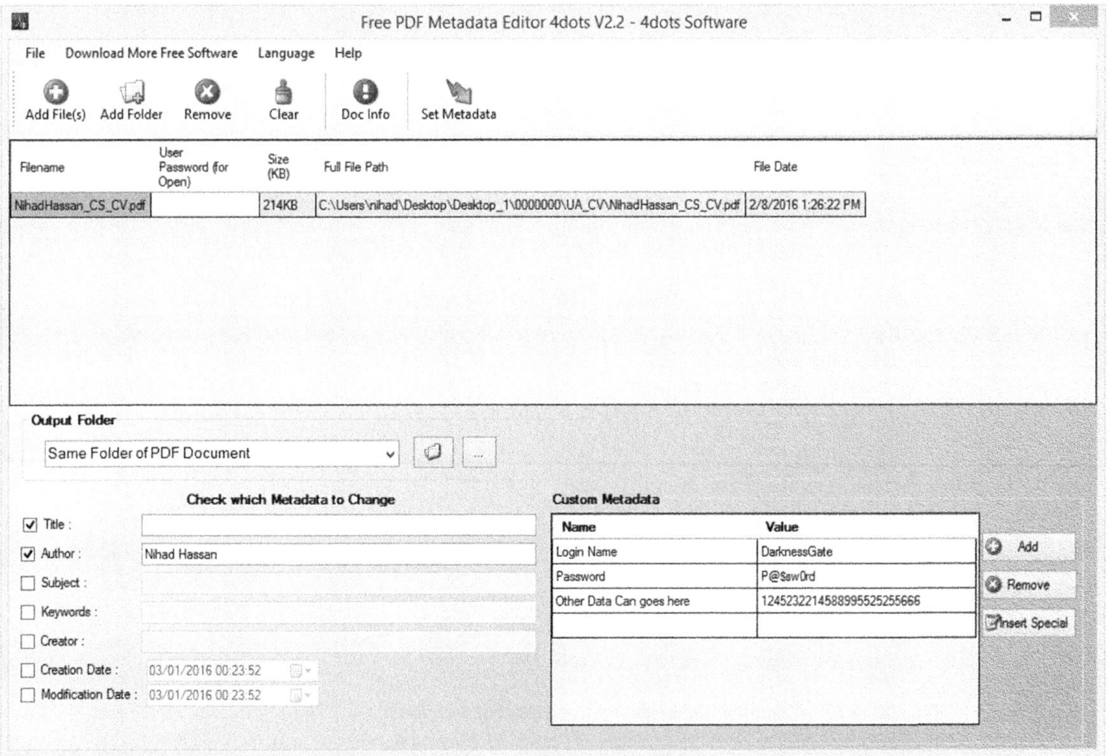

FIGURE 6.23 Using Free PDF Metadata Editor 4dots to view/update and add custom metadata to PDF files.

memory, your USB drive should have at least 7 GB of free space.)

2. Double-click the *DumpIt* tool to launch it and type "y" to confirm that you want to have a copy of your RAM memory. The captured RAM file will be stored in the same location where *DumpIt* resides (see Fig. 6.24). We note that the captured image is bigger than the acquired RAM (in this case we're capturing a PC with 4 GB of RAM; the image size is about 5 GB).

Belkasoft

Another free tool for capturing RAM memory is Belkasoft, a tiny free forensic tool that allows a reliable process of extraction of the entire contents of computer's volatile memory, even if protected by an active antidebugging or antidumping system. Separate 32-bit and 64-bit builds are available in order to minimize the tool's footprint as much as possible. Belkasoft can be downloaded from https://belkasoft.com/ram-capturer.

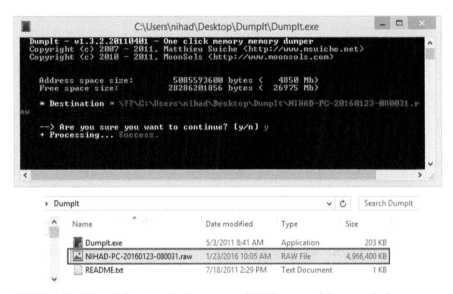

FIGURE 6.24 Using the DumpIt tool to have a copy of RAM memory of the current device.

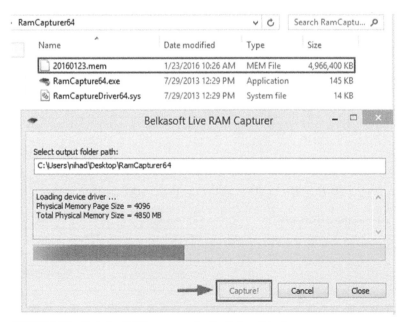

FIGURE 6.25 Capturing RAM memory using the Belkasoft tool.

Using *Belkasoft* is easy: just execute the program on the PC where you want to capture its RAM and click *Capture* (Fig. 6.25). If you are using it from a standard USB drive, make sure to have more storage than the size of the acquired RAM.

FTK® Imager

The third tool in our arsenal is FTK® Imager from AccessData™ available online from http://accessdata.com/product-download. You need to fill a simple registration form after which a download link will be sent to your registered email.

Unlike the previous two program, FTK Imager can be installed to the computer where it will be used, or it can be run from a portable device such as a USB thumb drive connected to a machine in the field.

After installing the program, launch it, then navigate to *File* menu » *Capture Memory….* A new window appears showing options for capturing the RAM memory of the current machine (see Fig. 6.26).

In Fig. 6.26 we select the destination path of the acquired image to be at *G:\RAM* (G:\ is a removable USB stick drive). We select to include *pagefile*, which is a reserved portion of a hard disk used as an extension for RAM for data in RAM that hasn't been used recently. After selecting these options, click *Capture Memory* to begin the capture process (see Fig. 6.27).

Once the memory dump has been completed, FTK Imager will tell you if the capture was successful, and you will see two files in the destination folder, one named *memdump.mem* for RAM and the second for the pagefile image named *pagefile. sys* (see Fig. 6.28).

In this section we've demonstrated how to capture RAM memory using three well-known free programs. The captured RAM image can be further analyzed to extract important information like passwords, temporary Internet files, deleted files, and other important artifacts.

Capture Disk Drive

Capturing the hard disk image is considered the main part of any computer forensic investigation as most data that may contain incriminating evidence will most probably be residing on it. In this section, we will briefly talk about how we can acquire a hard disk image in order to analyze it for concealed data and deleted files.

There are many tools that can be used to acquire hard disk images in Windows® OS: FTK Imager®, Pro Discover Basic®, Encase®, and X-Ways® Forensics all offers such capability.

Note that before acquiring the disk image, you need to *write-protect* the suspect hard disk before attaching it to your forensic workstation. Write-protection can be done using hardware tools or software programs. Many investigators prefers to boot from CD/DVD using a Linux forensic distribution that is preconfigured to disallow automatic disk mounting like CAINE (http://www.caine-live.net) and DEFT (http://www.deftlinux.net), and then acquire a suspect disk without any danger of manipulating the disk drive with data from external sources. If you want to know how to write-protect your investigated disk drive to safely acquire its image check my guide at http://www.darknessgate.com/computer-forensic/computer-forensic-prerequisites/windows-os-write-protection-with-usb-devices/.

Data can be captured and stored using different storage formats. The main ones are:

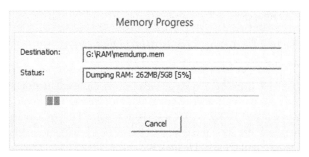

FIGURE 6.27   Capture RAM process while running using FTK Imager.

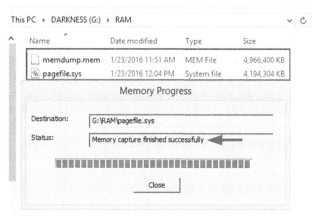

FIGURE 6.28   Resultant dump files captured with FTK Imager: one for RAM and the second for pagefile.

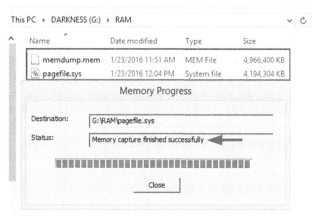

FIGURE 6.26   Capture RAM memory using FTK® Imager.

- Raw format
- Propriety format (Safeback by NTI, ILook Imager, ProDiscover)
- Advanced forensic format

Most computer forensic tools have the ability to read raw format, making it the most used tool. It has some disadvantages, though, such as it cannot integrate metadata into the image file, and it is not able to read bad sectors that may contain concealed information as we saw before in Chapter 4.

Disk acquisition can be performed using many methods:

1. Bit-stream disk-to-image file
2. Bit-stream disk-to-disk
3. Logical disk-to-disk
4. Spare data copy of a file

We will discuss the first option in this book. Bit-stream disk-to-image file is still considered the most used one in computer forensic investigation. This allows us to acquire the entire disk into an image file. It must be noted that this method will not copy the Host Protected Area (HPA) and Device Configuration Overlay (DCO). To include these areas in your image you need a tool capable of accessing the hard disk at the hardware level. The best tools able to perform this are hardware equipment's, but there are still a few software programs that can capture these areas such as PassMark OSForensics®. Later in this chapter we will show you how to acquire both HPA and DCO images.

Using FTK® Imager to Acquire Disk Drive

FTK® Imager is a data preview and imaging tool that allows computer investigators to quickly assess electronic evidence to determine if further analysis with a forensic tool such as AccessData® FTK® or EnCase® is justified. FTK® Imager can also create forensic images of digital evidence without making changes to the original evidence.

This software has the ability to make an image of the local hard drives, floppy diskettes, zip disks, CD/DVDs, and specific files or folders. It also has the ability to preview the contents of disk imager acquired through Windows Explorer exactly as if the user saw it on the original drive.

Note: When using FTK® Imager or any imaging software to create a forensic image of a hard drive or other electronic device, be sure you are using a hardware-based write-blocker or a specialized software for this purpose. This ensures that your operating system does not alter the original source drive when you attach it to your computer.

Now let us practice using this tool. We are using a machine with the Windows® 8.1 Enterprise edition installed. We will make an image of drive C:\ for practice.

1. Download FTK® Imager from http://accessdata.com/product-download. At the time of writing this chapter, version 3.4.2 was available for free download. Install this software following its simple steps. Note: FTK® Imager can be installed on a computer where it will be used, or it can be run from a portable device such as a USB thumb drive connected to a machine in the field. If you select to install FTK® Imager on a USB drive choose to download the lite version (at the time of writing FTK Imager Lite version 3.1.1 was available).
2. To launch this tool, go to *File* menu ≫ *Create Disk Image…*, and the disk image creation wizard appears.
3. The wizard window asks you to select the source evidence type (see Fig. 6.29). You have the following options:
   a. Physical drive: This will capture the entire local disk drive. If you are capturing a disk that has full disk encryption enabled, you will need to select this option.
   b. Logical drive: This option allows you to select individual disk partitions or CD/DVD and floppy disk drive.
   c. Image: Here you can select a disk image as the source. If you select this option, later you'll need to select the image type (DD, SMART, AFF, E01).
   d. The content of a folder: This option allows you to image the content of only one folder. The image created will include only logical files. It will not include any file system metadata, deleted files, unallocated space, and so on.
   e. Fernico Device (multiple CD/DVD)

In this case, we'll select *Logical Drive* **and click** *Next* **to continue.**

4. The wizard asks you to select your partition or CD/DVD from the drop-down menu. In our case we want to create an image of C:\ drive, where Windows® resides. After you click Select, click *Finish* to continue (see Fig. 6.30).
5. Once the *Create Image* dialog appears, click *Add* to *select the Image Type*. The type you choose will usually depend

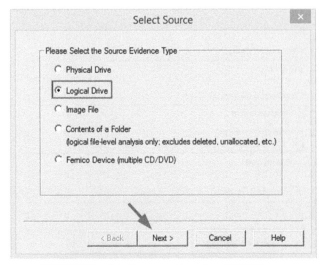

FIGURE 6.29 Select source evidence type in FTK Imager.

on what tools you plan to use on the image. In this case we will select the DD type as this format will work with more open source tools. But you might want SMART or E01 if you will primarily be working with ASR Expert Witness® or EnCase®. Click *Next* to continue (Fig. 6.31).

6. FTK Imager® asks you to specify evidence item information (see Fig. 6.32). All evidence item information is optional; if you select the raw DD format, the image metadata will not be stored in the image file itself.

7. The next dialog asks you to select image destination. You can also set the maximum fragment size of image split files. Click *Finish* to complete the wizard and to return back to the *Create Image* window. At this stage you can click *Start* to begin the acquisition process (see Fig. 6.33).

Now, a progress window will appear. When finishing the imaging process a summary window appears that contains a log of the acquisition process in addition to the checksum of the acquired image.

Congratulations! You have acquired your disk drive image. Later we will see how we can extract important information from it that can help us in our search for concealed data.

Deleted Files Recovery

Most deleted files can be recovered in Windows® OS if you tried to recover them fast enough before writing new data to the same disk holding them. When Windows® deletes a file, all it really does is mark the space on the hard drive that your deleted file occupied as free. When Windows® needs to store a new file, it may write data on top of this free space. This makes recovering the old file very difficult and time-consuming and in this case, you can only recover parts of the deleted file. So the sooner you work to recover a deleted file the better chance you will have in recovering it.

As we saw, Windows® does not delete the entire file immediately, it only deletes the pointer to this file; the data block of this file remains intact. This operation helps to speed up the deletion process and saves valuable time. For example, deleting a 9 GB file needs time equal to writing 9 GB of data to your hard drive. By removing only the pointer to the deleted file, its space will be freed up immediately (theoretically of course); however, data that belongs to deleted file blocks will remain on the disk and will not be removed until Windows® needs to write new data in their place.

Windows® deletes files using two methods: (1) by moving them to the recycle bin or trash, and (2) using the combination of Shift + Delete keys. Files deleted using both techniques can be recovered as we are going to see next.

The recovery of deleted files can be more successful if you:

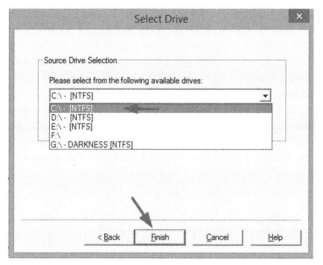

FIGURE 6.30 Select the drive whose image you want to capture.

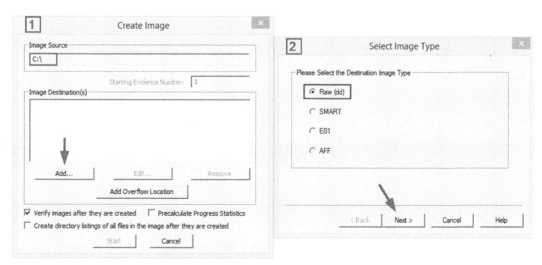

FIGURE 6.31 Select image type and other options.

- Recover the deleted files quickly before the user or Windows® writes data on top of the deleted file location in the hard disk.
- Shut down the PC immediately after deleting the file, and try to remove the hard drive that contains your deleted files and connect it to another PC that has an appropriate data recovery tool.

This discussion is only applicable to regular hard drives (mechanical disks with platters); new solid state drives (SSDs) use a different mechanism when handling deleted files. All modern SSDs utilize the TRIM command, when enabled. This command will remove deleted file data blocks instantly allowing for another file to take its space. The SSD uses this technique to speed the writing process next time the OS needs to write data onto disk. There are many approaches to implementing TRIM on SSD devices, which vary according to the operating system in use. Some operating systems will execute TRIM instantly after each file deletion, while others will execute TRIM at regular intervals. Windows® 7 and all its successors support TRIM with SSD drives, as do Mac® OS X 10.6.8+ and Android 4.3+.

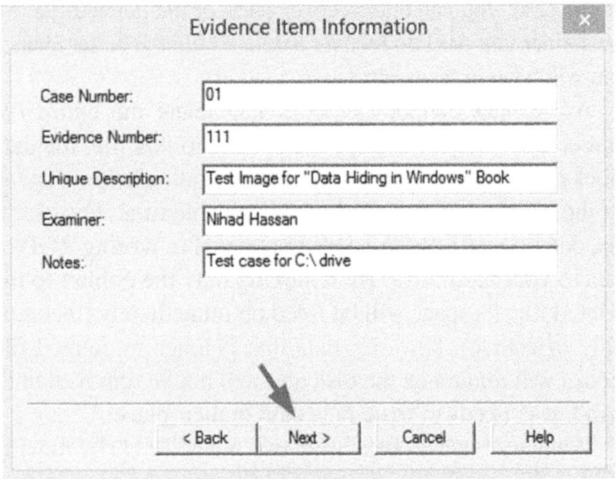

Recovering data from SSD with the TRIM command enabled is considered extremely difficult and in many situations it is impossible to achieve. Data can be recovered from such drives by using specialized tools, but in order to make the recovery possible, the device should be turned off immediately after the accidental deletion of the file, which may not be the case when investigating suspected devices for incriminating data.

There are numerous tools that can be used to recover deleted files or part of them. Some of these tools are better than others in recovering data, but for the purpose of this chapter, we are going to investigate recovery of deleted files using an image acquired from a USB zip drive. The same principles can also be applied to any image acquired from a hard disk drive and other USB memory sticks.

In a previous section we showed you how to acquire a hard disk image using FTK® Imager. In this example, however, we'll use another forensic tool, ProDiscover® Basic, to acquire and recover deleted files from a USB drive. Using multiple forensic tools will make this chapter richer. Note that almost all forensic suites offer deleted data recovery functions.

Acquiring Disk Drive Images Using ProDiscover Basic

Acquiring data using ProDiscover® Basic is very simple. Download the tool from http://www.arcgroupny.com/products/

FIGURE 6.32 Attach evidence item information with your captured image.

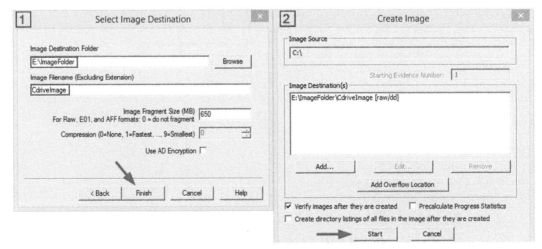

FIGURE 6.33 Select image destination and name and then start acquiring the image.

prodiscover-basic and install it using the following simple steps.

1. Launch ProDiscover® Basic. Dialog appears asking you to enter project details (number, name, and some description); you can ignore this by clicking *Cancel*.
2. Go to the *Action* menu » *Capture Image…*, fill in this dialog with the source drive, destination, and image format (in this case, select ProDiscover format). This dialog also allows you to compress the image to save space and to enter a password for protecting it. You can also enter the technician name and image number and some description. After filling in all these details, click Ok to begin image acquisition (see Fig. 6.34).

When ProDiscover® Basic finishes acquiring the image, click *OK* in the completion message window (see Fig. 6.35).

As we said before, the same procedures can be implemented on regular hard disk drives.

Analyzing the Digital Evidence for Deleted Files and Other Artifacts

The acquired image will contain the existing files, in addition to deleted files and other file fragments. As we said before, when you delete a file on a disk drive or USB, this file will not get deleted immediately. In this exercise we will recover deleted data from the image we already have.

1. Open ProDiscover® Basic, go to *File* » *New Project*, insert the project number and name in the dialog in addition to some comments if you want, and click *OK*.
2. From the tree view of the main window, click *Add* to expand this button, then click *Image File* to select the image you acquired in the previous section (see Fig. 6.36).
3. After opening your acquired image in ProDiscover®, go to *Content View* and expand it if necessary, then click to expand *Images*. Finally expand your image file by clicking

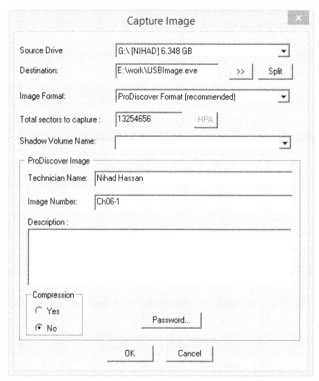

FIGURE 6.34 The capture image dialog window using ProDiscover® Basic.

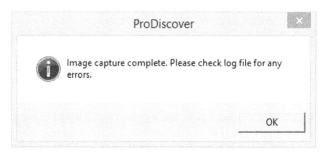

FIGURE 6.35 Dialog box launched by ProDiscover® Basic announcing that image acquisition is completed.

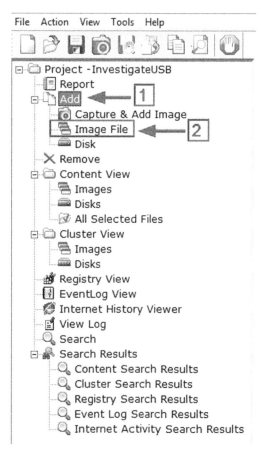

FIGURE 6.36 The tree view in ProDiscover® Basic.

the + sign on the left side of your selected image (see Fig. 6.37).

When clicking your acquired image, the ProDiscover® work area will be populated with the image file's contents. Below the work area you can see the *Data Area* where the content of each selected file in the *Work Area* appears (see Fig. 6.38).

You can note from Fig. 6.38 that the work area contains many deleted files that have not been overwritten yet and can be easily recovered. To recover a deleted file, right-click it and select *View* to view this file using the standard application associated with opening this type of file. You can also select *Copy* to copy the file to another location where you can store it for later use (see Fig. 6.39).

If your acquired images contain a large volume of data, investigating them may take a long time, which may not always be possible. For this reason, ProDiscover® Basic offers

a search facility that accepts both string and hexadecimal values as search keywords.

To test the search facility; go to the tree view and click *Search*. The search options dialog box appears. Select the *Content Search* tab (see Fig. 6.40). From this point, you can configure your search options by choosing your keyword type (hex or string), search inside metadata (like MS Office files metadata). You can also filter your finding by date (date created, modified, or accessed). The search dialog is rich and contains other tabs (the Cluster tab allows you to search for data at the cluster level). The Registry search is for searching inside the Windows® registry (this requires an image taken for the Windows® registry). The *Internet History Search* tab is for searching inside previous visited websites, and finally, the *Event Log Search* tab is for investigating inside Windows® log files.

For example, if we want to search for a name in all files, including their metadata, in the search option dialog, type the information shown in Fig. 6.40.

ProDiscover® Basic will conduct a search inside a selected image and show all files that contain the specified keyword (see Fig. 6.41).

You can view or save any file from the resultant search by right-clicking the file and then selecting *View* or *Copy File* as we did before. ProDiscover® allows you to conduct more than one search and open each search result in a separate panel allowing more flexibility for its users as shown in Fig. 6.41.

If you do not prefer to use this method to recover deleted data (acquire an image and then investigate for deleted files using computer forensic tools like ProDiscover® Basic), you can install data recovery software. There are many free programs that perform this function; keep in mind the following important things when using such tools:

1. When using a data recovery tool, make sure you install this tool on a PC other than the one you want to recover data from. It is better to unplug the hard drive of the PC you want to retrieve deleted files from then attach it to another PC that contains data recovery software. Recovering deleted data from one machine into itself may render your lost data permanently unrecoverable.

2. Not all data recovery software offers the facility to conduct a deep search as the one offered by many computer forensic tools. For example, ProDiscover® allows you to search inside file metadata for a specific keyword, which allows you to filter data very fast and save time.

3. You should select the data recovery software according to the file system used on the drive you are recovering data from. For example, most hard disks in Windows® PCs use the NTFS file system, however USB flash drives usually use some variant of FAT (FAT16, FAT32, or exFAT).

4. In order to record your findings in a legal digital forensic investigation, you must acquire a disk drive image using a reliable computer forensic tool such as ProDiscover® Basic, FTK® Imager, or any similar computer forensic

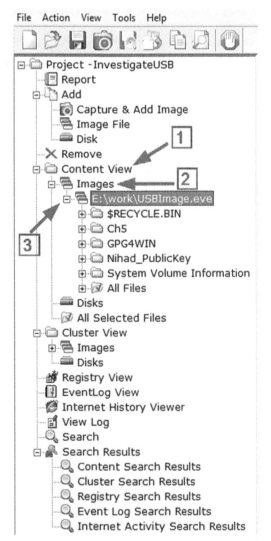

FIGURE 6.37 Expand Content View inside the ProDiscover® Basic main window to view image files.

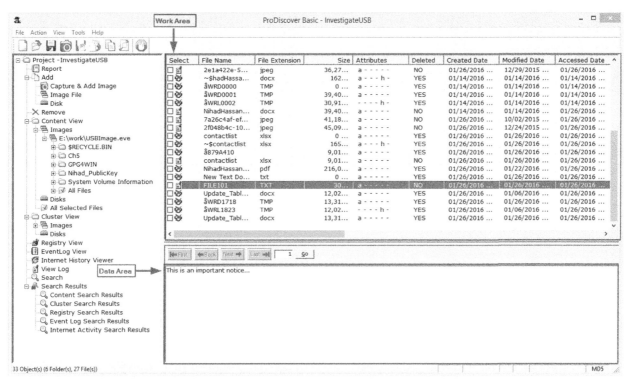

FIGURE 6.38   Selecting a file and viewing its contents in the data area.

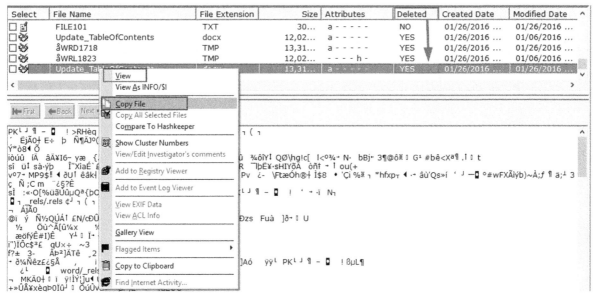

FIGURE 6.39   View or copy a deleted file using ProDiscover® Basic.

program and then perform your data recovery. This is one part of making your evidence stand in a court of law.

Some data recovery programs for Windows® are:

1. TestDisk: http://www.cgsecurity.org/wiki/TestDisk
2. PhotoRec: http://www.cgsecurity.org/wiki/PhotoRec
3. Recuva: https://www.piriform.com/recuva

4. EaseUS Data Recovery Wizard: http://www.easeus.com/datarecoverywizard/free-data-recovery-software.htm
5. A list of data recovery tools for Windows® OS is on the *Source Forge* website: http://sourceforge.net/directory/system-administration/storage/recovery/os:windows/; and another list exists on the Forensics Wiki website: http://www.forensicswiki.org/wiki/Tools:Data_Recovery

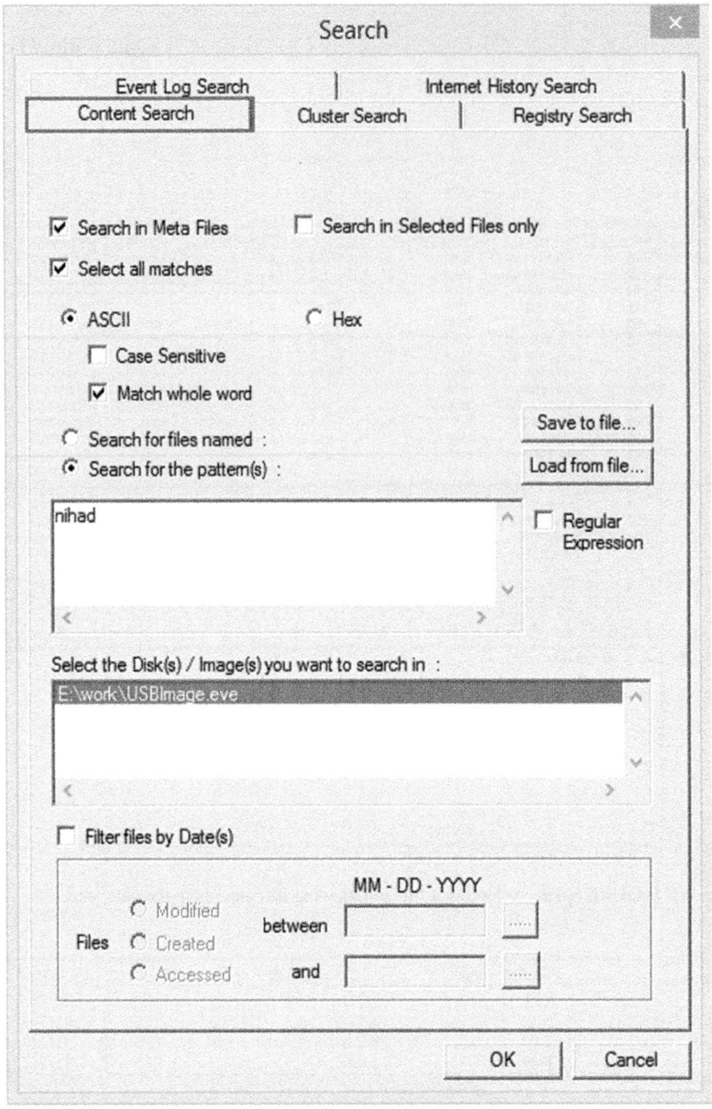

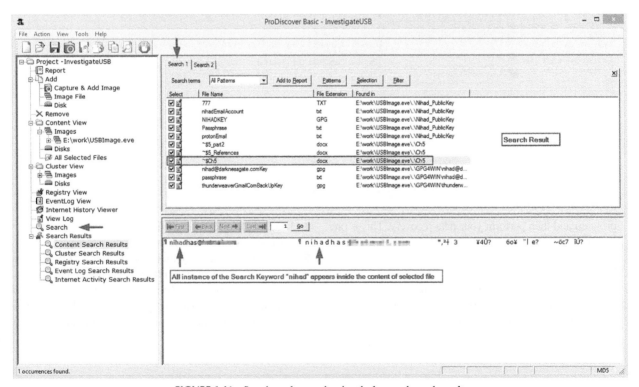

FIGURE 6.40 Searching for a specific keyword in the search dialog using ProDiscover® Basic.

FIGURE 6.41 Search result pane showing the keyword search result.

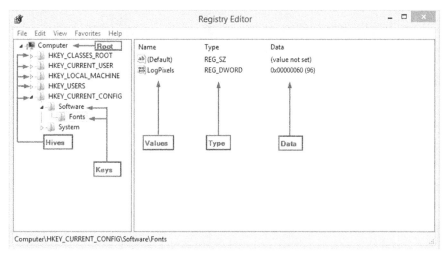

FIGURE 6.42 General structure of the Windows registry. *Image taken using Windows 8.1 registry.*

Windows Registry Analysis

Window® registry is a hierarchical database that stores the value of variables in Windows® and other applications and services that run on Windows® machines. Windows® registry allows Windows® OS to control hardware, software, user information, and GUI functionality of the system. Registry data is structured in a tree format. Each node in the tree is called a key.

Notably, a registry tree can be 512 levels deep only. Keep in mind that a registry key is a container object that plays the same role as a folder in normal Windows® naming. Registry values are noncontainer objects similar to files (cannot hold other objects). Also a key can contain other keys (subkeys) in addition to data values. It should also be noted that at its root level, Windows® registry is composed of a set of registry hives. The name Hive is given to the main parts of the registry that contain registry keys, subkeys, and registry values. Hives are considered the first folders in the registry (this is what distinguishes it from registry keys) and appear on the left side when you first open the registry editor; they appear as children of the parent root (Computer) (see Fig. 6.42). In order to open the registry editor, type *regedit* in the run dialog and press Enter (you can access the RUN window by pressing the combination keys **Windows + R**).

The following are common registry hives found in newer Windows® machines (Windows® XP+):

1. HKEY_CLASSES_ROOT
2. HKEY_CURRENT_USER
3. HKEY_LOCAL_MACHINE
4. HKEY_USERS
5. HKEY_CURRENT_CONFIG

Old versions of Windows® (ME, 98, and 95) contained a hive called HKEY_DYN_DATA; however, newer versions of Windows® discard this hive and stored its data inside the HKEY_LOCAL_MACHINE\HARDWARE hive.

We will limit our discussion about Windows® registry structure to this extent for now. Meanwhile, let's conduct some experiments to analyze the registry searching for interesting data that will help us in a criminal investigation.

Windows Registry Startup Location

Autorun programs are launched whenever Windows® boots; a Trojan, virus, or any malicious software can be attached to the autorun list of programs causing Windows® to load it automatically with each boot.

Windows® registry keeps a record of every program boot with Windows®. The list of such programs will be located in the registry keys listed in Table 6.2.

Microsoft has a great utility available to inspect all of these registry keys (see Fig. 6.43) called *Autoruns*, which provides a GUI that allows a user to easily investigate each program or DLL component that boots automatically with Windows® and disable it if necessary. This tool can be downloaded from https://technet.microsoft.com/en-us/sysinternals/bb963902.aspx.

Checking Installed Programs

Installed programs can reveal a great amount of detail about the programs that have been installed and used on a suspect's machine. Windows® uninstall function usually does not delete all leftovers of previously installed programs. Such traces can give clues about the existence of steganography and encryption programs that were previously installed on a suspect's machine.

Windows® keeps track of all installed software in the following locations in the registry:

TABLE 6.2 Windows Registry Startup Location Keys

No	Registry Key	Role
1	HKEY_LOCAL_MACHINE\System\CurrentControlSet\Services	Hardware device drivers—this boots first.
2	HKEY_LOCAL_MACHINE\System\CurrentControlSet\Services	Boot Windows-related services and drivers.
3	HKEY_LOCAL_MACHINE\Software\Microsoft\Windows\CurrentVersion\RunServicesOnce	This key used to start services automatically when Windows boots.
4	HKEY_LOCAL_MACHINE\Software\Microsoft\Windows\CurrentVersion\RunOnce HKEY_CURRENT_USER\Software\Microsoft\Windows\CurrentVersion\RunOnce	The programs listed in this key are used by setup programs and it is designed to run once and then get deleted.
5	HKEY_LOCAL_MACHINE\Software\Microsoft\Windows\CurrentVersion\Run HKEY_CURRENT_USER\Software\Microsoft\Windows\CurrentVersion\Run	Start programs automatically upon each boot.
6	HKEY_LOCAL_MACHINE\Software\Microsoft\Windows\CurrentVersion\Policies\Explorer\Run HKEY_CURRENT_USER\Software\Microsoft\Windows\CurrentVersion\Policies\Explorer\Run	Load programs according to user policy.
7	HKEY_CURRENT_USER\Software\Microsoft\Windows NT\CurrentVersion\Windows\load	Hardly used, but can load programs automatically on system boot.
8	HKEY_LOCAL_MACHINE\Software\Microsoft\Windows NT\CurrentVersion\Windows	All the DLLs that are specified in this value are loaded by each Microsoft Windows-based application that is running in the current log on session [13].
9	HKEY_LOCAL_MACHINE\SOFTWARE\Microsoft\Windows\CurrentVersion\ShellServiceObjectDelayLoad	The files under this key are loaded automatically by Explorer.exe when Windows® boots.
10	HKEY_LOCAL_MACHINE\SOFTWARE\Microsoft\Windows\CurrentVersion\Explorer\SharedTaskScheduler	Can run programs automatically. Only supported on Windows XP, NT, and 2000.

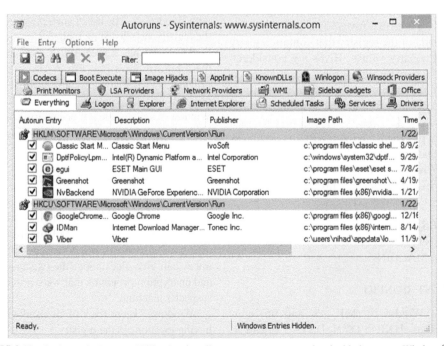

FIGURE 6.43 Sysinternals Autoruns Utility showing all autorun programs associated with the current Windows® boot.

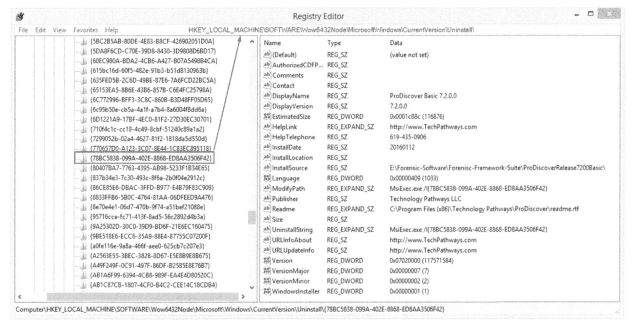

FIGURE 6.44   List of 32-bit programs installed on Windows® X64 version. *Image taken from Windows® 8.1 X64 version registry.*

HKEY_LOCAL_MACHINE\SOFTWARE\
MICROSOFT\WINDOWS\CURRENTVERSION\
UNINSTALL

Current user (HKEY_CURRENT_USER) hive also has similar key that you should look at:
HKEY_CURRENT_USER\SOFTWARE\
MICROSOFT\WINDOWS\CURRENTVERSION\
UNINSTALL

If the suspect's machine has more than one user, each user will have his/her own set of software installed at his/her own key under the (HKEY_CURRENT_USER) hive.

If you compare the list of programs installed on your Windows® machine, which appears in *Programs and Features* of the control panel, with the programs that appear in the registry keys we already mentioned, you will notice that not all programs appear in the registry keys. This is because when you install a 32-bit program on Windows® X64 version, such programs will not appear on the previous registry keys. In order to view such programs you need to check the following registry key (see Fig. 6.44):

HKEY_LOCAL_MACHINE\SOFTWARE\
WOW6432NODE\MICROSOFT\WINDOWS\
CURRENTVERSION\UNINSTALL\

Lastly, if the program was installed via an .MSI package, you also should check the following registry keys [14]:

HKEY_CLASSES_ROOT\INSTALLER\
PRODUCTS\<PRODUCT CODE>\SOURCELIST\NET

HKEY_CURRENT_USER\SOFTWARE\
MICROSOFT\INSTALLER\PRODUCTS\<PRODUCT
CODE>\SOURCELIST\NET

Free software by *nirsoft called RegScanner* will help you locate lost information such as parts of installed programs and applications left over or any data items that could be hidden inside Windows® registry.

According to its creator, "*RegScanner* is a small utility that allows you to scan the Registry, find the desired Registry values that match to the specified search criteria, and display them in one list. After finding the Registry values, you can easily jump to the right value in *RegEdit*, simply by double-clicking the desired Registry item. You can also export the found Registry values into a **.reg** file that can be used in *RegEdit*."

Download *RegScanner* from http://www.nirsoft.net/utils/regscanner.html. When you first execute this tool, a *search option* dialog will appear to enter your search criteria and specify search options (see Fig. 6.45).

Another tool for investigating the Windows® registry for hidden entries is *Registry Finder*. Hidden registry entries are the keys with the null character in its name. Such keys cannot be created, deleted, modified, or viewed by standard Windows® API, so they are not accessible by *regedit* and most other registry editors. *Registry Finder* claims an ability to find such keys. The software can be downloaded from http://registry-finder.com.

Note that not all applications need to have a registry key. There are many applications that do not need to be installed

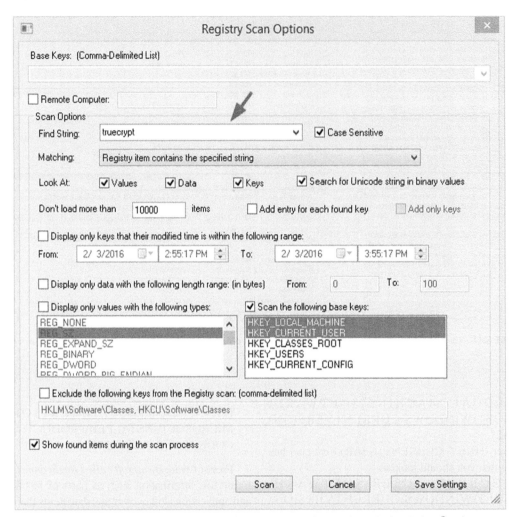

FIGURE 6.45   Registry scan options used by the RegScanner tool to search within the Windows® registry.

on the Windows® machine in order to work. For example, portable programs launched using U3 USB sticks can run without installing a registry key. To counter for this issue, we can check to see a list of USB devices that have been attached to this system previously. Later we'll check the Windows® Prefetch folder for such programs.

Connected USB Devices

Windows® keeps a history of all connected USB removable storage devices (thumb drives, iPods, digital cameras, external HDD, etc.). This information is vital to know which devices were previously (or currently) connected to the suspect's machine and by which user.

Windows® stores USB history-related information using five registry keys, and each one offers a different set of information about the connected device. When combining this information, investigators can formulate a clear view of how a suspect has used removable storage to commence an incident.

Windows registry stores information about each USB connected device in the following registry keys:

1. HKEY_LOCAL_MACHINE\SYSTEM\ CURRENTCONTROLSET\ENUM\USBSTOR: This key keeps a list of all USB storage devices that have ever been plugged into the system. It shows the USB device name, vendor name (manufacturer name), device serial number (note that if the second character of the device serial number is "&" it means the connected device does not have a serial number). See Fig. 6.46 for a list of previously connected USB devices on an author machine.

2. HKEY_LOCAL_MACHINE\SYSTEM\ MOUNTEDDEVICES: The MountedDevices subkey stores the database of mounted devices for the NTFS file system. This database matches the serial number of a USB device to a given drive letter or volume that was mounted when the USB device was inserted.

3. HKEY_CURRENT_USER\SOFTWARE\MICROSOFT\ WINDOWS\CURRENTVERSION\EXPLORER\ MOUNTPOINTS2: This key will hold information that

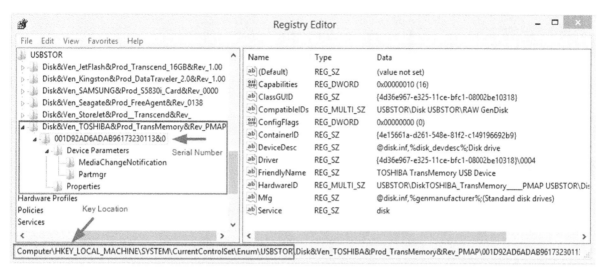

FIGURE 6.46 USB connected devices history.

states which user was logged into Windows® when a specific USB device was connected.

4. H K E Y _ L O C A L _ M A C H I N E \ S Y S T E M \ CURRENTCONTROLSET\ENUM\USB: This key views the USB device interface GUID, hardware ID, device class information about your device, and the last time this USB was connected to the current machine (see Fig. 6.47).

5. Check this file at C:\Windows\inf\setupapi.dev.log for Windows® Vista, 7, 8, and 10. On Windows® XP this file will be located at C:\Windows\setupapi.log. Keep in mind that you need to open this file and search for a particular USB device through its serial number to find when it was first connected to the system (see Fig. 6.48).

If you want to automate your work with USB mass storage discovery in Windows® OS, you can download a free tool by *nirsoft* that can perform all the manual tasks we already did called *USBDeview*. According to its creator, "USBDeview is a small utility software that lists all USB devices that currently connected to your computer, as well as all USB devices that you previously used. For each USB device, extended information will display: Device name/description, device type, serial number (for mass storage devices), the date/time that device was added, VendorID, ProductID, and more…" This tool can be downloaded from http://www.nirsoft.net/utils/usb_devices_view.html (see Fig. 6.49).

In Fig. 6.49, the *Last Plug/Unplug Date* represents the first time that the device was connected to the system. This date does not change when the same device is repeatedly reinserted. The second date appears: Created Date represents the last time that the same device was attached to the system.

Note that not all USB devices are connected and leave traces in Windows registry as we already described. Some modern USB devices use a media transfer protocol (MTP) when connecting with computers. New Android versions, Windows phones, and Blackberry all use this protocol, which does not leave traces in Windows registry keys we already talked about. For example, when an Android smartphone is connected to a computer running Windows® using the MTP, the Android device will not expose its contents to Windows® as USB mass storage, allowing it to have access to its raw file system. Instead the Android device will only allow Windows® to have access to a short list of media files that Windows® can see. If Windows® requests a file, the phone will respond by sending the file over the MTP connection.

What we want to conclude from this brief discussion is that USB devices connected through a MTP connection do not leave traces on the previously mentioned USB storage device registry keys. However, there are some forensic tools that can reveal such connected devices. Check your computer forensic tool feature list for such functions. Nicole Ibrahim has conducted research about MTP devices as a series of blog posts, which can be found at http://nicoleibrahim.com/part-1-mtp-and-ptp-usb-device-research.

Mostly Recently Used List

Windows keeps track of some user actions on the registry. There are many applications that run on Windows® that have most recently used (MRU) lists, which are lists of files that have been most recently accessed. Such lists are spread across the registry and store previous user actions on his/her PC. Incidentally, it is somewhat similar to IE history. The most common places for storing such lists are in the following registry keys [15]:

- H K E Y _ C U R R E N T _ U S E R \ S O F T W A R E \ MICROSOFT\WINDOWS\CURRENTVERSION\ EXPLORER\DOC FIND SPEC MRU
- H K E Y _ C U R R E N T _ U S E R \ S O F T W A R E \ MICROSOFT\WINDOWS\CURRENTVERSION\ EXPLORER\FINDCOMPUTERMRU

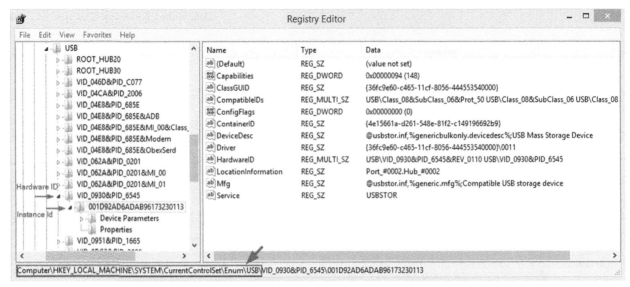

FIGURE 6.47 Viewing detailed information about all previously connected USB devices.

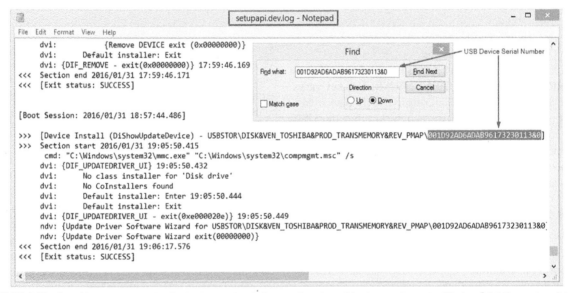

FIGURE 6.48 Searching setupapi.dev.log for the time a USB device was first plugged in. *Image taken using Windows® 8.1 Enterprise edition®.*

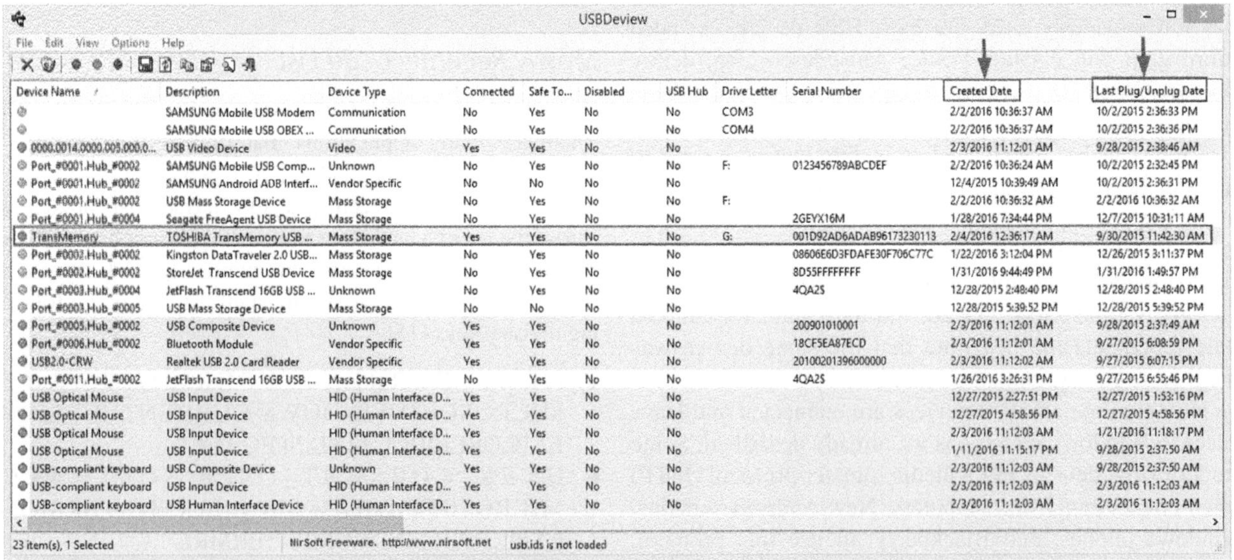

FIGURE 6.49 Using USBDeview to view USB hard drive artifacts.

- HKEY_CURRENT_USER\SOFTWARE\ MICROSOFT\WINDOWS\CURRENTVERSION\ EXPLORER\PRNPORTSMRU
- HKEY_CURRENT_USER\SOFTWARE\ MICROSOFT\WINDOWS\CURRENTVERSION\ EXPLORER\RUNMRU
- HKEY_CURRENT_USER\SOFTWARE\ MICROSOFT\WINDOWS\CURRENTVERSION\ EXPLORER\STREAMMRU
- SOFTWARE\MICROSOFT\WINDOWS\ CURRENTVERSION\APPLETS\REGEDIT
- SOFTWARE\MICROSOFT\WINDOWS\ CURRENTVERSION\APPLETS\REGEDIT\ FAVORITES
- SOFTWARE\MICROSOFT\WINDOWS\ CURRENTVERSION\APPLETS\PAINT\RECENT FILE LIST
- SOFTWARE\MICROSOFT\WINDOWS\ CURRENTVERSION\EXPLORER\COMDLG32\ OPENSAVEMRU

A complete list of MRU locations on major Windows® OS versions is available from http://forensicswiki.org/wiki/ List_of_Windows_MRU_Locations.

For example, if we want to check for previous commands run by the user using the RUN dialog window, we can go to the following registry key to see a list of previous commands (see Fig. 6.50): HKEY_CURRENT_USER\SOFTWARE\MICROSOFT\WINDOWS\CURRENTVERSION\ EXPLORER\RUNMRU.

In Fig. 6.50, RunMRU show that a *TrueCrypt* program was executed using the RUN dialog from within the USB zip drive. Further investigations for other keys in the registry can reveal the following information: user associated with this action, USB device used, and the time connection took place.

UserAssist Forensics

UserAssist keeps a record of all Windows® programs recently launched in addition to the files you've recently opened (MS Office, images, etc.).

Beginning from the date Windows® was installed on your machine, all programs launched on it will be recorded in the following registry key:

HKEY_CURRENT_USER\SOFTWARE\ MICROSOFT\WINDOWS\CURRENTVERSION\ EXPLORER\USERASSIST

Windows® will not only store the program name, but it will also record the last used date/time the program was executed in addition to the number of executions for each one. *UserAssist* will only record programs launched via Windows Explorer; programs launched through the command line will not appear in *UserAssist* registry keys.

Keynames associated with *UserAssist* keys are stored in an encrypted format using ROT-13 encoding schema. There are many tools that can automatically decrypt and investigate *UserAssist* data. A famous tool by *Nirsoft* called *UserAssistView* can reveal *UserAssist* stored data (see Fig. 6.51).

Aldeid offers a complete forensic analysis of the UserAssist feature in Windows® XP and 7; check their excellent guide at https://www.aldeid.com/wiki/Windows-userassist-keys.

Internet Programs Investigation

Internet applications already installed on Windows® can give important information about user actions performed previously on his/her computer. For example, if we investigate web browsers and see that the user was downloading or searching online for information on steganography and associated tools, this will give a clear sign that this user may use such tools to conceal secret data. In the following section we will describe how to investigate different Internet applications for evidence that can help discover whether there is any hidden data on a particular PC.

Internet Explorer

Internet Explorer comes preinstalled with all versions of Windows®. It has a registry key located at HKEY_CURRENT_USER\Software\Microsoft\Internet Explorer. You

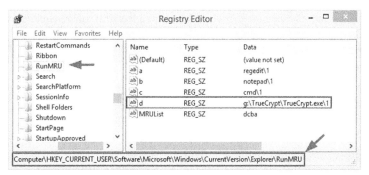

FIGURE 6.50 List of previous commands stored inside the RunMRU key.

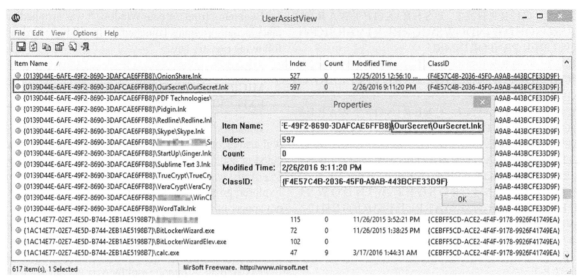

FIGURE 6.51 Viewing stored UserAssist registry key data using UserAssistView from Nirsoft.

will notice that under this key there are many keys; however, we are mainly concerned with:

- HKEY_CURRENT_USER\SOFTWARE\ MICROSOFT\INTERNET EXPLORER\MAIN: This key stores IE configuration settings like the home page, search bar, and so on.
    1. HKEY_CURRENT_USER\SOFTWARE\ MICROSOFT\INTERNET EXPLORER\ TYPEDURLS: The TypedURLs key maintains a list of the URLs the user types into the address bar in Internet Explorer (see Fig. 6.52).

In Windows®, the temporary Internet files folder, history, and cookies folder all contain a file called *index. dat*. This file keeps a coded record of the files in each of these folders. You can't delete this file using the regular Windows® *delete* function (you can do this through DOS only).

The location of this file can vary according to the version of Windows®.

Windows® XP:
    windows\documents and settings\%username%\local settings\temporary internet files\content.ie5
    windows\documents and settings\%username%\cookies
    windows\documents and settings\%username%\local settings\history\history.ie5
Windows® Vista, 7, 8, and 10:
    windows\users\%username%\appdata\local\micro-soft\windows\temporary internet files\
    windows\users\%username%\appdata\local\micro-soft\windows\temporary internet files\low\

You can automate the IE investigation task by using specialized tools. *Nirsoft* offers many tools that can simplify this issue; here is a list of IE forensic tools from *nirsoft*:

1. IEHistoryView: View IE history. http://www.nirsoft.net/ utils/iehv.html
2. IECacheView: Read the cache folder of IE. http://www. nirsoft.net/utils/ie_cache_viewer.html
3. IECookies: View all cookies that Internet Explorer stores on your computer. http://www.nirsoft.net/utils/iecookies. html
4. IE PassView: Reveal the passwords stored by Internet Explorer web browser. http://www.nirsoft.net/utils/internet_ explorer_password.html

Mozilla Firefox and Other Browsers

Firefox is considered among the most used browsers in the world. Firefox does not use Windows® registry the same way as the IE browser because it is not a native Microsoft application. Firefox stores its web history, download history, and bookmarks in a single file called *places.sqlite*. This file exists within your Firefox profile. You can access your profile by pressing the *Windows* key and typing the following: **%APPDATA%\Mozilla\Firefox\Profiles**. In the search box, your Firefox profile will appear in the search result as a folder; click to access it (see Fig. 6.53).

What we care about in our forensic search are the files surrounded with squares in Fig. 6.53. We'll describe each one briefly:

1. **Places.sqlite**: Holds bookmarks, websites, and download history.
2. **Cookies.sqlite**: Stores cookies planted by websites you already visited.
3. **Formhistory.sqlite**: Stores your search keywords used in Firefox search bar and your searches in Firefox website forms.
4. **Key3.db and logins.json**: Here is where Firefox saves your passwords.

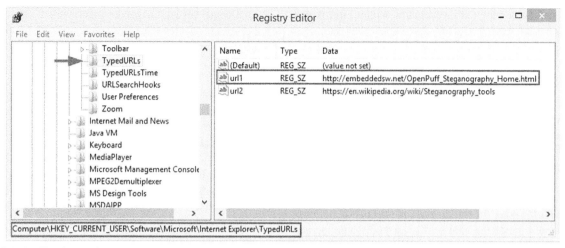

FIGURE 6.52 Showing previous URLs entered by a particular user using Internet Explorer. OpenPuff is a steganography tool; this should draw an investigator's attention that concealed data can be located on this machine within multimedia files.

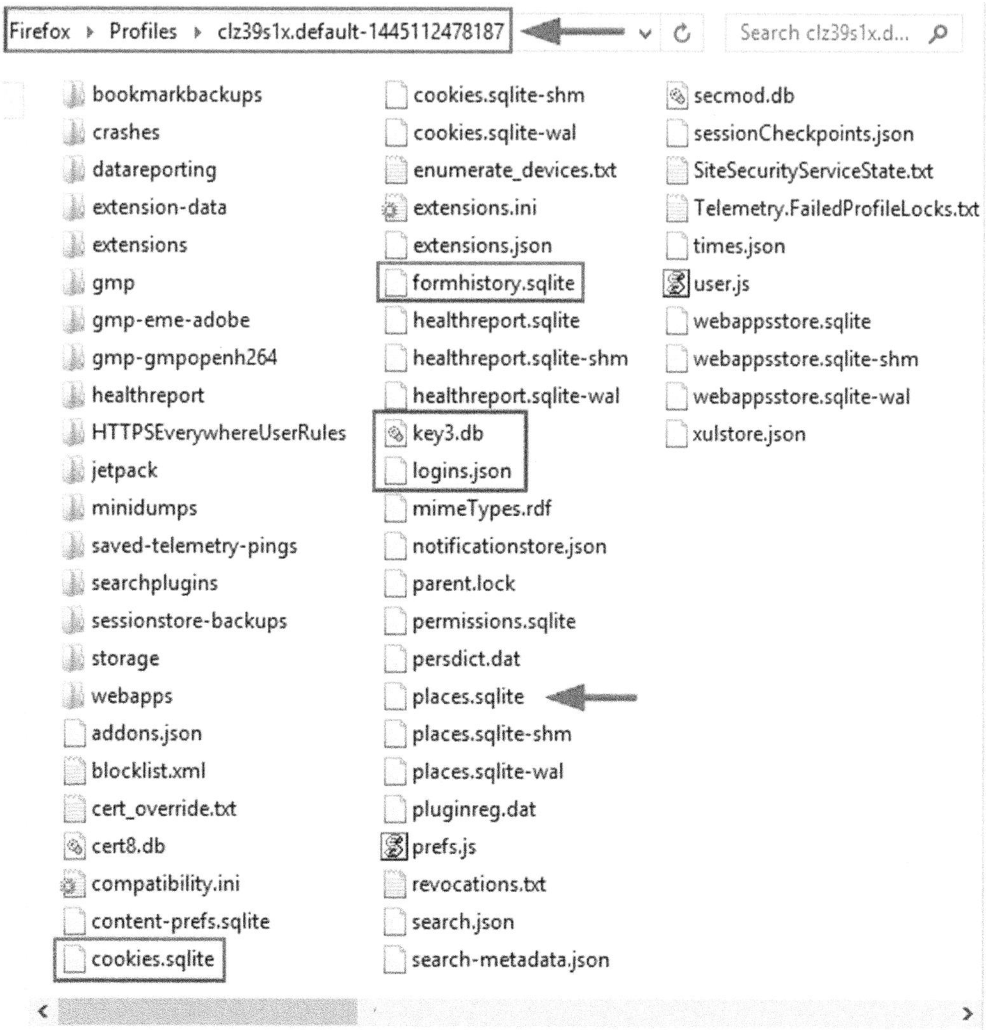

FIGURE 6.53 Firefox profile folder contents.

You can automate your investigation within Firefox and other browsers such as Opera®, Netscape® Navigator, and Chrome® using forensic tools, like *nirsoft*, which offers free portable tools for this issue:

- **MozillaHistoryView**: Reads history files of Firefox/ Mozilla/Netscape web browsers, and displays the list of all visited webpages in the last days. http://www.nirsoft. net/utils/mozilla_history_view.html
- **MozillaCacheView**: Reads the cache folder of Firefox/ Mozilla/Netscape web browsers, and displays the list of all files currently stored in the cache. http://www.nirsoft. net/utils/mozilla_cache_viewer.html
- **MozillaCookiesView**: It displays the details of all cookies stored inside the cookies file for both Netscape and Mozilla browsers. http://www.nirsoft.net/utils/mzcv.html
- **PasswordFox**: Password recovery tool that allows you to view the usernames and passwords stored by the Mozilla Firefox web browser. http://www.nirsoft.net/ utils/passwordfox.html
- **MyLastSearch**: Scans the cache and history files of four web browsers (IE, Firefox, Opera, and Chrome),

and locates all search queries made with the most popular search engines (Google, Yahoo, and MSN) and with popular social networking sites (Twitter, Facebook, MySpace). http://www.nirsoft.net/utils/my_last_search. html

- **SafariHistoryView**: Reads and parses the history file of Safari web browser (history.plist). http://www.nirsoft.net/ utils/safari_history_view.html
- **BrowsingHistoryView**: Reads the history data of four different web browsers (Internet Explorer, Mozilla Firefox, Google Chrome, and Safari) and displays the browsing history of all these web browsers in one table. You can use this tool instead of using a separate history viewer for each browser (see Fig. 6.54). http://www.nirsoft.net/utils/browsing_history_view.html

Other Internet Programs

There are many Internet applications worth investigating, but we limit our discussion here to the applications that a user may use in order to download encryption or/and steganography tools. The most used tools for downloading such

FIGURE 6.54 BrowsingHistoryView from nirsoft can display Internet history from major web browsers.

applications from hackers and criminals are torrent clients. Torrent websites are known as the biggest promoter of pirate software. In this section we will investigate the most used torrent client, *uTorrent*.

uTorrent uTorrent is a peer-to-peer program that uses metadata files (also known as torrent) to download files over the Internet from remote computers. *uTorrent* stores its previous downloaded files within the following path: **C:\Users\<user>\AppData\Roaming\uTorrent** (Windows® Vista, 7, 8,10). We are assuming of course that Windows® is installed on the *C:* drive.

In addition to previously downloaded files, the *uTorrent* folder contains program settings files that can be edited using programs like *BEncode Editor* (https://sites.google.com/site/ultimasites/bencode-editor).

If you come across a torrent file that doesn't have a meaningful name, you can investigate it and extract its contents using the tool *DumpTorrent*. This tool will show you uTorrent file information, including size, filenames, announce[-list], comment, publisher, and info_hash. It can also query (scrape) tracker for the current downloader count. You can

download it from http://sourceforge.net/projects/dumptorrent/ (see Fig. 6.55).

If you suspect a uTorrent client running on a Windows® machine and you want to confirm this process (uTorrent can

> Note: It is illegal to download pirated programs and other copyrighted materials through uTorrent clients. This test is made for exercise purposes only.

run from a USB stick), check the following registry key, which must store the firewall rule for all P2P clients (see Fig. 6.56):

HKEY_LOCAL_MACHINE\SYSTEM\Controlset001\Services\Sharedaccess\Parameters\Firewallpolicy\Firewallrules

Forensic Analysis of Windows Prefetch Files

Windows® Prefetch is a feature first introduced with Windows® XP. Beginning with Windows® Vista, the Prefetch feature has been extended by SuperFetch and ReadyBoost.

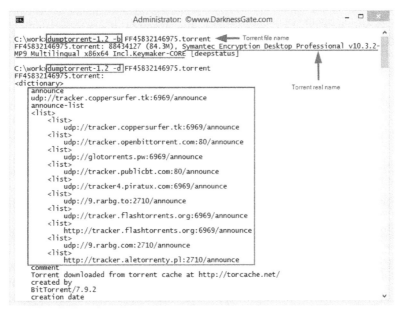

FIGURE 6.55 Extracting uTorrent file information using DumpTorrent.

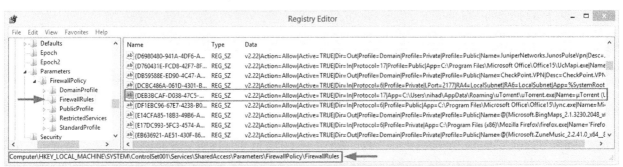

FIGURE 6.56 Check the uTorrent Firewall rule at Windows registry.

SuperFetch is a technology used by Windows® (Vista +) to preload commonly used applications into memory to reduce their load time.

ReadyBoost is a technology developed by Microsoft for its newer Windows® OS beginning with Windows® Vista. *Ready-Boost* enables Windows® to use NAND storage devices (like USB sticks and SD cards) to be used as a write cache between computer hard drive and RAM memory, resulting in increasing computing performance as a whole [16].

The Prefetcher's configuration is stored in the following Windows® registry key: HKEY_LOCAL_MACHINE\SYS-TEM\Currentcontrolset\Control\Session manager\Memory management\Prefetchparameters.

Windows® creates a Prefetch when a particular application runs from a particular location for the first time. A Prefetch file will contain information about which files are loaded as a part of the running application, a count of the number of times executable files run, and a timestamp indicating the last time any of these programs run. This information is used by Windows® to speed up the loading process of a particular application next time you run it.

Prefetch files are stored at *C:\Windows\Prefetch* (assuming Windows® is installed at C:\ partition).

Prefetch files are all named using common naming criteria. The name of the running application comes first, then an eight-character hash of the location where the application was run, and finally it ends with the **.PF** extension.

Determining from which location a particular application was run is easy. To reach this information, you need to populate a file with all possible saving locations inside Windows® hashed using the same hashing algorithm used by the Prefetch file. You then compare both hashes. This is a time-consuming process, however, and it is better to be automated. Each version of Windows® uses a different hashing algorithm. *Forensic Wiki* gives forensic investigators a method to calculate each hash to reveal its original location. Check their excellent guide on Windows® Prefetch files at http://www.forensicswiki.org/wiki/Prefetch.

What we care about as computer forensic experts searching for concealed data in Windows Prefetch files is that it tells us exactly which and when a specific application was executed on Windows®. Even if a specific application was uninstalled after running it, it will remain in the Windows® Prefetch folder. For example, if a user executes a portable image steganography tool (*OpenPuff*, for example) from a USB stick on a Windows® machine and uses this tool to conceal data and then unplugs the USB stick from the machine, if we search inside the Windows® Prefetch folder we can see that this steganography tool still exists within it, in addition to its last access date/time (Fig. 6.57).

We can automate our search inside the Windows® Prefetch folder using a simple, portable tool called *Win-PrefetchView* from *nirsoft* (http://www.nirsoft.net/utils/win_prefetch_view.html).

WinPrefetchView reads the Prefetch files stored in your system and displays the information stored in them. By looking at these files, you can learn which files every application is using, and which files are loaded on Windows® bootstrap (see Fig. 6.58). It can run on all versions of Windows® starting from XP through 10.

Windows Minidump Files Forensics

When your computer crashes with a Blue Screen of Death, the cause of the problem will be stored in *C:\Windows\minidump* or *C:\Winnt\minidump* depending on which version of Windows® you have.

Windows® minidump files can be read using a tool associated with Windows® called *Dumpchk.exe*. This is a command line utility that you can use to verify that a memory dump file has been created correctly. The *dumpchk* command is an external command that is available in Windows® 2000, XP, and 2003. Newer versions of Windows® can download this utility from http://go.microsoft.com/fwlink/?LinkID=156024.

What we care about as forensic examiners is that minidump files will usually contain the programs that were running/installed at the time when the crash happened. For example, if we were running a portable encryption tool to encrypt a secret file when the crash happened, this encryption tool name will appear in the dump file. This can effectively reveal previous user actions on the machine even though all protective measures mentioned in this chapter have been implemented to cover the user's previous tracks.

Nirsoft has a portable utility to investigate minidump files called *BlueScreenView*. This tool will scan all your minidump files created during crashes, and displays the information about all crashes in one table. For each crash, *BlueScreenView* displays the minidump filename, the date/time of the crash, the basic crash information displayed in the blue screen (Bug Check Code and 4 parameters), and the details of the driver or module that possibly caused the crash (filename, product name, file description, and file version) (see Fig. 6.59).

I will not mention how to antiforensic minidump files in the next chapter because of its simplicity. To avoid uncovering your previous program's usage, it is obvious that you should delete minidump files from your machine.

Windows Thumbnail Forensics

Windows® stores thumbnails of graphics files (JPEG, BMP, GIF, PNG, TIFF) and some document types (DOCX, PPTX) and movie files in the thumbnail cache file called *thumbs.db*. Even though a particular image or file has been deleted from our PC, its thumbnail view may still exist at thumbs.db. This helps us as forensic examiners to investigate previous files opened on a suspect machine.

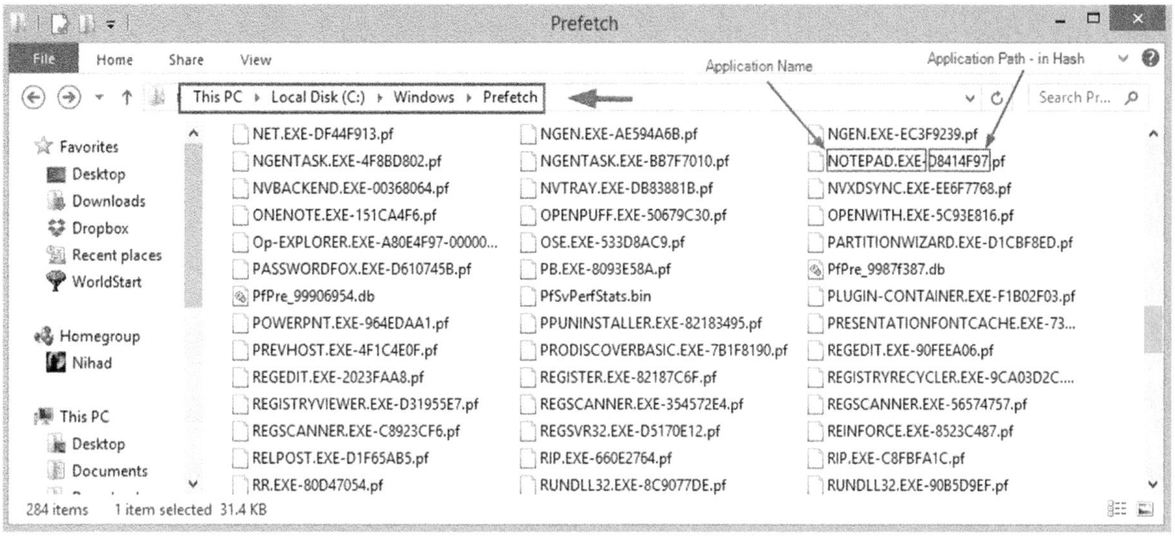

FIGURE 6.57 Contents of Windows Prefetch folder. *Image taken from Windows® 8.1 Enterprise.*

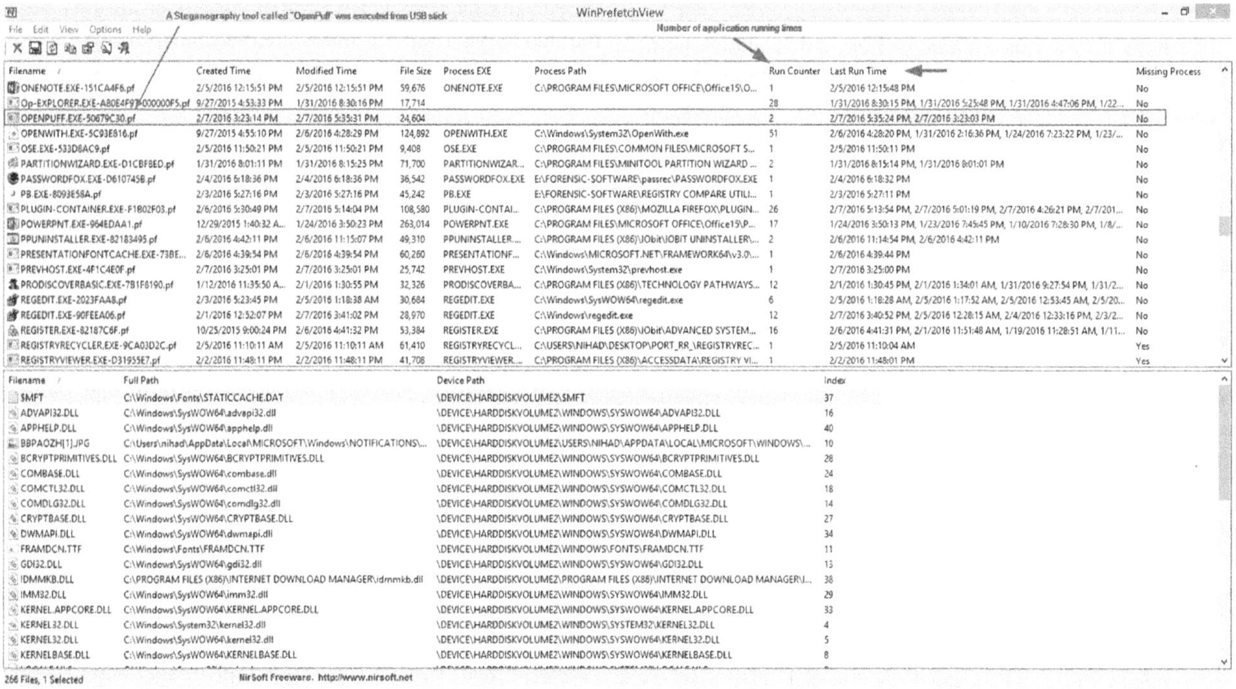

FIGURE 6.58 WinPrefetchView showing a steganography tool called OpenPuff was executed. It also shows the number of running times and last access time of each application.

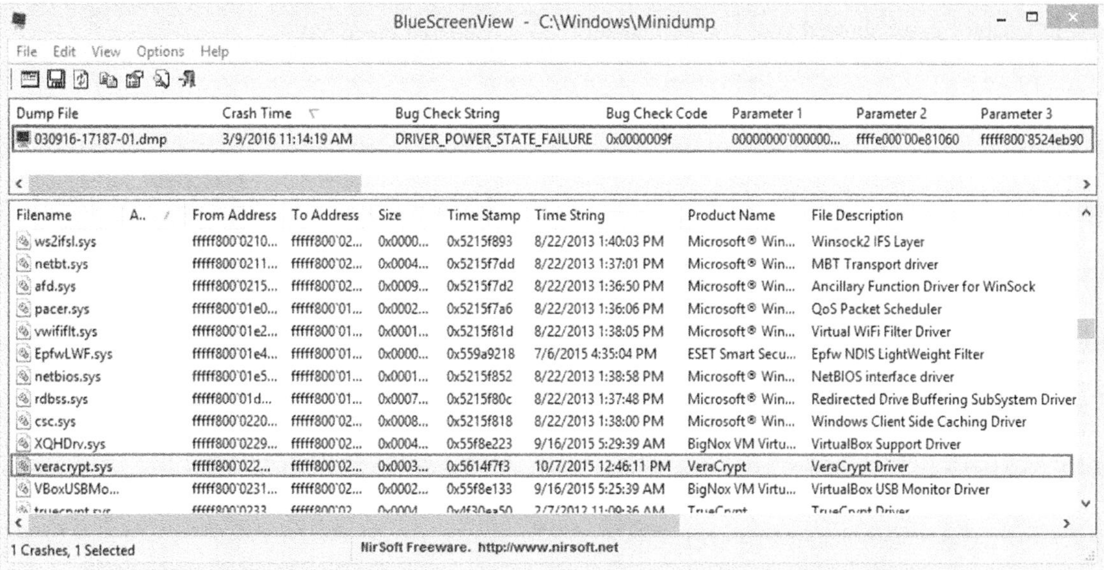

FIGURE 6.59 Using BlueScreenView to investigate for minidump files produced by Windows upon system crash.

Beginning with Windows® Vista, thumbnail previews are stored in a centralized location on the system. The cache is stored at *%userprofile%\AppData\Local\Microsoft\Windows\Explorer* as a number of files with the label thumbcache_xxx.db (numbered by size), as well as an index used to find thumbnails in each sized database [17].

> Please note that *Thumb.db* files come hidden, in order to view them you need first to show hidden files and folders by going to *Control Panel >> Folder Options>> View* tab and checking the option *Show hidden files, folders, and drives*. And uncheck the option *Hide protected operating system files (Recommended)*

There is a tool called *Thumbs Viewer* that allows us to extract thumbnail images from the Thumbs.db, ehthumbs.db, ehthumbs_vista.db, Image.db, Video.db, TVThumb.db, and musicThumbs.db database files found on various Windows® operating systems. You can download it from https://thumbsviewer.github.io (see Fig. 6.60) for a live demonstration.

If you are looking to open thumbcache_*.db files, there is another utility from the same developer called *Thumbcache Viewer*, which allows you to extract thumbnail images from the thumbcache_*.db and iconcache_*.db database files found in Windows® Vista, 7, 8, 8.1, and 10. You can download it from https://thumbcacheviewer.github.io. Such files are usually located at *C:\Users\<USER>\AppData\Local\Microsoft\Windows\Explorer* in Windows® Vista and above.

File Signature Analysis

A signature analysis is a process where file headers and extensions are compared with a known database of file headers and extensions in an attempt to verify all files on the storage media and discover those that may be hidden. As we know, each file under Windows® has a unique signature usually stored in the first 20 bytes of the file. We can check the original file signature of any file by examining it with Notepad®. In Chapter 2, we showed you how to manually investigate for hidden files by examining their signatures. In the following we will automate this process by using a free tool called HexBrowser.

HexBrowser is a tool that identifies file types. It does not care about file extensions, but opens each file to look for signatures inside them, which will be used to determine the exact type of each file. It now recognizes more than 1000 different file formats. *HexBrowser* shows detailed information about each file, or a hex or text dump of the beginning of each file. You can download this program from http://www.hexbrowser.com (see Fig. 6.61).

File Attributes Analysis

We saw in Chapter 2 how we can set the hidden attribute of any file under Windows® to make it extra hidden using the command line switch in Fig. 6.62.

McAfee™ has a set of Win32 command line tools that can help us examine the files on an NTFS disk partition. *HFind* is one of these tools that can reveal files which have their hidden attribute set (see Fig. 6.63). It can also reveal the last access time of files under investigation. Download the complete forensic bundle from www.mcafee.com/us/downloads/free-tools/forensic-toolkit.aspx.

Another tool that comes as a part of a *McAfee™* forensic bundle is *FileStat.exe*. This tool shows a quick dump of all file and security attributes. It works on only one file at a time (see Fig. 6.64).

Discover Hidden Partitions

Hard disk partitions can be hidden. Most Windows® machines contain at least one hidden partition used at startup. Most 64-bit versions of Windows® show a hidden boot partition labeled *System Reserve*. In order to discover whether a particular hard disk or USB stick contains hidden partitions we can do the following:

Go to *Control Panel≫≫Administrative Tools≫Computer Management*. Then click on Disk Management in the left pane (see Fig. 6.65).

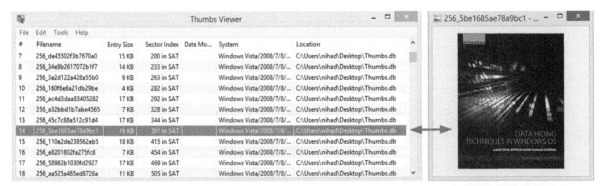

FIGURE 6.60 Viewing the contents of Thumbs.db located at Desktop showing all supported files' thumbnails previously opened at this location (including deleted files' thumbnails).

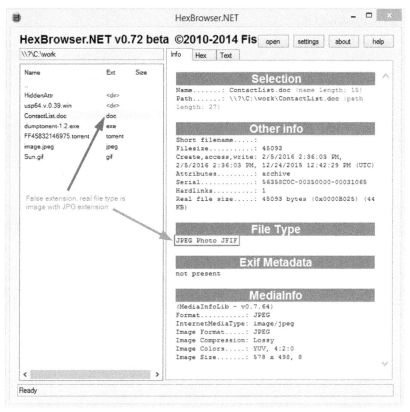

FIGURE 6.61 Using HexBrowser to discover a file hidden by changing its file extension.

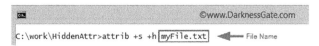

FIGURE 6.62 Setting hidden attribute for a TXT file to make it invisible in Windows OS.

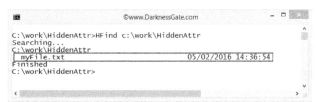

FIGURE 6.63 HFind can reveal files with the Hidden attribute set.

FIGURE 6.64 Dumping a file using the FileStat tool to view its security attributes.

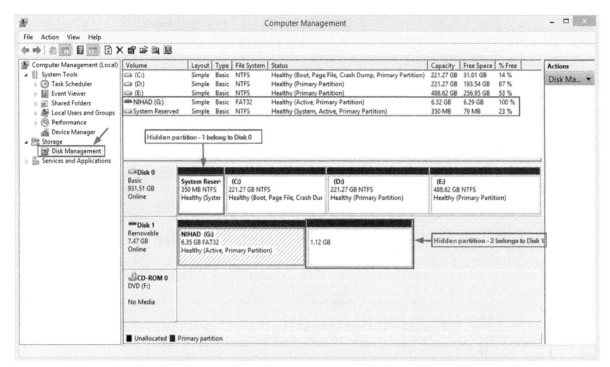

FIGURE 6.65　Hidden partition appears in the computer management console. *Image taken from a Windows® 8.1 machine.*

From Fig. 6.65 we can see that we have two disks attached to the running computer. On one hand, the first disk (labeled Disk 0) has one hidden partition created by Windows® called *System Reserved* that is 350 MB in size. On the other hand, the second disk (labeled Disk 1) has one hidden partition without a label that is 1.12 GB in size.

In order to open the system reserved hidden partition through Windows File Explorer, you can download a free portable utility that works on Windows® 7 and above (Enterprise, Ultimate, and Professional) called *OpenHiddenSystemDrive*. You can download this utility from http://www.coderforlife.com/projects/win7boot/extras/#OpenHiddenSystemDrive.

Double-click on the *OpenHiddenSystemDrive.exe file* to open the hidden *System Reserved* partition in Windows Explorer. Once the partition opens, it may look empty, but this is just because everything is well hidden. You must show hidden and protected system files to see them by going to *Control Panel≫ Folder Options≫ View* tab. You then select the option *Show hidden files, folders and drives.* You also need to uncheck the box beside the option *Hide Protected operating system files (Recommended).* This will make all drive contents appear (see Fig. 6.66).

Another method to check for hidden partitions under Windows® is by using the DiskPart command line utility, which comes as a part of the Microsoft Windows® family (Windows® 8, 8.1, 7, Vista, XP, and Server 2003®).

To launch this tool, open a DOS prompt, type DiskPart and press Enter. Type the following to check of hidden partitions:

1. Type *List disk* to view a list of connected hard disks to this PC and associated numbers.
2. In order to view the partition of each disk you first need to select it through the *select disk=n* command, where *n* points to the disk number that appears in the first command.
3. After selecting the disk, we type *list partition* to see a list of partitions that exist within this disk.

Fig. 6.67 shows you a complete demonstration of these steps.

In order to access any hidden partition (especially the one hidden inside the USB drive as we demonstrated in Chapter 4), you can use a free tool to check and investigate such drives.

MiniTool Partition Wizard Free Edition allows you to uncover hidden partitions and access them. Follow these steps to achieve this:

1. Download and install MiniTool Partition Wizard from http://www.partitionwizard.com/free-partition-manager.html and then install the software using its simple steps.
2. After you launch the program you will notice that all hidden partitions inside disk drives attached to this machine will appear. Hidden partitions will have an asterisk (*) at the front of their names. Right-click any

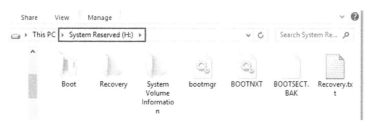

FIGURE 6.66 Accessing and viewing hidden Windows system reserved partition files.

FIGURE 6.67 Using DiskPart command to view hidden partitions within Windows OS.

hidden partition and select *Explore* to check its contents (see Fig. 6.68).

Detect Alternative Data Streams

This was covered thoroughly in Chapter 4 in the following subsections under the main section titled "*Data Hiding Using Alternate Data Stream*":

- How to Delete Alternate Data Stream Files
- Detecting Alternate Data Stream Files

Investigating Windows Volume Shadow Copy

In Chapter 4, we covered how we can use Windows® volume shadow copy (VSS) to conceal data inside it. We had also given detailed technical information about how VSS works. In this chapter, we will show you how to investigate Windows® restore points for data hidden and previously deleted files inside them.

We'll use two methods to analysis VSS copies, a tool called *ShadowExplorer* and using the *VSSadmin command line utility*. *ShadowExplorer* allows you to browse the *Shadow Copies* created by Windows® Vista, 7, and 8. VSS is included, and turned on by default, in all editions of Windows® Vista, 7, and 8. However, Windows Vista and 7 Home edition do not include the user interface (UI) that allows the user to recover older versions of file by right-clicking the intended File»*Properties»Previous Versions* tab (see Fig. 6.69).

Windows® 8 and 8.1 also lack the GUI portion necessary to browse them. According to Microsoft, previous versions were rarely used and negatively impacted the

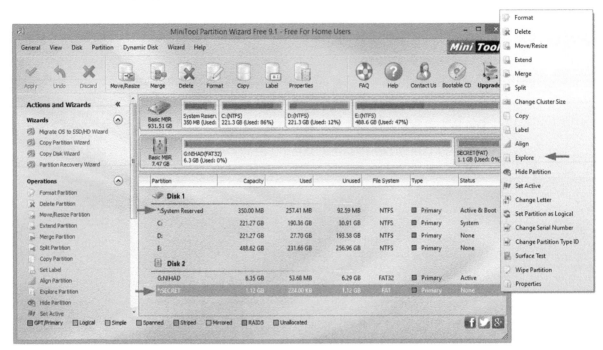

FIGURE 6.68 Viewing a hidden partition's contents using MiniTool free edition.

FIGURE 6.69 Windows® 7 (Professional, Enterprise, and Ultimate) support showing the Previous Versions feature on file properties.

overall Windows® performance. As a result the feature was removed, which is why in Windows® 8, these features are no longer available:

- The ability to browse, search, or restore previous versions of files through previous versions of UI.
- The ability to configure or schedule previous versions of files through UI system protection [18].

So, in cases where *previous versions* are not available, you can use the *ShadowExplorer* tool. This tool can also be used to access and investigate previous VSS copies—this is what we are going to do next.

1. Download *ShadowExplorer* from http://www.shadowexplorer.com. This program is portable; just click *ShadowExplorerPortable.exe* to launch the tool.
2. After you launch the program, select the drive letter from the top-left drop-down menu. Only partitions that have their *System Restore* activated can be selected to view their content. In this case, we selected *C:* drive. Now all C:\ drive contents will appear in the list on the right side. Go to *Users* ≫ <Your name> ≫ *Desktop*. From here you can view all files that were stored on the desktop even though you have previously deleted them (see Fig. 6.70). In the same way, data can be concealed by storing the files for a while and then deleting them. This will make these files of data available in VSS copies for some time, which can last for months if you are not using your PC on regular basis or saving/deleting files

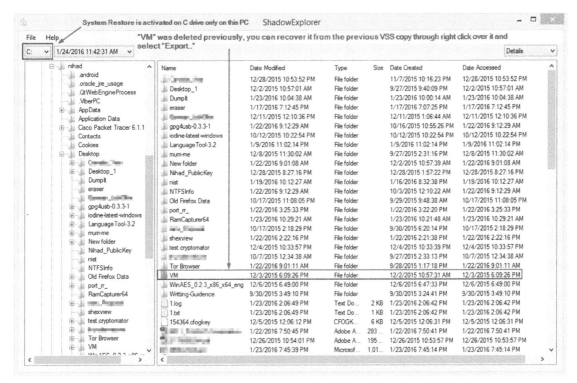

FIGURE 6.70 Using ShadowExplorer to retrieve deleted files and investigate for hidden data.

to it continually. These hidden files can be later retrieved by accessing VSS copies as we will see next. You can investigate the entire *C:* drive searching for concealed data using this tool; when you want to retrieve something, just right-click it and select *Export* ….

The second method to access and view VSS copies is to use the VSSadmin command line utility. Follow these steps to achieve this:

1. Launch the MS DOS prompt elevated as Administrator (right-click CMD and select *Run as Administrator*).
2. To list all existing shadow copies of a specified volume we need to use the command option, *VSSadmin list Shadows/for = C:*. Here we are listing the content of volume C:\ only (see Fig. 6.71). If we use the command, VSSadmin list Shadows, without parameters, it would list all volumes shadows on the PC. In this case, the drive C:\ has six restoration points saved.
3. Copy the shadow volume pathname (the one that you want to access) (see Fig. 6.72).
4. We need to create a symbolic link and save it in a specific folder (VSSCopies), which is our current working directory (C:\ drive). We also need to append a trailing slash (\) to the end of the name of the restoration point name in order to make sure it will work probably (see Fig. 6.73).

You can access this restore point from *C:\VSSCopies* (see Fig. 6.74).

You can access the remaining restore points one by one using the same method by creating a separate symbolic link for each one.

Virtual Memory Analysis

Virtual memory (also called swap space or pagefile) for your computer is hard drive space used by Windows® when it fills up the physical RAM. It resides by default on *C:\pagefile.sys* (*assuming the Windows® partition is on the C:\ drive*). Normally, Windows® sets the initial virtual memory paging file as equal to the amount of RAM you have installed. This feature works by allowing Windows® to use hard disk space as memory. When your machine RAM begins to fill up, parts of RAM files are moved from it into the virtual memory to free up more space.

Virtual memory can contain important information shifted from RAM. For example, fragments of decrypted files can still reside there, and encryption keys or passwords (or a fragment of it) can also be found here. Investigating inside pagefile requires specialized tools such as *pagefile.sys*, which is locked for exclusive use of the operating system and hence needs an imaging tool with low-level access to a disk drive. Data residing in virtual memory are usually stored in chunks of 4 KB or less; besides, these files are not saved sequentially. In addition to this, the capacity of the physical memory increases with the advance of

```
c:\>VSSadmin list Shadows /for=c:\
vssadmin 1.1 - Volume Shadow Copy Service administrative command-line tool
(C) Copyright 2001-2013 Microsoft Corp.

Contents of shadow copy set ID: {bcb41f61-494d-4350-9920-f4e75ccc6f8b}
   Contained 1 shadow copies at creation time: 1/24/2016 11:42:31 AM
      Shadow Copy ID: {d543d4b6-3782-4de0-adca-117d35dca550}
         Original Volume: (C:)\\?\Volume{c0ece30a-6570-11e5-824c-806e6f6e6963}\
         Shadow Copy Volume: \\?\GLOBALROOT\Device\HarddiskVolumeShadowCopy2
         Originating Machine: Nihad-PC
         Service Machine: Nihad-PC
         Provider: 'Microsoft Software Shadow Copy provider 1.0'
         Type: ClientAccessibleWriters
         Attributes: Persistent, Client-accessible, No auto release, Differential, Auto recovered

Contents of shadow copy set ID: {c976b059-ea28-4ab8-921f-b1b1b13d4ee4}
   Contained 1 shadow copies at creation time: 1/25/2016 3:09:47 PM
      Shadow Copy ID: {625c2d21-275c-4af1-9c48-0593b98fb5b5}
         Original Volume: (C:)\\?\Volume{c0ece30a-6570-11e5-824c-806e6f6e6963}\
         Shadow Copy Volume: \\?\GLOBALROOT\Device\HarddiskVolumeShadowCopy5
         Originating Machine: Nihad-PC
         Service Machine: Nihad-PC
         Provider: 'Microsoft Software Shadow Copy provider 1.0'
         Type: ClientAccessibleWriters
         Attributes: Persistent, Client-accessible, No auto release, Differential, Auto recovered

Contents of shadow copy set ID: {a00cfb82-bf46-4dda-8db1-2090d9f86c02}
```

FIGURE 6.71 Screen of shadow copies available on drive C:\ showing only the first two. There are six shadow copies on drive C:\ on the current testing machine.

```
c:\>VSSadmin list Shadows /for=c:\
vssadmin 1.1 - Volume Shadow Copy Service administrative command-line tool
(C) Copyright 2001-2013 Microsoft Corp.

Contents of shadow copy set ID: {bcb41f61-494d-4350-9920-f4e75ccc6f8b}
   Contained 1 shadow copies at creation time: 1/24/2016 11:42:31 AM
      Shadow Copy ID: {d543d4b6-3782-4de0-adca-117d35dca550}
         Original Volume: (C:)\\?\Volume{c0ece30a-6570-11e5-824c-806e6f6e6963}\
         Shadow Copy Volume: \\?\GLOBALROOT\Device\HarddiskVolumeShadowCopy2  ←
         Originating Machine: Nihad-PC
         Service Machine: Nihad-PC
         Provider: 'Microsoft Software Shadow Copy provider 1.0'
         Type: ClientAccessibleWriters
         Attributes: Persistent, Client-accessible, No auto release, Differential, Auto recovered

Contents of shadow copy set ID: {c976b059-ea28-4ab8-921f-b1b1b13d4ee4}
   Contained 1 shadow copies at creation time: 1/25/2016 3:09:47 PM
      Shadow Copy ID: {625c2d21-275c-4af1-9c48-0593b98fb5b5}
         Original Volume: (C:)\\?\Volume{c0ece30a-6570-11e5-824c-806e6f6e6963}\
         Shadow Copy Volume: \\?\GLOBALROOT\Device\HarddiskVolumeShadowCopy5  ←
         Originating Machine: Nihad-PC
         Service Machine: Nihad-PC
         Provider: 'Microsoft Software Shadow Copy provider 1.0'
         Type: ClientAccessibleWriters
         Attributes: Persistent, Client-accessible, No auto release, Differential, Auto recovered

Contents of shadow copy set ID: {a00cfb82-bf46-4dda-8db1-2090d9f86c02}
```

FIGURE 6.72 Copy shadow volume pathname to mount it as a regular disk drive in the next step.

```
c:\>mklink /D VSSCopies \\?\GLOBALROOT\Device\HarddiskVolumeShadowCopy2\
symbolic link created for VSSCopies <<===>> \\?\GLOBALROOT\Device\HarddiskVolumeShadowCopy2\

c:\>
```

FIGURE 6.73 Create a symbolic link for our restore point in order to mount it as a regular volume.

FIGURE 6.74 Accessing the restore point at C:\VSSCopies as any regular Windows folder.

computing power. This results in making the process of swapping decreased. All these issues result in low expectations of computer forensic investigators when investigating *pagefile.sys*.

Although the possibility of finding valuable data inside *pagefile.sys* is small, we can't omit its importance during an investigation. Some tools that can capture and analysis *pagefile.sys* files are:

1. *Rekall* memory analysis framework, which can capture and analysis *pagefile.sys* files: http://www.rekall-forensic.com/index.html.
2. *FTK Imager*, in order to include *pagefile.sys* in the captured RAM image (see Fig. 6.75).

There are additional computer forensic tools for investigating both *pagefile.sys* and hibernate file (*hiberfil.sys*). Consult the program feature list before buying the tool.

You can store your current work and opened programs on Windows® using one of the following power management options:

1. Sleep mode: This mode keeps the PC running in a low power state. You can resume it instantly after clicking any button.
2. Hibernation mode: Shuts down your PC, but before doing this, it copies all data from RAM memory onto a hard disk (*hiberfil.sys*). This saves the current state of the PC, so you can resume your work later when you power your PC on. *hiberfil.sys* can store a wealth of information about

the running machine. The following tools can investigate the *hiberfil.sys* file:

a. Volatility, free open source tool: https://code.google.com/archive/p/volatility/wikis/HiberAddressSpace.wiki
b. Belkasoft Evidence Center (commercial application): https://belkasoft.com

Windows Password Cracking

There are many ways in which A Windows® machine's password can be cracked. Actually, detailing how each cracking technique works will need a chapter of its own! In this section, we will give you a list of tools that you can use in order to crack Windows® passwords. Bear in mind that if the target machine uses full disk encryption, cracking it could be very difficult and even impossible in many cases. Review the section, "Discussion of Security Level in Disk Encryption" in Chapter 5 for detailed technical information about ways to attack full disk encryption and possible countermeasures.

Password Hashes Extraction

Windows® stores its password in a SAM file located at C:\WINDOWS\System32\Config. The registry key that corresponds to this file is located at HKEY_LOCAL_MACHINE\SAM. You have to remember that while Windows® is running you cannot access SAM files on either the registry or File Explorer, but you can still copy it out of the current PC by

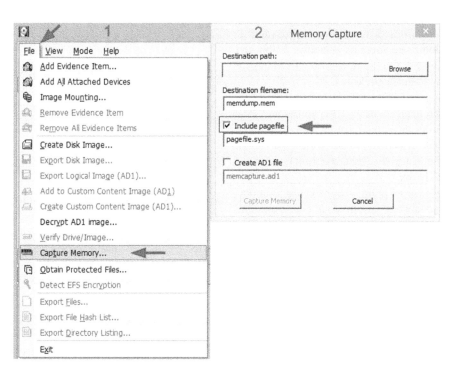

FIGURE 6.75   Capture pagefile.sys using FTK Imager.

booting from a Linux live CD. When Windows® is running, the System account is the only account that can read this part of the registry.

In order to crack a Windows® password, first you need to acquire the SAM file, decrypt it, and finally crack its hashes.

Windows® versions prior to Windows® NT used to store user passwords using the LM hash. Later versions of Windows® began to use NTLM hash, which is a security protocol suite for both Microsoft Windows® NT 4.0 and earlier Windows® versions. For backward compatibility reasons, Microsoft still supports NTLM in Windows 10, 8, 7, Vista, Windows Server 2003 and 2003 R2, Windows 2000, and Windows® XP.

The most well-known free tools that can be used to extract password hashes from current running Windows® are:

- Mimikatz (supports Windows® 10, 8)
- Quarks PwDump (supports Windows® XP, 2003, Vista, 7, 2008, 8): http://blog.quarkslab.com/quarks-pwdump. html
- Pwdump7: https://www.aldeid.com/wiki/Pwdump

Next, we will show you how to crack a Windows® password using a hash extraction technique.

Extracting Password Hashes from Windows 8, 8.1, and 10

Password hashes of newer versions of Windows® can be extracted and examined using two free portable tools, *Procdump* and *Mimikatz*.

Mimikatz is known to extract plaintext passwords, hash, PIN codes, and Kerberos tickets from memory. Mimikatz can also perform pass-the-hash, pass-the-ticket, build Golden tickets, play with certificates or private keys, and vault. It has two active versions: one supports Windows 32-bit and the second supports 64-bit. You can download it from https:// github.com/gentilkiwi/mimikatz/releases.

Procdump is a command line utility whose primary purpose is monitoring an application for CPU spikes and generating crash dumps during a spike that an administrator or developer can use to determine the cause of the spike. It can be downloaded from https://technet.microsoft.com/en-us/ sysinternals/dd996900.aspx.

Note: The exercise we are going to do next needs administrator privileges, so always launch your command line prompt using Administrator elevated privilege.

In the following exercise, we will use Procdump to dump the lsass.exe process, which contains the user password credentials, and then give this dump to Mimikatz in order to extract password hashes from it.

1. Launch the command line prompt elevated as Administrator, change the current working directory to where *Procdump* resides, then type the command seen in Fig. 6.76.

Here is a description of the command switches used in Fig. 6.76:

procdump.exe Used to launch the tool.
-ma Writes a dump file with all process memory. The default dump format includes only thread and handle information.
lsass.exe Is the process name, service name, or PID.
MyDump.dmp is the name of the dump file.

Now, we have the dump file. Launch the *Mimikatz* tool to extract password hashes from the dump file. Note that some antivirus software may recognize *Mimikatz* as a virus. In this case you need to disable your antivirus program until the extraction completes.

1. Open a new command prompt and navigate to where *Mimikatz* resides. Type its name and press Enter.
2. When working with the *lsass* process, *Mimikatz* needs some rights. Always start with the following two commands (press Enter after typing each command):

privilege:debug
log sekurlsa.log
3. Begin the extraction process by writing the following command:

sekurlsa:logonPasswords

Press Enter to extract the hashes of all Windows® accounts available in the dump file.

(See Fig. 6.77 for a complete demonstration of command flow.)

After we have the hash of each Windows® account, we can decrypt it. There are many tools (both commercial and free) for doing this. Cain & Abel is a famous program for doing this, and can be downloaded from http://www.oxid.it/ cain.html.

In our case, I'll use a free online service for decrypting my hash. Go to https://crackstation.net. Copy the previous hash and paste it into the hash text box on the page. Enter the simple Captcha to prove you are a human and finally click *Crack Hashes* (see Fig. 6.78).

Also in our case, we were able to crack the password instantly (Exact match) because we're using a simple password (as appears in Fig. 6.78); however, if the Windows® account is protected with a medium strength password, it will take a considerable amount of time to crack the password. This online service can only decrypt nonsalted hashes. For more information about the difference between salted and nonsalted hashes check the following links:

- Salted Password Hashing–Doing it Right: https://crackstation.net/hashing-security.htm
- Wikipedia website, Salt (cryptography): https://en.wikipedia.org/wiki/Salt_%28cryptography%29

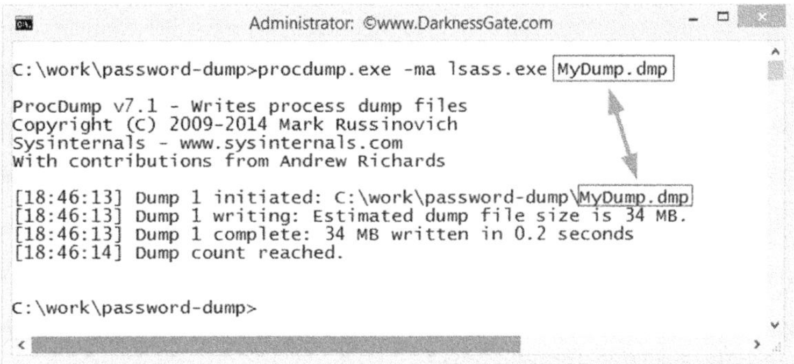

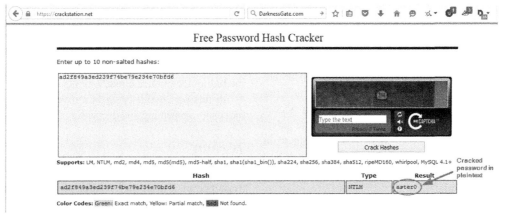

FIGURE 6.76 Dumping lsass.exe process using Procdump from Sysinternals.

FIGURE 6.77 Using Mimikatz to extract Windows password hashes from the lsass process.

FIGURE 6.78 Decrypting password hash using a free online service.

Ophcrack

Ophcrack is a free Windows® password cracker based on rainbow tables. It is a very efficient implementation of rainbow tables done by the inventors of the method. It comes with a GUI and runs on multiple platforms.

Using this tool is fairly simple:

1. Download the tool from http://ophcrack.sourceforge. net. It is supported by all versions of Windows® OS (free rainbow tables are only available for Windows® XP, Vista, and 7).
2. Burn the downloaded ISO image to a CD or DVD disk. You can use a free portable application for doing this called *CDBurnerXP* (https://cdburnerxp.se/en/home).

If you are going to crack the Windows® password on a machine that doesn't have a CD drive, such as a netbook, you can install *Ophcrack* on a USB drive using the universal USB creator from PenDrive Linux at http://www.pendrivelinux.com/universal-usb-installer-easy-as-1-2-3. (We showed you how to use this tool in Chapter 5 when we installed Tails OS on a USB stick.) You can download more rainbow tables from the *Ophcrack* website and extract these tables to *tables\vista_free* on the USB drive and they will be used automatically by *Ophcrack*.

3. Adjust the BIOS boot settings of the machine you want to crack, so you can boot from USB or CD/DVD. Once the machine is booted from USB/CD drive, *Ophcrack* should start automatically and will begin cracking the passwords for all the users on your computer.

Free rainbow tables can crack simple passwords. If Windows® is protected by a complex one you need to try the paid version of rainbow tables. It is available at http://ophcrack.sourceforge.net/tables.php.

Ophcrack uses a brute force attack to crack passwords. This may take a long time, especially for weak PCs (with low RAM and CPU speed).

Offline Windows Password and Registry Editor:Bootdisk/CD

This program will boot from a USB/CD, and will delete locked password account(s). This tool will not crack the old password; rather it will delete it so you can access Windows® without typing your login information or password. It works on all versions of Windows® starting from XP to Vista, 7, 8, and 10, both 32- and 64-bit versions. You can download this tool from http://pogostick.net/~pnh/ntpasswd/bootdisk.html.

> Note: Be careful. If a password is reset on users with EFS encrypted files and the system is XP or newer, all encrypted files for that user will be UNREADABLE! They cannot be recovered unless you remember the old password.

Trinity Rescue Kit

Trinity Rescue Kit is a free, live, command line Linux distribution that contains many programs. One of them allows you to reset Windows® passwords (winpass). This tool boots from a USB/CD or a network location. You can either delete your current Windows® password or create a custom one. About 150 MB in size, you can download this program from http://trinityhome.org/Home/index.php?content=TRINITY_RESCUE_KIT_DOWNLOAD&front_id=12&lang=en&locale=en. There are also many techniques where we can recover or reset a Windows® password using Linux OS live CD. Discussing this in more detail can take a long time, but we mentioned it in this section to make the user aware of its existence.

Host Protected Area and Device Configuration Relay Forensic

In Chapter 4, we talked about HPA and DCO. As a computer forensic investigator, what we care about these two areas is our ability to image them and later analyze them using a reliable forensic tool.

Not all computer forensic software vendors offer programs that can access these areas. The most reliable way, which still preferred by law enforcement professionals, is to use hardware tools in order to capture these areas.

In this section, we will show you a commercial application that claims an ability to capture and analyze HPA and DCO. This program is called *OSForensics*: http://www.osforensics.com (see Fig. 6.79).

Examining Encrypted Files

As we saw in the last chapter, different encryption tools can be used to create encrypted vaults or to encrypt existing data. Some of these tools do not use a specific file extension (or simply do not contain a file signature as other Windows® files). Such encrypted files can be difficult to find inside Windows® machines, especially if they are hidden using any of the hiding techniques already mentioned.

In this part, we'll bring in a diversity of tools and techniques for inspecting and decrypting files and secure volumes.

TCHunt

This is a portable command line tool that can reveal the existence of TrueCrypt® volumes in a specific directory or

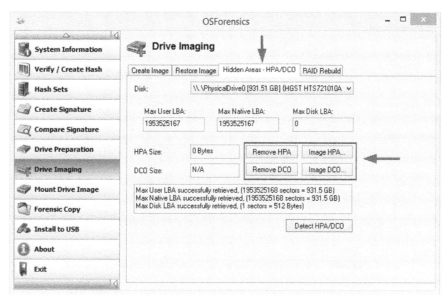

FIGURE 6.79 OSForensics can capture and remove both HPA and DCO.

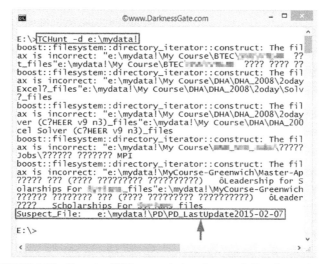

FIGURE 6.80 Executing TCHunt reveals the existence of a TrueCrypt volume.

partition even if they are not mounted on the system. Download the tool from http://download.cnet.com/TCHunt/3000-2094_4-75958483.html.

In spite of the fact that *TrueCrypt®* development has been disconnected, it remains used widely as a secure way to create encrypted vaults.

Launch a command line prompt, change your working directory to where *TCHunt* resides, and execute it using the following command switches:

TCHunt – d [directory] (see Fig. 6.80)

-d directory The directory you want to search; for example, -d e:\ to scan drive e

Cracking TrueCrypt Encrypted Volume Passwords

After we've discovered the existence of a *TrueCrypt®* container in the previous section, it's time to find a method to crack its password. There are multiple techniques for doing this; we will use a simple tool called *unprotect.info*. More advanced techniques employ manual extraction of encrypted container data and analyze it using special tools. This is outside the scope of this book.

unprotect.info is the password recovery software for Windows® (runs on Windows® XP, Vista, 7, and 8, both 32- and 64-bit) that you can use to recover a lost password for an

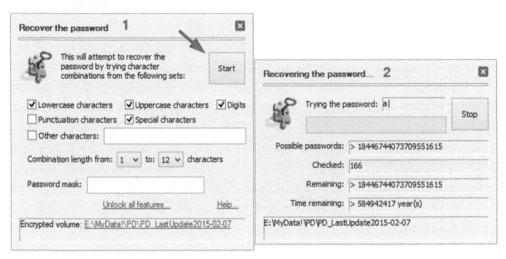

FIGURE 6.81   Using unprotect.info to crack TrueCrypt encrypted containers.

encrypted volume that you've previously created with the TrueCrypt® software.

To use *unprotect.info* follows these steps:

1. Download the tool from http://unprotect.info/download, then install it using its simple steps.
2. When launching the tool, the first window that will appear asks you to select your TrueCrypt volume. Select it and click *Begin*.
3. Enter the password search criteria. The more complex the password, the more time it needs. When you are ready, click *Start* (see Fig. 6.81).

The progress window displays the total number of possible passwords out of the character sets you've selected on the previous screen. The number of passwords that have been tried, the remaining number of the passwords to try, as well as the estimated time to completion is also displayed.

Password Cracking Techniques for Encrypted Files

Windows® users usually use a bundle of applications for their day-to-day work like MS Office documents, PDFs, and archive software. All of these documents can be protected with a password. In this section, we'll show you some tools to decrypt such files.

> Crack for 7-Zip: (Free) Recover (crack) your forgotten password on 7-Zip archives: http://www.crark.net/crark-7zip.html
> RAR Password Unlocker: (Commercial) Crack RAR archive passwords: http://codegena.com/extract-password-protected-rar-file-without-password/
> Advanced Office Password Recovery: (Commercial) Recovers MS Office applications passwords: https://www.elcomsoft.com/aopr.html

SUMMARY

This chapter was the reverse of Chapter 3. We presented different forensic techniques to investigate hidden data inside the Windows® OS file system and other digital media files.

We divided this chapter into two primary parts. The first one explained how to investigate data concealed in digital media files (text, image, and audio/video files). Different steganalysis tools were presented with a demonstration of how to use them with each file type. Also in the first part, we shed light on the concept of metadata, which comes associated with most digital files and can be used to conceal secret data. Different tools were discussed in this section too.

The second part of this chapter dealt with Windows® forensics, a broad topic that needs a book of its own. However, our focus was on presenting forensic techniques that can be used to investigate hidden data in Windows® OS. Forensic techniques presented in this part included acquiring disk and RAM images, Windows registry forensics, checking file attributes, virtual memory, investigating disk drives, and analyzing NTFS file systems for any concealed data using its attributes.

This was a rich chapter, like all chapters of this book. It was full of practical techniques. The next chapter discusses antiforensic techniques. Antiforensics is a new science that has only recently been recognized as a legitimate field of study. In the next chapter, you will learn how you can delete your traces when using steganography tools or exploiting Windows® features to conceal secret data. The antiforensic techniques chapter will teach you everything you need to know about maintaining your privacy and assuring confidentiality of data remains in your PC or digital files. Keep in mind that such techniques can also be used by criminals as countermeasures to a forensic analysis conducted by law enforcement.

REFERENCES

[1] Wikipedia Website, Digital Forensics [Online]. Available from: http://en.wikipedia.org/wiki/Digital_forensics (accessed 07.01.16).

[2] National Institute of Standards and Technology, Guide to Integrating Forensic Techniques Into Incident Response [Online]. Available from: http://csrc.nist.gov/publications/nistpubs/800-86/SP800-86.pdf (accessed 07.01.16).

[3] U.S. Department of Justice, Forensic Examination of Digital Evidence: A Guide for Law Enforcement [Online]. Available from: https://www.ncjrs.gov/pdffiles1/nij/199408.pdf (accessed 07.01.16).

[4] Wikipedia Website, Computer forensics [Online]. Available from: http://en.wikipedia.org/wiki/Computer_forensics (accessed 07.01.16).

[5] The Association of Chief Police Officers, ACPO Good Practice Guide for Digital Evidence [Online]. Available from: http://www.digital-detective.net/digital-forensics-documents/ACPO_Good_Practice_Guide_for_Digital_Evidence_v5.pdf (accessed 07.01.16).

[6] Wikipedia Website, Digital Forensic Process [Online]. Available from: https://en.wikipedia.org/wiki/Digital_forensic_process (accessed 07.01.16).

[7] The National Software Reference Library, (NSRL) Project Web Site [Online]. Available from: http://www.nsrl.nist.gov (accessed 07.01.16).

[8] EMC Corporation, The Digital Universe of Opportunities [Online]. Available from: http://www.emc.com/infographics/digital-universe-2014.htm (accessed 07.01.16).

[9] IEEE, Steganalysis of MSU Stego Video Based on Discontinuous Coefficient [Online]. Available from: http://ieeexplore.ieee.org/xpl/login.jsp?tp=&arnumber=5485297&url=http%3A%2F%2Fieeexplore.ieee.org%2Fxpls%2Fabs_all.jsp%3Farnumber%3D5485297(accessed 30.03.16).

[10] Cvedetails, Vulnerability Details: CVE-2007-0163 [Online]. Available from: https://www.cvedetails.com/cve/CVE-2007-0163 (accessed 30.03.16).

[11] Security Focus, A Major Design Bug in Steganography 1.7.x, 1.8 (Latest) (Updated Version) [Online]. Available from: http://www.securityfocus.com/archive/1/archive/1/456519/100/0/threaded (accessed 30.03.16).

[12] Peerj, Forensic Analysis of Video Steganography Tools [Online]. Available from: https://peerj.com/articles/cs-7/ (accessed 30.03.16).

[13] Microsoft, [Online]. Available from: https://support.microsoft.com/en-us/kb/197571 (accessed 30.03.16).

[14] Microsoft TechNet, About Windows Installer Source Location Manager [Online]. Available from: https://technet.microsoft.com/en-us/library/bb892810.aspx (accessed 30.03.16).

[15] Microsoft, How to Clear the Windows Explorer MRU Lists [Online]. Available from: https://support.microsoft.com/en-us/kb/142298 (accessed 30.03.16).

[16] Wikipedia, ReadyBoost [Online]. Available from: https://en.wikipedia.org/wiki/ReadyBoost (accessed 30.03.16).

[17] Wikipedia, Windows Thumbnail Cache [Online]. Available from: https://en.wikipedia.org/wiki/Windows_thumbnail_cache (accessed 30.03.16).

[18] Microsoft MSDN, Previous Versions UI Removed for Local Volumes [Online]. Available from: https://msdn.microsoft.com/en-us/library/windows/desktop/hh848072%28v=vs.85%29.aspx (accessed 30.03.16).

BIBLIOGRAPHY

[1] This is a List of Publicly Available Memory Samples for Testing Purposes [Online]. Available from: https://code.google.com/p/volatility/wiki/SampleMemoryImages (accessed 30.03.16).

[2] Mozillazine, Profile folder – Firefox [Online]. Available from: http://kb.mozillazine.org/Profile_folder_-_Firefox (accessed 30.03.16).

[3] Forensicfocus, A Forensic Analysis of the Windows Registry [Online]. Available from: http://www.forensicfocus.com/a-forensic-analysis-of-the-windows-registry (accessed 30.03.16).

[4] Windowsecurity, Extracting USB Artifacts From Windows 7 [Online]. Available from: http://www.windowsecurity.com/articles-tutorials/authentication_and_encryption/Extracting-USB-Artifacts-from-Windows-7.html (accessed 30.04.16).

[5] Milincorporated, What is in the Index.dat Files? [Online]. Available from: http://www.milincorporated.com/a3_index.dat.html.

[6] Geoffchappell, The INDEX.DAT File Format [Online]. Available from: http://www.geoffchappell.com/studies/windows/ie/wininet/api/urlcache/indexdat.htm?tx=20,78,83,84,88,89 (accessed 15.04.16).

[7] Ampsoft, Common Fonts to all Versions of Windows & Mac Equivalents [Online]. Available from: http://www.ampsoft.net/webdesign-l/WindowsMacFonts.html (accessed 15.04.16).

Chapter 7

Antiforensic Techniques

Chapter Outline

Introduction	**267**	Disable UserAssist	277
Antiforensics Goals	**268**	Disable Timestamp for Last Access to a File	277
Data Hiding General Advice	**268**	Disable Windows Hibernation	278
Data Destruction	**268**	Disable Windows Virtual Memory (Paging File)	278
Hard Disk Wiping	269	Disable System Restore Points and File History	280
Eraser	270	Disable Windows Thumbnail Cache	281
Moo0 Anti-Recovery	270	Disable Windows Prefetch Feature	281
SRM	271	Disable Windows Logging	285
Cipher Command	271	Disable Windows® Password Hash Extraction	285
Warning When Using Data Destruction Tools	271	**Clearing Digital Footprints**	**287**
Manipulating Digital File Metadata	272	Live CDs and Bootable USB Tokens	287
Changing File Timestamps	272	Virtual Machines	288
Erasing Document Metadata	273	VirtualBox	288
Windows Antiforensics Techniques	**275**	Windows Virtual PC	288
Configure Windows for Better Privacy	275	VMware Workstation Player	288
Disable Recycle Bin	276	Using Portable Applications	289
Registry Antiforensics	276	**Direct Attack Against Forensic Software**	**289**
Deleting the Leftovers of Uninstalled Programs	277	**Summary**	**289**
Connected USB Devices	277	**References**	**289**
Mostly Recently Used List	277	**Bibliography**	**290**

INTRODUCTION

Computer forensics tools and techniques allow investigators to gather intelligence about computer users, find deleted files, reconstruct artifacts, and try to gather as much evidence as they can. The outcome of using all these tools should be handled by professional computer forensic analysts in order to be admissible in a court of law. Antiforensics science, on the other hand, try to reverse the process. It uses tools and techniques to make investigation of computer crimes more difficult and time-consuming by performing many actions like intentional deletion of files, wiping disk space to prevent data recovery, putting false evidence to fool computer forensics tools, and increasing the analysis time in addition to using data hiding and encryption techniques to make uncovering secret data more difficult. The best compact definition of computer antiforensics comes from *Dr. Marc Rogers* of Purdue University who defined it as follows:

Attempts to negatively affect the existence, amount and/or quality of evidence from a crime scene, or make the analysis and examination of evidence difficult or impossible to conduct [1].

In relation to data hiding techniques, antiforensics will include all techniques related to hiding the truth of using a steganography tool on the suspect machine. It also includes all the protective measures that can be used in order to delete user traces on the target's machine like Internet activities, IP addresses, last-used programs, and anything that can be used to disclose the possibility of using steganography tools or/and data hiding techniques to conceal secret data.

The term antiforensics in a broad range includes both data hiding and encryption techniques. In fact, this entire book is about one branch of computer antiforensic techniques! Data hiding techniques (including encryption as a subtype of obscuring data) is the most used and advanced technique in the computer antiforensics family. Despite its great importance in computer security, few books about it are published, and few of these published books give such a practical approach as the one already in your hand.

In this chapter, we will practically teach you many techniques to hide your traces and make investigating your PC by professional computer forensic examiners very difficult

Data Hiding Techniques in Windows OS. http://dx.doi.org/10.1016/B978-0-12-804449-0.00007-5

and time-consuming. If the techniques presented in this chapter are combined with the appropriate data hiding and encryption techniques from the previous chapters, you will end up having a very strong approach to protect your confidential data to an extent that is impossible to break.

ANTIFORENSICS GOALS

The main goal of antiforensics is to make computer forensics very hard to achieve and time-consuming. Its ultimate goal is to mitigate the results of computer forensics and make acquiring evidence for a court of law inadmissible or, at least, debatable during a trial.

Many argue that antiforensics techniques are mainly used by criminals and terrorists to hide their traces and prevent law enforcement officers from capturing their communications and secret data. The fact of the matter is that this is true to some extent, but we cannot say that this branch of computer security is dedicated only to criminals. Many user segments also need to use such techniques to protect their communications and safeguard their privacy against unauthorized people. Legitimate users of computer antiforensics tools are:

1. Diplomats
2. Journalists
3. Human rights activists
4. Military and defense personnel
5. Computer users, to protect their privacy
6. Computer security professionals

Antiforensic techniques also help investigators gain considerable knowledge about the drawbacks available in currently used forensic tools, which help them develop better and more efficient forensic tools.

DATA HIDING GENERAL ADVICE

Before beginning our discussion on this topic, let us shed some light on steganography tools when concealing data.

As we saw in previous chapters, all steganographic tools that use media files need either images, audio files, or video files as carriers in order to store secret information inside them. When using such tools we should make sure we use private files as a carrier, and remove such files upon finishing with the embedding process. For example, do not download images or audio files from the Internet and use them as carrier files. Computer investigators can search the Internet and retrieve the original images/audio files to make a comparison between the one that existed on the suspect's machine and the original one retrieved from the Internet (**structural analysis**).

Do not save lots of images, audio files, and video files on your PC. Any computer that contains large amounts of media files will be suspicious.

It is better to store media files used as carriers of secret data on your USB drive, and store the output on the USB. Both will eliminate some traces from being recorded on your machine but will not eliminate everything should a professional investigator be involved. Later in this chapter you will learn how to eliminate all evidence from the Windows® registry.

Some steganographic and encryption tools offer a portable version. Always use such version when possible. It leaves a small footprint comparable to regular tools that come with their own installers.

Many steganographic tools offer the choice to encrypt the payload. Keep in mind that when selecting to encrypt the payload you need to use strong password. More details can be found in Chapter 5, "*Create and Maintain Secure Passwords*"

If you are not a computer professional, do not install advanced tools on your machine; hex editors, programming IDE, and system wiping and privacy cleaning tools may indicate that you have a good level of IT experience, which will make your PC more suspicious to investigators. The existence of a TOR browser, VPN software, and other anonymity tools are not recommended either.

Do not store tutorials, eBooks, or anything related to hacking, computer forensics, and antiforensic techniques; it goes without saying that this will draw attention to your activities.

Try to use modern solid state drives (SSDs) instead of the old magnetic disks. This kind of disk drive destroys deleted data permanently without user interference (depends on OS and type of SSD drive used—we talked about this in Chapter 5).

Do not search for steganography tools or download them using your regular Internet connection. Try to use an Internet café or public PCs where your identity is not known. If you cannot afford this use a TOR browser to download such tools (see Chapter 5 for best practices when using a TOR network).

It is always better to install and run steganography programs using virtual machines (VMs). This will eliminate all possible traces since you can delete the VM when done! In Chapter 5 we described how to install Linux OS using a portable VM inside an encrypted volume.

Do not store the emails you exchange with your correspondent that contain stego media files. It is advisable to delete such emails immediately after sending them.

DATA DESTRUCTION

This is the main area of antiforensics. It is concerned with making data completely unreadable and inaccessible or unusable for unauthorized purposes. We can categorize it as follows.

Hard Disk Wiping

This works by eliminating all bits inside the hard disk. There are three types:

Physical destruction: This includes physical destruction of hard drives, USB zip drives, CD/DVDs, tape drives, SD cards, and mobile phones in a way that makes them impossible to recover. There are many types of hard drive shredders; such equipment is used by business organizations and defense agencies. If you want to use such machines to destroy a few pieces, you can still use these services at some cost. If you prefer doing this destruction at home, all you need to do is to break the magnetic hard disk, remove the platters, smash them into pieces, and finally dip them in acid liquid. Physical destruction is the most effective and desirable solution to ensure total security for devices that contain critical data and need to be thrown away.

Degausser: This destruction technique works by exposing HDD and other storage devices into the powerful magnetic field of a degausser. This results in neutralizing data available on the disk, making it unrecoverable. Not all degaussers have the same magnetic field strength (the magnetic field strength of a degausser is measured in Gauss, or oersteds). It is crucial to check a degausser's ability to erase data completely before buying it. This will depend on the storage devices you intend to destruct. HDD usually require a degausser with a powerful magnetic field. After HDD is exposed to degaussing, it is no longer available for work again because the servo platter of the disk has been erased (leaving no head positioning information); this can be fixed only by the HDD manufacturer.

Logical destruction of data using wiping tools: This is the most commonly used technique to destroy data securely. It works by covering up old data on storage devices with new information supplied by the wiping tool. If such a technique is implemented correctly, recovering data from disk drives becomes impossible. This is a cost-effective solution as it only costs the eraser software price (some come free and they are reliable). In addition to this, you can reuse the storage media again or simply sell it as a used parts.

Wiping tools can be configured to erase specific parts of HDD like specific partition, folder, file, or fragments of deleted files to prevent future recovery.

The main disadvantage of wiping software is that it needs a long time to finish, especially for large disk drives, and it assumes that the HDD is already working and writable so false information can be written to it. Another challenge to wiping software comes when using it to wipe data stored using the RAID technology. This technology offers fault tolerance by spreading same data into multiple disk drives in different locations. In such a situation, the wiping tool should be run whenever data is located across all enterprise storage servers. This apparently will cost more money and time.

There are many standards developed to securely erase data; Table 7.1 describes the most commonly used one.

TABLE 7.1 Data Destruction Techniques

Erasing Method	Security Level	Overwriting Rounds	Pattern Used	Comments
Single overwrite	Low	1	Writes a zero	Can prevent software recovery tools from recovering data, but cannot stop hardware-based recovery tools from recovering deleted data.
NCSC-TG-025 (US National Security Agency)	High	3	All zeros, all ones, and finally writes a random character and verifies the write	Software recovery tool and most hardware-based recovery tools cannot recover data deleted this way. This technique is similar to HMG IS5 (UK) and DoD 5220.22-M (USA).
Gutmann	High	35	Writes a random character	This is an old technique invented in 1996; the encoding for HDD has changed since then. This method is not recommended for modern HDD.
Schneier	High	7	All ones, all zeros, random characters five times	Prevents software recovery tools and almost all hardware-based techniques from recovering data.
ISM 6.2.92	Medium	1	Random pattern (only for disks bigger than 15 GB)	Invented in 2014 by the Australian Department of Defense: Intelligence & Security. Prevents software recovery tools and most hardware-based techniques from recovering data.

There are many tools available out there for secure data erasing. Commercial tools usually offer more features and have a proven record of achievements, but in this book we are focusing on using free and open source tools. The following are the most reputable freely available ones.

Eraser

This is an advanced security tool for Windows® that allows you to completely remove sensitive data from your hard drive by overwriting it several times using different erasing standards according to user choice. Eraser is a free software and its source code is released under the GNU General Public License (http://eraser.heidi.ie).

You can run this software on the specified schedule to erase either files, folders, disk, partitions, unused disk space, or to securely move one file/folder from one place to another (see Fig. 7.1). Eraser integrates with Windows® context menu (right-click) to speed up the deletion process.

Moo0 Anti-Recovery

Another free popular utility for disk wiping is *Moo0 Anti-Recovery* (see Fig. 7.2). It destroys data by writing empty spaces once with pseudorandom data. The main drawback of this tool is that the filename is recoverable on FAT drives (we are using version 1.11). This tool can be downloaded from http://www.moo0.com/software/AntiRecovery.

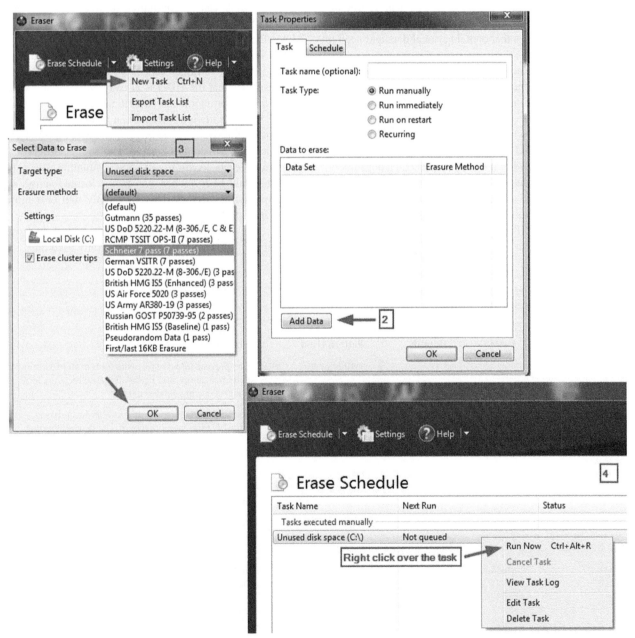

FIGURE 7.1 Using Eraser to delete unused disk space for partition C:\.

FIGURE 7.2 Moo0 Anti-Recovery software offers one method of data destruction suitable for most users.

SRM

The last tool we are going to talk about is **SRM** (see Fig. 7.3), which is a secure replacement for **RM(1)**. Unlike the standard **RM**, it overwrites the data in the target files before unlinking them. This prevents command line recovery of the data by examining the raw block device. It may also help frustrate physical examination of the disk, although it's unlikely that it can completely prevent that type of recovery.

It is, essentially, a paper shredder for sensitive files. **SRM** can be downloaded from http://srm.sourceforge.net.

Cipher Command

If you want to securely overwrite deleted data to avoid future recovery without using a third-party tool, then use *Cipher.exe*. This is a built-in command line tool in the Windows® OS that can be used to encrypt or decrypt data on NTFS drives. This tool also lets you securely delete data by overwriting it.

To use this tool, launch a command prompt and type **cipher.exe/w** and then specify the drive and the folder that identifies the volume that contains the deleted data that you want to overwrite. Data that is not allocated to files or folders will be overwritten. This permanently removes the data; furthermore, this can take a long time if you are overwriting a large space (see Fig. 7.4).

As we see in Fig. 7.4, after running *Cipher.exe* it overwrites the free space with three passes as follows on partition *E:* first with all zeroes (0x00), second with all 255s (0xFF), and finally, with random numbers.

Cipher.exe is supported on all Windows® versions beginning with Windows® 2000.

Warning When Using Data Destruction Tools

From the previous section, we can note that software antirecovery tools can offer a high level of security for personal users and companies; however, if you are dealing with top secret data, physical destruction is still the safest solution. To achieve the maximum security possible, it is important to be aware of the following issues when using wiping software tools:

- If you are deleting data that is scattered across many disk drives (RAID or mirroring disks), make sure to wipe all other locations to avoid leaving copies in other places.

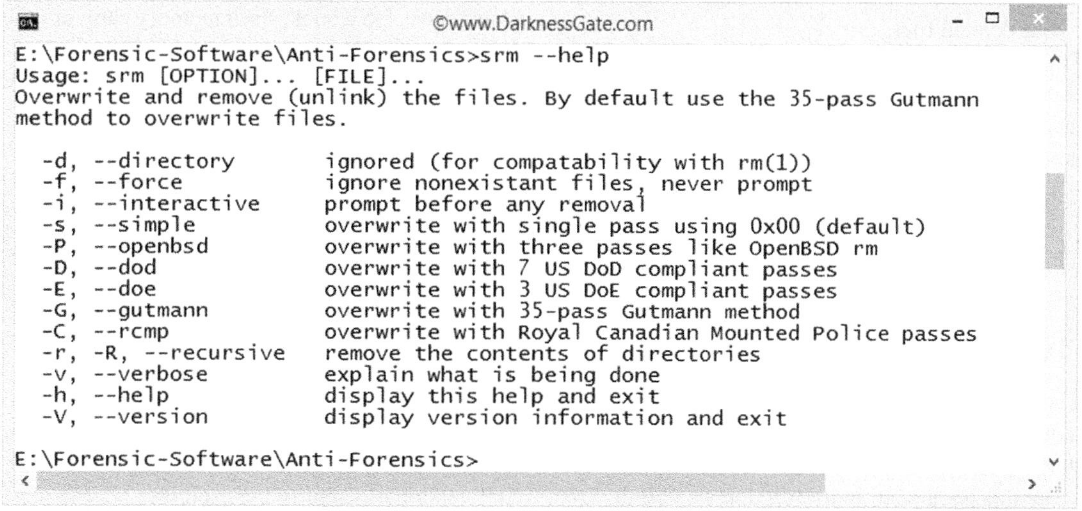

```
                                    ©www.DarknessGate.com                    _ □ ×
E:\Forensic-Software\Anti-Forensics>srm --help
Usage: srm [OPTION]... [FILE]...
Overwrite and remove (unlink) the files. By default use the 35-pass Gutmann
method to overwrite files.

    -d, --directory      ignored (for compatability with rm(1))
    -f, --force          ignore nonexistant files, never prompt
    -i, --interactive    prompt before any removal
    -s, --simple         overwrite with single pass using 0x00 (default)
    -P, --openbsd        overwrite with three passes like OpenBSD rm
    -D, --dod            overwrite with 7 US DoD compliant passes
    -E, --doe            overwrite with 3 US DoE compliant passes
    -G, --gutmann        overwrite with 35-pass Gutmann method
    -C, --rcmp           overwrite with Royal Canadian Mounted Police passes
    -r, -R, --recursive  remove the contents of directories
    -v, --verbose        explain what is being done
    -h, --help           display this help and exit
    -V, --version        display version information and exit

E:\Forensic-Software\Anti-Forensics>
```

FIGURE 7.3 SRM is a command line tool with powerful destruction capabilities for both Windows® and Linux® OSs.

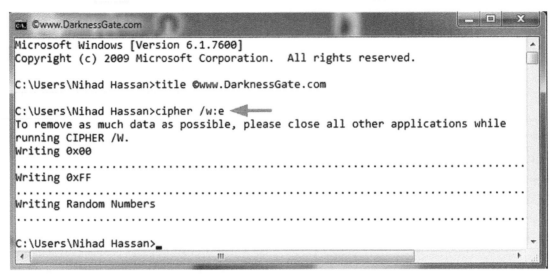

FIGURE 7.4 Using Cipher to overwrite deleted data space on partition E:\.

- Some files (like MS Office® documents) can have a previous version file stored somewhere other than the main file location that has been erased. To counter this issue, delete all previous restore points and file history. More details to follow.
- Make sure to delete all instances of a file; for example, a user may destroy a specific file and forget other copies in other locations.
- Hibernation and virtual memory (page files) files can contain IM chat, browser history, encryption passwords, decrypted documents, and other important data.
- RAM memory can be captured from a running PC, resulting in recovering important files and even passwords from it.
- Windows® by default stores thumbnails of graphics files and certain documents and movie files in the thumbnail cache file. Although thumbnail images are small, they still give sufficient information of any prior existence of the deleted file(s).
- Volume shadow copies and file history may contain copies of your deleted files.
- Windows event logs and registry can contain information about your PC usage. Such logs can give important evidence of your previous usage of Windows®. Registry antiforensics will be thoroughly discussed later.

As we note, data can be scattered in different locations on our disk drive; deleting a file and using a shredding tool may not be enough alone to securely destroy important data.

Manipulating Digital File Metadata

Metadata is a data about data. In digital file format metadata can contain a considerable amount of technical information about the document itself and the author and machine used to create this document. In this section we will discuss different techniques to manipulate digital files metadata to render its information useless or even misleading from a computer forensic perspective.

Changing File Timestamps

Digital files timestamps play a crucial role in any computer forensic investigation. It helps investigators limit their detailed investigation to a set of files at a particular timeframe, such as immediately before and after the data breach or occurrence of another suspected incident.

Manipulating a digital file's timestamp helps a suspect to backdate a document and try to pass it as if it were an older document. For example, a criminal can conceal a secret message inside a JPEG image. He/she can backdate its timestamp to look as if it were not accessed for a long time. This will effectively mislead any computer forensic investigator.

In a nutshell, timestamping means changing the created, modified, or accessed date of files within the file system of a hard drive, USB stick, flash memory card, or other storage device to mislead computer forensic investigators and their tools from capturing the real time a specific file was created, accessed, or modified.

There are many tools that can manipulate file timestamp attributes under the NTFS file system. In this experiment we will use one of the *Metasploit Anti-Forensics Project Tools*, called *Timestomp*. You can download it from https://www.bishopfox.com/resources/tools/other-free-tools/mafia.

Timestomp allows you to delete or modify all four NTFS timestamp values: Modified, Accessed, Created, and Entry Modified. This is a command line tool. However, there is a project called *Timestomp-GUI*, which as its name implies, offers a GUI for this tool; it can be downloaded from https://sourceforge.net/projects/timestomp-gui. We will use the GUI version to simplify the exercise.

After downloading both *Timestomp* and *Timestomp-GUI*, we execute the last tool to change the selected file time attributes as shown in Fig. 7.5.

The following describes the numbers in Fig. 7.5:

1. The location of *Timestomp.exe* tool.
2. The file whose timestamp attributes you want to change.
3. If you want to change the folder timestamp attribute instead of a file, click this button.
4. Here is the choice list; select the date attributes that you want to change.
5. Click this button to apply changes.

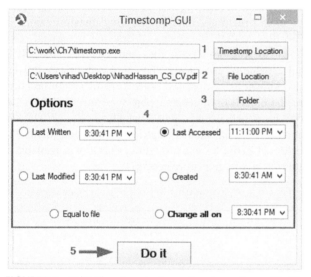

FIGURE 7.5 Using Timestomp to change time stamp of a specific file.

In Fig. 7.6 you can see the difference between the time attributes of the file used during the experiment, after and before applying this test. This clearly demonstrates how we can change the timestamp attributes of any file or folder in Windows® OS.

This technique can be used in different scenarios to conceal our conducted activities on a specific computer. Note that this technique can help you fool computer forensic experts and tools; however, if a professional expert suspects a file timestamp, he/she can perform a deep analysis of the suspected file timestamp attributes inside an MFT table, which will uncover that this file time attribute has been changed manually. Describing this technique is beyond this book's scope, but it is worth mentioning to draw user attention about this possibility.

Erasing Document Metadata

Metadata can contain sensitive information about document author and the machine used to produce it. This metadata is hidden from obvious view and it is automatically created and embedded in a computer file. In previous chapters we showed you how to use popular file types like PDF, MS Office® files, and images to conceal data inside them. The previous chapter also showed you how to investigate different files for metadata. In this section we will show you how to remove metadata from the most used file types using both application built-in functions and some third-party tools for advanced document sanitization.

We will only talk about MS Office® and PDF file types; if you want to remove metadata from other file types like

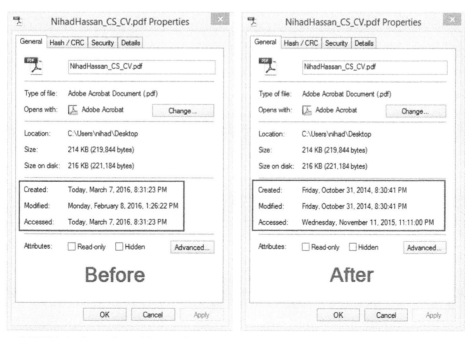

FIGURE 7.6 Comparison of the same file before and after changing its time attributes using Timestomp.

images, audio files, and video files, consult the section, "Digital Files Metadata Forensic" in Chapter 6, which contains information that can be used to remove metadata from most electronic files.

PDF Sanitization

With a single click, Acrobat® Reader allows you to delete all hidden data in a PDF file, including text, metadata, annotations, form fields, attachments, and bookmarks. Please bear in mind that free basic versions do not have PDF Sanitization activated. In the section, "Document Metadata" in Chapter 6, we mention some free tools that can be used to view/clear PDF document metadata. You can use it if your currently installed PDF Reader does not support the Sanitization feature.

Follow these steps to achieve this [2]:

1. Go to *View* menu >> *Tools* >> *Protection* (we're using Adobe® version 10.0.0).
2. The sanitation tools are listed under the heading *Hidden Information*.
3. To permanently remove items such as metadata, comments, and file attachments click *Sanitize Document* and then click OK in the confirmation pop-up windows (see Fig. 7.7).

4. You can also select *Remove Hidden Information* to have more control of what you want to remove.

According to an experimental test conducted by the *Australian Government, Department of Defense Intelligence and Security*, both *Sanitize Document* and *Remove Hidden Information* work as expected and have successfully removed all sensitive data from the tested PDF document. The full report is available at http://www.asd.gov.au/publications/adobe_acrobat_redaction_capability.pdf.

If you are a security paranoid person and don't trust the built-in sanitization feature offered by Adobe®, you can use *QPDF* to assure complete removal of all hidden contents inside your PDF files. *QPDF* is a command-line program that does structural, content-preserving transformations in PDF files. *QPDF* is capable of creating linearized (also known as web-optimized) files and encrypted files. It is also capable of converting PDF files with object streams (also known as compressed objects) to files with no compressed objects or to generate object streams from files that don't have them (or even those that already do). *QPDF* also supports a special mode designed to allow you to edit the content of PDF files in a text editor. This tool is available at https://sourceforge.net/projects/qpdf.

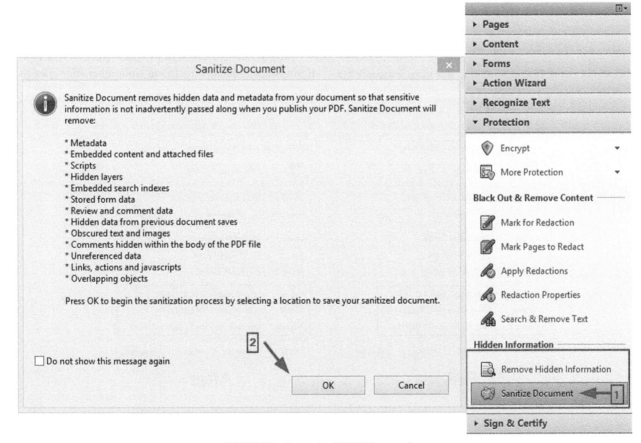

FIGURE 7.7 Destroying PDF hidden metadata.

MS Office Sanitization

It is widely known that Microsoft Word® is used for the preparation of documents, reports, notes, and other formal and informal materials across the commercial, government, and public sectors. Beginning with MS Office® 2007, Microsoft added the *Inspect Document* feature for MS Office® applications to destroy hidden metadata not viewed by the user. You can access this feature on MS Word® 2013/2010 from *File >> Info >> Check for Issues >> Inspect Document* (see Fig. 7.8). In MS Word® 2007 you can access this feature from *Office Button >> Prepare >> Inspect Document*.

If you belong to the old school and you are still using the old MS Word® application suite (Office Version 2003/XP), you need to be aware that Microsoft released an add-on similar to the inspect document feature to permanently remove hidden data and collaboration data. These features include options such as change tracking and comments, from MS Word®, MS Excel®, and MS PowerPoint® files. This add-on can be downloaded from https://support.microsoft.com/en-us/kb/834427.

WINDOWS ANTIFORENSICS TECHNIQUES

In this part of the chapter, we need to carefully hide traces of our computer usage of Windows® OS. As previously described, our ultimate goal is to hide our traces when using steganography tools or other hiding techniques already described in this book. Remember, should investigators discover what tools were used, all our efforts in hiding our data will be in vain.

Configure Windows for Better Privacy

Windows® can be configured to become more privacy friendly through a set of configurations of its functions; however, we cannot configure everything by modifying Windows® settings alone as this would be a daunting task and not suitable for average Windows® users. Some tools exist to make this process simple and easy as we are going to see next.

Using software, searching online using a web browser, checking your email, installing and uninstalling software, plugging a USB to your PC, and almost any task you perform on a Windows® machine will undoubtedly leave a trace. Experts can delete all traces manually, but this is not a viable solution because it requires good IT skills and even experts can miss a trace. Alternatively, privacy software will guarantee to wash our traces after we finish using our PC.

BleachBit is a free, open source software that does a very good job in maintaining user privacy (Fig. 7.9). It can free cache, delete cookies, clear Internet history, shred temporary files, delete logs, and discard junk you didn't know was there. It wipes clean thousands of applications including Firefox, Internet Explorer, Adobe Flash, Google Chrome, Opera, Safari, and many more. Beyond simply deleting files, *BleachBit* includes advanced features such as shredding files to prevent recovery, wiping free disk space to hide traces of files deleted by other applications, and vacuuming Firefox to make it faster.

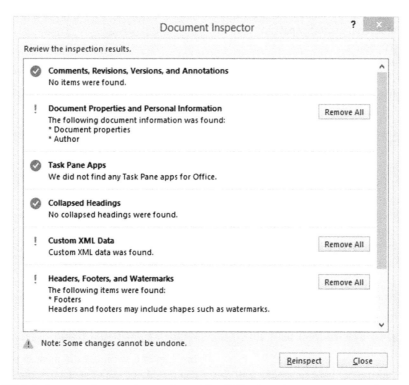

FIGURE 7.8 Document inspector feature of an MS Word® file allows the user to remove hidden metadata.

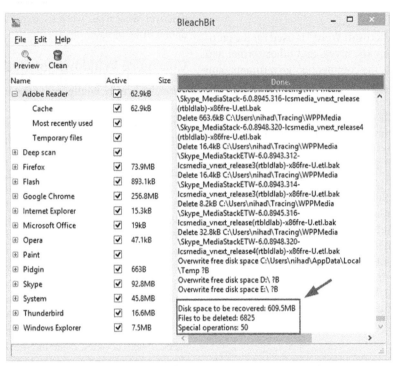

FIGURE 7.9 Using BleachBit to securely wash Windows® and installed programs from previous usage traces and personal data.

BleachBit also has a portable version and can be downloaded from https://www.bleachbit.org/download/windows.

BleachBit is an important arsenal in our bag for covering our tracks when using Windows® machines. You will find that professionals do not trust automated tools regardless of their strength. They will resort to manual configuration of Windows® and prevent it from creating specific types of data as a real robust protection.

Next, we will introduce some of these configurations in Windows®, which can help us to achieve maximum security and avoid detection when using stego tools and other hiding techniques.

Disable Recycle Bin

In Windows®, you can delete any file directly without sending it to the Recycle Bin by holding down the **SHIFT** key and deleting the file. This trick is useful if occasionally you decide to delete some files permanently. In case you want to force Windows® to perform this action on all deleted files and without holding down the **SHIFT** key, then you need to configure Windows® as follows:

1. On the desktop, right-click *Recycle Bin*, and then click *Properties*.
2. Click **Don't move files to the Recycle Bin. Remove files immediately when deleted**, and then click OK (see Fig. 7.10).

Now anything you delete on your machine will be deleted instantly without going to the *Recycle Bin*.

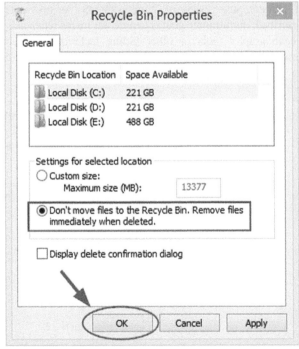

FIGURE 7.10 Configure Windows® to remove deleted files without sending them to the Recycle Bin.

Registry Antiforensics

In Chapter 6 we listed the most important registry keys that can reveal our use of steganography tools. In this section we will reverse the process and introduce different tweaks for the registry to avoid detection by any forensic examiner looking for evidence of using a stego tool on our machine.

Deleting the Leftovers of Uninstalled Programs

As we saw in the previous chapter, the registry keeps track of all installed programs on your machine; even when you uninstall a program, some parts of it may remain in the registry. There is no need to rewrite the registry keys that contain such information. Review Chapter 6 and make sure that no stego tool leftover still existed within your registry to avoid detection by forensic tools.

Connected USB Devices

Connected USB devices to Windows® can reveal important information about what happened and by which user. For example, a suspect can launch a stego tool from his/her USB stick and use images stored on his/her PC to conceal secret data, then move this image to his/her PC. By knowing that a USB device has been connected to a suspect's machine, investigators can assume that such an action has been conducted by the suspect. Registry keys that contain previous USB connected devices have been thoroughly covered by the suggested tool in the previous chapter. Subsequently in order to hide your USB from Windows®, delete the corresponding key in the registry.

Mostly Recently Used List

Clearly from its name, this is a list of files and programs that have been accessed recently. Windows keeps track of these lists in the registry. Such lists are spread across the registry and store previous user actions on the PC. The most common places for storing such lists inside the registry was described in the previous chapter. Remember to delete this list to cover your tracks. Most privacy tools empty these lists automatically from the registry (*BleachBit* performs this, for example).

Disable UserAssist

Windows® tries to keep track of all programs launched on your PC since its installation, including the number of times they have been running and the last execution date/time of each program. All this information is stored in an encrypted database in the following registry key:

HKEY_CURRENT_USER\Software\Microsoft\Windows\CurrentVersion\Explorer\UserAssist.

Note: In order to open the registry editor, type regedit in the Run dialog and press Enter (you can access the Run window by pressing the combination key **Windows** button+**R**).

As we saw in the previous chapter, there are many tools that can be used to explore *UserAssist*. We can use such tools to delete *UserAssist* entries and to automatically disable it (see Fig. 7.11) for a screen capture of *UserAssistView* by nirsoft (http://www.nirsoft.net/utils/userassist_view.html).

We can also access a *UserAssist* registry key directly and delete all its entries manually (see Fig. 7.12).

To disable *UserAssist* logging we can create a new DWORD in a *UserAssist* key, name it *NoLog*, and assign a value of **1** to it.

Disable Timestamp for Last Access to a File

This is a setting that keeps track of the last time a file was accessed. Disabling it will make investigating your

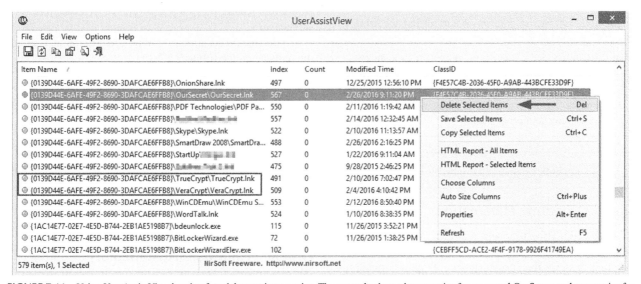

FIGURE 7.11 Using UserAssistView by nirsoft to delete registry entries. The example above shows entries for stego tool OurSecret and two entries for TrueCrypt and VeraCrypt encryption tools.

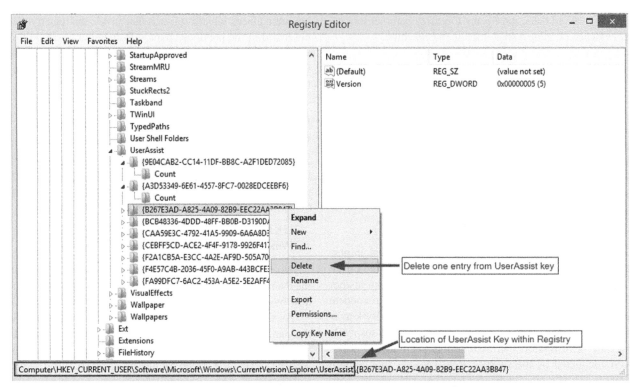

FIGURE 7.12 Deleting UserAssist entries manually using the Windows® registry.

computer for when you last accessed a file or program too difficult to know.

To disable the last access launch of a command prompt, elevated as Administrator, type the information in Fig. 7.13 and press Enter.

In order for it to take effect you must restart your computer. Now try to open any file on your PC, right-click it, select *Properties* >> then check *Accessed* attribute (see Fig. 7.14). Although I already opened this document (my current date is **Wednesday, March 9, 2016, 01:10: 11 AM**), its previous last access date was not modified accordingly.

> **Warning: If you have a backup program scheduled to perform an automatic backup of files, the last access time attribute will be necessary in order for it to function properly. To reenable this feature, type the following in a command prompt window and press Enter:**

> **fsutil behavior set disablelastaccess 0**

Disable Windows Hibernation

Hibernate file (Hiberfil.sys) is a hidden system file located in the root folder of the drive where the operating system is installed. It stores the current state of Windows® machines. In other words, it is a copy of system RAM memory stored on hard disk at specific times (when the user selects to hibernate his/her PC). This file can contains a wealth of

FIGURE 7.13 Disable the last access time of files in Windows® OS.

information for computer forensics investigators, so disabling this feature may be a good choice as a counterforensic measure.

To disable hibernation on a Windows® machine through the registry do the following:

1. Navigate to the following registry key: HKEY_LOCAL_MACHINE\SYSTEM\CurrentControlSet\Control\Power.
2. Give **HibernateEnabled** a value of 0 to disable hibernation (see Fig. 7.15).

To disable hibernation through the command prompt, launch a command prompt elevated as Administrator, type the information in Fig. 7.16, and press Enter.

To reenable it type **powercfg/hibernate on**.

Disable Windows Virtual Memory (Paging File)

In Chapter 5 we described the concept of a paging file (also called virtual memory), which is used by Windows® to

compensate for the shortage of RAM memory. Paging is considered a security risk for many reasons. For example, if you have a file encrypted or stored inside an encrypted container, when you want to read this file you first need to decrypt it. This decrypted file may still exist in the paging file long after the user logs off. In addition to this, some third-party programs can temporarily store unencrypted passwords or other sensitive information in memory. Fragments of this data may go to paging in some cases. For this reason it is better to disable paging in Windows® for maximum protection.

To disable paging on a computer running Windows® 8.1 (also applies to Windows® 7) follow these steps (see Fig. 7.17):

Control Panel >> System >> Advanced system settings >> Advanced tab >> from the Performance section, choose Settings… >> Advanced tab >> Virtual memory section then click Change…

FIGURE 7.14 The file access time attribute will not change when accessing the file after implementing this tweak.

FIGURE 7.16 Disable Windows® hibernation through a command prompt.

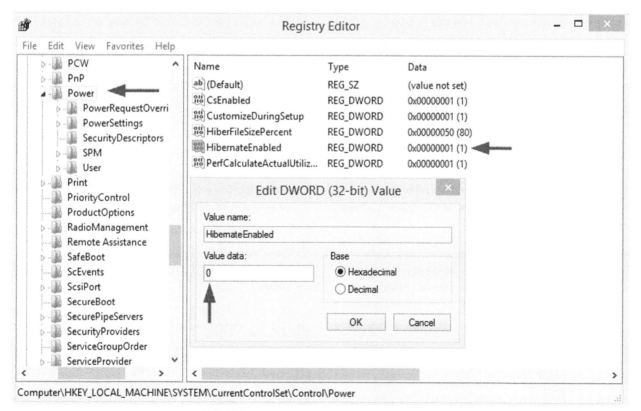

FIGURE 7.15 Disable hibernation through the registry.

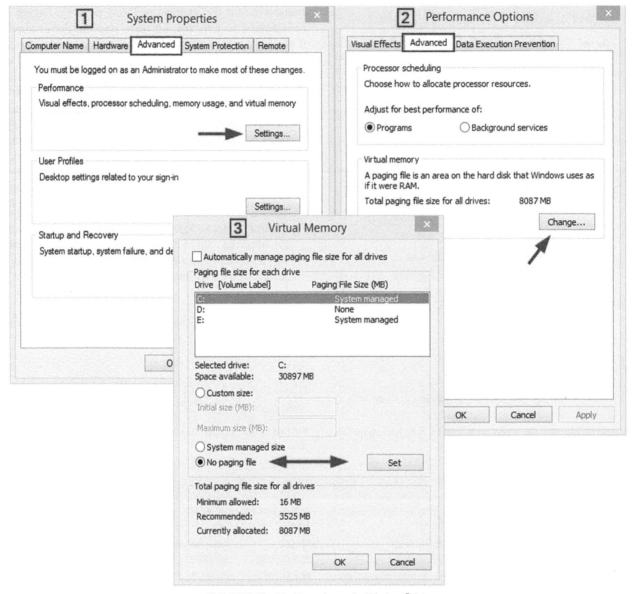

FIGURE 7.17 Disable paging under Windows® 8.1.

From this menu you can select the drive where you want to disable the paging file by checking the option *No paging file* and then clicking *Set*.

In computers with low RAM memory (less than 4 GB), disabling the paging file may cause performance degradation. To counter for such cases we can leave paging file enabled while configuring Windows® to empty the paging file automatically upon shutdown. To achieve this, follow these steps:

1. Access the registry (press the **Window** button+**R** to launch the Run window, type *regedit* inside it, and press Enter).
2. Navigate to the following registry key:

HKEY_LOCAL_MACHINE\SYSTEM\Current ControlSet\Control\Session Manager\Memory Management

3. Change the data value of the **ClearPageFileAtShutdown** value to a value of **1** (see Fig. 7.18).

If the value does not exist, add the following value [3]:

Value Name: ClearPageFileAtShutdown
Value Type: REG_DWORD
Value: 1

Restart your PC for the changes to take effect. After implementing this registry tweak, shutdown time will increase a bit.

Disable System Restore Points and File History

As we have already seen during previous chapters, system restore points can contain hidden data and previously deleted

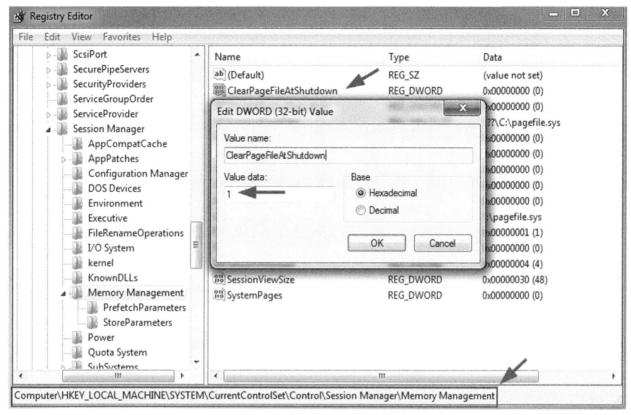

FIGURE 7.18   Enable empty paging file upon shutdown.

files. This imposes security risks because our previous data and deleted files can be easily recovered from previous restore points. To disable this feature in Windows® 7 do the following:

Go to *Control Panel >> System >> System Protection*

Select the partition where you want to disable protection and click *Configure*. A new window appears; select the option *Turn off system protection*, and finally click *OK* to apply changes (see Fig. 7.19).

Repeat the same process for all disks/partitions where you want to disable system restore.

In Windows® 8 and 10, you need also to disable *File History*, which is a modern Windows® feature that backup all your default and custom libraries, Contacts, Documents, Music, Pictures, Videos, Desktop and the OneDrive files available offline on your PC.

This feature is disabled by default in Windows® and it only saves its backup copies to external drives. In case it is enabled, however, follow these steps to disable it:

Go to *Control Panel >> File History*

If it is already enabled, click *Turn Off* (see Fig. 7.20).

Disable Windows Thumbnail Cache

It is a known fact that Windows® stores thumbnails of graphics files (JPEG, BMP, GIF, PNG, TIFF), some document types (DOCX, PPTX), and movie files in the thumbnail cache file called *thumbs.db*. The thumbnail can reveal previously deleted/used files on your machine. For example, if you use a specific image to conceal data inside it and then deleted this image, a thumbnail of this image will still exist in *thumbs.db* and this can reveal the fact that a deleted image was used previously on the system.

Beginning with Windows® XP, Windows® allows users to turn off this feature. To disable it, do the following:

Go to *Control Panel >> Folder Options >> View* tab, check the option *Always show icons, never thumbnails*, and click *OK* (see Fig. 7.21).

In case you are using a PC that has its thumbnail feature activated and you have security concerns, you can delete the previous *thumbs.db* on the Windows® partition following the steps in Fig. 7.22.

Disable Windows Prefetch Feature

In Chapter 5, we talked about Windows® *Prefetch*, which was first introduced in Windows® XP. Its name was later changed to SuperFetch in Windows® Vista. This feature helps boost Windows® performance by predicting which applications a user is likely to launch and then works by loading the necessary files into RAM memory to increase application loading.

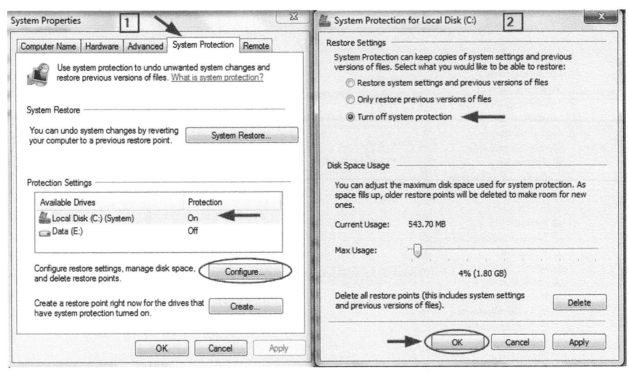

FIGURE 7.19 Disable Windows® restore feature.

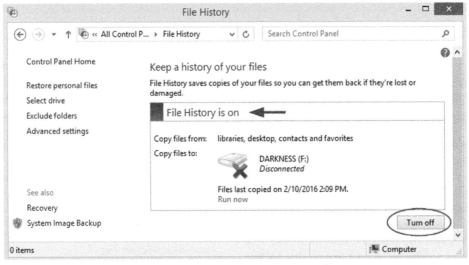

FIGURE 7.20 Turn off file history in Windows® 8.1.

You will be keen to know that even if a user used an application once and then uninstalled it, a copy of the application Prefetch file will remain in the Prefetch folder. The same issue also happens to portable applications. The location of the Prefetch file is under *C:\Windows\Prefetch* (assuming Windows® is installed at C:\partition).

We can get rid of applications loaded into the Prefetch folder by simply deleting them, but this may not always happen. For example, what if we forget to do this? A computer forensics can recover deleted Prefetch files from HDD if these files were not deleted securely as we described earlier.

To achieve maximum security (although this will increase the launch time of your Windows® applications) you should disable the Prefetch feature. Follow these steps to achieve this (this tweak is applicable to Windows® Vista, 7, 8, 10, and Server versions 2008+):

1. Press **Windows+R** to launch the Run dialog.
2. Type **services.msc** to access the Windows® services console.
3. Search for the service named **Superfetch** and double-click to access it. Go to *Startup type*, change it to

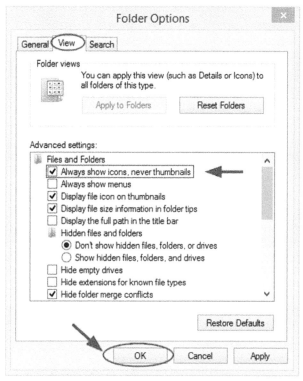

FIGURE 7.21 Disable thumbnail from folder options.

Disabled, click *Stop* to stop this service, and finally click *OK* and you are done (see Fig. 7.23).

We can also disable the *Prefetch* feature using the Windows® registry following these steps:

1. Access the registry editor as we did many times during this book.
2. Navigate to the following registry key:

HKEY_LOCAL_MACHINE\SYSTEM\ CurrentControlSet\Control\Session Manager\Memory Management\PrefetchParameters

Right-click the **EnablePrefetcher** value and change its **Value Data** to one of the following (see Fig. 7.24):

0 – Disables Prefetch
1 – Enables Prefetch for applications only
2 – Enables Prefetch for boot files only
3 – Enables Prefetch for boot and application files

To disable Prefetch, insert **0** in the value data of the **EnablePrefetcher** value. Restart your machine to apply changes.

As we mentioned earlier, disabling Prefetch can significantly increase boot (if disabled) and application launch time.

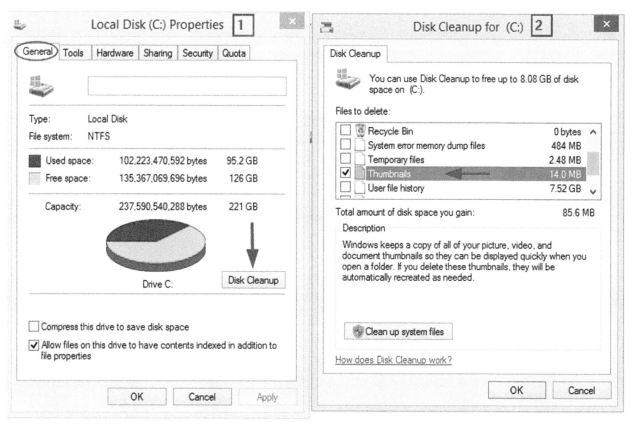

FIGURE 7.22 Delete thumbnails using the Disk Cleanup utility.

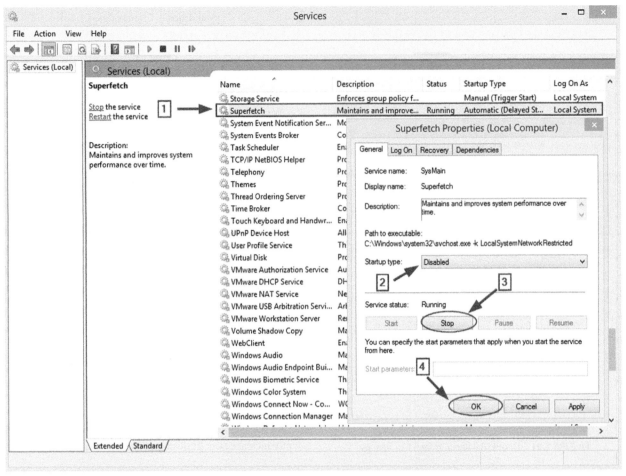

FIGURE 7.23 Disable Windows® SuperFetch service using the Windows® Service Manager.

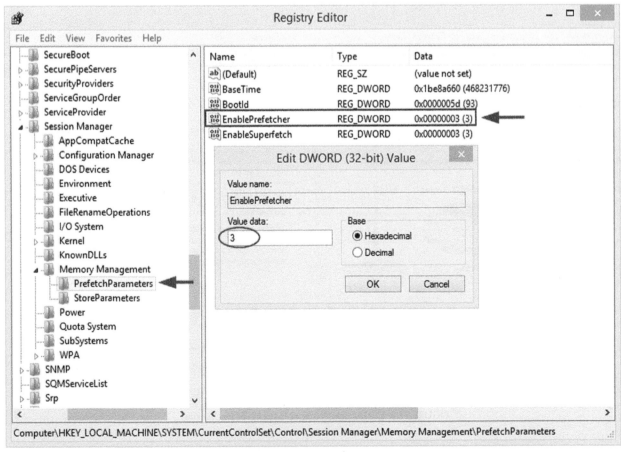

FIGURE 7.24 Disable Prefetch using the registry editor.

Disable Windows Logging

Event logs are special files that record specific events when they happened within Windows® OS. For example, when a user halts an application, an error event will be recorded in the application log. In the same way, when a user fails to log in to Windows® another event will be saved in the security log event. Windows® has a special console that presents these events to the end user in a user-friendly way. You can access the event viewer from *Control Panel >> Administrative tools >> Event Viewer.*

The event viewer tracks information in several different logs. According to Microsoft, Windows® logs include [4]:

Application (program) events: Has three types: errors, warning, or information. An error is a significant problem, such as loss of data. A warning is an event that isn't necessarily significant, but might indicate a possible future problem. An information event describes the successful operation of a program, driver, or service.

Security-related events: These events are called audits and are described as successful or failed depending on the event, such as whether a user trying to log on to Windows® was successful.

Setup events: For computers configured as domain controller.

System events: System events are logged by Windows® and Windows® system services, and are classified as error, warning, or information.

Forwarded events: These events are forwarded to this log by other computers.

Now, with regard to our antiforensic work, we are concerned with deleting our previous traces and anything that may point back to our previous action on our PC. Windows® event logs may contain a wealth of information about our PC usage; for example, in Fig. 7.25 you can see that there is an error generated by *TOR Browser.* For obvious reasons this error is recorded in application logs. Despite that fact that we previously deleted all traces of using *the TOR browser* from our machine, we can clearly see that it is still there. This gives any computer forensic investigator a clear clue of any previous use of *TOR Browser.*

You can manually clear any event log by right-clicking on the button. Choose *Clear log…* from the right-click menu (see Fig. 7.26).

Deleting the event log will not affect Windows® performance and will help you to better cover your tracks when using Windows® machines for data concealment activities.

If you prefer to use automated tools to clean your event logs and other traces in Windows®, there is a portable tool from *nirsoft* called *CleanAfterMe* (Fig. 7.27). According to its inventor, it allows you to easily clean files and registry entries that are automatically created by the Windows® OS during your regular computer work. It can also clean the

cookies/history/cache/passwords of Internet Explorer, the *Recent* folder, Registry entries that record the last accessed files, the temporary folder of Windows®, the event logs, the Recycle Bin, and more.

Automated tools are a simple and fast choice that require no advanced IT skills, although it is also necessary to know what Windows® logs your actions. It is essential to know where these logs are stored in order to assist those with security concerned users to check manually for any traces left on their machines even after using automated tools to clear traces.

Disable Windows® Password Hash Extraction

In the previous chapter, we have demonstrated a method to crack Windows® passwords using *Procdump* to dump the lsass.exe process, which contains user password credentials. It then gives this dump to *Mimikatz* in order to extract password hashes from it. In this section we will reverse the process and harden our Windows® machine to defend against *Mimikatz* and prevent it from stealing our password hashes.

Mimikatz can act differently in each version of Windows®; explaining how to halt this tool attack needs a long description and is beyond the scope of this book. We will mention some measures to harden your Windows® installation against the most common attacks of this tool.

1. Make sure to update your antivirus software regularly. According to the Virus Total Website (https://www. virustotal.com), *MimiKatz* was detected as a malicious software by 32/55 antivirus engines (test done on March 17, 2016). The major antivirus software recognized this tool as a hacking tool.
2. Make sure that the value of *UseLogonCredential* is set to **0** (see Fig. 7.28) in the following registry key to prevent *clear-text* passwords from being stored in LSASS: HKEY_LOCAL_MACHINE\SYSTEM\CurrentControlSet\Control\SecurityProviders\WDigest

    Windows® 8.1/2012 R2/10 do not have a *UseLogonCredential* DWORD value. **If this value is available on the registry this may indicate a warning**. In all previous versions of Windows® this value should be set to 0. However, if your Windows® version is set to have automatic updates, you will not suffer from this vulnerability as Microsoft has released a security update for all Windows® versions prior to 8.1 to fix this issue. The description of this update can be found on https://support.microsoft.com/en-us/kb/2871997.

    By default, the *UseLogonCredential* DWORD value won't appear in the registry on all versions of Windows® 8.1 or later. Earlier versions that have installed KB2871997 security update also will not have this value appearing in their registry, meaning that this value is set to **0**.

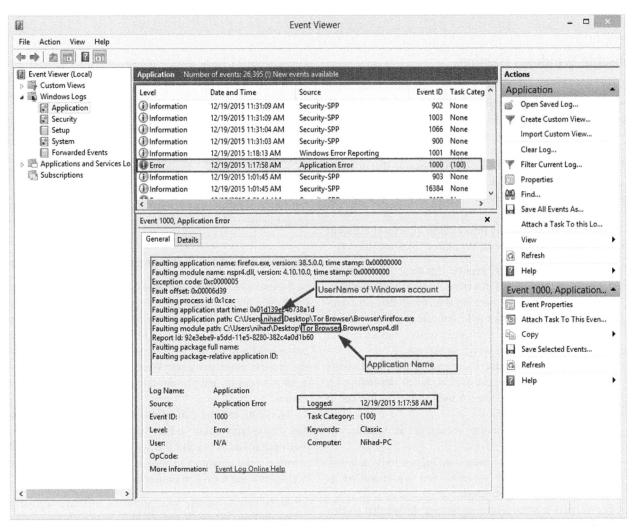

FIGURE 7.25 Investigating Windows® event logs shows an error generated by TOR Browser.

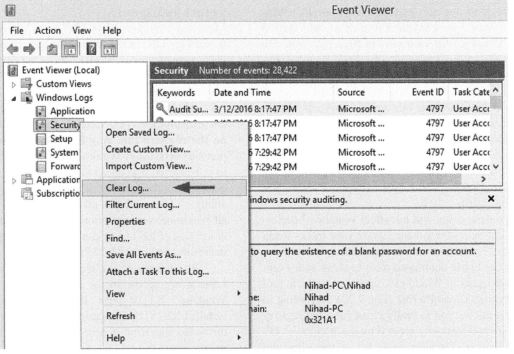

FIGURE 7.26 Clearing windows logs.

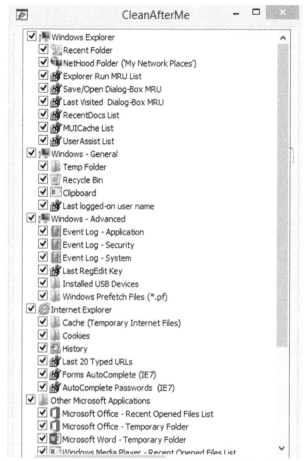

FIGURE 7.27 CleanAfterMe tool can delete most user traces from Windows® machines automatically.

CLEARING DIGITAL FOOTPRINTS

We already talked in Chapter 5 about hiding our digital footprints; in fact, most techniques in this book focus on this particular issue. Clearing our footprints will include the following and more:

1. Become anonymous online by using the TOR network for both surfing and file sharing.
2. Use no log VPN service to encrypt online communications.
3. Use a search engine that doesn't record your search history.
4. Use a secure email provider located in a country where user privacy is respected.
5. Boot from USB drives or live CDs.
6. Use virtual technology.
7. Use encryption techniques to protect your data.
8. Clear your previous tracks on a Windows® machine using the techniques already mentioned in this chapter.
9. Be paranoid and assume that you are targeted by a different third party. Work online according to this fact.

Additional best practices also exist to protect our identity online and prevent outside attackers from knowing important information about us such as:

1. Deactivate social media accounts like Facebook, Twitter, and the like. If using such services is necessary, make sure to check the privacy settings and set your personal details and contact information available only to your friend list.
2. If you already have a social media account on a specific service that does not allow you to delete it (disable it), you can simply update it with false information about yourself.
3. Do not use your work email or phone number to subscribe to commercial, sport, or any other mailing list. Use a dedicated email address for such services and populate it with false information.
4. Do not store any data related to you on portable USB drives or laptop/tablet without encryption.

Personal computer security awareness is crucial to mitigate most risks online and to prevent others from successfully investigating and acquiring information about you.

Live CDs and Bootable USB Tokens

Live CDs and USBs offer a secure and easy way to use a PC without leaving traces on it. (Some will leave traces on the host hard disk drive. If you need to achieve the maximum anonymity and security online, review Chapter 5 thoroughly. Pay special attention to the section, "Anonymous Operating System" for a complete discussion of this issue.) In this section we will list some tools that can be used to create bootable USB zip drives:

- Windows USB/DVD download tool: https://wudt.codeplex.com
- Rufus: https://rufus.akeo.ie
- UNetbootin: https://unetbootin.github.io
- Universal USB installer: http://www.pendrivelinux.com/universal-usb-installer-easy-as-1-2-3
- WiNToBootic: http://www.wintobootic.com
- WinToFlash: https://wintoflash.com/home/en
- WinUSB Maker: http://joshcellsoftwares.com/products/zotacwinusbmaker

Windows® OS can also be booted from within a CD/DVD. *WinBuilder* is a tool for creating bootable Windows PE operating systems that you boot from a CD/DVD or from a USB/HDD (http://winbuilder.net). Most Linux distributions can be booted using a CD/DVD using the tools just mentioned. *DistroWatch* lists nearly all Linux distributions available in the world today; you can download the ISO image of any distribution and burn it into the CD/DVD to boot from https://distrowatch.com.

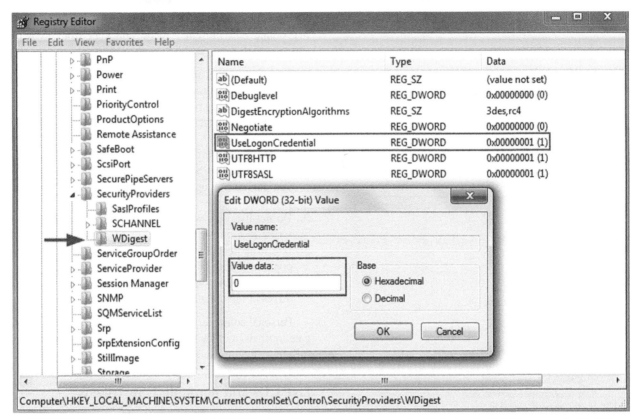

FIGURE 7.28 Setting UseLogonCredential DWORD value to 0 to avoid storing logon credentials in clear-text in LSA memory for this SSP.

Virtual Machines

A VM is a fake OS running in your real computer OS. Each VM (also called guest OS) will take a portion of your host PC RAM memory and CPU speed in order to work. You can have many VMs installed on a single computer and running at the same time. Each of these VMs will use its own hard disk, which is simply a file on your actual host HDD. In fact, most cloud storage servers are based on VM technology.

Using virtualization software, we can use the Internet, download files, visit dangerous websites, open attachments, and test software downloaded from random websites with limited possibility of being hacked compared to using a regular machine. In case malicious software got installed on our VM, it will have no access to our host machine files. The VM can effectively help us to lower our digital footprint as we can customize our guest OS installation according to our needs and then delete it with one click when needed to destroy all previous tracks.

In Chapter 5 we also talked about how we can use a portable version of *VirtualBox* to run a portable OS from within a USB drive. In this section we will list some virtual software that can be used to run VMs in Windows® OS.

VirtualBox

VirtualBox is a powerful ×86 and AMD64/Intel64 virtualization product for enterprise as well as home use. It runs on Windows®, Linux, Macintosh®, and Solaris® hosts and supports a large number of guest operating systems (https://www.virtualbox.org).

Windows Virtual PC

Developed by Microsoft, it can be used to run more than one operating system at the same time on one computer, and to run many productivity applications in a virtual Windows® environment (https://www.microsoft.com/en-us/download/details.aspx?id=3702).

VMware Workstation Player

This is famous virtualization software that can run multiple operating systems and corporate desktops in an isolated and protected environment on modern hardware. These applications also offer a free version for personal use (https://www.vmware.com/products/player).

Using Portable Applications

Portable applications can run without the need to install them into the system. This will effectively reduce our digital footprint, although some traces will remain in Windows® OS after executing such tools. However, we have thoroughly covered how we can delete an application's previous use at the beginning of this chapter. There are many websites offering portable applications; some have grouped a large number of portable applications and organized them in one suite. The following are some well-known portable application suites:

- PortableApps.com Suite, 300+ Apps: http://portable-apps.com/suite
- Lupo PenSuite, 160 Apps: http://www.lupopensuite.com/suite.htm
- Liberkey, 296 Apps: http://www.liberkey.com/en
- OpenDisc, 1.57 GB: http://www.theopendisc.com
- NirLauncher, a package of more than 180 portable freeware utilities for Windows®, all of them developed for the *NirSoft* website during the last few years: http://launcher.nirsoft.net
- Sysinternals Suite, all Sysinternals utilities in one package: https://technet.microsoft.com/en-us/sysinternals/bb842062.aspx

DIRECT ATTACK AGAINST FORENSIC SOFTWARE

A new approach to fight against computer forensic tools and techniques is using specialized tools to attack the forensic software itself instead of attacking the forensic process. Such tools are not widely documented, but it is worth mentioning them to draw user attention to their existence.

A famous old-school attack against computer forensic software is the ZIP bomb. A ZIP bomb, also known as a decompression bomb, is designed to crash/freeze any application trying to read it. Originally created to attack antivirus software, for example, when a forensic imaging software tries to take an image for an HDD that contains this ZIP bomb, it is highly likely that the forensic tool will freeze and stop working while trying to read each layer of the zipped package. This should effectively lower the forensic investigation speed and waste valuable time while investigating the cause of this problem. You can download a ready ZIP bomb called *42.zip compression bomb (42.374 bytes zipped)* from https://www.unforgettable.dk. Upon extracting the 42.zip bomb, a 4.5 PB file size will be produced resulting in probably consuming all available disk space on the forensic examiner's machine.

Another attack is Hash Collision. Hash function is an algorithm used to create unique fixed value strings from any file.

This process is irreversible. Hashing is very important during a computer forensic trial because it ensures that data was not tampered with. If two different files have the same hash, this will heavily affect the credibility of digital evidence and may render it unacceptable in a court of law. *BishopFox* has a tool for generating MD4 and MD5 hash collision based on *Xiaoyun Wang's* method. *Wang* is considered the first researcher who managed to create the same hash outputs from the two different sets of inputs [5]. The MD5 and MD4 Collision Generators can be downloaded from https://www.bishopfox.com/resources/tools/other-free-tools/md4md5-collision-code.

With the advance of computing, more antiforensic tools directed to attack computer forensic software will be developed. Such tools will mainly work on exploiting vulnerabilities in forensic software. This could be a problem for the first sight; however, this fact will force computer forensic software vendors to create better and more secure tools.

SUMMARY

This chapter was the reverse of the previous one. Antiforensics techniques may seems as if they are targeted against law enforcement, but this is not always true. Ordinary computer users seeking privacy can benefit from such techniques to cover their tracks and protect personal data.

As computing advances, more antiforensics tools will be developed. This will impose real challenges for computer forensic investigators to have their skills up to date. Computer forensic software vendors also need to stay one step ahead to make sure their tools are not vulnerable and that digital evidence acquired by their tool is still reliable and acceptable in a court of law.

Experts predict that antiforensic techniques will gain more attention in the near future, opening the door widely to a new branch in computer security, *computer antiforensics*.

REFERENCES

[1] D.M. Rogers, Anti-forensic Presentation Given to Lockheed Martin, 2005 (San Diego).

[2] Adobe® Acrobat® XI, Sanitization—Remove hidden data from PDF files with Adobe® Acrobat® [Online] Available from: https://www.adobe.com/content/dam/Adobe/en/products/acrobat/pdfs/adobe-acrobat-xi-pdf-sanitization-remove-hidden-data-from-pdf-files-tutorial-ue.pdf (accessed 17.03.16).

[3] Microsoft, How to Clear the Windows Paging File at Shutdown [Online] Available from: https://support.microsoft.com/en-us/kb/314834 (accessed 17.03.16).

[4] Microsoft, What Information Appears in Event Logs? (Event Viewer) [Online] Available from: http://windows.microsoft.com/en-us/windows/what-information-event-logs-event-viewer#1TC=windows-7 (accessed 17.03.16).

[5] Wikipedia, Wang X. [Online] Available from: https://en.wikipedia.org/wiki/Wang_Xiaoyun (accessed 17.03.16).

BIBLIOGRAPHY

[1] Microsoft TechNet, Cipher Command [Online] Available from: https://technet.microsoft.com/en-us/library/bb490878.aspx (accessed 17.03.16).

[2] Microsoft Office, Remove Hidden Data and Personal Information by Inspecting Documents [Online] Available from: https://support.office.com/en-us/article/Remove-hidden-data-and-personal-information-by-inspecting-documents-356b7b5d-77af-44fe-a07f-9aa4d085966f#__toc312143396 (accessed 17.03.16).

[3] Forensics Wiki, Timestomp [Online] Available from: http://forensic-swiki.org/wiki/Timestomp (accessed 17.03.16).

[4] Windows Explored, A Quick Glance at The UserAssist Key in Windows [Online] Available from: http://windowsexplored.com/2012/02/06/a-quick-glance-at-the-userassist-key-in-windows/ (accessed 17.03.16).

Chapter 8

Future Trends

Chapter Outline

Introduction	291	Streaming Protocols	295
The Future of Encryption	292	Wireless Networks and Future Networking Protocols	296
Data Stored in Cloud Computing	293	Data Hiding in Mobile Devices	297
Virtualization Technology	293	Anonymous Networks	297
Data Hiding in Enterprise Networks	294	Summary	298
Data Concealment	294	References	298
Data Leakage Prevention	295	Bibliography	298

INTRODUCTION

Steganography has been used since ancient times with the first record of its use in 500 BC. Old civilizations used different steganographic techniques to protect their military communications. Some used it to hide kings' secrets and treasures; other ancient civilizations considered steganography as a kind of magic, raising serious suspicions of anyone who mastered it at that time.

Beginning in the 20th century, the emphasis was on using digital steganographic techniques to conceal diplomatic, espionage, and military communications. As we mentioned at the beginning of this book, steganography can be considered a subbranch of cryptography. The ultimate objective is to obscure secret messages to outside observers. However, with the development of computing and the emergence of different techniques to conceal data digitally, steganographic techniques have become a branch of their own. Nevertheless, steganographic techniques can be further strengthened by encrypting payloads before concealing them in the overt object file.

As computing technology develops, we can expect to see more methods of digital steganography in the near future. More IT devices are shifting toward using wireless connections. In the near future, you will be able to perform nearly all of your office work wirelessly including but not limited to printing, Internet connection, sharing files and streaming media, security cameras, Internet TV, and many more examples of devices that can use wireless connections to accomplish their tasks. This increase in using wireless technology opens endless possibilities to conceal and transfer secret data among wireless devices. Hiding data in audio

and video files is expected to have a boost, especially with continued research to develop new methods for hiding in multimedia files other than images. As more methods to detect copyright piracy in audio/video files are continually developed, we can expect to see more advanced techniques developed to bury invisible watermarks in such files using more sophisticated ways than those currently available.

At the time of writing this book, there was a great debate in the United States about whether IT companies who create security software, operating systems, and any software that can process data in an encrypted format (including smartphone manufacturers) should handle decryption keys or simply leave backdoors in their products to allow law enforcement to break into user devices in some cases (criminal, terrorist, or victims when their devices are seized as evidence). For example, many US states propose legislation to prevent encryption of data on a mobile phone. California and New York introduced a bill that prevents the sale of smartphones with unbreakable encryption. The new California bill issued on January 20, 2016 would require a smartphone that is manufactured on or after January 1, 2017, and sold in California, to be capable of being decrypted and unlocked by its manufacturer or its operating system provider [1]. More states are expected to issue similar bills to govern the usage of full device encryption features in smartphones.

The main cause of setting such bills that prevents data encryption in mobile phones is that terrorist organizations, drug dealers, and global criminal organizations are considered among the main users of encryption techniques these days. Of course, legal users also exist and they still form the greatest percentage of encryption technique users worldwide. With the continual growth in terrorist threats all over the world, nothing indicates that this debate will end soon in favor of protecting personal privacy and civil liberty of end users.

Data hiding techniques could be the remaining solution in such situations where encryption is prohibited by law. Like arms, everything in computer security can be used by both parties, good guys and bad guys. What we care about in this book is to offer the good people a method to protect their private data from unauthorized access, at the same time drawing law enforcement officials' attention to such techniques that can be used by the bad guys for incriminating purposes. Partnerships between governments and giant IT companies are crucial to find a compromise that assures users' privacy and at the same time prevents criminals and terrorists from using advanced technology to bring devastation to our societies. Trust is the magic word that can certainly solve this dilemma between the affected triangle of governments, IT products manufacturers, and end users (customers).

In the last chapter of this book, we are going to foresee the future and talk about advances in steganographic and encryption technologies. We will also talk about some mitigation measures that can help enterprises prevent illegal information leakage conducted with the use of steganographic techniques.

THE FUTURE OF ENCRYPTION

As we all know, the greatest danger that modern encryption schemes face is losing the encryption key used to decrypt the data and make it readable again.

Most algorithms that are used today in security products to encrypt data are very strong and can be completely robust by today's security standards if implemented correctly in the encryption product. But no matter how strong the encryption algorithm is, it will be breakable in a fraction of a second when the decryption key gets revealed to an outside attacker.

Modern studies have addressed this fact. They suggest alternative ways for protecting encryption keys in transit to prevent outside eavesdropping from breaking our security system.

Fully homomorphic encryption is a modern encryption technique created by *Craig Gentry*, a graduate student supported by the National Science Foundation (NSF) in 2010 as a thesis for his PhD. We can summarize his approach in one sentence: **Find a way to process encrypted data without ever decrypting it**.

According to the NSF [2], *To explain this concept, Craig invented an imaginary character named Alice who owns a jewelry store. Alice doesn't trust her workers with her expensive gems, so she gets an impenetrable box for which only she has the key.*

When Alice wants her employees to make a new piece of jewelry, she locks the materials inside the box and hands it off to her workers. Using special gloves, employees can work on the gems inside the box, but can't get them out. Once the work is done, Alice opens the box with her key and takes out the finished jewelry. In this way, her workers process raw materials into jewelry without ever truly having access to the materials themselves.

We can give a more practical example related to our IT world using *homomorphic encryption*. For example, we can query a homomorphic-enabled search engine using an encrypted query; the search engine will compare this query with an index of encrypted websites and finally return the result back to the user. In this way the search engine will not see or process user query plaintext at all, making this approach highly secure.

Homomorphic encryption needs immense computational power in order to process encrypted data on both sides. *Craig* estimates that his idea would need a decade or more to become practically usable in our daily communications (he proposed his technique in 2009). If serious improvements are added to this technique, we can expect to begin seeing it in the near future as an additional secure communication channel.

Another type of modern data encryption techniques is the *Honey Encryption*, proposed in 2014 by *Ari Juels* and *Thomas Ristenpart*. This new encryption works by producing a ciphertext, which, when decrypted with an incorrect key as guessed by the attacker, presents a plausible-looking yet incorrect plaintext password or encryption key [3,4].

Functional encryption is another development in data encryption techniques. It is a type of public-key encryption in which a key holder knows the specific function of encrypted data without knowing anything else about the data. For example, given an encrypted program a secret key may enable the key holder to have a specific output from the program depending on the input without knowing anything else about the program itself [5].

The last modern encryption technique we are going to talk about is *quantum cryptography*. The security of this technique relies on the physical characteristics of the transmission channel to send data across it rather than depending on the mathematics as all traditional encryption algorithms do.

Quantum cryptography uses elementary particles such as photons (each photon represents a single bit of data, either 0 or 1) to generate a cryptographic key and transmit it to a receiver using a suitable communication channel like lasers and fiber optic wires. The physical characteristics of the photon assure that no one can intercept the connection without alerting both communication parties, the sender and receiver.

Quantum cryptography is acting as the light and can be used to assure secret message secrecy for a long time.

Distributing encryption keys is highly secure using *quantum cryptography*. In fact if an eavesdropper wants to intercept the connection, he or she must do this in real time (of course, this also can be detected). He or she cannot intercept the encrypted connection and store a copy of it in order to decrypt it later (maybe after years, when the technology development can make this possible). *Quantum cryptography* does not allow copying data while in transit, since any change in the location of any photon during transit will raise an alert.

A number of banks and finical institutions began using the *quantum key distribution* (QKD) technique in Europe, especially Switzerland, to exchange secret encryption keys to protect high-value data; however, its adoption is still very limited in the United States. The high-security measures implemented by QKD will make it a favorable solution for all private and public organizations that aim to protect their high-value data for a long time.

A recent approach to protecting enterprises' confidential data through encryption is by using a special software solution that keeps all data encrypted on corporate computers and mobile devices until it is requested by the user. This software will then decrypt the fetched data on the fly and present it to the end user. This will effectively lower data leakage from corporate enterprises since no data is stored unencrypted on corporate hard disks.

DATA STORED IN CLOUD COMPUTING

According to Forester research, the value of the public cloud market is expected to reach at least $191 billion by 2020 [6].

Originally, cloud service began when a number of web hosting providers sold parts of their extra storage space to consumers for saving their personal data. Later, as more customers joined this service, giant companies like Amazon™ and Google™ realized the importance of offering web storage service for their customers to increase profits and customer retention.

To briefly define cloud storage, it is a set of data storage servers usually located at different physical locations. While cloud storage providers maintain and protect data (both physically and logically from viruses and cyber threats), these servers continue to insure that data stored on them are available and accessible to their legal owners 24/7.

With the advance of smartphone technology and the reduction of hard disk drives prices, more people are willing to use cloud storage to store their private data. Nowadays, with a single click, people can upload all personal data stored on their mobile phones to their cloud storage accounts through specialized applications available for different OS versions. Dropbox™ and Google™ drive are examples of such widely used services.

Cloud storage is not only limited to storing private user data but many storage providers offer additional cloud service models that can be exploited in digital steganography:

- **Infrastructure as a service (IaaS)**: In this model a user can have access to a cloud storage server, which comes preloaded with a specific operating system. The OS allows remote user access to the IaaS as if it was his/her local desktop PC. The user can access the system using a specific application or emulator. Examples of such services are *Amazon™ Web Services* and *Google™ Computer Engine*.

- **Software as a service (SaaS)**: In this model, the user can have access to cloud storage servers that come preloaded with the user's favorite applications. Users can use these applications as if they were installed on their local machines. Examples of such services are *Google™ Apps for Education* and *Microsoft Office 365*.

Law enforcement agencies will have their hands full when trying to investigate criminal cases with evidence stashed on cloud storage units. A user can simply encrypt data using any technique and upload the encrypted container or file to a cloud storage account. A user can also use any data hiding technique mentioned in this book and implement it using either the **IaaS** or **SaaS** cloud storage model. This will effectively hide user tracks from the local machine, resulting in extending a search warrant to the cloud, which can make criminal investigation more challenging and even impossible in many cases.

Cyber law jurisdiction extends to cloud storage. What if a US citizen uploads his/her incriminating data to a cloud storage provider that is located in Switzerland? If this user was a part of a criminal case, can the US cyber enforcement agency demand that the Swiss provider hand over a copy of the user data?

Data stored in cloud storage may become a privacy issue for end users. For instance, what if a user wants to delete his/her previously uploaded data from a cloud storage provider? Can the provider assure that all data have been deleted completely and securely?

Recently it has emerged that Apple™ is storing some of its users' iCloud data on Google's computer servers [7]. Most cloud storage providers use virtualization and RAID disks to assure high availability of data. Can cloud storage users assure that their data have been deleted from all locations? Our advice for cloud storage users is that encrypting your data before uploading to the cloud is a must.

The usage of the cloud storage service is expected to grow explosively in the near future. This will impose additional challenges for law enforcement and end users at the same time.

VIRTUALIZATION TECHNOLOGY

Virtualization technology has a huge impact on the IT industry, especially in data centers to save costs and increase performance. On the data hiding side, the virtual machine can be used and launched from within a USB zip drive. This imposes great risks to organizations trying to fight against data leakage. A user can fully launch an OS from a USB stick, allowing him/her to use steganography tools without leaving any traces on the host machine. If accessing a USB is prohibited by an organization's security policy (and this is an excellent security measure that must be implemented without exception), a user can use the **IaaS** model of cloud computing and install VM software on the host account. Then he/she can perform stego actions on the remote server, thus bypassing all network security measures related to fighting against data hiding techniques.

The virtual machine can also impose a real challenge to forensic investigators. A user can conduct a criminal activity or conceal data using VM and then delete it from the host machine. Recovering deleted VM files (especially after performing data wiping on HDD) and then retrieving data from it is too difficult, and impossible in many situations.

To recap, to enhance security in an organization, regular actions performed by regular users must be restricted. For instance, it is better to prohibit accessing all models of cloud services and technically prevent users from attaching USB sticks and all removable devices to the corporate network. It is also recommended to prevent users from synchronizing their mobile phones with work PCs and using corporate Internet connections on their mobile devices.

Virtualization technology is advancing rapidly, while more developers are aiming to build cloud-friendly applications. All these advances can be explored later to simplify data hiding techniques and data leakage.

DATA HIDING IN ENTERPRISE NETWORKS

According to a *TechDay* report on EMC's Digital Universe study, the world's data is expected to multiply tenfold between 2013 and 2020, from 4.4 trillion gigabytes to 44 trillion gigabytes. Most of these data are produced by corporate and government organizations, and a large percent of it contains private data that should be held confidential [8].

The FBI says that corporate espionage is the greatest risk that enterprises face. It costs the American economy hundreds of billions of dollars per year. The FBI estimates that hundreds of billions of dollars are lost to foreign competitors every year because of this kind of espionage. These foreign competitors deliberately target economic intelligence in advanced technologies and flourishing US industries [9].

Data Concealment

Data concealment techniques are the main method of storing and smuggling corporate data out of company walls. Other penetration attacks also get benefits from such techniques to attack their targets silently, thus avoiding real-time detection. Corporations invest millions of dollars in network security devices to protect their assets and prevent data leakage.

No single solution can protect corporate networks completely. Companies need to have many solutions installed and configured properly to protect their precious data. Some network devices that can protect companies against data concealment techniques and prevent data leaks are:

Intrusion detection systems and software firewalls: Prevent users from downloading steganography tools and/or encryption software.

Antivirus software: Detect and delete downloaded steganographic tools and warn network administrator if a user tries to download/install such applications.

Next-generation firewall (**NGFW**): A very intelligent device that can detect steganographic software by its signature in addition to performing advanced content filtering. This kind of firewall has the ability to detect anomalies in network protocols to help investigate data hidden in network protocols (eg, data hiding in a TCP/IP protocol header). NGFW has the ability to perform deep packet inspection of data passing across the network, enabling it to detect and block access to underground networks like the TOR and I2P networks. It can also be integrated with third-party software like Active Directory in Windows® server to determine what traffic each user (according to his/her group permission) is allowed to send and receive using the company network.

NGFW is application software that acts as a filter in limiting traffic to only approved applications. To understand this better let us compare it with the traditional firewall solutions. Traditional firewall systems have a list of common ports used by each application. These ports use a list to determine which applications are running in any NGFW device. Running applications are not determined according to the used port; instead, the firewall will monitor all traffic passing across the network from layers 2 through 7 [in an open systems interconnection (OSI) model], making necessary decisions as to what type of traffic is allowed to pass. This feature is very important in fighting against steganography tools that can be configured to mask traffic with innocent-looking ports to smuggle data outside a corporate network. For example, if an employee wants to smuggle confidential data outside the corporate network, he/she can use any technique mentioned in previous chapters to conceal the data inside an innocent-looking file and then try to upload this file to a remote FTP server. If for any reason the FTP port was blocked, he/she can open an encrypted tunnel through port 80 (port 80 is traditionally used for HTTP traffic only, and usually comes open in most network organizations to allow Internet access) and send data across it. As expected, traffic will tunnel through the port as if it is

END-point Data Leakage Prevention Solution

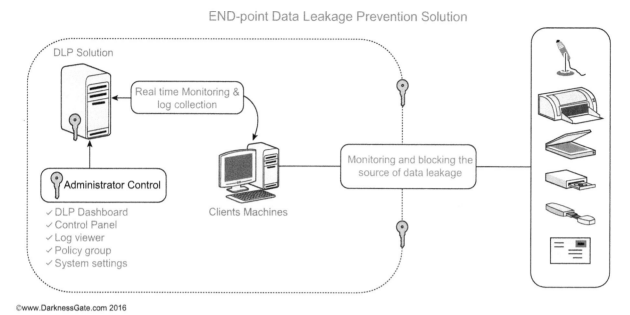

©www.DarknessGate.com 2016

FIGURE 8.1   Endpoint DLP solution.

traditional HTTP data. A traditional firewall allows this traffic because it considers it HTTP web traffic; however, in an NGFW device, it will have the ability to investigate this traffic and block it if it is not allowed to pass by the NGFW preset policy.

Data Leakage Prevention

This solution helps companies identify confidential data and investigate document metadata in transit to make sure that no confidential information hidden in this area is leaving the company network. Modern data leakage prevention (DLP) software also offers application monitoring, email monitoring, malware protection, and user access control.

There are three main DLP solutions:

- **Network-based DLP solution**: This protects data in transit layer. DLP network solution is installed on network edges to monitor travelled data to and from a company network. Its monitoring activity includes email traffic, IM chat, SSL traffic, and more. These solutions should first be configured according to a predefined information disclosure policy to differentiate confidential data from ordinary data.
- **Storage-based DLP solution**: This monitors data at rest status. It works by checking how data is stored on storage servers and whether it adheres to the company's secure storage policy. It sends a warning to the administrator when a policy violation occurs.
- **Endpoint DLP solution**: This monitors individual user devices like laptops, desktops, and tablets for actions that may lead to data leakage such as copying files to

USB or CD/DVD media, printing confidential data on paper, attaching files to emails, or uploading files to social media websites, ftp sites, cloud storage, and so on. Endpoint DLP solutions can also be configured to block illegal user actions actively and warn the administrator immediately after each policy violation (see Fig. 8.1).

The future will bring more intelligent devices that are more content conscious and have the ability to classify their own data automatically. Such tools will effectively fight against data hiding techniques and will have the ability to perform fast scanning of all incoming and ongoing traffic to prevent unauthorized disclosure of data by creating and enforcing disclosure policies set by companies.

STREAMING PROTOCOLS

As streaming media increased after the wide spread of the Internet, many streaming protocols have been mainly developed to simplify the transfer of multimedia content to end user. The word streaming itself means in the domain of computer science, the ability to send and receive media data (usually audio and video) and start processing this data by the end user before the download completes. Video clips on YouTube are a clear example.

Real-time transport protocol (RTP) is one of these streaming protocols, which has been around a long time (its first draft was launched at 1996). RTP is a network protocol for delivering audio and video over IP networks. RTP is used extensively in communication and entertainment systems that involve streaming media, such as telephony, video teleconference applications, television services, and web-based push-to-talk features [10]. There is a tool (that only supports Linux OS) that can be used to exploit RTP protocol to conceal data, called *SteganRTP–RTP Covert Channel*. It works by establishing a full-duplex steganographic data transfer protocol utilizing RTP packet payloads as the cover medium. The tool provides interactive chat, file transfer, and remote shell access; you can download it from https://sourceforge.net/projects/steganrtp.

Modern streaming protocols are continually developed to stay in line with future computing and networking development. *BitTorrent Live Streaming* is a new protocol mainly developed by *Bram Cohen* (*BitTorrent* inventor) that allows the public to send a video stream to millions of people without having to invest in expensive bandwidth [11]. To date, little information is available about this protocol; however, such protocols are expected to grow, opening possibilities for more places to conceal data in transit.

HTML5 supports embedding audio/video contents in its source page. Although HTML5 works on the application layer and has nothing to do with the rest of OSI model layers, its native support for JavaScript and DOM to control multimedia content embedded on HTML pages can be exploited to conceal secret data.

WIRELESS NETWORKS AND FUTURE NETWORKING PROTOCOLS

According to a Cisco report titled, "Global Mobile Data Traffic Forecast Update, 2015–2020" [12], the following forecasts are estimated for mobile data traffic:

- Global mobile data traffic will increase nearly eightfold between 2015 and 2020.
- Mobile network connection speeds will increase more than threefold by 2020. The average mobile network connection speed (2.0 Mbps in 2015) will reach nearly 6.5 Mbps by 2020. By 2017, the average mobile network connection speed will surpass 2.0 Mbps.
- The average smartphone will generate 4.4 GB of traffic per month by 2020.
- By 2020, 66% of all global mobile devices could potentially be capable of connecting to an IPv6 mobile network.

We can confidently conclude that the future will show mobile devices connecting to Internet through high-speed wireless connection at least for the next phase to come, which we already witnessing now. Most traffic generated will be real-time video and multimedia files requiring increased bandwidth and fast connection. This tremendous traffic can be exploited to deliver secret messages with limited possibility of being discovered.

As new generations of mobile telecommunication networks are developed (4G and 5G), we can expect to witness a huge increase in Internet connection speed. This speed is crucial to allow development of more secure steganographic algorithms. As increasing steganographic algorithm efficiency will require more bandwidth and high-speed connection to transmit its data and stego keys, which is expected to be longer than the currently used to increase its security. Future steganographic algorithms will be more efficient and secure, which will require more computation power. Future computing devices, including smartphones, will have more CPU to process such algorithms.

Modern telecommunication mobile networks, especially the coming fifth generation, which is expected to become available to end users by 2020, will introduce advanced security standards in addition to its high speed data rates (10 MB per second).

As more content will be delivered wirelessly in the future like video streaming, concealing data in wireless protocols will become an ideal solution especially with the huge amount of transferred data in the air. Network monitoring devices like NGFW and IDS should be configured properly to scan wireless traffic to mitigate this risk.

In this book we did not discuss data concealment in network protocols; however, it is worth noting that different methods already exist to conceal data in TCP/IP packet headers. *Craig H. Rowland* has created a program called *covert_tcp*, which happens to be a simple utility written for use on Linux systems only and has only been tried on Linux running version 2.0 kernels. *Covert_tcp* is a proof-of-concept application that uses raw sockets to construct forged packets and encapsulate data from filenames given on the command line. You can read the full paper describing how to cover data in TCP/IP along with *covert_tcp* program source code at http://firstmonday.org/ojs/index.php/fm/article/view/528/449.

Another modern technique to conceal data in TCP/IP protocol suites is through time-based covert channels. A specialized program developed for this issue is called *Time-shifter*. This program allows you to transmit and receive data by modifying the time intervals between packets. You can check the program source code at https://www.anfractuosity.com/projects/timeshifter.

Based on *covert_tcp* and *Timeshifter* programs, we can exploit different networking protocols for covert communication as many future protocols that are designed to work in the Transport layer still build based on TCP/IP protocol suite structure. This allows optional fields to exist in its data packets (eg, utilizing free/unused or not strictly standard defined fields) and that can be exploited to conceal secret data. Stream control transmission protocol is an example of a future protocol expected to offer networking services similar to transmission control protocol (TCP) and user datagram protocol (UDP).

TABLE 8.1 Currently Available Mobile Steganography Tools

Program Name	Operating System	License	Location
StegDroid	Android	Free	https://github.com/fredley/StegDroid
Hide It In	Apple	Free	https://itunes.apple.com/en/app/hide-it-in/id401162613?mt=8
Secret Tidings	Android and Windows phone	Free	https://www.microsoft.com/en-us/store/apps/secret-tidings/9wzdncrdcb84
Steganography+	Windows phone	Free	https://www.microsoft.com/en-us/store/apps/steganography/9wzdncrfjtbj
My Secret	Android	Free	https://play.google.com/store/apps/details?id=ro.tipspedia.mysecret&hl=en

DATA HIDING IN MOBILE DEVICES

Nowadays, most people, especially computer geeks, use social networking services and check their emails using smartphone devices. The dominant two mobile OSs in markets today are Apple™ and Android™. There are many tools developed to conceal data in smartphones using some of the steganographic methods already mentioned in this book. To name a few, Table 8.1 lists available tools for data hiding in mobile phones.

You do not need to have a specialized application to conceal data in smartphones. You can conceal data on your Windows® PC and then shift the stego object to your mobile phone for delivery when needed. Despite the fact that this approach will require the use of two devices, it will effectively hide your tracks on your mobile device if it were subject to criminal investigation.

Currently, more than 50% of Internet users use smartphones in daily communication and Internet browsing. Future smartphones will have even more processing power and increased memory than what is available now. This will enable them to use more efficient steganographic algorithms with better embedding techniques.

ANONYMOUS NETWORKS

In the future we can expect to see more anonymous networks that allow Internet users to conceal their online identity similar to TOR. Apparently many secret documents revealed by NSA's previous employee *Edward Snowden*, were mass surveillance programs, not imaginary programs. Different governments are heavily involved in such programs and have already invested billions of dollars for this task. Giant companies are also interested in knowing user behavior and habits in order to bury them with targeted advertisements. Anonymity online is becoming a need for any Internet user caring about his/her privacy.

At the time of writing this book, TOR privacy network was dominating the Internet as the most used anonymous network currently available; however, serious attempts have undergone to deanonymize TOR hidden services. At 2014 Russia's interior ministry offered up to 3.9 m rubles ($110,000) for a technological solution that would allow police officers to identify Internet surfers who are using the TOR anonymizer network [13]. Both NSA and UK government intelligence services try to crack TOR according to top secret documents released by *Edward Snowden* [14]. This clearly shows that TOR is a big target for top secret services worldwide and this may lead to weaken or even revealing its anonymity services one way or another in the future.

New research is ongoing to create more secure anonymizing networks. Here is a list of main anonymizing projects currently under development:

HORNET: According to its creators, "HORNET is a system that enables high-speed end-to-end anonymous channels by leveraging next generation network architectures. HORNET is designed as a low-latency onion routing system that operates at the network layer thus enabling a wide range of applications. This system uses only symmetric cryptography for data forwarding yet requires no per-flow state on intermediate nodes. This design enables HORNET nodes to process anonymous traffic at over 93 GB/s. HORNET can also scale as required. Adding minimal processing overhead per additional anonymous channel." The official paper of this project is available at http://arxiv.org/abs/1507.05724v1.

Vuvuzela: A new scalable messaging system that offers strong privacy guarantees, hiding both message data and metadata. Vuvuzela is secure against adversaries that observe and tamper with all network traffic, and that control all nodes except for one server. Vuvuzela's key insight is to minimize the number of variables observable by an attacker, and to use differential privacy techniques to add noise to all observable variables in a way that provably hides information about which users are communicating. Check complete system descriptions published by its developers in this paper: https://davidlazar.org/papers/vuvuzela.pdf. The project website is at https://github.com/davidlazar/vuvuzela.

SUMMARY

During this book, we've discussed how to use steganographic techniques to conceal private data; however, bear in mind that these same techniques can be exploited as a part of a malicious attack. Trojan, Botnets, keylogger, Spyware, Rootkits, Bootkits, and viruses can all use steganographic techniques (some can encrypt themselves to avoid antivirus detection) to conceal their existence before launching an attack.

The science of digital steganography is expected to draw more attention in the future. Its use can benefit wide arrays of user segments. Nearly all people who use computers, tablets, and smartphones need to use at least one hiding technique in order to protect their private data. Encryption as a form of data obscuration continues to take the lead in the press today. Nevertheless, the art of hiding data without encryption will have the major focus in the future, as more bills are issued in many countries against allowing people to have full disk encryption on their personal IT devices. These people leave steganography as the last hope for people trying to protect their privacy without breaking the law.

REFERENCES

[1] California Legislative Information, AB-1681 Smartphones [Online]. Available from: https://leginfo.legislature.ca.gov/faces/billTextClient.xhtml?bill_id=201520160AB1681 (accessed 26.03.16).

[2] National Science Foundation, The Future of Encryption [Online]. Available from: https://nsf.gov/discoveries/disc_summ.jsp?cntn_id=136673&org=NSF (accessed 26.03.16).

[3] Threat Post, Honey Encryption Tricks Hackers with Decryption Deception [Online]. Available from: https://threatpost.com/honey-encryption-tricks-hackers-with-decryption-deception/103950/ (accessed 26.03.16).

[4] Wikipedia, Honey Encryption [Online]. Available from: https://en.wikipedia.org/wiki/Honey_Encryption (accessed 26.03.16).

[5] Stanford University, Functional Encryption: Definitions and Challenges [Online]. Available from: https://crypto.stanford.edu/~dabo/pubs/abstracts/functional.html (accessed 26.03.16).

[6] ZDNet, Forrester: Public Cloud Market Will Reach $191B by 2020 [Online]. Available from: http://www.zdnet.com/article/forrester-public-cloud-market-will-reach-191b-by-2020/ (accessed 26.03.16).

[7] BBC, Apple Stores iCloud Data with Google [Online]. Available from: http://www.bbc.com/news/technology-35837692 (accessed 26.03.16).

[8] IT Brief, EMC: World's Data Doubling Every Two Years [Online]. Available from: http://itbrief.co.nz/story/emc-worlds-data-doubling-every-two-years (accessed 26.03.16).

[9] The FBI, Economic Espionage [Online]. Available from: https://www.fbi.gov/about-us/investigate/counterintelligence/economic-espionage (accessed 26.03.16).

[10] Wikipedia, Real-time Transport Protocol [Online]. Available from: https://en.wikipedia.org/wiki/Real-time_Transport_Protocol (accessed 26.03.16).

[11] TorrentFreak, BitTorrent's Bram Cohen Patents Revolutionary Live Streaming Protocol [Online]. Available from: https://torrentfreak.com/bittorrent-s-bram-cohen-patents-revolutionary-live-streaming-protocol-130326 (accessed 26.03.16).

[12] Cisco, Visual Networking Index: Global Mobile Data Traffic Forecast Update, 2015–2020 White Paper [Online]. Available from: https://www.cisco.com/c/en/us/solutions/collateral/service-provider/visual-networking-index-vni/mobile-white-paper-c11-520862.html (accessed 26.03.16).

[13] RT, Russian Interior Ministry offers $111k to crack TOR network [Online]. Available from: https://www.rt.com/news/175408-russia-internet-tor-service (accessed 26.03.16).

[14] Dailydot, NSA Attempted to De-anonymize Tor, with Little Success [Online]. Available from: http://www.dailydot.com/news/nsa-tor-crack-anonymize-snowden-slides (accessed 26.03.16).

BIBLIOGRAPHY

[1] Wired, The Future of Security: Zeroing In On Un-Hackable Data With Quantum Key Distribution [Online]. Available from: http://www.wired.com/insights/2014/09/quantum-key-distribution (accessed 22.03.16).

[2] Introduction to Quantum Cryptography and Secret-Key Distillation [Online]. Available from: http://gva.noekeon.org/QCandSKD/QCandSKD-introduction.html (accessed 22.03.16).

[3] The Chromium Projects, SPDY: An Experimental Protocol for a Faster Web [Online]. Available from: https://www.chromium.org/spdy/spdy-whitepaper (accessed 25.03.16).

[4] The Protocol Engineering Laboratory (PEL)- University of Delaware – Comparison of HTTP over TCP and SCTP in High Delay Networks [Online]. Available from: https://www.eecis.udel.edu/~leighton/firefox.html (accessed 17.04.16).

Index

'*Note*: Page numbers followed by "f" indicate figures, "t" indicate tables and "b" indicate boxes.'

A

ADS. *See* Alternate data stream (ADS)
AES crypt, 159
AIFF format, 83
ALAC. *See* Apple lossless audio codec (ALAC)
Alternate data stream (ADS), 98, 214. *See also* Stealth ADS
  data hiding using
    calc.exe process, 102f
    creating hidden ADS file, 99f
    default unnamed stream, 99f
    deleting files, 104
    detecting files, 104
    hiding data, 101f
    hiding executable code, 100–102
    to hiding files, 98–99
    hiding *mspass.exe*, 103f
    NTFS, 98
    opening hidden alternate data stream file, 100f
    TXT file, 99f
  detection, 255
  notes about, 102–104
Amazon™ Web Services and Google™ Computer Engine, 293
"Amnesic" tails, 136
Analog signal, 82
Anonymity, 21
Anonymity online. *See also* Email communications encryption
  anonymous search engine, 180–181
  data encryption and data hiding techniques, 169
  using proxy server, 179–180
  secure anonymous file sharing, 183
    OnionShare, 184–185, 185f
  SSH tunneling, 179
  using TOR Browser, 169–170
    Access Grams search engine, 172f
    dark web, 170–171
    error message, 176f
    launching, 171f
    TOR bridges, 172f
    traffic through, 169f
    update privacy and security level in, 175f
    warnings, 171–176
  VPN, 176–179
  web browser privacy add-ons, 180–181
Anonymous calling service using *GHOST CALL*, 199
Anonymous networks, 297–298. *See also* Wireless networks
Anonymous operating system (Anonymous OS), 135, 287
  advice, 138–140
  Linux, 135
  other security distributions, 138
  portable stick computer, 140
  tails, 135–137
  UPR, 137–138
Antiforensic techniques, 267
  clearing digital footprints, 287–289
  data destruction, 268
    hard disk wiping, 269–272
    manipulating digital file metadata, 272–275
  data hiding general advice, 268
  direct attack against forensic software, 289
  goals, 268
  Windows antiforensics techniques, 275–287
Antiforensics, 264
  science, 267
Antipiracy techniques, 19
Antivirus software, 294
APE. *See* Monkeys audio (APE)
Apple lossless audio codec (ALAC), 83
Application events, 285
Aspect ratio, 89
Association of Chief Police Officers, 208
aswMBR Rootkit scanner, 164
Asymmetric cryptography, 13f
Asymmetrical encryption. *See* Public key cryptography
Atbash cipher, 2
  ciphertext alphabet for, 3t
Audio files, 82–84
  data hiding, 81–90
    analog signal, 82
    common audio file types, 83–84
    digital signal, 82–83
    format types, 83
    steganography types, 84–90
Audio forensics, 219
Audio sample rate, 89
Audio steganography, 84
  data hiding inside video files, 89–90
  echo hiding, 89
  LSB encoding encoding, 84–85
  parity coding, 85–88
  phase coding, 88
  spread spectrum, 89
Audio/video metadata, 223–226, 225f–226f

Audio/video steganography, 19
AutoKey cipher, 5
Automated tools, 285
Autoruns, 239

B

Backbone security, 216
Belkasoft, 230–231, 230f
BIOS software, 138–139
BishopFox, 289
Bit depth, 70, 70t
Bit order, 23
Bit-shifting data hiding, 23–26
  accepting default settings and shift bits, 25f
  activating bit-shifting toolbar in Hex Workshop, 24f
  generating checksum for opened files, 26f
  MD5 hash using Hex Workshop, 26f
  open text file using Hex Workshop, 24f
  shift Left button to shift data, 25f
  text scrambled after bit shifting, 25f
Bit-to-bit image, 208–209
BitLocker, 140–141
  encrypting partitions using, 141
    changing BitLocker settings, 144f
    on data disk drive, 142f
    data drive disk encryption, 142–143
    error message, 144f
    types, 142
    windows partition encryption, 143–145
    Windows® versions, 141
    wizard before BitLocker
    processing system disk encryption, 146f
  removing protection, 146f
Bitmap graphics, 71
Bitmap images (BMP), 72–73, 73f, 76f
  hidden data could be embedded, 74t
  LSB substitution using, 74–76
Bitrate, 89
BitTorrent Live Streaming, 296
BleachBit, 275–276, 276f
BlueScreenView files, 250
BMP. *See* Bitmap images (BMP)
Book cipher, 10
Boot attack, 140
Bootable USB tokens, 287
Bootdisk/CD, 262
Bootkit attacks, 164
Browser fingerprint checking, 181–182
BrowserLeaks. com, 181
Brute-force sign-in attacks, 164

C

"-C" command, 66, 77
CA. *See* Certificate authority (CA)
Caesar shift, 2
  ciphertext alphabet for, 3t
calc.exe process, 102f
Capture disk drive, 231
  FTK® imager to acquire disk drive, 1 using, 232–233, 232f–233f
Capture volatile memory, 228
  Belkasoft, 230–231, 230f
  DumpIt tool, 228–230, 230f
  FTK® Imager, 231, 231f
CDR. *See* CorelDraw® (CDR)
Certificate authority (CA), 187
Check disk (CHKDSK), 127
Chi-square attack. *See* Specific statistical analysis
CHKDSK. *See* Check disk (CHKDSK)
Chosen message attack, 210
Chosen stego attack, 210
Chromebit, 140
Chrominance, 78
Cipher, 2
  command, 271
CipherShed, 147
Classical ciphers, 2
  Book cipher, 10
  English language
    distribution of letters in, 11f
    frequency of letter combinations, 11t
  Morse code, 9–10
  one-time pad, 9
  practicing old ciphers using modern computing, 12
  substitution cipher, 2–8
  substitution *vs.* transposition cipher, 10–12
  transposition cipher, 8–9
CleanAfterMe tool, 285
Clearing digital footprints, 287
  live CDs and bootable USB tokens, 287
  portable applications, 289
  VM, 288
Cloud computing, data in, 293
Cloud storage, 293
Cloud storage encryption, 161–162. *See also* Single file encryption
Cluster size, 114
Codec, 89
Cold Boot attack, 164
Columnar transposition, 8–9, 9t, 12
COM Structured Storage, 35–37
Compressed file, 28
  accessing Windows® built-in utility for file compression, 28f
  combine zip folder inside image, 30f
  create new RTF document, 29f
  hiding data in, 28–29
  secret file inside *SecretFolder*, 29f
Compressed objects, 274
Computer antiforensics, 267
Computer forensics, 208. *See also* Windows forensics
  differences between computer forensics and computing domains, 209

  need for digital evidence, 209–210
  process, 208, 208f
    acquisition, 208–209
    analysis, 209
    reporting, 209
    seizure, 208
Computer hardware level, data hiding under, 128
  in DCO, 130–131
  inside HPA, 129–130
Computer security, 209
CorelDraw® (CDR), 71
Corporate surveillance, 134
Covered cipher, 17–18
covert_tcp and Timeshifter programs, 296
covert_tcp program, 296
CPU-Z tool, 168
Cryptanalysis, 210
Cryptography, 1, 12
  cryptographic hash function, 14
  digital signature, 14, 14f
  public key cryptography, 13–14
  secret key cryptography, 13, 13f
  steganography *vs.*, 15, 16t
Cryptomator, 162
CrypTool, 12, 12f
  CT1, 12
  CT2, 12
CryptSync
  automatically encryption, 163f
  for cloud storage encryption, 161–162
  to synchronizing MyFiles folder, 163f
Crypture steganography tool, 75
Crypture tool, 74, 75f
Cyber law jurisdiction, 293

D

Dark web, 170–171. *See also* TOR Browser
Data concealment techniques, 294–295
Data destruction, 268
  hard disk wiping, 269–272
  manipulating digital file metadata, 272–275
  warning when using, 271–272
Data drive disk encryption, 142–143
Data hiding, 23
  audio files, 81–90
    analog signal, 82
    common audio file types, 83–84
    digital signal, 82–83
    format types, 83
  bit-shifting data hiding, 23–26
  in compressed files, 28–29
  using digital media types, 90–94
    PDF documents, 91–94
    program binaries, 94
  in enterprise networks, 294
    data concealment techniques, 294–295
    DLP, 295
  through file splitting, 31–33
  general advice, 268
  in HTML
    by exploiting whitespaces using snow program, 66–67

  files by modifying attribute, 65, 65f
  in HTML/XML files using tag attributes, 65, 65f
  using HTML5 tags, 64–65
  in image attributes, 40–42
  in Microsoft® office documents, 33–39
    hidden data within document attributes, 34–35
    hidden text, 34
    hiding data by exploiting OLE structured storage, 35–37
    hiding inside MS Excel® spreadsheet, 38–39
    self-encrypt MS Office® document, 37–38
    White font, 35
  in mobile devices, 297
    mobile steganography tools, 297t
  MS office® documents on OOXML file format, 49–50, 50t, 51f–52f
    through image cropping, 57–58, 57f–58f
    OOXML document structure, 52–54
    using OOXML markup compatibility and extensibility, 59–63
    OOXML replacement images, 58
    reducing image and chart dimensions, 1 by, 57, 55–57, 56f–57f
    understanding package relationships, 51, 52f
    xml comments, 58–59
    zipped container comments field, 54–55, 55f
  renaming files, 27–28
  RTF documents, 26
  secret messages inside twitter updates, 67–68, 68f
  inside spam messages, 48
  steganography types, 84–90
  techniques, 267, 292
  using text acronyms, 49t
Data hiding forensics
  computer forensics
    differences between computer forensics and computing domains, 209
    need for digital evidence, 209–210
    process, 208–209, 208f
  steganalysis, 210–211
    digital media files, 211–227
  windows forensics, 227
    capture disk drive, 231–233
    capture volatile memory, 228–231
    deleted files recovery, 233
    windows registry analysis, 239–249
Data leakage prevention (DLP), 295
  endpoint DLP solution, 295f
Data recovery, 209
DCO. *See* Device configuration overlay (DCO)
DCT. *See* Discrete cosine transform (DCT)
Decompression bomb. *See* ZIP bomb
Decryption, 5
Deep packet inspection technique (DPI technique), 173–174
Default stream, 98

Degausser, 269
DES key, 66
Device configuration overlay (DCO), 130, 131f, 232
Device security, 134
Dictionary attacks, 164
Digital audio files, 82
Digital evidence, 209–210
Digital files, 46, 68, 91
  metadata forensic, 222
    audio/video metadata, 223–226, 225f–226f
    digital images metadata, 223
    document metadata, 226–227, 227f–228f
    file system metadata, 222–223, 222f–224f
  metadata manipulation, 272
    changing file timestamps, 272–273
    erasing document metadata, 273–275
    MS Office sanitization, 275
    PDF sanitization, 274
Digital forensics, 207
Digital images, 69–73, 214
  bit depth, 70
  graphic file
    format, 72–73, 73t
    types, 71
  image compression types, 71–72, 73t
  metadata, 223
  monitor resolution, 70
  pixel, 69–70
Digital media
  data hiding using, 90–91
    PDF documents, 91–94
    program binaries, 94
  steganalysis of digital media files, 211–227
  steganography tools, 81
    free image steganography tools, 82t
Digital signal, 82–83, 83f
  digital sampling works, 83
Digital signature, 14, 14f, 186–187
Digital steganography, 18–20. *See also* Linguistic steganography; Technical steganography
Digital text files, 46
Digital watermark, 20
Direct attack against forensic software, 289
Direct memory access (DMA), 164–165
Disconnect search, 181–182
Discrete cosine transformation (DCT), 72, 78, 216
Disk acquisition, 232
Disk bad blocks, data hiding in, 127–128
Disk encryption, 140. *See also* Email communications encryption
  cloud storage encryption, 161–162
  encrypted vaults creation, 145–159
  encrypting partitions using BitLocker, 141
    changing BitLocker settings, 144f
    on data disk drive, 142f
    data drive disk encryption, 142–143
    error message, 144f
    types, 142
    windows partition encryption, 143–145
    Windows® versions, 141

security level in, 162–163
  countermeasures, 165–169
  full disk encryption attack, 163–165
  Windows 8.1 startup process, 166f
  single file encryption, 159–161
Disk platter, 114
DiskPart tool, 122
DLP. *See* Data leakage prevention (DLP)
DMA. *See* Direct memory access (DMA)
docProps, 51
Document metadata, 226–227, 227f–228f
  erasing, 273–275
document.xml, 51
Double transposition, 9
Down-bit ordering, 23
DPA. *See* Swiss Federal Data Protection Act (DPA)
DPI technique. *See* Deep packet inspection technique (DPI technique)
DPO. *See* Swiss Federal Data Protection Ordinance (DPO)
DUCKDUCKGO search engine, 181
Dumpchk.exe, 250
Dumping, 228
DumpIt tool, 228–230, 230f

E

EaseUS Partition Master Free tool, 118
Echo hiding, 89
Electronic documents, 46
Email communications encryption, 185. *See also* Disk encryption
  using *Gpg4Win*, 186
    decrypting encrypted message, 190
    digital signature, 186–187
    encrypting emails in MS Outlook®, 189–190
    PGP keypair certificate creation, 187–188
    prerequisites to sending and receiving encrypted emails, 188–189
    public and private key concept in encryption, 186
    talking with correct person, 190
  using *OpenPGP*, 190–192
  secure web mail providers, 192–195
Encapsulated PostScript (EPS), 71
Encoding, 46
Encrypted vaults creation
  encrypted volume creation using VeraCrypt, 147–150
  formatting drive, 151f
  hidden volume
    creation, 153–155
    practical notes, 158–159
  installing *tails* inside hidden VeraCrypt volume, 156–158
  installing virtual machine OS, 150–159
  Portable-VirtualBox tool, 155–156, 155f
  tools from TrueCrypt, 147
  TrueCrypt, 145–147
  VeraCrypt volume, 150
    direct mode selection, 153f
    mounting, 152f

Encryption
  algorithm, 66
  future, 292–293
Encryption techniques, data hiding using, 134
  anonymity online, 169–185
  anonymous operating system, 135–140
  creating and maintaining secure passwords, 201
    password best practice, 201–202
    password generation tools, 202
    password manager tools, 202
    password-saving techniques, 202
  disk encryption, 140–169
  Email communications encryption, 185–195
  encrypting instant messaging, video calls, and VOIP sessions, 195
    anonymous calling service using *GHOST CALL*, 199
    off-the-record-messaging and Pidgin, 195–198
    Pidgin IM program, 196f
    Retroshare secure social platform, 199
    Ricochet, 201
    risks, 195
    TOR messenger, 199–200
    video calling service using *Gruveo*, 198–199
  security awareness corners, 134–135
  security hints and best practices, 203–204
Encryptr, 203
End-of-file marker (EOF marker), 18
Endpoint DLP solution, 295
English language
  distribution of letters in, 11f
  frequency of letter combinations, 11t
Enigma machine, 7–8
EOF marker. *See* End-of-file marker (EOF marker)
EPS. *See* Encapsulated PostScript (EPS)
Eraser, 270
Event logs, 285
Evil Maid attacks, 163–164
Exchangeable Image File Format data (EXIF data), 40
Exif Pilot, 40, 223
Exit relay, 169–170
Extended partition, 114
Extensible Markup Language (XML), 50
  data hiding using, 58–59
Extensible Metadata Platform (XMP), 40

F

FAT. *See* File allocation table (FAT)
FDE. *See* Full disk encryption (FDE)
File
  archive encryption, 160–161
  attributes analysis, 252
  extensions, 27–28
  Metadata, 222
  signatures, 27–28
    analysis, 252
  slack space, 117
  system metadata, 222–223, 222f–224f

File allocation table (FAT), 98, 114–115. *See also* Master file table ($MFT)
  changing working directory, 115f
  file slack space, 117
  restoring hidden file, 115–117
File splitting, hiding data through, 31–33
  launching GSplit portable edition, 31f
  selecting file to split, 32f
  set size of each piece, 32f
  splitting selected file, 33f
  viewing file parts after splitting, 33f
  viewing splitting log, 33f
File timestamps, changing, 272–273
  timestomp to change time stamp, 273f
File's slack space, hiding in, 112
  FAT, 114–117
  understanding hard disk drives, 112–114, 114t
FileStat.exe, 252
FLAC. *See* Free lossless audio codec (FLAC)
Forensic Toolkit® (FTK®), 209
  Imager, 231–232, 231f
Format-based steganography, 46–47
  character coding, 46, 46f
  hiding text within text, 47, 48f
  line-shift coding, 46
  white space manipulation, 46–47
  word-shift coding, 46
42.zip compression bomb, 289
Forwarded events, 285
Frame rate, 89
Frame size, 89
Free lossless audio codec (FLAC), 83
Frequency analysis technique, 11
FTK®. *See* Forensic Toolkit® (FTK®)
Full disk encryption (FDE), 140
  attack, 163–165
    countermeasures against, 165–169
Fully homomorphic encryption, 292
Functional encryption, 292

G

General public license (GPL), 84–85
Generation method, 20
GHOST CALL, anonymous calling service using, 199
GhostMail, 195
GIF. *See* Graphics Interchange Format (GIF)
GIFSHUF, 77
Gifshuffle, 77, 77f
Global mobile data traffic, 296
Glow text effects, 60, 60f
GNU Privacy Guard (GnuPG), 186
Google Talk, 200
Google™, 180
Apps for Education and Microsoft Office 365, 293
Gpg4Win, 185–186
  email encryption using, 186
    decrypting encrypted message, 190
    digital signature, 186–187
    encrypting emails in MS Outlook®, 189–190
    PGP keypair certificate creation, 187–188
    prerequisites to sending and receiving encrypted emails, 188–189

    public and private key concept in encryption, 186
    talking with correct person, 190
GPL. *See* General public license (GPL)
Graphic file
  format, 72
    BMP, 72–73
    GIF, 72
    JPEG, 72
    PNG, 72
    RIF, 72
    TIFF, 72
    types, 71, 71t
      bitmap graphics, 71
      metafile graphics, 71
      raster graphics, 71
      vector graphics, 71
Graphics Interchange Format (GIF), 72
Grayscale images, 77
Grille cipher, 18
Gruveo, video calling service using, 198–199
GSplit, 31
Guest OS, 288
GUI tool, 51, 78

H

Hard disk, 112
  cluster size determination, 117b
  drive, 112–114, 113f, 114t
Hard disk wiping, 269
  cipher command, 271
  data destruction techniques, 269t
  degausser, 269
  eraser, 270
  logical destruction of data, 269
  Moo0 anti-recovery, 270
  physical destruction, 269
  RAID technology, 269
  SRM, 271
  tools, 269
  warning when using data destruction tools, 271–272
Hardware bad sector, 127
Hash function, 14, 289
Hashing, 14, 289
  Hash/CRC tool, 15f
Hex editor (HxD), 220
Hex Workshop®, 24
HexBrowser tool, 28, 252
Hibernate file, 278
Hibernation mode, 259
Hidden attribute, 64
Hidden data, destroying, 211
Hidden file, restoring, 115–117
Hidden Message box, 68
Hidden partitions, 117–118, 119f
  creating within USB zip drive, 118–119
    access USB zip drive properties, 119f
    install USB drive software, 121f
    uncovering hidden partitions, 122, 123f
    update USB zip drive driver software, 121f
  discovery, 252–255
  under Windows® OS, 118

Hidden text, 34
  activating show hidden text, 34f
Hidden volume
  creation, 153–155
  installing *tails* inside hidden VeraCrypt volume, 156–158
  practical notes, 158–159
Hiding data. *See* Data hiding
Hiding information, 84
High level programming language, 24
Homomorphic encryption, 292
Honey encryption, 292
HORNET system, 297
Host protected area (HPA), 129–130, 129t, 130f, 232
  data hiding
    IDE controller, 129
    operating systems, 129
    partition on disk drive, 129f
HTML, 50, 64t
  HTML attribute written state, forensics of data hidden by modifying, 214
  HTML5 tags, 296
    data hiding using, 64–65, 65f
    forensics of data hidden using, 213–214
HTTP proxies, 180
HTTPS Everywhere, 182
Huffman encoding stage, 78
Human security, 134
Human-authored video metadata, 225
HxD. *See* Hex editor (HxD)
Hybrid brute-force attacks, 164

I

IaaS. *See* Infrastructure as a service (IaaS)
ICE. *See* Information concealment engine (ICE)
IDE controller, 129
IDENTIFY_DEVICE, 129
Ignorable attributes, 61, 62f
Image compression types, 71
  lossless, 72
  lossy, 71
Image cropping
  data hiding through, 55–57, 56f
  forensics of data hidden through, 213
Image domain, 74
  LSB substitution using bitmap image, 74–76
  LSB using palette-based images, 76–78
Image file types, 73, 73t, 81t
Image forensics, 214. *See also* Video forensics
  comparing files, 216f
  comparing images, 216f
  modifications to HTML file, 215f
  signature analysis, 216
    StegSpy, 216–217
  statistical analysis, 217
    Stegdetect tool, 217–219
    StegExpose tool, 217
  visual detection, 216
Image metadata, 40–42, 81
  adding new EXIF tag to picture, 42f
  editing picture metadata, 42f
  EXIF metadata to picture, 41f
  selecting image EXIF metadata, 41f

Image steganography, 19, 68–69. *See also* Text
      steganography
   digital image, 69–73
   digital media steganography tools, 81
   techniques, 73–81
      image domain, 74–78
      transform domain, 78–79
Imperial period, 1
In-band registration, 200
index.dat, 246
Information concealment engine (ICE), 66
Infrastructure as a service (IaaS), 293–294
Injection technique, 73
Injunction, 20
Inspect Document feature, 275
International Organization for Standardization
      (ISO), 147
International Press Telecommunications
      Council (IPTC), 40
Internet Explorer, 245–246
   URLs entering, 247f
Internet programs investigation, 245
   Internet applications, 248–249
   Internet Explorer, 245–246
   Mozilla Firefox and other browsers, 246–248
   uTorrent, 249
Internet Service Provider (ISP), 174
Intrusion detection systems, 294
Invisible ink, 16–17
Invisible watermark, 21
IPTC. *See* International Press Telecommunica-
      tions Council (IPTC)
ISO. *See* International Organization for
      Standardization (ISO)
ISP. *See* Internet Service Provider (ISP)
IT devices, 291

J

Jargon code, 17
Jargon code hiding technique, 211–212
Java–jar, 217
Joint Photographic Experts Group (JPEG), 72,
      79f–80f
   compression, 78
   JPHS, 80f
   steganography, 78–79
   stego image, 80f
JPEG. *See* Joint Photographic Experts Group
      (JPEG)
JPHIDE programs, 78
JPSEEK programs, 78

K

Kaspersky TDSSKiller tool, 164
KeePass, 202–203
KeePassX, 136
Key, 239
Keyword cipher, 2
   ciphertext alphabet for, 3t
Kleopatra program, 187–188, 190
   export private key from, 191f
   import certificates, 189f
Known cover attacks, 210
Known message attack, 210
Known stego attack, 210

L

LADS program, 104
Law enforcement agencies, 293
Least significant bit (LSB), 18, 74, 216
   using bitmap image, 74–76
   encoding encoding, 84–85, 84t
   using palette-based images, 76–78
Line-shift coding, 46
Linguistic data hiding techniques, 211
Linguistic method forensics, 211–212
   change word misspellings, 212f
Linguistic steganography, 17. *See also*
      Technical steganography
   open codes steganography, 17–18
   semagrams, 17
Linguistic-based methods, 48–49
   acronym, 49
   change of spelling, 49, 49t
   synonyms, 48–49
Linux, 135
Live acquisition, 208
Live CD, 287
Logical destruction of data, 269
Lossless compressed format, 83
Lossless compression algorithm
      (LZW), 72
Lossy compressed format, 83
Lossy compression algorithms, 78
LSB. *See* Least significant bit (LSB)
LZW. *See* Lossless compression algorithm
      (LZW)

M

Mailvelope extension
   import keypair into, 191f
   OpenPGP encryption for webmail,
      190–192
Man-in-the-middle attack, 174–175, 176f
Markup Compatibility and Extensibility
      mechanisms (MCE), 60
Master boot record (MBR), 164
Master file table ($MFT), 98
Master file table, 123f. *See also* File allocation
      table (FAT)
   data hiding within, 123–127
      destroy hidden message, 128f
      extract secret message, 128f
      metadata files, 125t
      zone, 126f
Master Password, 203
MBR. *See* Master boot record (MBR)
McAfee *Stinger*, 164
McAfee™, 252
MCE. *See* Markup Compatibility and Extensi-
      bility mechanisms (MCE)
Mechanical substitution ciphers, 7–8
Media transfer protocol (MTP), 243
MediaInfo tool, 225–226
Message security, 135
MessnPass tool, 102
Meta-Clean tool, 226
Metadata, 23, 34, 40, 61, 61f–62f, 98, 222,
      272–273. *See also* Image metadata
   Audio/video, 223–226, 225f–226f
   document, 226–227, 227f–228f

files, 125
source, 225
Metafile graphics, 71
Metasploit Anti-Forensics Project Tools, 272
$MFT. *See* Master file table ($MFT)
Microdots, 17
Microsoft Word, 275
Microsoft® office documents, 23
   hiding data in, 33
      hidden data within document attributes,
         34–35
      hidden text, 34
      hiding data by exploiting OLE structured
         storage, 35–37
      hiding data inside MS Excel® spreadsheet,
         38–39
      self-encrypts MS Office® document, 37–38
      White font, 35
Mimikatz, 260, 285
   to extract Windows password, 261f
Misspellings, 17
Mobile devices, data hiding in, 297
   mobile steganography tools, 297t
Monitor resolution, 70
Monkeys audio (APE), 83
Monoalphabetic ciphers, 2
Moo0 anti-recovery, 270
Morse code, 9–10
   letters and numerals, 10f
Moscow State University (MSU), 220
Most recently used lists (MRU lists), 243
Mozilla Firefox® browser, 182, 246–248
   Disconnect, 182
   Firefox profile folder contents, 247f
   HTTPS Everywhere, 182
   Privacy Badger, 182, 184f
   Random Agent Spoofer, 183, 184f
   Self-Destructing Cookies, 182–183
   uBlock Origin, 183
MP3. *See* MPEG-1 Level 3 (MP3)
MP3Stego tool, 87, 87f–88f
MP4 video file, 90, 90f
MPEG-1 Level 3 (MP3), 83–84
MRU lists. *See* Most recently used lists (MRU
      lists)
MS Excel® spreadsheet
   hide sheet3 using VBE, 40f
   hiding data inside, 38–39
MS Office sanitization, 275
   document inspector feature of an MS Word,
      275f
MS office® documents
   on OOXML file format, 49–50, 50t, 51f–52f,
      64t
      data hiding OOXML document structure,
         52–54, 53f
      through image cropping, 57–58, 57f–58f
      inspect document feature, 54f
      using OOXML markup compatibility and
         extensibility, 59–63
      OOXML replacement images, 58, 58f
      by reducing image and chart dimensions,
         55–57
      understanding package relationships, 51,
         52f

MS office® documents (*Continued*)
    xml comments, 58–59
    zipped container comments field, 54–55, 55f
MS Outlook®, encrypting emails in, 189–190
MS Word® 2010, 34
MSU. *See* Moscow State University (MSU)
MTP. *See* Media transfer protocol (MTP)
Multimedia files, 81

N

National Institute of Standards and Technology (NIST), 147
National Science Foundation (NSF), 292
NATO. *See* North Atlantic Treaty Organization (NATO)
Network security, 135
Network steganography, 19–20
Network-based DLP solution, 295
New technology file system (NTFS), 97–98, 98f, 123
Next-generation firewall (NGFW), 294–295
Nirsoft, 102, 250
NIST. *See* National Institute of Standards and Technology (NIST)
Normal bit direction, 23
North Atlantic Treaty Organization (NATO), 49
Norton identity safe password generator, 202
Notepad®, 99
NSF. *See* National Science Foundation (NSF)
NTF-SInfo tool, 124, 124f
NTFS. *See* New technology file system (NTFS)
NTLM hash, 260
Null cipher, 17–18

O

OCR programs. *See* Optical character recognition programs (OCR programs)
Off-the-record security (OTR security), 195
Off-the-record-messaging and Pidgin, 195
    authenticate buddy screen, 198f
    authenticating contacts identification, 197–198
    generating private key, 196
    Pidgin IM program, 196f
    practice using OTR, 197
Office Open XML (OOXML), 50–51
    data hiding inside MS office® documents on, 49–50, 50t, 51f–52f
    data hiding OOXML document structure, 52–54
    through image cropping, 57–58, 57f–58f
    using OOXML markup compatibility and extensibility, 59–63, 59f
    OOXML replacement images, 58, 58f
    by reducing image and chart dimensions, 55–57, 56f
    understanding package relationships, 51, 52f
    xml comments, 58–59
    zipped container comments field, 54–55, 55f
Offline windows password and registry editor, 262
OLE objects, 55

OLE structured storage, 35–37
    hiding data by, 35–37
    merging different Office documents, 37f
One-time pad, 9
Onion routing, 169
OnionShare, 184–185, 185f
    downloading file, 185f
OOXML. *See* Office Open XML (OOXML)
OOXML format document forensics, 212
    forensics of data hidden
        through image cropping, 213
        using OOXML exchanging images feature, 213
        using OOXML markup compatibility and extensibility feature, 213, 213f
        by reducing image and chart dimensions, 212–213
        using XML comments, 213
        in zipped container comments field, 212
    structure, 212
OPC. *See* Open packaging conventions (OPC)
Open codes steganography, 17–18
Open Crypto Audit Project, 146–147
Open packaging conventions (OPC), 51
Open space technique forensics, 211
Open systems interconnection model (OSI model), 294–295
OpenHiddenSystemDrive.exe file, 254
OpenPGP standard, 187
    encryption for webmail using Mailvelope extension, 190–192
    OpenPGP. js, 185–186
OpenPuff tool, 222
Operating systems, 129
Ophcrack, 262
Optical character recognition programs (OCR programs), 47, 47b
OSForensics, 262
OSI model. *See* Open systems interconnection model (OSI model)
OTR security. *See* Off-the-record security (OTR security)
OurSecret tool, 220

P

"-p" command, 66, 77
Pagefile. *See* Virtual memory
Pagefile.sys, 166, 259
Paging, 166
Palette-based images, 76t
    LSB using, 76–78
Panopticlick, 182, 183f
Parity coding, 85–88, 87f
Passwords, 201
    best practice, 201–202
    cracking techniques, 264
    generation tools, 202
    hashes extraction, 259–262
    manager tools, 202–203
    -saving techniques, 202
Payload, 210
PCM. *See* Pulse code modulation (PCM)
PDF. *See* Portable Document Format (PDF)
PeaZip free archive and file compressor, 160
    file archive encryption, 160–161
Personal iterations multiplier (PIM), 149–150

PGP keypair certificate creation, 187–188
Phase coding, 88
Photons, 292
Physical destruction, 269
Pidgin application, 136
PIM. *See* Personal iterations multiplier (PIM)
Pixel, 69–70, 69f–70f, 75t
places. sqlite, 246
Playfair cipher, 5, 11
    ciphertext, 7t
    decrypt using, 7
    encrypt using, 6
    encryption rules, 6
    with keyword LONDON, 6t
PNG. *See* Portable Network Graphics (PNG)
PoDoFo, 91, 92f
Polyalphabetic ciphers, 2, 11
    AutoKey cipher, 5
    Vigenère cipher, 2–5
Polygraphic ciphers, 5, 11
    Playfair cipher, 5–7
Portable applications, 289
Portable Document Format (PDF), 71
    PDF Metadata Editor 4*dots*, 226–227
    sanitization, 274
        destroying PDF hidden metadata, 274f
    structure, 91–94, 91f, 93f–94f
        change formatting, 91
        embedding objects, 91
        hidden file, 93f
Portable Network Graphics (PNG), 72
    interlacing supported by, 72
Portable stick computer, 140
Portable-VirtualBox tool, 155–156, 155f
Portable-VirtualBox.exe, 155
Primary partitions, 114
Privacy Badger, 182, 184f
Private key
    in encryption, 186
    steganography, 18
Procdump, 260, 285
ProDiscover Basic, 236
    acquiring disk drive images using, 234–235
ProDiscover Basic®, 28
ProtonMail, 193–194, 193f
    non-ProtonMail user, 194f
Proxy server, 179–180, 179f
Public key
    cryptography, 13–14, 186
    in encryption, 186
    steganography, 18–19
Pulse code modulation (PCM), 82
Pure steganography, 18
PuTTY, 179
PWGen, 202

Q

QKD technique. *See* Quantum key distribution technique (QKD technique)
QPDF, 274
Quantum cryptography, 292–293
Quantum key distribution technique (QKD technique), 293
Qubes OS, 138

R

RAID. *See* Redundant array of independent disks (RAID)
Rail Fence, 8
  imaginary table, 8t
Random Agent Spoofer, 183, 184f
RANDOM. ORG server, 202
Raster graphics, 71
Raw image files (RIF), 72
RDS. *See* Reference Data Set (RDS)
READ_NATIVE_MAX_ADDRESS, 129
ReadyBoost technology, 250
Real-time transport protocol (RTP), 295–296
Redundant array of independent disks (RAID), 97
  disks, 293
  technology, 269
Redundant bits, 69, 69f
Reference Data Set (RDS), 209
Registry, 110
  forensics, 264
Registry antiforensics, 276–277
  connected usb devices, 277
  deleting leftovers of uninstalled programs, 277
  disable timestamp for last access to file, 277–278
    file access time attribute, 279f
  disable *UserAssist*, 277
    deleting entries manually using Windows® registry, 278f
    nirsoft to delete registry entries, 277f
  mostly recently used list, 277
RegScanner, 241
rels, 51
Remapping process, 127
Remove hidden information work, 274
Renaming files, 27
  matching file signatures and file extensions, 27–28
    searching for EXE, 28f
  Windows bitmap files, 27
Retroshare secure social platform, 199
Reverse bit direction, 23
Revision identifiers tags, 63
Rich text format documents (RTF documents), 23
  hiding data in, 26
Ricochet, 201
RIF. *See* Raw image files (RIF)
Root certificate, 186–187
Rootkit attacks, 164
RTF documents. *See* Rich text format documents (RTF documents)
RTP. *See* Real-time transport protocol (RTP)
run.exe, 102

S

SaaS. *See* Software as a service (SaaS)
SAFDB. *See* Steganography application fingerprint database (SAFDB)
Sampling rate, 83
Sanitize document, 274
Scalable vector graphics (SVG), 71
Scytale system, 8
SD Formatter tool, 122

Search engines, 134
  anonymous, 180–181
Secret key cryptography, 13, 13f, 186
Secret writings, 16
Secret-Folder, 28
Sectors, 114
Secure socket layer (SSL), 23, 135
Security
  awareness corners, 134–135
  operating systems, 138–140
  security-related events, 285
Seganalysis scanners, 216
Self-Destructing Cookies, 182–183
Self-encrypts MS Office® document, 37–38
  selecting option encrypt with password, 38f
Semagrams, 17
SET_MAX_ADDRESS, 129
Setup events, 285
7-zip tool, 28
SHA-256 hashing algorithms, 147
SHA-512 hashing algorithms, 147
Signature analysis, 216
  StegSpy, 216–217
Signature-based steganalysis, 215
Single file encryption, 159
  AES Crypt, 159
  file archive encryption, 160–161
Slacker, 115
Slacker.exe tool, 115
Sleep mode, 259
Snow program
  hidden formatting marks, 68f
  HTML by exploiting whitespaces, 66–67, 66f–67f
SNOW tool, 214
SOCKS proxy, 180
Software as a service (SaaS), 293
Software bad sector, 127
Software firewalls, 294
Solid state drives (SSDs), 234, 268
Source metadata, 225
Spammimic website, 20
Spatial domain. *See* Image domain
Specific statistical analysis, 217
Splitting files, 33
Spread spectrum, 89
SRM tool, 271
SSDs. *See* Solid state drives (SSDs)
SSL. *See* Secure socket layer (SSL)
StartPage, 180–181, 181f
Statistical analysis, 217
  Stegdetect tool, 217–219, 218f
  StegExpose tool, 217
Stealth ADS. *See also* Alternate data stream (ADS)
  data hiding using, 104–106
    creating a file, 106f
    reading a file, 106f
Steganalysis, 210
  destroying hidden data, 211
  of digital media files, 211
    audio forensics, 219
    digital files metadata forensic, 222–227
    image forensics, 214–219
    text document steganalysis, 211–214

video forensics, 219–222
  methods, 210–211
  and steganography main process, 210f
Steganographic techniques, 46
  data hiding inside audio files, 81–90
  data hiding using digital media types, 90–94
  image steganography, 68–81
  text steganography, 46–68
Steganography, 1, 15, 291
  cryptography *vs.*, 15, 16t
  digital steganography techniques, 20
  protocols types, 18–19
  tools, 216, 267
  types, 15–16, 16f
    according to host file type, 19–20
    digital steganography, 18–20
    linguistic steganography, 17–18
    technical steganography, 16–17
  watermarking *vs.*, 21
Steganography application fingerprint database (SAFDB), 216
SteganRTP–RTP Covert Channel, 295–296
StegExpose tool, 217, 217f
StegExpose. jar, 217
Steghide screen capture, 85, 85f–86f
Stego Video tool, 220
Stego-image, 19
Stego-key, 18
Stego-only
  attack, 210
  technique, 215
StegoMft tool, 125
StegoMft64 tool, 126
StegoStick Beta, 90
StegSpy, 216–217
Stoned Boot attack, 164
Stoned Bootkit, 164
Storage-based DLP solution, 295
Stream control transmission protocol, 296
Streaming protocols, 295–296
Streams.exe from SysInternals, 104
Structural detection, 215
Substitution, 20
Substitution cipher, 2. *See also* Transposition cipher
  mechanical substitution ciphers, 7–8
  monoalphabetic ciphers, 2
  polyalphabetic ciphers, 2–5
  polygraphic ciphers, 5–7
  transposition cipher *vs.*, 10–12
SuperFetch technology, 250, 281
SVG. *See* Scalable vector graphics (SVG)
Swap space. *See* Virtual memory
Swapping, 166
Swiss Federal Data Protection Act (DPA), 193
Swiss Federal Data Protection Ordinance (DPO), 193–194
Symmetrical encryption. *See* Secret key cryptography
System events, 285
System restore points and file history, disable, 280–281
  disable Windows restore feature, 282f
  turn off file history in Windows 8.1, 282f
*System*32 directory, 27

T

Tagged Image File Format (TIFF), 72
TagScanner tool, 225
Tails, 135, 138f, 139–140
    boot Start menu, 137f
    Greeter screen, 138f
    installing hidden VeraCrypt volume, 156–158
    TOR network, 135–137
    on USB stick, 137f
TCHunt, 262–263
TCP. *See* Transmission control protocol (TCP)
TechDay report, 294
Technical steganography, 16. *See also*
        Linguistic steganography
    invisible ink, 16–17
    microdots, 17
Text document steganalysis, 211
    linguistic method forensics, 211–212
    OOXML format document forensics,
        212–213
    open space technique forensics, 211
    webpages text documents steganalysis,
        213–214
Text semagrams, 17
Text steganography, 19, 46–68, 47f, 211. *See*
        also Image steganography
    data hiding inside MS office® documents,
        49–64, 50t, 51f
    format-based, 46–47
    linguistic-based methods, 48–49
    random and statistical generation, 47–48
    webpage, 64–67
Thumbcache Viewer, 252
Thumbnail cache file, 281
Thumbs Viewer tool, 252
TIFF. *See* Tagged Image File Format (TIFF)
Time-shifter programs, 296
Timestamp for last access to file, disable,
        277–278
    file access time attribute, 279f
Timestomp, 272
    Timestomp–GUI, 272
TOR bridges, 171–172, 172f
    configuration wizard, 173f
TOR Browser, 169–170, 285
    Access Grams search engine, 172f
    dark web, 170–171
    error message, 176f
    launching, 171f
    TOR bridges, 172f
    traffic through, 169f
    update privacy and security level in, 175f
    warnings, 171–176
TOR messenger, 199–200
TOR network, 135–137
TOR privacy network, 297
torrent. *See* uTorrent
TPM. *See* Trusted platform module (TPM)
Transform domain, 78
    data hiding
        end-of-file marker, 79–80, 80f–81f
        image metadata, 81
        zip files image, 81
    JPEG
        compression, 78
        steganography, 78–79

Transmission control protocol
        (TCP), 296
Transposition cipher, 8, 12. *See also*
        Substitution cipher
    columnar transposition, 8–9
    double transposition, 9
    rail fence, 8
    substitution cipher *vs.*, 10–12
Trinity Rescue Kit, 262
True Color, 70
TrueCrypt program, 137, 145–146
    cracking encrypted volume passwords,
        263–264
Trusted platform module (TPM), 140–141,
        163–164
24-bit color image, 69, 70t, 75t

U

uBlock Origin, 183
Ubuntu Privacy Remix (UPR), 135, 137–138,
        139f
Ubuntu version, 140
UDP. *See* User datagram protocol (UDP)
UEFI. *See* Unified extensible firmware interface
        (UEFI)
Uncompressed format, 83
Uncompressed videos, 90
Unified extensible firmware interface
        (UEFI), 165
Universal statistical analysis, 217
unprotect.info, 263–264, 264f
Up-bit ordering, 23
UPR. *See* Ubuntu Privacy Remix (UPR)
USB zip drive, creating hidden partition within,
        118–119
    access USB zip drive properties, 119f
    install USB drive software, 121f
    uncovering hidden partitions, 122
    update USB zip drive driver
        software, 121f
USBDeview, 243
User datagram protocol (UDP), 296
UserAssist, disabling, 277
    deleting entries manually using Windows®
        registry, 278f
    nirsoft to delete registry entries, 277f
UserAssist forensics, 245
UserAssist-View, 245
uTorrent, 249
    Firewall rule, 249f

V

VBE. *See* Visual Basic Editor (VBE)
VBinDiff hex editor, 29, 31f
VBR. *See* Volume boot record (VBR)
Vector graphics, 71
Venona project, 9
VeraCrypt, 147
    encrypted volume creation
        using, 147–150
    hidden volume creation, 153–155
    installing *tails* inside hidden VeraCrypt
        volume, 156–158
    installing virtual machine OS, 150–159
    pop-up message, 155f

volume, 150
    direct mode selection, 153f
    mounting, 152f, 157f
Viber™ foundation, 195
Video calling service using *Gruveo*, 198–199
Video files, data hiding, 89–90
Video forensics, 219. *See also* Image forensics
    location of OurSecret signature, 221f
    location of password, 221f
    16-byte user-defined password, 220, 221f
    steganalysis
        of digital media files, 222
        of video files, 219
        of video steganography programs, 220–222
    video steganography tools, 220t
Vigenère cipher, 2–5
    ciphertext alphabet for, 5t
    Vigenère table, 4t
Virtual machines (VMs), 135, 268, 278–279,
        288, 294
    VirtualBox, 288
    VMware Workstation Player, 288
    Windows Virtual PC, 288
Virtual memory, 257
    analysis, 257–259
Virtual private networks (VPNs), 23, 135,
        176–179
    services, 170
    working process, 177f
VirtualBox tool, 155–156, 155f, 288
    contents of portable version, 156f
    launching, 157f
Virtualization, 293–294
Visible watermark, 20
Visual Basic Editor (VBE), 38
Visual detection, 216
Visual semagrams, 17
VMs. *See* Virtual machines (VMs)
VMware Workstation Player, 288
Volume boot record (VBR), 164
Volume shadow copy service (VSS), 106–107
VPNBook, 177–178, 178f
VPNs. *See* Virtual private networks (VPNs)
VSS. *See* Volume shadow copy service (VSS)
Vuvuzela system, 297–298

W

Watermarking, 20
    steganography *vs.*, 21
    types, 20
        invisible watermark, 21
        visible watermark, 20
WAV, 83, 88f–89f
WbStego4open, 91, 93f
Web browser privacy add-ons, 181
    browser fingerprint checking, 181–182
    Mozilla Firefox privacy add-ons, 182–183
Web mail providers, 192
    GhostMail, 195
    ProtonMail, 193–194, 193f
Web proxy, 179
    types, 180
Webpage text steganography, 64–67
    data hiding
        in HTML by exploiting whitespaces using
            snow program, 66–67

in HTML files by modifying attribute, 65, 65f
in HTML/XML files using tag attributes, 65, 65f
using HTML5 tags, 64–65
secret messages inside twitter updates, 67–68
Webpages text documents steganalysis, 213
forensics of data hidden
by exploiting XML/HTML tag attributes, 214
in HTML by exploiting whitespaces, 214
using HTML5 tags, 213–214
by modifying HTML attribute written state, 214
Whirlpool hash algorithm, 147
White font, 35
Whitespaces
forensics of data hidden in HTML by exploiting, 214
manipulation, 46–47
Whonix, 138
WinBuilder, 287
Windows antiforensics techniques, 275
configure Windows for better privacy, 275–276
configure Windows to remove deleted files, 276f
disable recycle bin, 276
disabling system restore points and file history, 280–281
disabling Windows
hibernation, 278
logging, 285
password hash extraction, 285–287
prefetch feature, 281–283
thumbnail cache, 281
virtual memory, 278–280
registry antiforensics, 276–278
connected USB devices, 277
deleting leftovers of uninstalled programs, 277
disabling timestamp for last access to file, 277–278
disabling *UserAssist*, 277
mostly recently used list, 277
Windows forensics, 214, 227. *See also* Computer forensics
alternative data streams detection, 255
BlueScreenView, 251f
capture disk drive, 231–233
capture volatile memory, 228–231
deleted files recovery, 233
acquiring disk drive images using ProDiscover Basic, 234–235, 235f
analyzing digital evidence for deleted files and artifacts, 235–239, 235f, 237f–238f
using DiskPart command, 255f
examining encrypted files, 262
cracking *TrueCrypt* encrypted volume passwords, 263–264
password cracking techniques, 264
TCHunt, 262–263
file attributes analysis, 252
file signature analysis, 252
hidden partitions discovery, 252–255

host protected area and device configuration, 262
virtual memory analysis, 257–259
Windows minidump files forensics, 250
Windows password cracking, 259–262
Windows Prefetch files forensic analysis, 249–250
windows registry analysis, 239–249, 239f
Windows thumbnail forensics, 250–252
Windows® VSS, 255–257
WinPrefetchView, 251f
Windows hibernation, disabling, 278
through command prompt, 279f
through registry, 279f
Windows logging, disabling, 285
CleanAfterMe tool, 287f
clearing windows logs, 286f
investigating Windows® event logs, 286f
Windows metafile (WMF), 71
Windows minidump files forensics, 250
Windows partition encryption, 143–145
Windows password cracking, 259
offline windows password and registry editor, 262
Ophcrack, 262
OSForensics, 263f
password hashes extraction, 259–262
Trinity Rescue Kit, 262
Windows prefetch feature, disabling, 281–283
disable Prefetch using registry editor, 284f
disable Windows® SuperFetch service, 284f
Windows Prefetch files forensic analysis, 249–250
Windows registry, 239
analysis, 239, 239f
checking installed programs, 239–242, 241f–242f
connected USB devices, 242–243, 243f–244f
internet programs investigation, 245–249
MRU lists, 243–245, 245f
UserAssist forensics, 245
windows registry startup location, 239
hiding data, 109–112, 112f, 112t
startup location, 239
keys, 240t
sysinternals autoruns utility, 240f
Windows thumbnail cache, disabling, 281
delete thumbnails using disk cleanup utility, 283f
disable thumbnail from folder options, 283f
Windows thumbnail forensics, 250–252
Windows virtual memory, disabling, 278–280
disable paging under Windows 8.1, 280f
enable empty paging file upon shutdown, 281f
Windows Virtual PC, 288
Windows® 7 version, 107, 141
Windows® 8 version, 107, 141
Windows 8.1 startup process, 166f
Windows® 8.1 version, 141, 165
Windows® 8.1/2012 R2/10, 285
Windows® 10 version, 107, 141

Windows® Media Audio (WMA), 83–84
Windows® OS file structure, 27
data hiding
using ADS, 98–104
under computer hardware level, 128–131
in disk bad blocks, 127–128
in file's slack space, 112–117
within $MFT, 123–127
using stealth ADS, 104–106
Windows® registry, 109–112, 112f, 112t
Windows® restoration points, 106–109
hidden partitions, 117–118
under Windows® OS, 118, 119f
Windows® password hash extraction, disable, 285–287
setting UseLogonCredential DWORD value, 288f
Windows® passwords (winpass), 262
Windows® *Prefetch*, 281
Windows® restoration points
hiding data, 106–109
configuring restore points under Windows® 7, 108f
executing *mspass.exe*, 108f
Windows® version, 140
Windows® Vista version, 141
Windows® volume shadow copy (Windows® VSS), 255–257
Windows® VSS. *See* Windows® volume shadow copy (Windows® VSS)
Windows®, 118
winpass. *See* Windows® passwords (winpass)
WinPrefetchView, 250
WinRAR tool, 28
Wiping tools, 269
Wireless networks, 296
WMA. *See* Windows®; Media Audio (WMA)
WMF. *See* Windows metafile (WMF)
Word-shift coding, 46
Word/media folder, 60, 61f

X

X.509 certificate, digital signature using, 186f
Xiaoyun Wang's method, 289
XML. *See* Extensible Markup Language (XML)
XML comments, forensics of data hidden using, 213
XML-based file structure, 50
XML/HTML tag attributes, forensics of data hidden by exploiting, 214
XMP. *See* Extensible Metadata Platform (XMP)
XnViewMP, 42

Y

YUV color, 78

Z

ZIP bomb, 289
Zipped container comments field, data hiding in, 54–55, 55f
Zipped folder. *See* Compressed file

Printed and bound by CPI Group (UK) Ltd, Croydon, CR0 4YY

03/10/2024

01040324-0019